CRITICAL INCIDENTS IN MANAGEMENT

DECISION AND POLICY ISSUES

CRITICAL INCIDENTS IN MANAGEMENT

DECISION AND POLICY ISSUES

Sixth Edition

John M. Champion, Ph.D.
John H. James, D.B.A.
both of the University of Florida

1989

Homewood, Illinois 60430

© RICHARD D. IRWIN, INC., 1963, 1969, 1975, 1980, 1985, and 1989

Acquisitions editor: *William R. Bayer*
Project editor: *Paula M. Buschman*
Production manager: *Carma W. Fazio*
Cover designer: *Maureen McCutcheon*
Compositor: *Eastern Graphics*
Typeface: *10/12 Caledonia*
Printer: *Malloy Lithographing, Inc.*

Library of Congress Cataloging-in-Publication Data
Champion, John M.
    Critical incidents in management.

    Bibliography: p.
    1. Industrial management.   2. Personnel management.
I. James, John H., 1929-   .   II. Title.
HD31.C455   1989   658.4   88-624
ISBN 0-256-06825-9 (pbk.)

Printed in the United States of America

    4 5 6 7 8 9 0 ML 6 5 4 3 2 1

Dedicated to our colleagues who wrote critiques
for the incidents included in this edition.

Preface

The first edition of *Critical Incidents in Management* was published over 20 years ago. Since that time, the value of incidents as an experiential tool in management development and education has become increasingly accepted and recognized. The related use of critiques, or commentaries, written by outstanding academicians from leading universities throughout the country remains a unique feature of this book. Analysis and discussion of issues raised in each incident and its accompanying critiques provide the vehicle or mechanism for stimulating students in all stages of professional development to discover principles, truths, and generalizations which can be applied to business situations. While the level of professional maturity and background may vary among students, this purpose of the incident analysis remains the same. As we complete the materials for the sixth edition, the rationale for its development is as follows.

First, one of the most characteristic tasks of any manager is decision making and the consideration that must be given to policy implications associated with those decisions. The typical manager is often confronted with decisions for which there are no precedents, no policies, no formulas, no procedural manuals, no established principles, and few, if any, factual premises. These decisions call for a knowledge of managerial principles as well as a philosophy of thought, a personal system of values, a professional code of ethics, and a view of what constitutes business morality. Thus, in a method of instruction which incorporates this book, students of the management process are encouraged to develop their own perspective, frame of reference, or method of thinking necessary to cope effectively with the value premises needed in making managerial decisions, formulating policies, and implementing those policies. In this way, each student is motivated to formulate his or her own personal "philosophy" of management.

Second, experience indicates that greater student interest in assigned reading materials and increased classroom participation can be achieved when theoretical concepts are related to practical situations that are likely to confront managers in day-to-day operations. Therefore, in this book, a series of managerial incidents that are behavioral or human resource oriented is presented, each involving some management principle, issue, or practice. For most of the incidents, there are two critiques written by university professors of management or related disciplines. The critiques address the incident's basic issues and usually express some position regarding decisions made, decisions to be made, relevance of operational or functional area policies, and problems associated with policy implementation. In most instances, the critiques present differing views and opinions. These conflicting views and opinions were not discouraged because they not only reflect reality but they also encourage students to develop their own philosophy of management and to exercise their own judgment in an environment of uncertainty. In addition, they lead students to form a decision-making, policy-formulating, and policy-implementation position. Comprehensive reading lists are included for incidents that are accompanied by critiques. Supplementary assignments in books and professional journals can be drawn from these lists. Students will be intrigued by the issues covered in the incidents and by the views expressed in the critiques, and they will find the materials necessary to justify their position to be stimulating reading.

In this sixth edition, suggestions from university instructors and industrial trainers having experience with the fifth edition were incorporated. A revised introduction chapter acquaints readers with the format of the book and the rationale basic to its use. Two additional chapters have been written. They serve the purpose of providing readers with concepts that will enable them to more effectively cope with the decision-making, policy-formulation, and policy-implementation aspects of the incidents and their critiques. All of the incidents and critiques have been subjected to revision. Some incidents and critiques have been deleted and others have been added.

The total number of incidents remains essentially the same. They are all drawn from a variety of organizational settings including business, government, health care, and education. Forty of the 50 incidents are accompanied by a total of 80 critiques. The incidents and critiques introduce readers to a variety of current issues varying from abusive discharge to sexual harassment. Suggested reading lists have been completely revised and updated and include only the latest editions of books and the most recent articles in professional journals. Finally, 10 incidents have been included without analytical critiques and reading lists in order to give readers a few incidents unstructured by the formal analysis of others.

Critical Incidents in Management: Decision and Policy Issues can be used as a basic text with assigned readings from the reading lists or as a supplement to some standard textbook. It can easily be adapted for use in courses concerned with management development, but it is particularly useful in such courses as Principles of Management, Strategy and Policy, Personnel Administration, Organizational Behavior, and Industrial Psychology. It may be especially relevant in instances where no cases or incidents are included in the textbook being used, where the instructor is not happy with the cases in the adopted textbook, where it is desirable to emphasize the behavioral problems a typical manager can expect, where operational policy formulation and implementation are emphasized in human resource management, or where an instructor desires to utilize the pedagogical power of analytical critiques of the incidents prepared by outstanding professionals in the field. Additionally, organizations conducting management training programs will find an application for this book. Whether the reader is a business trainee or a college student, the analysis of incidents and critiques provides a challenging experience in diagnosing managerial situations, making decisions, formulating policies, and implementing policies.

The presentation of these materials leaves us indebted to many people. In particular, we are grateful to those who so enthusiastically responded when asked to write and revise critiques for the incidents. The incidents are based on situations related by managers who have participated in various management development programs that we have either conducted or attended. Names have been changed to avoid the possibility of association with actual persons or organizations. Most of the 80 critiques were contributed by distinguished university professors from many of the leading colleges and universities throughout the United States. They are actively instructing courses in such diverse disciplines as management, business policy, organizational behavior, economics, health care administration, psychology, sociology, labor relations, strategic management, industrial engineering, and business ethics. Some hold administrative positions in their respective universities, and a few are retired from their previous academic positions but remain active as consultants. Most have written and published widely, and most have consulting and management experience. Without their depth of insight this book's approach to education for the management process could not have been achieved. Biographical information for each critique writer appears in a special section at the end of this book. To them we dedicate this sixth edition.

John M. Champion
John H. James

Contents

Incidents without Critiques

CHAPTER 1

Introduction

Even though the first edition of *Critical Incidents in Management* was published in 1964 and the book is now in its sixth edition, it remains rather unique. The purpose of this chapter is to introduce readers to its nature and format. The basic unit of the book consists of the following: (1) a description of a managerial incident; (2) two critiques or commentaries for each incident expressing the views of knowledgeable academicians or consultants regarding the decisions, actions, and issues reflected in the incident; (3) statements indicating some observations on the part of the authors of the book; (4) comprehensive lists of suggested readings from leading textbooks and professional journals; (5) thought-provoking discussion items; and (6) biographical information for each critique writer. An elaboration of each of these follows.

(1) Incidents

The incidents, based on actual situations are short, generally three or four paragraphs, but precisely stated so that decisions and discussions can be generated from the information given. The typical incident begins with a brief description of the situation, develops a decision-making environment, and then focuses the responsibility for making a decision on the reader and/or a central figure in the incident. This is usually followed by the recognition of a need for well-articulated operational policies in human resources management, and then by policy and strategy implementation considerations. Decisions to be made do not necessarily represent crisis situations or even success or failure for the firm, but they usually do place the decision maker in a critical situation. Managers face such incidents daily, and they require an attitude and an analytical process that hopefully can be developed through an instructional approach such as the one suggested in this book.

There are 50 incidents illustrating situations that have developed from managerial efforts to plan, organize, control, and direct others in organizational situations. Fundamental issues in the incidents represent a broad range of problems and situations such as overlapping lines of authority, violation of company policies, whistleblowing, appropriate uses of authority, resistance to change, sexual harassment, and invasion of privacy. Every effort has been made to include incidents that typify decision-making problems facing key operating managers. In practically every incident, the key figure is faced with making a decision regarding a situation that has no precedent in that organization.

The incidents are presented alphabetically with titles that, in most instances, reflect some major management issue. For the following reasons no attempt has been made to provide a functional classification of the incidents, such as planning, controlling, and so forth. Each incident may have a primary focus in a particular functional area, but it will require consideration of a broad range of issues representing many functional areas. Additionally, in the accompanying critiques, many issues and concepts are raised that create overlap between functions. Many incidents and critiques are deceptive in appearance, and, like icebergs, more is hidden underneath than appears on the surface. An incident may be selected for use by an instructor simply to introduce a specific topic for class discussion and analysis. On the other hand, choice of an incident could be a result of the instructor's analysis of course objectives, student sophistication, the incidents, critiques, supplementary reading lists, and the subject matter areas suggested by the introductory "What This Incident Is About" statements. Incident selection may also depend on whether an instructor wishes to emphasize a decision-making situation, a policy-formulation situation, a policy-implementation situation, a policy-violation situation, or an incident involving all of these.

(2) Critiques

The inclusion of critiques, or commentaries, written by knowledgeable academicians and consultants make this a unique book. Previous classroom experience with incidents and cases has revealed that students have a tendency to seek the opinion of an "authority" or an "expert" regarding issues and concepts presented. When confronted with practical situations and faced with the task of recommending alternative courses of action, students will also often seek publications of academicians known for their work in organization, if it is an organization problem, or policy if it is a policy issue. A result is that students often view an authoritative opinion as representing the last word on the matter. They too readily accept the judgment of a learned writer as beyond question. However, as they read further and their thought processes begin to mature, they soon realize other authorities have different opinions. There are different ways to view the issues and there are alternative approaches to a problem, each usually having some merit. Students become alert to the fact that there is not necessarily one "correct" answer. They begin to realize that management is an "art" as well as a "science," and realize the necessity of developing their own philosophy of management. They discover that seldom is there only one alternative in the actual situation. Otherwise, a standard operating manual could be developed and used as a substitute for the interpretation of the situation, which is the real contribution of the manager. There would be no need for management development programs, academic work at the collegiate level, or experience on the "firing line."

This maturation process is facilitated through the use of critiques. Forty incidents are accompanied by two critiques each. Therefore, a total of 80 individuals recognized as knowledgeable on the subject, university professors of business administration or management consultants, have written short critiques giving their views on the basic issues in the incident, opinions about the actions that should be taken, explication of how the incident might have been avoided, and recommendations regarding policy formulation and implementation. The critique writers are brief in order to provide readers with latitude in their own analysis. The critiques are, however, thoughtfully written and focus on major concepts, issues, and perceptions reflected in the incident. Critiques vary in their pattern of analysis. Each represents one possible approach or interpretation. Thus, there are always assumptions, problems, and points of elaboration not included in the critiques. The perceptions and views of one critique writer often will conflict and be in disagreement with those of the other critique writer. Upon seeing two "authorities" holding diverse views about a situation, the student begins to realize that in the final analysis, each individual must develop his or her own personal managerial attitude, perception, value structure, or philosophy.

A critique should not be construed as suggesting a right answer or the correct way of doing things. It represents a point of view, often in conflict with the point of view someone else has taken. The critique does, however, provide guidelines, understanding, insights, and structure to discussions and the resulting point of view that a student is encouraged to formulate. In order to permit class discussion and exploration of issues without the stimulation of critiques or discussion questions, 10 incidents are presented without critiques, questions, or reading lists. This avoids any structuring other than the information provided in the incident and more closely simulates conditions of managerial decision making by placing students more on their own.

(3) Observations

For each of the 40 incidents that are accompanied by critiques and suggested readings, the authors of the book make some general comments that attempt to achieve one or more of the following: (1) relate the incident and its two critiques to each other, (2) relate the incident and its critiques to one or more of the suggested readings, (3) emphasize points made in the critiques, (4) emphasize points not made in the critiques, (5) relate the incident and its critiques to theoretical concepts, (6) suggest further points to consider, and (7) focus on the identification of additional issues.

(4) Suggested Readings

For each of the 40 incidents that are accompanied by critiques, comprehensive reading lists have been prepared. These suggested readings will assist in developing the reader's own critical potential and lead to a justifiable decision-making position. The suggested readings have been taken from textbooks, representative journals and periodicals, and involve the reader in basic issues and concepts discussed in the incident and its critiques.

(5) Discussion Items

The discussion items that accompany each incident and its critiques are thought-provoking in nature. They may or may not be used to provide some additional analysis and structure to the incident and its critiques. In many instances the discussion item is actually an exercise requiring the student to make and justify a decision, to formulate a policy, to modify an existing policy, or to submit a policy implementation plan.

(6) Critique Writer Biographical Information

In a separate section of the book biographical information is given for each of the 80 persons writing critiques. This is a group of individuals whose professional credentials are impressive. Knowing something about the interests and accomplishments of each one is helpful in gaining additional insights regarding their views and perceptions.

In summary, *Critical Incidents in Management: Decision and Policy Issues* consists of a series of managerial incidents, most of which have critiques written by recognized knowledgeable professionals, and suggested reading lists to supplement the student's knowledge of the issues and concepts reflected by the incidents. Student responsibility becomes clear when analyzing an incident: (1) review the incident and the views provided in the critiques, (2) use the suggested reading list to supplement views already provided for in the critiques, (3) make decisions and recommendations regarding actions that were taken or should have been taken, (4) consider implications relative to policy formulation and implementation, and (5) justify the views taken. Such an analysis will often proceed in accordance with a sequential pattern in which the student will define the problem, state the primary and secondary issues, recommend decisions and actions to be taken, specify how the problem or issue could have been avoided, make suggestions relative to ways of avoiding similar incidents, formulate policies to be used as guides in future situations, and make recommendations regarding the process of implementing decisions, strategies, and policies.

All incidents reflect decision-making and policy issues that allow alternative courses of action. The analysis and discussion of alternative actions, additional reading for the purpose of justifying positions taken, and the further consideration of facts, issues, and concepts suggested by the incident and its critiques make the incident-analysis experience dynamic and challenging.

CHAPTER 2

Incident analysis

In both the preface section and Chapter 1 readers are provided with an introduction to the rationale and format of this book. This chapter suggests an analytical approach to analysis of the incidents and critiques based on a sequence of considerations ranging from decision making through policy implementation.

While the preferred approach to incident analysis will vary among instructors, it seems important to emphasize several things about the incidents and critiques. First, they serve as the basis for discussion rather than to illustrate effective or ineffective handling of a particular problem or situation. Second, while all the incidents involve the reader in decision-making situations, most of the incidents can be extended to lead into some aspect of policy formulation and policy implementation. Thus, the emphasis and orientation of each incident will differ but will always lead readers through a sequential process by placing major emphasis on one or more of the following four categories: (1) decision-making considerations, (2) policy-formulation considerations, (3) policy-implementation considerations, and (4) policy-violation and/or noncompliance considerations. Each of these areas of emphasis will be discussed in the remainder of this chapter.

(1) Decision-Making Considerations. A review of basic management textbooks will reveal the emphasis currently placed on the supervisor or manager's role as a decision maker. In their attempts to define the term *management*, many authors take the position that decision making is one of the manager's most characteristic tasks. This is particularly true of decisions relating to actions that must be taken to achieve the firm's objectives, strategies to be selected as a means of achieving those objectives, and policies to be formulated and later implemented. It follows, then, that managerial development programs should provide not only for the comprehension of established principles and concepts of professional management but also for the development among participants of a personal system of values, a philosophy of thought, and a pattern of thinking needed to cope effectively with the value premises present in most executive decisions. For many of the decisions that a supervisor or manager must make daily, there exist no precedent, no formula, no procedural manual, no ten tried and true principles. Yet, a manager's ability to cope with such situations effectively may largely determine his or her status and progress in an organization.

Attempts to instill in students an appreciation for a self-developed philosophy concurrent with the comprehension of managerial principles and concepts has coincided with the emergence of situational and contingency theories of management. Contingency theories explicitly recognize that organization designs, models of leadership, and other management-related concepts become appropriate or inappropriate in relation to the situation in which they are applied. Contingency approaches to management include methods for identifying, classifying, and weighting those dimensions of the situation that are significant for managerial decisions. Through exposure to incidents and critiques, students can improve their ability to analyze situations, balance conflicting requirements, identify and combine options, select from alternative courses of action, and design plans for effectively implementing desired actions.

Faced with the realities of specific job situations reflected by an incident, students recognize that theories must be adapted to the specific needs of each situation. Thus, incident analysis brings realism to situational and contingency theories of management, provides opportunities for students to practice situational analysis, and develops managerial skills for making decisions and taking decisive action.

Each incident and its accompanying critiques should be read and studied. Then, based on assigned supplementary readings, students are prepared to give their own views, decisions, and recommended courses of action regarding the issues of the incident. Attention must always be focused on good management practices and on steps that can be taken to avoid the occurrence of similar incidents in the future.

Thus, all incidents are structured in such a way that a decision is called for and actions must be taken on someone's part with respect to certain basic issues or problems. It is not so important what decision is reached, but it is essential that all aspects of the situation be considered, that the decision-making process be taken into account, and that various values and perceptions be expressed and examined. The incidents serve as "discussion starters," they are issue oriented, and they require that various alternatives be identified, that recommendations be made, and that support for recommendations be provided.

For example, the incident entitled "Abusive Discharge" places major emphasis on the necessity of generating a decision. The principal character in the incident, an attorney employed by a firm, must make a choice between three alternative courses of action. In making her choice she must, of course, examine her values as well as the consequences of each alternative. The incident "False Report" requires that a decision be made with regard to a group of employees that have turned in false documents regarding their expenses and performance activities. "Invasion of Privacy" involves an incident in which three fourths of a firm's employees have indicated their refusal to abide by a policy. Decisive action on the part of management is clearly called for. In some incidents the responsibility for making a decision is on management. In other incidents, such as the "Whistleblowing" incident, the onus for making a decision is on the employee.

(2) **Policy-Formulation Considerations.** After analyzing the decision-making aspects of an incident, the next step will logically be one of identifying any policy-formulation implications suggested by the incident and its critiques. It will be obvious that some of the problems reflected in an incident might have been avoided, or reduced in seriousness and intensity, if clearly stated policies had been previously adopted relating to the situation. This provides students with opportunities to examine the usefulness of policies, to determine how they should be stated, and to give them practice in writing them. The incident "A Sexual Harassment Policy" establishes a situation in which the newly appointed president of a firm realizes no policy exists regarding a major issue which he, his managers, and his employees may likely encounter. The issue is one of sexual harassment, and he requests that his director of human resources formulate a policy statement to be included in the firm's policy manual that addresses some six questions that will reflect the firm's philosophy on the issue. In the incident "An Exam for Mrs. Smith" it readily becomes clear from the incident and from the critiques that accompany it that if a policy had been previously adopted regarding psychological testing of spouses, an awkward and unpleasant incident might have been avoided. The incident not only calls for a decision but also calls for adoption of a policy in order to avoid repetition of the incident.

(3) **Policy-Implementation Considerations.** A third step in this sequential pattern of incident analysis is to focus attention on the development of plans for the execution or implementation of policies. Merely announcing a policy, or even publishing it in written form, will not ensure that it will be implemented. While all of the incidents can serve as the basis for discussing the implementation of decisions, strategies, and policies, there are some incidents in which the primary or major emphasis is on the need for an effective implementation plan. These incidents stress policy implementation as opposed to decision execution.

In the "Equal Pay for Comparable Worth" incident the director of a rehabilitation hospital is considering the adoption of an employee compensation policy based on the value or worth of jobs in the hospital. The basic question to be discussed is whether such a policy could ever be fairly and effectively implemented due to the difficulty of measuring the value or worth of most jobs. The incident "Implementing Strategic Change" has been especially written to provide the basis for considering various facets of introducing change in an organization that has adopted turnaround strategies. The "Travel Policy Dilemma" incident focuses particular attention on the development of a specific plan for implementing a policy regarding ownership of gifts and bonuses received by employees from a frequent-flier program.

(4) Policy-Violation/Noncompliance Considerations. In many of the incidents it will be obvious that difficult problems have arisen from, and in, noncompliance with specific orders, directives, and procedures. Some incidents have been specifically written to focus on considerations to be taken into account when someone in the organization violates or fails to comply with an adopted policy. Such an incident may involve a situation in which it is a subordinate that has violated or not complied with the policy, or it may be the supervisor that is in violation or noncompliance with the policy. Still other incidents may reflect situations in which policies existed but may have been so poorly written that they fail to serve any useful purpose and therefore are in need of revision, modification, or even elimination. The incident "Heroic Banker" provides an interesting situation in which there exists a policy calling for the immediate discharge of anyone not complying with a procedure for reacting to bank robbery attempts. It so happens that the employee violating the policy is seen in the eyes of the public as a hero. A discussion of what the bank president should do will inevitably lead to the conclusion by many that the policy should have provided for management flexibility by stating that employees violating the policy would be "subject to" termination. That, however, leads many to question the value or usefulness of policies that provide for too much flexibility. "Moonlighting Policy" describes a situation in which a company has adopted a policy prohibiting employees from becoming involved in any business venture that could be in conflict or in competition with the employer. The incident calls for an examination of the desirability of such a policy when it is found that some employees have violated it. A different situation occurs in the incident entitled "Performance Appraisal Policy" in which it is the supervisor rather than the subordinate that is not in compliance with a stated policy.

The preceding discussion is an elaboration of the point made earlier that incidents included in this book have been selected in accordance with the major emphasis each may place on a decision-making situation, on a policy-formulation situation, on a policy-implementation situation, or on a policy-violation/noncompliance situation. It has been emphasized that many of the incidents can be used to lead into a sequential process involving all of these categories. For example, the first incident in the book, "A Sexual Harassment Policy," requires first of all that certain decisions be made regarding the need for a sexual harassment policy and with respect to how sexual harassment is defined. Once those decisions are made, a policy statement must be formulated and stated, preferably in written form. Then all the ramifications of developing a plan for the policy's implementation must be considered. Finally, the question of the action to be taken in the event of violation or noncompliance is a major consideration. Other incidents such as "Conflict of Interest," "Reverse Discrimination," and "Illegal Drugs Policy" will be found to be suitable for such a sequential analysis.

In the interest of making an incident analysis more meaningful, several suggestions are offered. First, Professor James P. Logan, in his critique of the incident "Resistance to Change," points out some common errors to avoid in the decision-making aspects of an incident analysis. While the errors are specific to that particular incident, they can be generalized to all the incidents. Second, with respect to policy formulation and implementation aspects of an incident analysis, Chapter 3 should be studied carefully. The chapter provides some basic information that should be helpful in considering such issues as the need for policies, how and under what circumstances policies should be written, and how policies can be effectively implemented or executed. Third, the Incident Analysis Classification Matrix presented on pages 366–67 reflects our views regarding the major and secondary emphases that an incident may place on one or more of these four categories in the sequential process.

CHAPTER 3

Policy analysis

The previous chapters pointed out that analysis of the incidents and critiques included in this book will almost always lead readers into decision-making situations. Most, if not all, of the incidents can be analyzed further by extending the reader's involvement into a policy-formulation and implementation process. It will prove useful, therefore, to examine certain factors that should be taken into consideration when discussing policy-formulation and implementation issues suggested by an incident and its critiques.

SOME DEFINITIONS

The relationship and distinction between strategic decisions and policy decisions at various levels in a firm must be clarified if the analysis of the incidents is to be profitable for the reader. There is a noticeable lack of consensus among textbook authors writing on this subject as to the meaning of various terms. We define the term *strategy* as the method or means of achieving a firm's mission, goals, or objectives. The term *policy* is defined as a decisional guide for assisting in the execution of a strategy. Policies enhance effective implementation or execution of strategies. For purposes of this discussion it is important to note that in most firms there exists a hierarchy of strategies and policies. In the typical diversified multibusiness firm strategic decisions and policy decisions will occur at three levels: (1) the corporate level, (2) the business level, and (3) the functional area or departmental unit level.

Corporate Level. Strategic decisions made at the corporate level are those relating to such questions as to what businesses should the firm's scarce physical, fiscal, and human resources be allocated. Such decisions represent top management's overall game plan for the firm. Corporate-level policy decisions, on the other hand, serve as broad guidelines to be followed in order to effectively implement corporate-level strategies. For example, a firm that has established controlled growth as an objective might make a strategic decision to achieve that growth through acquisition of additional existing businesses. A policy decision might be made to only acquire businesses that will provide a synergistic, or mutually reinforcing, effect. Such a policy would make decisions regarding corporate acquisition strategies easier for those persons in the firm responsible for implementing such strategies.

Business Level. Strategic decisions made at the business level reflect various means or methods that have been adopted to achieve the mission, goals, and objectives of a single business, or division, of the firm. At one time Holiday Inns, Inc., consisted of five distinctive business groups organized as divisions. They were the (1) Motel Division, (2) Transportation Division, (3) Restaurant Division, (4) Products Division, and (5) Casino Gambling Division. Corporate-level strategic decisions at Holiday Inns often centered on which of those businesses or divisions would receive or be denied resource allocations. Business-level strategic decisions occurred within each of the businesses and applied specifically to the particular division. For example, business-level strategic decisions in the Motel Division focused on such questions as the best locations for additional motels, the desired ratio between company-owned and franchised motels, and diversification opportunities in high-priced and low-priced segments of the lodging industry. Policies were formulated at this level in order to provide guidance and direction for managers in the Motel Division attempting to implement such strategic decisions. An example of a business-level policy decision pertaining to the Motel Division's strategy of finding the best locations for future growth was one of building only in locations where occupancy rates could be expected to exceed 80 percent.

Operational Level. Strategic decisions made at the operational level serve as the means for achieving goals and objectives in such functional areas an manufacturing, finance, marketing, engineering, and human resources as well as in departments such as production, sales, research and development, finance, and personnel. They will also provide the means for supporting higher level goals, objectives, and strategies at the business and corporate levels. Policies are adopted at this level to operationalize the implementation of strategies designed to maximize productivity, efficiency, and effectiveness in the functional areas and departmental units. We refer to policies adopted at this level as operational policies. These operational-level policies provide direction to supervisors and middle managers and result from the need to effectively implement corporate, business, and operational-level strategies. It is necessary to elaborate on several points suggested by these definitions.

First, it should be recognized that in diversified multibusiness firms this three-level hierarchy exists, but in single-business firms like Safeway or Coors, the corporate and business levels are one and the same. Therefore, no distinction should be made between corporate-level and business-level strategy and policy decisions in single-business firms.

Second, the need for policies can arise anywhere in the organization. Policies that originate at the corporate level may apply to the entire firm, while policies originating at the business level may apply to a single business, and policies originating at the functional, or departmental, level may apply operationally to activities at that level and/or the entire firm. A policy prohibiting sexual harassment may have originated in the personnel department but applies to every employee in the entire firm. Policies at the operational level are, however, usually more concerned with implementation, whereas policies at the corporate and business levels may be more concerned with planning.

Third, the majority of incidents in this book focus on policy formulation and implementation at the operational level and generally involve the functional area of human resource management. They do, however, serve as a vehicle or mechanism for examining policy formulation and implementation at all levels and in all functional areas. This is because the considerations that one must take into account in formulating and executing policies at the operational level in the functional area of human resource management are much the same for all levels and functional areas of the firm. The basic difference in policy formulation at the corporate/business levels and policy formulation at the operational level is that operational policies must be consistent and compatible with corporate/business-level policies and with policies in other functional areas. All other considerations and suggestions included in this chapter are applicable.

EXAMPLES OF OPERATIONAL POLICIES

Earlier, *policy* was defined simplistically as a decision statement that serves as a guide to behavior and assists in the implementation of strategies. Some elaboration on the definition and some examples of operational policies seem desirable at this point. While policies are supportive of goals and objectives and are needed to make strategies work, they do not generally dictate specific actions to be taken in specific situations. They only define the ground rules, specify the framework, establish the boundaries, and provide the direction within which objectives are to be pursued and strategies implemented. Some latitude in the implementation of a policy is usually considered desirable and necessary. If no latitude is provided for, it becomes a procedure or a rule rather than a policy.

In an "ideal" situation policies result from some perceived need and have been subjected to a rational decision process. This is not always the case. Some policies exist as a result of an arbitrary "on-the-spot" decision on the part of some supervisor and manager, from what is perceived by individuals in the firm to be traditional, or what seems to be desired on management's part. Thus, a policy may not necessarily be a formally written statement; it may be verbal, or even implied. The advantages and disadvantages of written policy statements will be examined later in this chapter; first, some examples of operational policies are given for selected functional areas or departmental units.

1. "Employees in the production department will be offered an opportunity to work a maximum of 15 hours per week overtime."
   This production policy was adopted by an automobile parts manufacturer facing bankruptcy. It supported a survival objective through the adoption of a strategy calling for increased production with existing employees.
2. "All stores will be open 8:00 A.M. to 10:00 P.M. Monday through Sunday."
   This marketing policy, adopted by a chain of retail stores, supports an objective of increasing sales volume through a strategy of keeping stores open for longer periods of time.
3. "All wage increments will be based on merit."
   This personnel department policy was adopted by a large hospital chain and supports an objective of increasing employee productivity through a strategy of providing rewards for high performance, and no rewards for low performance.
4. "No dividends will be paid in any year that is not profitable."
   This financial policy was adopted by a firm in the airline industry and was intended to contribute to the achievement of profit objectives through a strategy of increasing available funds for internal use.
5. "In budget requests priority will always be given to research and development activities."
   This business-level policy, adopted by a newly organized firm in the computer industry, reflects a strategy of emphasizing product development as a means of achieving higher levels of competitiveness.
6. "No person who smokes cigars and/or cigarettes will be permitted to work for this firm."
   This corporate policy was recently adopted by a large company in the construction supply industry. It is not clear what objectives or strategies such a policy supports or is intended to achieve.

POLICY FORMULATION AND IMPLEMENTATION

There are a number of questions to consider when faced with the task of formulating and implementing operational policies. What are the purposes served by policies? Should they be written or not written? How can they best be implemented or executed?

Purposes Served. There are those who argue that a chaotic condition would exist without operational policies, and there are those who argue that policies stifle and restrict individuals in the firm. Those who support the need for clearly written policy statements do so on the basis of the following:

1. Policies provide for internally consistent and standardized performance of activities and implementation of strategies. They are needed to guide, support, and communicate how strategies are to be executed. A policy statement indicating behaviors to be expected reduces conflicting and inconsistent actions of individuals in the firm, and thereby reduces time spent by supervisors and managers on repetitive or recurring problem situations. Policies leave less room for misinterpretation and doubt, and help avoid decisions that are shortsighted and based on expediency. The chance that individual judgment is likely to be exercised in each instance is reduced, and this helps to ensure that similar situations are handled consistently.

2. Individuals in the firm, especially in operational units, are more likely to know what is expected of them if carefully stated policies exist. A policy defines, provides direction, and indicates the boundaries of acceptable behavior. It reduces uncertainties that may exist when individuals face some problem, issue, or question that is unprecedented for them. Placing limits on independent actions contributes to fair and equitable treatment of all individuals in the firm.

3. Policies facilitate and accelerate decision making. Due to time and other restraints managers find it impossible to render a decision on every problem or issue arising from implementing a particular strategy. Policies serve as guides to those charged with implementing the strategy and reduce the quick "made-on-the-spot" decisions that are usually inferior to those that have received prior thoughtful analysis. The need to obtain approvals is reduced if the policy reflects appropriate decisional approaches to the problem, issue, or situation. The policy statement may reflect a generally acceptable predetermined approach to the question, thereby reducing the amount of time managers spend making the same decisions repeatedly.

4. Resistance is reduced. It has been found that employees are more accepting of policies they believe were given thoughtful analysis and considerate attention before being adopted. Publication in a policy manual suggests the policy was not derived in an arbitrary manner, and that it represents a considered judgment.

5. Policies can be used to indicate the sanctions or penalties that will be invoked in instances of violation, noncompliance, or attempts to circumvent them. Just as policies may be used to establish what can be done in

the implementation of strategies, they may also be used to indicate what cannot be done and what will be the penalties for not following the policy.

6. Policies may serve to reduce the potential liability of a firm in areas such as sexual harassment and illegal drug use.

7. Policies may reflect the philosophy, values, and ethics of management and the firm's desired corporate image.

Although there are very few legitimate arguments for having no written policy statements in the firm, there is justification for holding them to a minimum. This perception is based on the idea that it is best to let employees do things their own way as long as that way works. Too much policy can be as stifling as the wrong policy, and creativity is preferred to standardization and strict conformity. Both uniformity and conformity work against creativity and effective implementation. Obviously, managers must decide for themselves if they want more policies, less policies, or different policies. It would seem apparent that having no policies can be chaotic. It is also evident that having a thick omnibus policy manual that is seldom revised is questionable. Just as with most questions of this type, perhaps an eclectic or middle position is the best approach.

The amount of policy making will most likely vary with firms according to size, complexity, and views of managers within the firm. A few policies will suffice for a small firm, whereas a large multibusiness firm may have volumes. Additionally, in a small firm most policies may be verbal; in a large firm they are more likely to be formally written and revised periodically.

Written, Implied, Verbal Policies.   Formulation of policies essentially involves trying to determine in advance what problems or issues can be expected to occur in the implementation of strategies and then developing guides that will resolve the problems or issues in order to facilitate strategy implementation. In doing so the question arises of whether or not policies that have been adopted should be written. Most of those who choose putting policies in written form argue on the basis of the following:

1. Written policies reduce the possibilities for misunderstanding and ambiguity. A written communication of the policy is less likely to result in alteration and ambiguity than would a verbal statement. Written policies will more clearly indicate where the policy originated and designate its source of authorization. It is often useful for those affected by the policy to know whether the policy was internally derived or if it results from the firm's efforts to comply with external forces such as laws, courts, or agencies such as the Equal Employment Opportunity Commission.

2. Written policies will be more likely to have been thoroughly and comprehensively analyzed with regard to meaning, content, and usage than if verbally stated with no attempt made to write out the statement. The writing of a policy is not necessarily an easy task and may require much analysis and thought. A written policy will also serve as the basis for revisions in the event modifications are needed.

3. Written policies will reduce the tendency for employees in the firm to imply policies from their observation of managerial actions, activities, and decisions. Such observations may have never been intended to be interpreted as policies.

One persuasive argument against committing to written form policy statements is that in a firm concerned with security of information a written policy statement will reveal corporate secrets and give competitors insights into the firm's goals, objectives, and strategies. Another argument frequently heard against written policies is that flexibility and latitude are needed in the execution of policies and that many individuals in the firm may feel bound and restricted by written policy statements. Finally, some would argue that since it is impossible to determine in advance all the problems and issues for which policy statements are needed, the effort is a futile one. The mere absence of a written policy statement may erroneously suggest that the firm has taken no position with regard to a particular problem and issue, and that any form of behavior is acceptable or condoned.

Policy Execution. The question of effective policy implementation is one that cannot be comprehensively treated within the limits of this chapter. Though the formulation of clearly written policy statements will require some thought and effort, it is a relatively easy task when compared with the enormous amount of effort and leadership skill required to effectively implement policies. There is no one easy formula, or 10 tried and true rules, that can be offered to ensure effective execution of policies. Perhaps the best advice to those charged with effective implementation of policies is to be sure the following questions have been addressed in the initial formulation of the policy. Taking into account such considerations when first adopting a policy may facilitate more effective implementation.

1. Can the policy be implemented? This is the most crucial and most basic of all the questions one should consider when formulating policy statements. There are some policies that simply cannot be executed, and it would be best not to adopt them in the first place. The no-smoking policy given as an example of an operating policy earlier in this chapter is one that the company adopting it will find very difficult, if indeed not impossible, to implement. The company proposes to implement the policy by conducting pulmonary function tests that measure lung capacity in order to determine if employees are smoking in their homes and backyards. The legality, cost, employee acceptance, and accuracy of such testing are factors that raise serious doubts as to whether or not the no-smoking policy will ever be successfully executed.

2. Does the policy meet some realistic need? A policy should not exist unless there is some justifiable reason for its existence. This question also suggests that there should be some established mechanism for periodic review of all policies to determine if they continue to meet some need. Policies are generally written with the long view in mind. They usually live

a long life; perhaps too long without review and revision. They often outlive the strategies that caused their creation. A change in strategy should be followed quickly by a change in policy. Policies that are seldom, if ever, used should be eliminated.

3. Is the policy consistent, compatible, and supportive of the firm's corporate- and business-level goals, objectives, and strategies? Also, is it consistent with other operational policies in other functional areas and departmental units of the firm? Is it in conformity with applicable federal, state, and local laws?

4. Does the policy facilitate, or block, strategy implementation? Since implementation of policies can determine the success or failure of strategic decisions, efforts must be made to determine if policies exist in appropriate number in key areas critical to the firm's success.

5. Is the policy understandable, or is it so vaguely written that it cannot be effectively communicated to all affected by it and those who are responsible for its effective execution? It must be clear who the policy applies to and who is responsible for executing it. For effective implementation, individuals within the firm must be able to understand what the objective of the policy is, why it is important, and what it entails. Otherwise, the following reaction occurs: "What is the reason?" "There is no reason; it's company policy."

6. Is the policy reasonable, timely, and practical given existing or unexpected problems, issues, and situations?

7. Does the policy cover recurring problems, issues, or situations that can be expected to occur?

8. Does the policy reflect desired company practices, culture, and values?

9. Does the policy appropriately limit and constrain employee behavior, yet provide latitude and flexibility to behavioral actions and activities? The question often arises as to whether or not it is appropriate to include as part of the policy statement itself the disciplinary measures that will be taken in cases of violation, noncompliance, or circumvention.

10. Does the policy provide for exceptions? There are instances when, in spite of valid arguments for following a policy as stated, arguments can justifiably be made for making exceptions. Some argue that a policy should never be so inflexibly stated that exceptions are prevented; especially when good reasons for making an exception exist. On the other hand, arguments against making exceptions are made on the basis that exceptions establish precedents and render a policy meaningless. The danger is that exceptions result in an undermining and gradual erosion of policy execution. Some mechanism for permitting exceptions probably needs to be established. However, when the record indicates that a lot of exceptions are being made to the policy, it is time for reevaluation of the need for the policy.

Football coach Vince Lombardi is said to have made the statement that, "The best game plan in the world never blocked or tackled anybody." His statement suggests that just being able to conceive, write, and formulate a policy is not enough. Carefully developed policies mean very little in the absence of appropriate and effective implementation. A good policy does not guarantee effective execution of the policy. The value of any policy depends not only on its content and structure but equally on whether it can be successfully implemented. Effective leadership is the major component in assuring that policies will be implemented effectively and that a follow-through on that implementation occurs.

WHAT THIS INCIDENT IS ABOUT:
This incident examines various issues related to
sexual harassment in the workplace, a form of
employee behavior that is discriminatory according
to Equal Employment Opportunity Commission
(EEOC) guidelines. Emphasis is placed on actions
that will result in the formulation and implementation of policies for the prevention and control of
such activity.

1

A sexual harassment policy

INCIDENT

Ralph Wilson, director of human resources for the Williams Publishing
Company, knew he could no longer delay responding to a memorandum he
had received a few days earlier from his new boss, Fred Clements. The
memorandum read as follows:

DATE: December 1, 1987

TO: Mr. Ralph Wilson, Director of Human Resources, Williams Publishing
Company

FROM: Mr. Fred Clements, President, Williams Publishing Company

SUBJECT: Need for a Sexual Harassment Policy

Shortly after assuming my present position, I thoroughly reviewed the
company's policy manual for which your department is responsible. I was
appalled at the absence of a policy statement relating to the subject of sexual
harassment. Perhaps my reaction is a result of an uncomfortable situation I
experienced just before leaving my previous employer. I will briefly review
that situation in order to emphasize my concern with the sexual harassment
issue.

My position with the other company was as division sales manager. It was
often necessary for my regional and district sales managers, positions staffed
by both men and women, to travel together for various reasons. One regional
manager, a female, initiated a formal complaint against her district manager
—accusing him of sexual harassment whenever both were traveling together
and especially when attending meetings and conferences together. Heated
accusations were exchanged between both individuals, and at one point it

even appeared the incident might reach a point where the company could be held liable for both compensatory and punitive damages. I was able to eventually resolve the situation to almost everyone's satisfaction, but only after it became painfully obvious that the matter could have been handled much more expeditiously if there had existed a definitively stated policy regarding such issues. Therefore, I want you to immediately consider the following questions and respond to each:

1. Is it desirable to have a specific statement in the policy manual addressing the issue of sexual harassment?
2. What constitutes sexual harassment? Certain acts, such as unwanted sexual invitations, amorous advances, and unwelcome physical contacts, may be obvious examples. But what about suggestive looks and gestures, unsolicited attention, demeaning remarks, intimidation, distasteful comments, flirting, dirty jokes, persistent requests for dates, and so forth?
3. Is it possible to establish external policies and rules governing complex male-female relationships where men and women must work together cooperatively and harmoniously?
4. Because the Williams Publishing Company has both men and women in positions of authority, is there a question of "gender" harassment? Should any policy we adopt be broadened to address this issue?
5. What procedures should employees be encouraged to follow when making sexual harassment charges? Will our existing grievance procedures suffice?
6. How best can we implement any newly formulated and adopted policies? Who will be responsible for implementing them? When and under what circumstances should they be implemented? What will be the desired results of their implementation?
7. What action(s) should be taken in the event of violation, or noncompliance?

Wilson decided to respond to President Clement's memorandum by sending him a memo of his own. In it, he would provide his views regarding each of the seven categories of questions. He would also formulate a statement to be included in the policy manual that would address each of the questions posed by Mr. Clements. He recognized this was no small task, but it was his responsibility as director of human resources to do so. Furthermore, he had been told to do so by his boss.

CRITIQUES

VIRGINIA G. MAURER
Associate Professor of Business Law
and Legal Studies
University of Florida

The president's concern is well based. The problem of sexual harassment is real, and it has both legal and business aspects. Legal cases under

Title VII of the Civil Rights Act of 1964 and a recent U.S. Supreme Court case have established that certain forms of sexual harassment constitute prohibited sex-based discrimination—for which the firm may be liable in damages. The Equal Employment Opportunity Commission has defined prohibited sexual harassment to include not only unwanted sexual advances and requests for sexual favors, but also verbal or physical conduct of a sexual nature that unreasonably interferes with work performance or creates an intimidating, hostile, or offensive working environment. Moreover, the pervasiveness of sexual harassment in the workplace, and the effect of such harassment on morale and job performance, is well documented. The firm cannot tolerate behavior that undermines its own personnel policies. Therefore, the firm needs a well-conceived and well-developed policy, backed up by an appropriate training program. Wilson should respond to the president's memo with a memo indicating a proposed follow-up action and then draft a policy and training component for the president's consideration.

The task is not simple because the subject involves sensitive human interaction. Many people fail to distinguish between behavior appropriate to their personal lives and behavior appropriate to their professional lives. And because of the diversity of values and ethics in our society, one cannot expect general agreement on the meaning or the appropriateness of sexual behavior on the job—all the more reason why the firm must clearly define its interests and communicate what behavior is and is not acceptable.

As a starting point, Wilson should consider whether, in this firm, it is ever appropriate for a superior to have sexual intercourse with a subordinate, or to make unmistakably romantic overtures to such a person, whether or not the intercourse or overture was posed as a job condition or wanted by the subordinate. A strong argument can be made that such behavior is invariably inappropriate, for the same reason that it is inappropriate to supervise a spouse or a close relative in the firm; the relationship poses a conflict of interest, it raises the suspicion of favoritism, it engenders mistrust among coworkers, and it usually interferes with judgment about the subordinate's performance and development. In short, it is unmistakably bad for the firm. Holding the superior absolutely liable, with no "consent" defense, effectively assures that the behavior will not occur often. Punishing the subordinate for sexual behavior with a superior only assures that the policy will not be very effective. Swift and visible enforcement may effectively remove sex as a desired object in the work relationship. If unambiguous sexual behavior is unambiguously taboo, harmonious and cooperative male-female work relationships in the firm are more easily fostered.

The other problems—the behavior that falls into the broader category of sexual harassment, the general, systematic disparagement of women, or the sexual relationships that do not involve authority relationships—are not so simple. The firm's policy should be stated clearly: every employee is valued, and behavior that demeans or degrades a colleague or subordinate on account of his or her sex will not be tolerated. In fact, this is a complex area of life and of human communication where uncertainty about what will or will not offend may be genuine. Therefore, it is particularly important to establish clear and reasonable expectations for both men and women, so that male-female working relationships are not unnecessarily strained by sexual harassment or by the sexual harassment policy. The fear of false accusation should be confronted head-on: that the policy is enforced justly, and that very few subordinates jeopardize their positions to make *true* accusations, much less *false* ones. Supervisors must be sensitized to the dynamics of this problem. Fortunately, many policy and training models exist and can be adapted to the firm's circumstances.

Finally, procedure must be considered carefully. The problem with perceiving the remedy as lying solely in a grievance procedure is that it misses the point that the capacity to support the organization's goals and policies is a matter of professional competence, not of personal morality or ethics alone. Sexual harassment is not simply a personal offense that happens to occur on the job. Responsibility for identifying the problem and acting on it should lie with the offender's supervisor. It is his or her job to pick up on a subordinate problem of this nature, to demand the facts and relevant information from knowledgeable parties (not simply accept what is voluntarily forthcoming), to make fair judgments, and to act. To leave the matter to a grievance procedure, in which the subordinate has the burden of proof and makes the accusation at his or her peril, assures that the organization's policy will be underenforced. Nevertheless, the offense is unlikely to surface unless the subordinate or his or her co-workers have a clear route to an effective decision maker. Therefore, the firm must establish and identify such a route in the policy. A grievance procedure may be one such route.

JOHN R. SCHERMERHORN, JR.
Professor of Management
Southern Illinois University at Carbondale

Ralph Wilson faces a situation that is timely in respect to both the specific issue at hand, sexual harassment, and the general circumstance in which it arises, managerial decision making. I will address both facets of the incident in this critique.

To begin, Wilson is clearly experiencing the challenges of being a manager. He is being held accountable by his supervisor for the development and implementation of policies appropriate to his area of organizational responsibility—human resources. Ideally Wilson would not be caught in this position of having to *react* to the requests of his boss. Rather, Wilson should be sufficiently alert to organizational needs and environmental trends so that he can take the initiative in suggesting new and revised policies over time. Part of his current dilemma may very well relate to the fact that he is a bit embarrassed to be caught in a situation where the *new* boss feels Wilson has been slow in taking action to fill a void in the company's operating policies.

When we shift our attention more specifically to the sexual harassment policy, Wilson should recognize that he needs to help formulate and implement a policy that fits both the issue at hand, that is, protection of individual rights in the workplace, and the specific work environment of the Williams Publishing Company. Fred Clements appears to be acting on the basis of a problematic situation encountered in a different organization. He may be tempted to transfer both the perceived problem and the proposed solution from that setting to his new company. Wilson, on the other hand, should know Williams Publishing and its history, climate, and culture. He should be alert to and accept his responsibility to help his boss learn all about Williams Publishing and understand it as a unique work environment within which policies, such as one on sexual harassment, must be developed and implemented.

From Wilson's perspective, the proposed new policy should be pursued with full consideration of the company's responsibility to act in an ethical and socially responsible way to protect the rights of its employees. Wilson should also recognize that the best policy will be one that satisfies this goal and one that proves acceptable to company employees. Thus, he should start by developing a brainstorming document that frames a tentative policy around answers to the seven questions raised by Clements. Then, he should convene a representative task force of company employees to react to and further refine the document. This revised document should be shared with Clements for further review and modification.

The task force should include persons from various levels in the company and should include a mixture of males and females. Use of this task force would allow for inputs and perspectives from employees during the policy-formulation phase. This will help ensure that an appropriate policy is formulated and also establish a good framework for eventual policy implementation. Everyone is sure to benefit from this strategy.

In summary, Wilson should respond immediately to Clements and tell him a policy will be quickly formulated, but that he (Wilson) plans to do so with the active participation of a representative group of company employees. This should satisfy Clements for the moment and give Wilson time to proceed in a planned and systematic manner. Next he should convene a task force to help formulate a suggested policy on sexual harassment. Based on the suggestions of this task force, he should respond in writing to the president, addressing each of the seven points raised in the memo. When discussing the proposal with Clements, Wilson should act in a polite and responsible way to ensure the policy that is developed and implemented is truly correct for Williams Publishing Company. That is, he should strive for a policy that is appropriate in its ethical/social legal protections and is consistent with the climate/culture of the company as a whole.

Finally, Wilson should make a personal commitment *not* to be caught having to *react* to such initiatives from the president in the future. This means he should act as a "problem *finder*" and not just a "problem *solver*." The former is a proactive manager; the latter is a reactive one. This whole situation is a good developmental opportunity for Wilson. It is a chance to "learn" from experience and adopt a more progressive managerial style. Wilson's goal, therefore, should be twofold: (1) to successfully respond to the president's expressed desire for a sexual harassment policy, and (2) to personally become more active in managing his department and conducting himself so that the department becomes the primary source of initiatives for policy development in human resources management for Williams Publishing. Only then will Wilson be able to say that he is a "manager" in the true sense of the term!

OBSERVATIONS

The president of a major university recently appointed one of the critique writers, Professor Virginia Maurer, to chair a campuswide committee to study various forms of sexual harassment reportedly occurring on that campus. Ms. Maurer, as a result, has developed considerable expertise on the subject, and her point that a firm may be liable for damages that occur from sexual harassment is one that should not be considered lightly. A firm is especially vulnerable if it has been negligent in establishing clearly articulated policies for the prevention and control of sexual harassment.

Curtiss Behrens, author of one of the suggested readings, emphasizes that an employer must do more than demonstrate the existence of a policy prohibiting such conduct. The firm is liable when it knows, or should have known, of the harassment and took no immediate and corrective action. The steps that can be taken to develop a sexual harassment policy suggested by Professor John Schermerhorn in his critique and the recommendations regarding implementation of such policies found in other suggested readings have special relevance to individuals, such as Ralph Wilson and Fred Clements, who have responsibilities in this sensitive area.

DISCUSSION ITEMS

1. Ralph Wilson decided to respond to President Clement's memorandum by sending him one of his own. Write the memorandum you think Wilson should send.

2. Evaluate Professor Schermerhorn's recommendation that a task force be appointed to refine a document for President Clement's review and modification.
3. In his article that appears on the suggested reading list, Curtiss Behrens states that discipline for those guilty of sexual harassment must be immediate and sufficiently severe to discourage such behavior in the future. How would you determine the appropriateness of disciplinary action in relation to the nature of the offense?

SUGGESTED READINGS

BOOKS

Arnold, Hugh J., and Daniel C. Feldman. *Organizational Behavior*. New York: McGraw-Hill, 1986, chaps. 4, 15, 16.

Callahan, Robert E.; C. Patrick Fleenor; and Harry Knudson. *Understanding Organizational Behavior*. Columbus, Ohio: Charles E. Merrill Publishing, 1986, chaps. 1–3.

Davis, Keith, and John W. Newstrom. *Human Behavior at Work*. 7th ed. New York: McGraw-Hill, 1985, chaps. 18–20.

Donnelly, James H.; James L. Gibson; and John M. Ivancevich. *Fundamentals of Management*. 6th ed. Plano, Tex.: Business Publications, 1987, chaps. 4, 9, 20, 23.

Ewing, David W. *Do It My Way or You're Fired*. New York: John Wiley & Sons, 1983.

French, Wendell L. *The Personnel Management Process*. 6th ed. Boston: Houghton Mifflin, 1987, chaps. 1, 8.

Griffin, Ricky W. *Management*. 2nd ed. Boston: Houghton Mifflin, 1987, chaps. 5, 21.

Heneman, Herbert G.; Donald P. Schwab; John A. Fossum; and Lee D. Dyer. *Personnel/Human Resource Management*. 3rd ed. Homewood, Ill.: Richard D. Irwin, 1986, chaps. 1, 2, 11.

Megginson, Leon C. *Personnel Management: A Human Resources Approach*. 5th ed. Homewood, Ill.: Richard D. Irwin, 1985, chap. 4.

Miner, John B. *People Problems: The Executive Answer Book*. New York: Random House, 1985, pp. 1–320.

Robertson, Cliff. *Staying Out of Court: A Manager's Guide to Employment Law*. Lexington, Mass.: D. C. Heath, 1985, pp. 1–177.

Rue, Leslie W., and Lloyd L. Byars. *Management: Theory and Application*. 4th ed. Homewood, Ill.: Richard D. Irwin, 1986, chaps. 5, 10, 15, 16.

Schermerhorn, John R. *Management for Productivity*. 2nd ed. New York: John Wiley & Sons, 1986, chaps. 1, 4, 9, 21.

JOURNALS

Behrens, C. W. "Co-Worker Sexual Harassment: The Employer's Liability." *Personnel Journal* 63, no. 5 (May 1984), pp. 12–14.

Brief, A. P., and S. J. Motowidlo. "Prosocial Organizational Behaviors." *Academy of Management Review* 11, no. 4 (October 1986), pp. 710–25.

Chusmir, Leonard H. "Job Commitment and the Organizational Woman." *Academy of Management Review* 7, no. 4 (October 1982), pp. 595–602.

Cohen, L. R. "Nonverbal (Mis)Communication between Managerial Men and Women." *Business Horizons* 26, no. 1 (January–February 1983), pp. 13–17.

Collins, Eliza C. "Managers and Lovers." *Harvard Business Review* 61, no. 5 (September–October 1983), pp. 142–53.

Collins, G. C., and T. B. Blodgett. "Sexual Harassment: Some See It, Some Won't." *Harvard Business Review* 59, no. 2 (March–April 1981), pp. 76–95.

Curry, Lynne. "Legal Hot Water: The Hint of Sex." *Administrative Management* 48, no. 12 (December 1985), p. 59.

Faley, Robert H. "Sexual Harassment: Critical Review of Legal Cases with General Principles and Preventive Measures." *Personnel Psychology* 35, no. 3 (Autumn 1982), pp. 583–99.

Hemming, Heather. "Women in a Man's World: Sexual Harassment." *Human Relations* 38, no. 1 (January 1985), pp. 67–79.

Jamison, Kaleel. "Managing Sexual Attraction in the Workplace." *Personnel Administration* 28, no. 8 (August 1983), pp. 45–51.

Linenberger, Patrice, and T. J. Keaveny. "Sexual Harassment: The Employer's Legal Obligation." *Personnel* 58, no. 6 (November–December 1981), pp. 60–68.

Motowidlo, S. J. "Does Job Satisfaction Lead to Consideration and Personal Sensitivity?" *Academy of Management Journal* 27, no. 4 (December 1984), pp. 910–15.

Powell, Gary N. "Sexual Harassment: Confronting the Issue of Definition." *Business Horizons* 26, no. 4 (July–August 1983), pp. 24–28.

Sherwin, D. S. "The Ethical Roots of the Business System." *Harvard Business Review* 61, no. 6 (November–December 1983), pp. 183–92.

Wesman, Elizabeth C. "Shortage of Research Abets Sexual Harassment Confusion." *Personnel Administration* 28, no. 11 (November 1983), pp. 60–65.

Wymer, John F. "Damages for Sexual Harassment." *Personnel Journal* 62, no. 3 (March 1983), pp. 181–82.

WHAT THIS INCIDENT IS ABOUT:
Though the major issue in this incident is one of
managerial prerogatives, the specific focus is on the
power of bosses to fire arbitrarily as contrasted with
the social need for job protection.

2

Abusive discharge suit

INCIDENT

Mary O'Shea had been looking forward to assuming her new position as
head of the newly created legal department of the Mid-Western Telephone
Company. The department had been established as a result of a massive
company reorganization brought about because of divestiture from a large
holding company. Once on the job, O'Shea realized she would be quite
busy for some time due to an enormous number of requests for her legal
opinion. Many of the requests resulted from questionable management
practices in the past and other requests were from managers given newly
acquired authority due to decentralization and separation from the parent
company.

One request, which O'Shea realized must be given high priority and
immediate attention, came from the company president himself. It seems
that just prior to divestiture, a company vice president, acting in accord
with what he thought was the parent company policy, discharged the
manager of an area telephone exchange, Randy Bishop. Documents revealed that when Bishop filed for divorce and moved in with a female
co-worker, he was fired on the grounds of adultery. Bishop filed an abusive
discharge suit against the company contending he was dismissed unfairly
merely because he was living with a female while separated from his wife.
He argues this violates federal discrimination laws because the company
would not fire single employees who cohabitate. Bishop further argues the
company has no right to impose its own moral standards on an employee's
private life. The vice president who fired Bishop contends that management should be allowed to fire any nonunion member that it chooses. He
emphasizes that our society distinguishes adultery from sex between two
single adults, and that his company should have the prerogative of doing so
as well. He also maintains that the use of different standards for married

28

and single employees does not violate laws pertaining to discrimination in employment.

O'Shea was aware the issue involved more than the company's right to involvement in how employees conduct their private lives, although she felt the private behavior of employees should be of no concern to the employer. She knew that in recent years some companies have been hit with these new "abusive discharge" suits, and she was aware that the courts, reflecting a growing sensitivity to personal rights and a growing awareness of the social need for job protection, are increasingly curbing the power of employers to fire employees arbitrarily. The courts have, in effect, told employers they cannot fire employees, union or nonunion, if the terminations are unfair. O'Shea realized there were basically three alternatives; but she could only recommend one to the company president. One idea was to support the action taken by the vice president. Another plan was to reinstate Bishop and admit a mistake was made. The third idea was to negotiate an out-of-court settlement. The first would involve costly and time-consuming legal maneuvers with possible substantial damages awarded to the claimant. The second and third alternatives might be construed as an admission of wrongdoing, although O'Shea guessed the company president would like to avoid litigation and dispose of the case in the least expensive way possible. Whatever alternative she decided to recommend, she was convinced the company should adopt a policy stipulating the circumstances in which meddling in employees' private lives is, or is not, justified.

CRITIQUES

WILLIAM P. ANTHONY
Professor of Management
Florida State University

When an organization takes action against an employee because of incidents that have occurred in the employee's personal life, the company walks on very thin legal ice. In this case, the termination of a manager for an increasingly common practice—one might even argue it is a practice that is becoming accepted in society—places the company in a difficult legal position. With increasing support from the courts and federal regulatory agencies for the protection of employee rights, including the right to privacy, the company will likely have a time-consuming and expensive effort to make its ruling stick in court.

The situation is further complicated by the recent divestiture. In all likelihood, the newly formed company has not yet formulated an overall policy on employee rights related to rights and expectations of the employer. Such a broad based policy is important today—the specific application of the policy to perceived "adultery" and other moral cases is but one area where application is needed. There are many other off-the-job situations where such a policy would have application, such as off-the-job use of alcohol and drugs, political or special interest group membership, moonlighting, and so on.

Since Mary O'Shea believes the company wishes to avoid litigation, the first alternative—making the termination stick even if it means court action—should be rejected. Such action would be time-consuming and costly, and in view of recent court decisions, the company would likely lose the case. Because of attention focused on telephone companies, the wide publicity surrounding the case would be damaging.

The second option—reinstatement with an apology—also may cause a problem because of the loss of credibility on behalf of the vice president and the company. Thus, we are left with the third option. An out-of-court settlement would likely be quick and inexpensive compared to court action. The company saves face and minimizes bad publicity. If such a settlement is not accepted by the dismissed employee, then a hard-nosed stance of "we'll fight you through the courts" should be taken.

Finally, the firm needs to get its act together on formulating an employee rights policy. This broad policy statement should deal with employees' rights as they are affected by both on and off-the-job behavior. Such a policy would provide guidance for future management decisions in this area and would lessen the chances of a similar problem arising.

R. EDWARD FREEMAN
Visiting Associate Professor
of Business Administration
The Darden School
University of Virginia

There are three major issues in considering abusive discharge suits as illustrated by the incident described at Mid-Western Telephone: (1) Does management have the right to fire employees at will? (2) Is it good management practice to fire employees, such as Randy Bishop, at will? and (3) Should management tolerate a diversity of values from its stakeholders?

The doctrine of "employment at will" states that employees enter into voluntary contracts with their employers. Some of these contracts are explicit, but many of them are implicit. The doctrine holds that one contract provision is that employees serve at the pleasure of employers. Management has a responsibility to the firm's owners and other stakeholders to run the firm as efficiently and effectively as possible. This can occur only if they have control over the hiring and firing of employees. Now labor law protects unionized workers from abuses of the doctrine of employment at will, but there is no such protection for the roughly 70 percent of the workforce that is not unionized, except in cases of discrimination, and so forth. But the issue must be addressed in terms of "employment at will." Is this doctrine generally a good idea? What are the potential abuses? How can these abuses be prevented?

Is it good practice to fire an employee such as Bishop? While management may have the right to fire Bishop, it is not smart for management to exercise that right. Management has an obligation to the stockholders and stakeholders of Mid-Western Telephone. Bishop's contract with the company should be based on his performance. If management is smart, it will not care if Bishop has three heads and lives and sleeps with 45 men and women, if he gets the job done well and if his personal life does not unnecessarily interfere with his performance. How management gets out of this pickle is exactly Mary O'Shea's role: to interpret the law and give management the best advice. I would recommend an out-of-court settlement that may include reinstating Bishop. The argument to be given inside the company is that while the vice president was following company policy, the policy itself needs revision to keep up with the changing nature of personal relationships.

This case raises a fundamental management issue. In today's business environment, with a host of stakeholder groups making claims on the firm, it is imperative that management and company policies be tolerant of a multiplicity of values. Indeed, a good principle is one proposed by philosopher Immanuel Kant: Treat other persons with respect, as ends in themselves, not as means to your own ends. This "liberal" principle is embodied in the stakeholder approach to management—whereby stakeholders pursue their projects through their interactions with the firm. Management must realize that stakeholder groups have rights to autonomy, and that they have some control over important matters in their lives. On the other hand, stakeholders must see management as autonomous agents pursuing their own projects through the firm.

It is only by treating each other as persons worthy of respect, each with the right to determine her or his own future, that incidents such as abusive discharge suits can be avoided. This principle goes beyond any legal actions and must become a norm of business ethics and professional management. Until we do so, there will be many Bishops, many long and expensive court cases, a proliferation of lawyers such as O'Shea, who make strategic decisions for companies on legal rather than business grounds, and a lot of frustration for managers.

OBSERVATIONS

An article published in *The Wall Street Journal* related the experience of a 26-year-old female attorney for Westinghouse Electric Corporation, who accepted an invitation to dance with a co-worker on a business trip. Her supervisor, upon learning of this, admonished her for unprofessional behavior and then lectured her on her tight and flashy clothes. When she threatened to relate his actions to a company vice president, she was fired. She sued her supervisor, claiming sex discrimination, and a federal court judge awarded her $121,670.

Both Professors Anthony and Freeman astutely observe that incidents such as the one at Westinghouse and the one facing Mary O'Shea place a firm in a difficult legal position. Bills were recently introduced in a number of state legislatures designed to prohibit employers from firing workers except for "just cause," and there is speculation that the growing debate about employee rights versus managerial prerogatives may lead to a push for federal legislation to prohibit "unjust firings." A theme reflected in several of the suggested readings is that the incentive for legislation will diminish only if employers quickly develop equitable internal policies and practices to protect employees against arbitrary treatment.

DISCUSSION ITEMS

1. Discuss examples of other ways that employers get involved in the private lives of their employees. When is it acceptable and when is it not acceptable?
2. A Michigan legislator was quoted as saying that "Someday the idea that an employee can be fired at whim will be viewed as uncivilized." Evaluate that statement based on your own perceptions.
3. Mary O'Shea has reduced her options to three. Both Professors Anthony and Freeman seem to favor the option of negotiating an out-of-court settlement between Mid-Western Telephone and Randy Bishop. What do you think would be acceptable to each party? Which option do you favor? Why?

SUGGESTED READINGS

BOOKS

Arnold, Hugh J., and Daniel C. Feldman. *Organizational Behavior*. New York: McGraw-Hill, 1986, chaps. 1, 14.

Callahan, Robert E.; C. Patrick Fleenor; and Harry Knudson. *Understanding Organizational Behavior*. Columbus, Ohio: Charles E. Merrill Publishing, 1986, chap. 8.

Davis, Keith, and John W. Newstrom. *Human Behavior at Work*. 7th ed. New York: McGraw-Hill, 1985, chaps. 16, 18.

Donnelly, James H.; James L. Gibson; and John M. Ivancevich. *Fundamentals of Management*. 6th ed. Plano, Tex.: Business Publications, 1987, chaps. 9, 10–12, 20.

Farley, Lin. *Sexual Shakedown: The Sexual Harassment of Women on the Job*. New York: McGraw-Hill, 1978.

Freeman, R. Edward. *Strategic Management: A Stakeholder Approach*. Hagerstown, Md.: Ballinger Publishing Co., 1984.

French, Wendell L. *The Personnel Management Process*. 6th ed. Boston: Houghton Mifflin, 1987, chap. 8.

Griffin, Ricky W. *Management*. 2nd ed. Boston: Houghton Mifflin, 1987, chaps. 1, 10, 21.

Heneman, Herbert G.; Donald P. Schwab; John A. Fossum; and Lee D. Dyer. *Personnel/Human Resource Management*. 3rd ed. Homewood, Ill.: Richard D. Irwin, 1986, chaps. 2, 11.

McFarland, Dalton E. *Management and Society*. Englewood Cliffs, N.J.: Prentice-Hall, 1982, chap. 14.

Megginson, Leon C. *Personnel Management: A Human Resources Approach*. 5th ed. Homewood, Ill.: Richard D. Irwin, 1985, chaps. 1–4.

Rue, Leslie W., and Lloyd L. Byars. *Management: Theory and Application*. 4th ed. Homewood, Ill.: Richard D. Irwin, 1986, chaps. 3, 10, 16.

Schermerhorn, John R. *Management for Productivity*. 2nd ed. New York: John Wiley & Sons, 1986, chaps. 9, 14, 20.

JOURNALS

Carter, A., and N. Foy. "Will 1990 Mark the End of the Will to Work—Or the Right to Manage?" *Long-Range Planning* 14, no. 2 (April 1981), pp. 42–48.

Condon, T. J., and Richard Wolff. "Procedures that Safeguard Your Right to Fire." *Harvard Business Review* 63, no. 6 (November–December 1985), pp. 16–18.

"Curtailing the Freedom to Fire." *Business Week*, March 19, 1984, pp. 29–30.

Ewing, David W. "Your Right to Fire." *Harvard Business Review* 61, no. 2 (March–April 1983), pp. 32–44.

Hambrick, D. C., and P. A. Mason. "Upper Echelons: The Organization as a Reflection of Its Top Managers." *Academy of Management Review* 9, no. 2 (April 1984), pp. 193–206.

Harrison, Edward L. "Legal Restrictions on the Employer's Authority to Discipline." *Personnel Journal* 61, no. 2 (February 1982), pp. 136–40.

Hatano, Daryl G. "Employee Rights and Corporate Restrictions: A Balancing of Liberties." *California Management Review* 24, no. 2 (Winter 1981), pp. 5–13.

"It's Getting Harder to Make a Firing Stick." *Business Week*, June 27, 1983, pp. 104–5.

Leap, T. L., and M. D. Crino. "How to Deal with Bizarre Employee Behavior." *Harvard Business Review* 64, no. 3 (May–June 1986), pp. 18–25.

Matusewitch, Eric. "Employment Rights of Ex-Offenders." *Personnel Journal* 62, no. 11 (December 1983), pp. 951–54.

Nobile, R. J. "Employee Searches in the Workplace: Developing a Realistic Policy." *Personnel Administrator* 30, no. 5 (May 1985), pp. 89–98.

Oliver, A. T. "The Disappearing Right to Terminate Employees at Will." *Personnel Journal* 61, no. 12 (December 1982), pp. 910–17.

O'Toole, James. "Employee Practices at the Best-Managed Companies." *California Management Review* 28, no. 1 (Fall 1985), pp. 35–66.

Posner, Barry, and Warren H. Schmidt. "Values and the American Manager: An Update." *California Management Review* 26, no. 3 (Spring 1984), pp. 202–16.

Summer, C. W. "Protecting All Employees against Unfair Dismissal." *Harvard Business Review* 58, no. 1 (January–February 1980), pp. 132–39.

Wooten, B. E., and Lynn Godkin. "The Specter of Malpractice: Are Personnel Managers Liable for Job-Related Actions?" *Personnel* 60, no. 6 (November–December 1983), pp. 53–58.

WHAT THIS INCIDENT IS ABOUT:
This incident provides the vehicle for an examination of a variety of issues such as the influence of
a spouse on the manager, ethical considerations in
personality testing, staffing, executive stress, policy
formulation, and policy implementation.

3

An exam for Mrs. Smith

INCIDENT

The president of Lincoln, Inc., asked the director of development to
recommend from within the organization the person most suitable for
promotion to the position of plant manager. Lincoln, a producer of electrical appliances, controlled 16 plants throughout 11 states. The vacant
position involved a plant employing 2,300 individuals in Dallas.

Extensive evaluation of personnel records revealed the name of John
Smith, assistant manager of a company plant in Little Rock, Arkansas.
Smith was a graduate of a leading university with a master's degree in
business administration. He had six years of industrial experience and four
years of military service when he joined the company. During his seven
years with Lincoln, he had progressed rapidly and was highly regarded
throughout the company.

An invitation was extended for Smith to visit the central office in Philadelphia. Company officials requested him to bring his wife so that they
might meet her. The president welcomed the Smiths at the airport and
escorted them to his club for dinner and conversation. He was quite
impressed by Smith, and with a single qualification, he was inclined to
offer him the plant manager post. His qualification was a recommendation
to the director of development that Mrs. Smith be asked to submit to a
psychological examination before Mr. Smith was tendered a definite offer.
The president believed that Mrs. Smith exhibited certain traits of a neurotic or psychotic nature.

Mr. Smith was noticeably disturbed and offended when he learned of
this suggestion. He thereupon stated that he had no intention of following
the president's request. He stated further that he believed that his wife's
health did not bear upon his employability, and that an apology for a

serious breach of decorum was due from the company president. If he received no such apology, he felt he would have to submit his resignation before returning to Little Rock.

The director of development was faced with either approaching the president for an apology or supporting him in his contention that Mrs. Smith required a psychological examination. The director felt that while his personal philosophy was closely attuned to the president's, the absence of a clearly stated policy requiring psychological examinations of all spouses was a factor that should influence his decision. He finally decided, however, to accept Mr. Smith's resignation.

CRITIQUES

JOHN M. CHAMPION
Professor of Management and Adminstrative
Sciences
University of Florida

Confronted with an immediate decision, the director of development chose the correct and proper course of action. The president of Lincoln, Inc., was fearful that Mrs. Smith was suffering from some mental disturbance, and he was thus within his rights in requesting a psychological examination for her. Psychologists have based much of their work on the premise that human behavior is the product of various influences — such as heredity, religious and home environments, and education. Hence, John Smith's wife is an influence who could conceivably adversely affect his performance as plant manager. It is also questionable whether Mrs. Smith is currently capable of performing her function as a plant manager's wife.

One must also consider that Mr. Smith's behavior, upon learning of the president's request, may represent a somewhat immature reaction. To consider the president's view that Mrs. Smith is ill as insulting, and to dogmatically demand an apology, must have suggested to the director of development the undesirability of placing Mr. Smith in a position of trust, responsibility, and leadership.

Some may feel that the president created an undesirable and embarrassing incident in requiring of Mrs. Smith an examination not asked of others in the past and that, as a layman, he was not qualified to designate Mrs. Smith as neurotic. It appears, too, that the company should have anticipated the possibility of an incident, such as the one involving Mrs. Smith, and formulated a policy for this eventuality. Nevertheless, the president had no alternative course of action if, sensitive to the responsibility of his post, he was fearful that Mrs. Smith's health might affect her husband's performance as plant manager.

It is emphatically recommended that the director of development immediately reexamine and evaluate the company policy for such visits. Before another interview is planned, he should minutely examine the practices and procedures of other companies in an effort to formulate his organization's policy. The requirement of a psychological evaluation of both husband and wife by a qualified examiner should be seriously considered as a routine step in the Philadelphia visit.

WILLIAM M. FOX
Professor of Industrial
Relations and Management
University of Florida

This problem has several dimensions that deserve special attention. The first has to do with the inadequacy of evidence with which the president jumped to his conclusion about Mrs. Smith and the possible misinterpretation of what little evidence he had. Mr. Smith has been with the company for seven years and it is most unlikely that during this time his wife had been in limbo. Probably, discreet contact with appropriate company personnel and others would have yielded important information as to her adjustment and standing in Little Rock and elsewhere.

Even if her behavior in Philadelphia was unquestionably neurotic (and we may question the president's competence to classify it), was it the result of serious maladjustment or merely temporary anxiety based upon a different social background and overconcern for her husband's promotional chances? The president does not realize that Mrs. Smith's everyday behavior in Little Rock would probably provide a much better basis for judging her stability and personality. Certainly, he has given us strong reason to suspect rashness and insensitivity to the needs of others on his part by his seeming disregard for his offense to Mr. and Mrs. Smith and failure to realize that, were he right about Mrs. Smith, he would jeopardize his chances of retaining Mr. Smith in the Little Rock position where, evidently, Mrs. Smith's qualifications were relatively irrelevant to her husband's performance!

If a discreet investigation had been conducted and the president's suspicions confirmed, and *if* it were clear that her role as a plant manager's wife would make demands upon her that would be significant to the company's interests, then a tactful discussion of the problem with Mr. Smith might have been fruitful. Such a discussion could have explored Mr. Smith's awareness of his wife's condition and its relevence to his present position, the proposed position, and so on. Presumably, this approach would have left an acceptable "out" to maintain the status quo as well as an opportunity to explore various courses of action without offending Mr. Smith, if handled with perception and tact. (This is quite hypothetical, of course, for the president, from the little we know of him, seems incapable of this role!)

It is interesting to speculate as to whether or not the president and his chief lieutenants have ever really analyzed the basic policy issue in the case: What demands can and should the company reasonably make with regard to spouses? And should certain demands be made across the board or merely with respect to certain specific positions, or both?

We are told that the director of development was faced with the decision of either approaching the president for an apology or supporting him in his contention that Mrs. Smith requires a psychological examination. What about the alternative of making the president aware of Mr. Smith's reactions, to see if he might wish to reexamine his position? There is an obvious need here to develop sound policy for present and future action.

In any event, the director of development appears oblivious to the sizable costs of losing a valuable employee and of having unfavorable publicity concerning the president's action spread throughout the company and beyond. It is unlikely that Mr. Smith will refrain from letting the cat out of the bag before his departure from the company. The insecurities and resentment engendered by this will probably go a long way toward making even a reasonable approach to the questions of "wife qualifications," as well as other matters, very difficult to sell to company personnel in the future. Esprit de corps is hard to attain initially and, once forfeited, doubly hard to regain.

OBSERVATIONS

A basic purpose of this book is to emphasize that students of management must develop their own "philosophy" as a basis for their decisions and actions when faced with the issues similar to those reflected in this incident. It is unrealistic to believe that conflicting views regarding decisions and actions will not take place and that any particular view will necessarily be correct or "right." In this incident the director of development must take a position regarding Mr. Smith's demand that the president of Lincoln, Inc., apologize for stating that Mrs. Smith exhibited traits of a neurotic or psychotic nature. Conflicting views will arise from discussions of this incident and its critiques. Professor Champion believes that any factor relating to a manager's employability should be explored and that management should retain that right. Others may believe that the company president is in the wrong and the information he seeks is an invasion of Mr. and Mrs. Smith's privacy. The question of who is right is not nearly as important as recognizing that it will be the perceptions developed as a result of discussing the incident that will be important when students are faced with managerial issues of this type.

While there may be no necessarily correct action in this incident, Professor Fox makes a point on which there should be little disagreement. He states there is an obvious need to develop sound policy for present and future action.

DISCUSSION ITEMS

1. In his critique, Professor Champion indicates that management should have the prerogative to investigate any factor relating to the employability of a candidate for a managerial position. Do you agree or disagree? Why?
2. What responses do you have to Professor Fox's questions regarding the basic policy issues in this incident? They are: (*a*) What demands can and should a company reasonably make with regard to spouses? (*b*) Should certain demands be made across the board or merely with respect to certain positions, or both?
3. Do you think the director of development was correct in accepting Mr. Smith's resignation? If not, what do you think he should have done? Justify your response based on your own philosophy of management.

SUGGESTED READINGS

BOOKS

Arnold, Hugh J., and Daniel C. Feldman. *Organizational Behavior*. New York: McGraw-Hill, 1986, chaps. 15, 16.

Callahan, Robert E.; C. Patrick Fleenor; and Harry Knudson. *Understanding Organizational Behavior*. Columbus, Ohio: Charles E. Merrill Publishing, 1986, chap. 4.

Davis, Keith, and John W. Newstrom. *Human Behavior at Work*. 7th ed. New York: McGraw-Hill, 1985, chaps. 16, 19–21.

Donnelly, James H.; James L. Gibson; and John M. Ivancevich. *Fundamentals of Management*. 6th ed. Plano, Tex.: Business Publications, 1987, chaps. 9, 13.

Freeman, R. Edward. *Strategic Management: A Stakeholder Approach*. Hagerstown, Md.: Ballinger Publishing Co., 1984, chap. 9.

French, Wendell L. *The Personnel Management Process*. 6th ed. Boston: Houghton Mifflin, 1987, chaps. 11–14.

Griffin, Ricky W. *Management*. 2nd ed. Boston: Houghton Mifflin, 1987, chaps. 10, 16, 21.

Heneman, Herbert G.; Donald P. Schwab; John A. Fossum; and Lee D. Dyer.

Personnel/Human Resource Management. 3rd ed. Homewood, Ill.: Richard D. Irwin, 1986, chaps. 8–12.

Megginson, Leon C. *Personnel Management: A Human Resources Approach.* 5th ed. Homewood, Ill.: Richard D. Irwin, 1985, chaps. 6–7.

Pastin, Mark. *The Hard Problems of Management: Gaining the Ethics Edge.* San Francisco: Jossey-Bass, 1986.

Rue, Leslie W., and Lloyd L. Byars. *Management: Theory and Application.* 4th ed. Homewood, Ill.: Richard D. Irwin, 1986, chaps. 10, 17.

Schermerhorn, John R. *Management for Productivity.* 2nd ed. New York: John Wiley & Sons, 1986, chap. 9.

JOURNALS

Dipboyle, Robert L. "Self-Fulfilling Prophecies in the Selection-Recruitment Interview." *Academy of Management Review* 7, no. 4 (October 1982), pp. 579–86.

Dransfield, Ann. "The Uneasy Life of the Corporate Spouse." *Fortune* 110, no. 4 (August 20, 1984), pp. 26–32.

Dreher, G. F. "The Impact of Extra-Work Variables on Behavior in Work Environments." *Academy of Management Review* 7, no. 2 (April 1982), pp. 300–304.

Drucker, Peter. "How to Make People Decisions." *Harvard Business Review* 63, no. 4 (July–August 1985), pp. 22–29.

Fox, Harold W. "Better Hiring Decisions." *Personnel Journal* 62, no. 12 (December 1983), pp. 966–70.

Glicken, M. D., and Katherine Janka. "Executives under Fire: The Burnout Syndrome." *California Management Review* 24, no. 3 (Spring 1982), pp. 67–72.

Jackson, S. E.; Sheldon Zedeck; and Elizabeth Summers. "Family Life Disruptions: Effects of Job-Induced Structural and Emotional Interference." *Academy of Management Journal* 28, no. 3 (September 1985), pp. 574–86.

Kiechel, Walter. "Psychological Tests for Managers." *Fortune* 107, no. 3 (February 7, 1983), pp. 113–16.

London, Manuel, and Stephen A. Stumpf. "Effects of Candidate Characteristics on Management Promotion Decisions." *Personnel Psychology* 36, no. 2 (Summer 1983), pp. 241–59.

Martin, T. N., and J. R. Schermerhorn. "Work and Nonwork Influences on Health." *Academy of Management Review* 8, no. 4 (October 1983), pp. 650–59.

McCroskey, Jacquelyn. "Work and Families: What Is the Employer's Responsibility?" *Personnel Journal* 61, no. 1 (January 1982), pp. 30–38.

Moore, Thomas. "Personality Tests Are Back." *Fortune* 115, no. 7 (March 30, 1987), pp. 74–82.

Pfeffer, Jeffrey, and Jerry Ross. "The Effects of Marriage and a Working Wife on Occupational and Wage Attainment." *Administrative Science Quarterly* 27, no. 1 (March 1982), pp. 66–80.

Reilly, P. R., and G. T. Chao. "Validity and Fairness of Some Alternative Employee Selection Procedures." *Personnel Psychology* 35, no. 1 (Spring 1982), pp. 1–61.

Scott, Sid. "Finding the Right Person." *Personnel Journal* 62, no. 11 (November 1983), pp. 894–902.

WHAT THIS INCIDENT IS ABOUT:
When a power struggle erupts in a highly charged
confrontation precipitated by digruntled employees,
production comes to a halt. This incident involves
motivation of productive human behavior, grievance
handling, control, decision making, and power.

4

Assembly line protest

INCIDENT

On Tuesday morning at 6 A.M., two young automobile assembly line
workers, disgruntled over failing to get their supervisor transferred, shut
off the electric power supply to an auto assembly line and closed it down at
Consolidated Automobile Manufacturers, Inc.

The electric power supply area, containing transformers, switches, and
other high-voltage electrical equipment, was positioned near the center of
the plant in a 6 × 7 foot area. Enclosing this area was a 10-foot high chain-
link fence with a locked gate of equal height, which together formed a
protective cage around the facility and provided a measure of security.

The two assembly line workers, William Strong and Larry Kane, gained
access to the electric power supply area simply by scaling the fence. Once
inside, they halted the assembly line by opening the switches and cutting
off the electrical power.

Strong and Kane, who worked as spot welders, took matters into their
hands when the union's grievance procedure did not work fast enough to
satisfy them. Fellow workers, idled by this dramatic protest and by the
motionless assembly line, grouped themselves around the fenced area,
shouting encouragement to the two men inside. In response, Strong and
Kane were chanting, "When you cut the power you've got the power."
They were in the process of becoming folk heroes to their fellow workers.

Sam Winfare, who supervised Strong and Kane and who was the target
of the protest, had been supervisor for only a short time. In explaining the
events that led to the power cage protest, Winfare said that production on
the assembly line had been chronically below quota before he took charge.
At the time Winfare was made supervisor, the plant manager had plainly
told him that his job was to improve the production rate. Production had
improved markedly in the short time that he was supervisor.

41

Winfare told the plant manager that his transfer would set a damaging precedent. "The company's action to remove me would create a situation where the operations of the plant were subject to the whims of any employee with a grudge," he said. This possibility was emphasized by the comment of a union steward who said there were other conditions in the plant that needed improving—such as the cafeteria food and relief from the more than 100-degree heat in the metal shop. Moreover, the steward said, there was at least one other supervisor who should be removed. He implied that, if successful, the power cage protest would facilitate attaining both these ends. The union steward's final comment was that two men on an unauthorized, wildcat strike might accomplish the same thing as a full-blown strike.

Each passing minute was costing the company a production loss of one automotive unit valued at $6,000. The cost of each lost production hour, therefore, was $360,000.

As he began a staff meeting, the plant manager felt stress and time pressure to accomplish two objectives: (1) to restore production on the motionless assembly line (but he was uncertain about the best way to do this), and (2) to develop policies for preventing future production interruptions by assembly line workers.

CRITIQUES

LARRY L. CUMMINGS
Distinguished Research Professor
Northwestern University

There are two basic managerial and behavioral themes underlying this incident. Both represent significant and recurring issues in the management of persons and organizations.

The first theme centers on the bases of *influence* and *power* within organized systems. The second theme focuses on the *motivational bases* or *origins* of behavior within organizations.

Strong and Kane exhibit power-seeking behaviors arising from implicit frustration with their inability to exert influence upward within the organization. Their behavior illustrates a basic proposition of psychology; that is, aggression is a frequent consequence of frustration (blockage of goal-directed behavior). It is likely that Strong and Kane either found the legitimate appeal system provided by the company and the union to be ineffective, or perhaps they failed to perceive that such a system could be used to seek redress against a supervisor. Control over resources is the fundamental mechanism underlying the development and use of power within organizations. Organizations allocate this control through formal structures, reward allocations, and status systems. Lower level participants like Strong and Kane frequently are allocated little or no power through these means. Thus, some sort of upward-influence or upward-power mechanism is necessary to integrate all participants into the organization. Frequently, management provides such a system (grievance procedures, open-door policies, suggestion systems, and so forth) and/or relies upon the unions representing the organization's employees to provide such a system. So the appropriate questions to ask on this issue as they relate to this incident are:

1. Who has the primary responsibility to provide upward channels of influence in large, bureaucratic, unionized organizations—management or union?
2. What reasons might be suggested for why the management and union channels failed to function effectively in this case?

The second theme prevalent in this incident concerns the range of motivations reflected in the behaviors of the participants—particularly Strong, Kane, Winfare, the plant manager, and the steward. The motivational bases for willing cooperation and self-control within a large organization are quite complex and often precarious. Organizations assume that participants will either identify with the goals of the larger system and/or see the system's goals or objectives as logical means of achieving individual goals or objectives. In other words, if participants act in their own self-interest, organizational aims will be achieved. In most large organizations, however, this model is unrealistic for one or more of the following reasons:

1. The goals of the organization are not clear or are misperceived by participants.
2. The goals of the organization are inconsistent with those of the participants.
3. The paths or means provided by the organization for attaining participant aims are not clear.
4. The organization's structure and technology cause the participant to feel that his or her personal efforts are unrelated to achieving organizational goal and performance.

How would you analyze and "explain" the behaviors of Strong, Kane, Winfare, the plant manager, and the steward, utilizing these four reasons?

HENRY L. TOSI
Professor of Management
University of Florida

When those two employees were in the power cage holding the rest of the plant as hostage, it was no different from a person holding a gun to another persons's head and making extreme demands. An immediate solution is needed in this crisis situation. There is no question about the high costs of shutting down the plant for any extended period to negotiate. What other ways are there to deal with this problem? Let's speculate. Could we get the union involved in talking these two workers out of the power cage? Should we make vague and ambiguous concessions to the two workers, which we later will claim to be unlawful?

The more relevant question now is what are the issues involved for the future? There are basically two questions that must be considered. The first one is, What should be the fate of Winfare? There is a serious question of equity here. Apparently there was a set of problems which existed when Winfare took the supervisory position. I believe it is irresponsible to take an inexperienced or untrained person, put him or her under pressure, not provide much assistance, and then hold the person responsible. Sinking or swimming is not an acceptable way to operate a firm. It may well be that Winfare was the victim of many previous unfair circumstances and events. If that is true, then every effort should be made to place him in another similar position without prejudice.

There is another important dimension that should not be overlooked. The act of taking over the power cage is an extreme one. It is equivalent to holding a gun to management's head. Unless there is reason to believe that the two workers are seriously and emotionally disturbed, such an act suggests that there are serious problems to which the management must attend. It is time to look hard at the circumstances in which the workers must perform. An evaluation of working conditions, eating facilities, pay systems, and supervisory practices is clearly in order. If there are more hazardous and extreme working conditions that precipitated this act of aggression against management, they must be removed. If not, there will be another retaliatory event at some unpredictable time in the future that may be more serious.

OBSERVATIONS

Unauthorized occupation of the power cage and stoppage of the plant's production presents an unstable and crucial situation for plant management. The outcome of this state of affairs will make a decisive difference for better or worse; thus, management faces a crisis. Since continued downtime is economically costly and erodes management's capacity to manage, restoration of production deserves top priority for management attention. Conditions must be created to ensure that Strong and Kane depart the power cage within an acceptable time frame, either voluntarily or involuntarily. It is desirable to achieve this departure efficiently and with minimum negative impact on factors such as work force motivation and cooperation, which are essential for regaining "normal" plant operation.

When facing a crisis, the manager tends to feel lonely. Management theory and research provide small guidance or comfort. Experience is unlikely to offer sufficient direction since each crisis has some unique dimensions. Moreover, one's superiors, assuming they can be contacted, are likely to simply say "handle it."

Professors Cummings and Tosi have shown that management and behavioral theory provide an analytical framework that may be useful in answering questions such as, "What really went wrong?"; "How might this crisis have been avoided?"; and "What needs to be done to repair fractured relationships and to restore productive harmony between workers and management?"

DISCUSSION ITEMS

---

1. Identify the options open to the plant manager. Discuss the potential costs and benefits of each.
2. Is it necessary to control the workers idled by the shutdown? Explain your position. What instructions, if any, would you issue to them?
3. What should be the plant manager's number one priority? Recommend operational plans for its achievement.

SUGGESTED READINGS

BOOKS

Arnold, Hugh J., and Daniel C. Feldman. *Organizational Behavior*. New York: McGraw-Hill, 1986, chap. 4.

Callahan, Robert E.; C. Patrick Fleenor; and Harry Knudson. *Understanding Organizational Behavior*. Columbus, Ohio: Charles E. Merrill Publishing, 1986, chap. 8.

Davis, Keith, and John W. Newstrom. *Human Behavior at Work*. 7th ed. New York: McGraw-Hill, 1985, chaps. 11, 17.

Donnelly, James H.; James L. Gibson; and John M. Ivancevich. *Fundamentals of Management*. 6th ed. Plano, Tex.: Business Publications, 1987, part 3.

French, Wendell L. *The Personnel Management Process*. 6th ed. Boston: Houghton Mifflin, 1987, chaps. 8, 25.

Griffin, Ricky W. *Management*. 2nd ed. Boston: Houghton Mifflin, 1987, chap. 16, pp. 536–44, 670–74.

Heneman, Herbert G.; Donald P. Schwab; John A. Fossum; and Lee D. Dyer. *Personnel/Human Resource Management*. 3rd ed. Homewood, Ill.: Richard D. Irwin, 1986, chap. 17.

Megginson, Leon C. *Personnel Management: A Human Resources Approach*. 5th ed. Homewood, Ill.: Richard D. Irwin, 1985, chap. 12.

Rue, Leslie W., and Lloyd L. Byars. *Management: Theory and Application*. 4th ed. Homewood, Ill.: Richard D. Irwin, 1986, chaps. 13, 17.

Schermerhorn, John R. *Management for Productivity*. 2nd ed. New York: John Wiley & Sons, 1986, chaps. 17, 18, 25.

JOURNALS

Barnard, Janet. "The Foreman's Role in the New Management." *Advanced Management Journal* 49, no. 2 (Spring 1984), pp. 13–19.

Beck, Arthur C., and Ellis D. Hillmar. "Bad Vibes in the Workplace . . . What Managers Can Do to Turn around Negative Attitudes in the Organizations." *Management Review* 73, no. 1 (January 1984), pp. 22–25.

————. "The Power of Positive Management." *Personnel Journal* 62, no. 2 (February 1983), pp. 126–31.

Elahorn, Hillel J., and Robin M. Hogarth. "Decision Making: Going Forward in Reverse." *Harvard Business Review* 65, no. 1 (January–February 1987), pp. 66–70.

Fox, Harold W. "Eliciting Latent Productivity." *Business Horizons* 26, no. 6 (November–December 1983), pp. 37–45.

Fulmer, William E. "How Do You Say, 'You're Fired'?" *Business Horizons* 29, no. 1 (January–February 1986), pp. 31–38.

Goddard, Robert W. "How to Avoid Employees' Complaints that Could Lead to Litigation." *Management Review* 73, no. 2 (February 1984), pp. 58–61.

Greenhalgh, Leonard. "Managing Conflict." *Sloan Management Review* 27, no. 4 (Summer 1986), pp. 45–52.

Novit, Mitchell. "Employer Liability for Employee Misconduct: Two Common Law Doctrines." *Personnel* 59, no. 1 (January–February 1982), pp. 11–19.

Simon, Herbert A. "Making Management Decisions: The Role of Intuition and Emotion." *The Academy of Management Executive* 1, no. 1 (February 1987), pp. 57–64.

Slatter, Stuart St. P. "The Impact of Crises on Managerial Behavior." *Business Horizons* 27, no. 3 (May–June 1984), pp. 65–68.

Stanton, Erwin S. "A Critical Reevaluation of Motivation, Management, and Productivity." *Personnel Journal* 62, no. 3 (March 1983), pp. 208–14.

Stoner, Charles R., and Fred L. Fry. "Developing a Corporate Policy for Managing Stress." *Personnel* 60, no. 3 (March 1983), pp. 208–14.

Yukl, Gary, and Tom Taber. "The Effective Use of Managerial Power." *Personnel* 60, no. 2 (March–April 1983), pp. 37–44.

WHAT THIS INCIDENT IS ABOUT:
The specific instance of a policy relating to board
member conflict of interest provides a basis for a
more comprehensive examination of corporate
governance.

5

Conflict of interest

INCIDENT

Robert Winkle, the newly appointed headmaster of Riverside Academy, was busy preparing for his first regular meeting of the school's board of directors. In a previous conference with the board's chairman, items that needed to be placed on the meeting's agenda were determined. One item concerned the school's present insurance coverage. Winkle was surprised at the total cost of the coverage, which in his opinion appeared to be well above the average. In addition he noted that all of the insurance coverage was being purchased from one firm owned by none other than the chairman of his board. Further investigation revealed that the firm had held the school's coverage for the past nine years.

Winkle had recently reviewed in detail the school's constitution and bylaws and the operating policy manual that had been adopted and approved by the board of directors. He was familiar with sections in the bylaws and the policy manual that stated "no director, while serving as a member of the board of directors of Riverside Academy, shall derive personal financial gain or reward from serving on the board because of membership." Winkle felt that he should prepare recommendations for board action regarding what he perceived to be a clear case of conflict of interest and policy violation on the part of at least one member of the board of directors.

CRITIQUES

ROBERT E. ENGEL
Associate Professor of Foundations
and Higher Education
University of Iowa

There are two critical aspects of this incident as far as the headmaster is concerned. The more important aspect may not be the most obvious one. The obvious problem is the apparent conflict of interest. It could be dealt with in a somewhat abstract way without regard for the subjects. Apparently this is what Winkle intends to do. Before preparing recommendations for board action, however, he should ascertain (probably from the school's legal counsel) whether or not the organization's constitution and bylaws and policies in fact have been infringed. If there are violations, corrective action should be taken.

Perhaps the less obvious but more crucial problem for both the headmaster and the school is how to handle this situation. In protecting the organization's best interests, Winkle will not want to do it greater harm, nor would he wish to embarrass a school director unnecessarily or damage his reputation. Consequently, the headmaster has a communication and human relations challenge, and a probable legal problem. Questions of power, authority, and role are foremost, along with the issue of institutional stability. This is the most crucial aspect of this incident as far as the organization's welfare is concerned.

The headmaster may be somewhat handicapped by his newness to the situation. He may not know the chairman well enough to be sure how he would react to a query about this issue. On the other hand, there can be an advantage in being new on the scene. Apparent innocence based on lack of acquaintance with a situation is often excused. An example is the child who pointed out that the emperor was wearing no clothes.

The dynamics of the situation and the personalities of people involved will largely determine how the headmaster will broach the subject. But there is no question that he must raise the issue with the chairman before he presents recommendations for board action. (Unless, of course, he finds that he is mistaken.) Whether or not the board policies are being infringed, prudent attention to the issue will legitimize the headmaster's authority as the chief executive of the school. It will demonstrate his thoroughness as an administrator. In any case, to ignore the issue would amount to administrative malfeasance.

While the headmaster is considering how to approach the chairman, and while he is (perhaps) gaining expert counsel on the interpretation of the bylaws and policies, he ought to seek some simple facts himself. For example, the school has purchased its insurance from this firm for nine years. Also, the bylaws and policy state that no director while serving shall derive financial gain or reward. It may be that the chairman was elected to the board after the school purchased the insurance coverage and no one has thought about it. Perhaps the chairman is not familiar with all the policies. Oversight and lack of information are frequently the reasons for problems of this nature, in which case the problem may be easily resolved. Typically, a reasonable person will be grateful for being informed and for being saved embarrassment.

Or it may be that in spite of Winkle's observation that the insurance costs seem too high, the coverage from this firm is the best deal available. It may be that a different policy states that such services must be purchased after a bidding process and that this firm's bid was the lowest for the kind of coverage desired. Since school trustees or directors of private schools (as one assumes this school is) are typically expected to make financial as well as service contributions to the school, the chairman may wish to return his profit from the sale of insurance to the school. Or perhaps he (or his company) is already doing this, but the headmaster does not know it.

These comments and examples suggest that: (1) the incident is critical both as an apparent legal conflict of interest and as a communication challenge relative to the exercise of role, power, and authority in the organization, (2) the situation may not be what it seems to be and, therefore, the headmaster must not jump to conclusions, and (3) one should not take precipitous action which might be unnecessary and which could generate a greater crisis for the organization and for the people involved than the apparent problem itself. Nevertheless, it is clear that the headmaster cannot ignore the issue.

JAMES E. INMAN
Professor of Business Law and
Director of Graduate Programs in Business
University of Akron

The Riverside Academy incident presents a policy issue that should be brought to the board's attention and resolved by the board. It also exemplifies a problem situation in which Winkle must: (1) define the scope of the problem, (2) gather relevant information, (3) evaluate alternatives to address/solve the problem, and (4) make recommendations to the board for implementation.

The headmaster and the directors, like many administrative officers, are often unfamiliar with the particulars of law. Hence, they recognize the importance of obtaining legal counsel. The board undoubtedly obtained legal counsel in the preparation of the board's bylaws. The bylaws provide the board with guidance in conducting its business so as to avoid violations of the law through ignorance. Indeed, it is the bylaws that alert Winkle to the possibility of legal problems in this situation. After becoming aware of the problem, Winkle should not act hastily. Instead, he should determine if the academy has paid too much for insurance coverage, and he should consult with the academy's attorney concerning the legal implications.

The attorney would inform Winkle that educational institutions like Riverside Academy are created in one of two legal forms: trusts or non-profit corporations. If the academy is a trust organization, the trustee's (chairman's) duty of loyalty to the trust prohibits any self-dealing like the chairman's voting for the academy to buy insurance coverage from his own insurance agency. In contrast, if the academy is organized as a nonprofit organization, its directors are not prohibited from self-dealing. Instead, the law only prohibits self-dealing that is detrimental to the corporation. It is presumed that the corporation obtained a "fair deal" if the self-dealing director makes a full disclosure to the board and refrains from voting on the transaction. In the absence of prior disclosure and disassociation from voting, a self-dealing director is liable to the corporation unless he can sustain the burden of proving that the transaction was fair.

Despite the clear theoretical distinctions between a trust and a nonprofit corporation, courts often have had difficulty in deciding whether to apply the fiduciary duties of the trustee (no self-dealing allowed) or of the director (permitting "fair" deals). If a trust standard is applied in this instance, the self-dealing chairman must return any profits obtained from the insurance transactions. If the standard for corporate directors is applied, the chairman must sustain the burden of proof that the transaction was a fair deal if he did not make prior disclosures of self-dealing. If this burden cannot be sustained, the chairman is liable to the academy for the unfair profits. Besides the academy's right to bring suit, the state attorney general is often empowered to initiate legal action to protect the assets of nonprofit corporations from unfair self-dealing by directors. Also, the academy's tax-exempt status is threatened because tax law prohibits the diversion of corporate revenues to the benefit of any private individual.

If the chairman disclosed his interests in the insurance agency and disassociated himself from voting, the situation probably involves "fair dealing." However, if the board awarded the contract to the chairman at a price higher than that submitted by competitors, the board should substantiate its reasons for choosing the higher bid so as to avoid the obvious inference of harmful self-dealing. But, in the future, it would be better to avoid this *apperance* of unfair self-dealing by having the board adopt a new policy of awarding contracts only to outsiders, unless the self-dealing director can supply products or services at less-than-market rates as a gesture of goodwill toward the academy.

If the attorney advises that wrongdoing occurred, Winkle should privately approach the chairman emphasizing the imperative of the academy's integrity and its ability to exemplify moral leadership. The moral integrity of the institution requires restitution of unfairly paid funds. Winkle should suggest that the chairman voluntarily return any "unfair profit" to the academy. The bylaws should be amended to adopt the policies of competitive bidding and "less-than-market" prices by insiders.

If wrongdoing occurred and the chairman refuses to cooperate, Winkle's obligation to the academy requires that he present his findings of self-dealing and recommendations for bylaw changes to the board of directors. He also should seek the election of a new chairman. It then becomes the board's responsibility to take corrective actions, that is, to seek recovery and implement policies to prevent recurrence of illegal self-dealing. Should the board refuse to remedy the situation, Winkle must resign the headmaster position to avoid his culpability in this legal wrongdoing and to maintain his moral integrity as a headmaster of this or any other academy. In addition, Winkle's ethical obligations to society include the necessity of supplying information about this illegal self-dealing to the state attorney general and to the IRS.

OBSERVATIONS

The setting of this incident is a private school, Riverside Academy, but it could occur in any number of other organizations in which it is illegal or improper for a director to profit from his or her service on the board. At issue is a possible conflict of interest, which provides the basis for a much broader study of corporate leadership. Professor Stanley Vance, author of *Corporate Leadership: Boards, Directors and Strategy*, has made an exhaustive study of corporate leadership, and his book presents a timely contribution to the literature. In one section, he reports on a study conducted to determine causes for legal action against directors. They were:

Misleading representation, 21.4 percent.

Collusion or conspiracy to defraud, 13.6 percent.

Civil rights denial, 7.9 percent.

Antitrust violations, 7.6 percent.

Failure to honor employment contract, 6.5 percent.

Improper expenditures, 6.2 percent.

Breach of duty to minority stockholders, 6.0 percent.

Conflict of interest, 4.6 percent.

Nine other specified causes, 23.5 percent.

Professor Vance states the sum of these figures exceeds 100 percent since some claims involved more than one set of allegations. Another interesting point he makes, regarding director liability, is that most director and officer liability insurance policies sold today have exclusions, meaning they won't cover any losses arising from risks such as: libel or slander, personal profit, short-swing profit, excess remuneration, dishonesty, and claims arising from payments to foreign government officials.

An excellent article from the book *Business Ethics*, authored by Hoffman and Moore, relates rather specifically to this incident and more broadly to board composition. The point is made that there are some people who do not belong on boards—members of management, outside counsel, investment bankers, and suppliers. All of these people must be excluded until a mechanism is designed whereby they can establish their ability to function on an independent basis.

DISCUSSION ITEMS

1. Why is it desirable, or not desirable, to have a policy that no director will derive financial gain from serving on the board? Are there any instances when such a provision would be detrimental to the organization? Elaborate.
2. Formulate a board policy that will provide as much assurance as possible that situations similar to this incident will not occur. Be specific regarding how your policy should be implemented.
3. What action do you think Mr. Winkle should take regarding the perceived conflict of interest? Why?

SUGGESTED READINGS

BOOKS

Arnold, Hugh J., and Daniel C. Feldman. *Organizational Behavior*. New York: McGraw-Hill, 1986, chaps. 1, 9, 10.

Braiotta, Louis, and A. A. Sommer. *The Essential Guide to Effective Corporate Board Committees*. Englewood Cliffs, N.J.: Prentice-Hall, 1987.

Callahan, Robert E.; C. Patrick Fleenor; and Harry Knudson. *Understanding Organizational Behavior*. Columbus, Ohio: Charles E. Merrill Publishing, 1986, chaps. 8, 9.

Davis, Keith, and John W. Newstrom. *Human Behavior at Work*. 7th ed. New York: McGraw-Hill, 1985, chaps. 1–3, 19, 20.

Donnelly, James H.; James L. Gibson; and John M. Ivancevich. *Fundamentals of Management*. 6th ed. Plano, Tex.: Business Publications, 1987, chaps. 14, 20.

French, Wendell L. *The Personnel Management Process.* 6th ed. Boston: Houghton Mifflin, 1987, chaps. 1–5.

Griffin, Ricky W. *Management.* 2nd ed. Boston: Houghton Mifflin, 1987, chaps. 1, 3, 7.

Heneman, Herbert G.; Donald P. Schwab; John A. Fossum; and Lee D. Dyer. *Personnel/Human Resource Management.* 3rd ed. Homewood, Ill.: Richard D. Irwin, 1986, chaps. 1, 2.

Hoffman, W. Michael, and Jennifer M. Moore. *Business Ethics.* New York: McGraw-Hill, 1984, chap. 9.

Megginson, Leon C. *Personnel Management: A Human Resources Approach.* 5th ed. Homewood, Ill.: Richard D. Irwin, 1985, chaps. 1–4.

Mueller, R. K. *Behind the Boardroom Door.* New York: Crown Publishers, 1984.

Rue, Leslie W., and Lloyd L. Byars. *Management: Theory and Application.* 4th ed. Homewood, Ill.: Richard D. Irwin, 1986, chaps. 3, 9, 16.

Schermerhorn, John R. *Management for Productivity.* 2nd ed. New York: John Wiley & Sons, 1986, chap. 20.

Vance, Stanley C. *Corporate Leadership: Boards, Directors, and Strategy.* New York: McGraw-Hill, 1983, chaps. 1–6.

JOURNALS

Cressey, D. R., and C. A. Moore. "Managerial Values and Codes of Ethics." *California Management Review* 25, no. 4 (Summer 1983), pp. 53–75.

Frederick, W. C. "Why Ethical Analysis Is Indispensable and Unavoidable in Corporate Affairs." *California Management Review* 28, no. 2 (Winter 1986), pp. 127–41.

Freeman, R. E., and D. L. Reed. "Stockholders and Stakeholders: A New Perspective on Corporate Governance." *California Management Review* 25, no. 3 (Spring 1983), pp. 88–106.

Henderson, V. E. "The Ethical Side of Enterprise." *Sloan Management Review* 23, no. 3 (Summer 1982), pp. 37–47.

Herzel, Leo; R. W. Shepro; and Leo Katz. "Next-to-Last Word on Endangered Directors." *Harvard Business Review* 65, no. 1 (January–February 1987), pp. 38–43.

Jones, T. M., and L. D. Goldberg. "Governing the Large Corporation: More Arguments for Public Directors." *Academy of Management Review* 7, no. 4 (October 1982), pp. 603–11.

Kesner, I. F.; Bart Victor; and B. T. Lamont. "Board Composition and the Commission of Illegal Acts." *Academy of Management Journal* 29, no. 4 (December 1986), pp. 789–99.

Magnet, Myron. "The Decline and Fall of Business Ethics." *Fortune* 114, no. 13 (December 8, 1986), pp. 65–72.

Menzies, Hugh D. "The Boardroom Battle at Bendix." *Fortune* 105, no. 1 (January 11, 1982), pp. 54–64.

Mizruchi, Mark S. "Who Controls Whom? An Examination of the Relation between Management and Boards of Directors in Large American Corporations." *Academy of Management Review* 8, no. 3 (July 1983), pp. 376–86.

Nash, John. "Tailoring a Board to Your Company Size and Circumstance." *Advanced Management Journal* 48, no. 1 (Winter 1983), pp. 51–58.

Perkins, R. B. "Avoiding Director Liability." *Harvard Business Review* 64, no. 3 (May–June 1986), pp. 8–17.

Von Glinow, Mary Ann, and Luke Novelli. "Ethical Standards within Organizational Behavior." *Academy of Management Journal* 25, no. 2 (June 1982), pp. 417–36.

Williams, Oliver F. "Business Ethics: A Trojan Horse?" *California Management Review* 24, no. 4 (Summer 1982), pp. 14–23.

Wokutch, R. E., and B. A. Spencer. "Corporate Saints and Sinners." *California Management Review* 29, no. 2 (Winter 1987), pp. 62–77.

WHAT THIS INCIDENT IS ABOUT:
A decision-making situation is established regarding
three candidates for a managerial position. Topics
including leadership styles, performance appraisal,
use of consultants, and projective tests are raised for
discussion.

6

Consultant's report

INCIDENT

The Harlee Company, manufacturer of office supplies, decided to establish a branch plant in a large southeastern city. The plant was to be staffed with 16 managers, 34 secretaries and stenographers, and 78 skilled and semiskilled workers. Most of the managers and a few of the skilled workers were to be transferred from other plants. The remaining employees were to be obtained locally.

The position of production manager was one in which staffing was considered to be of utmost importance. Managers of Harlee decided to utilize the services of a psychological consulting firm for assistance, and a firm was selected from advertisements in the yellow pages of the telephone book. The consultants advised that candidates for the position would be given both a projective personality test and an in-depth interview.

After the initial screening and evaluation of personnel records, three candidates were sent to the consultants. They seemed to be equally qualified on factors such as age, education, experience, motivation, and intelligence. The major difference between the three seemed to focus on their attitudes toward subordinates. It was this characteristic that Harlee managers asked the consulting firm to investigate and report on. A digest of the reports on each candidate returned to Harlee within two weeks follows:

D. M. — This candidate appears to believe the average human being has an inherent dislike for work, will avoid responsibility when possible, cannot be trusted, has little ambition, and above all desires security. He thinks that all persons must be coerced, controlled, directed, and threatened with punishment or rewarded in order to obtain on-the-job efficiency. D. M. appears to have no trust or confidence in his subordinates.

J. C.—This candidate appears overly suspicious, has delusions of persecution, and may even be losing contact with reality. The little subordinate interaction that he would grudgingly permit is likely to be
accompanied with suspicion and mistrust. His leadership style is
expected to be dictatorial. The prognosis is that J. C. will probably
become an alcoholic.

F. J.—This candidate believes that all persons are kindly, inherently
noble, and self-sacrificing, and that it is possible to influence and modify any person's behavior by logic and reason. F. J. holds that once
the shortcomings of individuals are pointed out to them, they will try
to correct the problems. F. J. is convinced that all workers are or can
be made to feel happy, content, and dedicated to company goals. He
appears to have complete trust and confidence in his subordinates.

Although the assessments were diverse, Harlee managers felt that a good
decision regarding the best candidate could be made. Just prior to doing
so, however, they received a caustic memorandum from J. C. criticizing
and questioning the competency of the psychological consultants and
Harlee's policy of using them for employee assessment.

CRITIQUES

ROBERT T. GOLEMBIEWSKI
Research Professor of Political Science
and Management
University of Georgia

Harlee's management should be cautious in making decisions that rest
substantially on the projective tests, and only after being satisfied about
the validation research underlying the tests in relation to the position of
production manager. More and more "personnel decisions" end up in the
courts nowadays. The digest of the report on J. C. may be a prelude to just
such an action, especially since it is very unlikely that any projective test is
validated for the position of production manager. Several Supreme Court
decisions seem to require just such validation of a test in predicting success
in a specific job.

At a minimum, then, Harlee's management should intimately know the
testing and interview techniques employed by their consultant. The
tenuous reliability and validity of most projective techniques, particularly,
do not encourage easy acceptance of any consultant's report, especially a
consultant chosen from the classified ads who completes three specific
analyses "within two weeks." In addition, judicial decisions cast serious
doubt on the use of any testing techniques whose reliability and validity for

the specific job in question have not been established beyond reasonable doubt.

Despite such concerns about the consultant's report, one can see how its information could be used *in combination with* the company's purposes and structure to determine the selection of the production manager.

A negative decision seems obvious in the case of J. C. What organization could possibly risk such a hire? Sad to say, even individuals more extreme than the consultant's description of J. C. have been recruited and trained to handle certain administrative programs, for example, the tragic mass murder of the Jews during World War II.

Since the Harlee Company no doubt will not be a congenial home for J. C., assuming the consultant's description is valid, the choice lies between D. M. and F. J. Two rudimentary organization charts help make this choice:

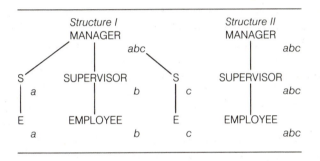

Many factors suggest that D. M. is suited to be a manager in Structure I. The span of control must be narrow, for only the manager "gets all the way around" the discrete subassembly *abc*, and he must closely monitor the three separate organization units performing each operation. Therefore, only trivial matters can be delegated, which is consistent with D. M.'s beliefs. In addition, supervisors would tend to "kick decisions upstairs," of which D. M. would approve. Employees performing only a single process or operation with close supervision also suits D. M.'s distrust of people.

Structure II, in contrast, requires a manager like F. J. The span of control can be wide, and delegation can be substantial, since each supervisor controls an entire discrete subassembly. The style of supervision, consequently, can be general. Indeed, Structure II assumes that trained and motivated employees are substantially self-controlling, an assumption reinforced by making individuals responsible for some total subassembly (as supervising or performing operations *abc* versus *a* or *b* or *c*).

Other advantages often are attributed to Structure II. Decisions are made closer to the action level, and would probably move quickly; employees and supervisors receive valuable training; and the implied job enrichment will probably increase satisfaction and output.

Harlee's management does not seem inclined toward Structure II, however. To support the point, Harlee's managers planned on 112 employees and 16 managers. The span of control is seven, within the limits usually prescribed for Structure I. Candidate D. M. seems the most appropriate person for Harlee's management structure.

LYLE F. SCHOENFELDT
Professor of Management
Texas A&M University

The Harlee Company was wise to seek to fill the important production manager position of a new plant from current employees. Such an approach provides promotional opportunities for top performers and ensures that the position will be filled by someone with a track record with Harlee. Beyond that, there are several problems with the implementation of this plan.

While it may have been desirable to evaluate candidate attitudes toward subordinates, the use of a consultant was not necessary and, in any case, was not pursued in the appropriate manner. From a cost-benefit perspective, the use of the consultant was an expensive method of obtaining inferior information. The optimal source of information about attitudes of candidates for the production manager position toward subordinates would be from the observation of manager-subordinate relationships over an extended period of time. Top management of the new Harlee plant was fortunate in having this inexpensive source of rich information available, and would have done well to take advantage of the opportunity through careful discussion with colleagues of the candidates.

Had the use of a psychologist been indicated, Harlee officials should have proceeded in a different manner. The one-size-fits-all approach was backwards. Harlee managers should have screened candidates and decided on the role of the psychologist *before* seeking to locate a consultant and settling on a personality test and in-depth interview as the basis for assessment. However names of psychologists were obtained, Harlee managers should have talked to several and should have expected each to be explicit about the approach to be taken along with anticipated results. Psychologists observing the guidelines of the profession for consultation would insist on such a discussion, including the possible negative or unanticipated consequences that seem to have occurred. As a final step, Harlee managers should have talked to officials of organizations for whom each psychologist provided similar services before proceeding to make a final decision on a consultant. The approach taken was analogous to waking up with a severe headache, deciding that brain surgery was necessary, locating a surgeon from the yellow pages, and reporting to the hospital for preoperative care. The potential for harm to the candidates and liability of Harlee was almost as great.

Were the assessments of the three candidates accurate? It is hard to tell from the summaries, but there is reason to question the results. While it is true that a candidate evaluated as "overly suspicious" and as having "delusions of persecution" might be inclined to write a caustic memorandum criticizing the competency of the consultant, there is another possible explanation for the events. Individuals who, on the basis of education and experience, are qualified for an important production manager position would, in general, have difficulty seeing the need for psychological evaluation. This would suggest J. C. was suspicious even before his meeting with the psychologist, and became more so as a result of the interaction with a professional inexperienced in such assessments. The diversity of the three assessments should also be a tip-off to potential inaccuracies, especially in light of each candidate's prior evaluation by Harlee on the basis of performance.

One way or another, Harlee officials have a problem. Either they have a high-level employee with potentially dangerous tendencies or, more likely, they have three well-regarded employees with varying degrees of uneasiness about the decision process and the organization. It is not clear who in the Harlee organization decided on the selection process for the production manager position. However, the problem created could have corporate-wide impact and involve potential legal liability. Those at the highest levels, including the corporate human resources officer and legal counsel, need to be consulted before anything further is done. Legal issues aside, the hiring manager, presumably the manager of the new plant, should seek to verify the assessments by talking to the other Harlee personnel acquainted with the individuals. If the assessments are found to be off target, as is suspected, the plant manager should personally explain the situation to each candidate through face-to-face discussion. At the same time, the continuing interest of each candidate can be assessed and the optimal process indicated earlier can be initiated, either with these candidates or with others.

Depending on the organization and culture at Harlee, there is also a more serious problem. The manager who made the decision on screening candidates for the production manager position exercised poor judgment, and inadequate organizational controls existed to double-check the procedure adopted. Senior managers need to decide if the gap in judgment was an isolated event or was a window to a more serious blind spot on the part of the manager involved. Procedures for obtaining information on current Harlee employees being considered for advancement need to be put in place and to be communicated to all hiring managers.

In summary, the process used to obtain needed information on candidates for the production manager position was suboptimal and was carried out in an unprofessional way. As a result, the assessments on one or more of the three candidates may well be inaccurate. Harlee managers need to proceed along two fronts: (*a*) square things with the three candidates and (*b*) put in place acceptable procedures for internal hiring.

OBSERVATIONS

This incident and its accompanying critiques lead to the consideration of a variety of concepts that are discussed in some of the books and journals on the suggested reading list. Among them are the Theory X and Theory Y concept advanced by Douglas McGregor, the authoritarian versus the democratic leadership style, the traitist approach to leadership, Blake and Mouton's Managerial Grid®, and Frederick Herzberg's motivation-hygiene theory.

In one of the suggested readings, Stephen Stumpf and Manuel London add a pragmatic orientation to the decision-making situation by discussing individual and organizational factors influencing the management selection and promotion process. Their basic thesis is that promotions are judgmental decisions that are often based on ambiguous criteria and numerous sources of information, much of which is subjective. Even though promotions are central to the quality of leadership in most large organizations, they argue that little is known about the process or effectiveness of management promotion decisions. With respect to formal promotion policies, Stumpf and London state that there are both advantages and disadvantages. Such policies can increase the opportunities for, and ensure fairer treatment of, employees, and inform managers about salient promotion criteria. However, formalization may limit the decision maker's discretion and increase the time required to fill a vacancy.

DISCUSSION ITEMS

---

1. Which of the three candidates would you prefer? Justify your response.
2. How are the concepts of Douglas McGregor, Frederick Herzberg, Blake and Mouton, and others found in the suggested reading list related to the decision that Harlee Company officials must now make in selecting a production manager?
3. Professor Golembiewski emphasizes the situational or contingency aspect of the organization's structural influence on leadership style. What is your evaluation of his thesis?

SUGGESTED READINGS

BOOKS

Arnold, Hugh J., and Daniel C. Feldman. *Organizational Behavior*. New York: McGraw-Hill, 1986, chaps. 5, 11, 15.

Callahan, Robert E.; C. Patrick Fleenor; and Harry Knudson. *Understanding Organizational Behavior*. Columbus, Ohio: Charles E. Merrill Publishing, 1986, chap. 5.

Davis, Keith, and John W. Newstrom. *Human Behavior at Work*. 7th ed. New York: McGraw-Hill, 1985, chaps. 5–8.

Donnelly, James H.; James L. Gibson; and John M. Ivancevich. *Fundamentals of Management*. 6th ed. Plano, Tex.: Business Publications, 1987, chaps. 8, 9, 12.

French, Wendell L. *The Personnel Management Process*. 6th ed. Boston: Houghton Mifflin, 1987, chaps. 7, 10, 12, 13.

Griffin, Ricky W. *Management*. 2nd ed. Boston: Houghton Mifflin, 1987, chaps. 1, 7, 9, 10, 13, 14, 21.

Heneman, Herbert G.; Donald P. Schwab; John A. Fossum; and Lee D. Dyer. *Personnel/Human Resource Management*. 3rd ed. Homewood, Ill.: Richard D. Irwin, 1986, chaps. 8–12.

Matheny, Philip R. *Critical Path Hiring: How to Employ Top-Flight Managers*. Lexington, Mass.: D. C. Heath, 1986, pp. 1–224.

McFarland, Dalton E. *Management and Society*. Englewood Cliffs, N.J.: Prentice-Hall, 1982, chaps. 8–10.

McGregor, Douglas. *The Human Side of Enterprise*. New York: McGraw-Hill, 1960, pp. 1–244.

Megginson, Leon C. *Personnel Management: A Human Resources Approach*. 5th ed. Homewood, Ill.: Richard D. Irwin, 1985, chaps. 9, 11.

Rue, Leslie W., and Lloyd L. Byars. *Management: Theory and Application*. 4th ed. Homewood, Ill.: Richard D. Irwin, 1986, chaps. 1, 2, 10, 14.

Schermerhorn, John R. *Management for Productivity*. 2nd ed. New York: John Wiley & Sons, 1986, chaps. 1, 10.

JOURNALS

Bennis, Warren. "Good Managers and Good Leaders." *Across the Board* 21, no. 10 (October 1984), pp. 7–11.

Carbone, T. "Theory X and Theory Y Revisited." *Managerial Planning* 29, no. 6 (May–June 1981), pp. 24–27.

Carroll, S. J., and D. A. Gillen. "Are the Classical Management Functions Useful in Describing Managerial Work?" *Academy of Management Review* 12, no. 1 (January 1987), pp. 38–51.

Clarke, N. K. "The Sadistic Manager." *Personnel* 62, no. 2 (February 1985), pp. 34–37.

Edwards, M. R., and T. E. Bartlett. "Innovations in Talent Identification." *Advanced Management Journal* 48, no. 4 (Autumn 1983), pp. 16–24.

Fairholm, Gilbert. "Power Tactics on the Job." *Personnel* 62, no. 5 (May 1985), pp. 45–50.

Flax, Steven. "The Toughest Bosses in America." *Fortune* 110, no. 3 (August 6, 1984), pp. 18–23.

Gerstein, Marc, and Heather Reisman. "Strategic Selection: Matching Executives to Business Conditions." *Sloan Management Review* 24, no. 2 (Winter 1983), pp. 33–37.

Graeff, Claude L. "The Situational Leadership Theory: A Critical View." *Academy of Management Review* 8, no. 2 (April 1983), pp. 285–91.

Grant, Floyd H. "When You Call in a Consultant." *Advanced Management Journal* 48, no. 1 (Winter 1983), pp. 31–37.

Levesque, J. D. "Selecting and Managing Competent Managers." *Personnel Administrator* 30, no. 3 (March 1985), pp. 63–72.

O'Neal, M. A. "Managerial Skills and Values—For Today and Tomorrow." *Personnel* 62, no. 7 (July 1985), 49–55.

Rowan, Roy. "America's Most Wanted Managers." *Fortune* 113, no. 3 (January 3, 1986), pp. 18–25.

Slavenski, Lynn. "Matching People on the Job." *Training and Development Journal* 40, no. 8 (August 1986), pp. 54–57.

Stumpf, Stephen, and Manuel London. "Management Promotions: Individual and Organizational Factors Influencing the Decision Process." *Academy of Management Review* 6, no. 4 (October 1981), pp. 539–49.

Szilagyi, A. D., and D. M. Schweiger. "Matching Managers to Strategies." *Academy of Management Review* 9, no. 4 (October 1984), pp. 626–37.

Wells, Ronald G. "What Every Manager Should Know about Management Consultants." *Personnel Journal* 62, no. 2 (February 1983), pp. 142–48.

WHAT THIS INCIDENT IS ABOUT:
Security is breached when master keys disappear,
and the decision to incur immediate costs or future
liabilities is made more difficult by conflicting and
professionally self-serving staff advice. This incident
focuses on decision making, responsibility, controls,
goals and objectives, ethical considerations, and
contradictory staff recommendations.

7

Contradictory staff
advice

INCIDENT

The administrator of the state mental hospital learned that keys to
security wards for dangerous criminals had been lost or stolen when he
received an early morning telephone call on May 1 from the hospital's
night administrator. Since duplicate keys were available in the hospital
safe, the administrator, Mr. Jackson, knew the loss of the keys would not
interfere with the hospital's routine functioning, but he decided to call a
general staff meeting the next morning to consider the problem.

At the meeting, Jackson explained about the missing keys and asked for
suggestions. The assistant administrator suggested that the matter be kept
confidential among the staff since public knowledge could lead to damaging
publicity and a possible investigation by Department of Health and Rehabilitative Services officials.

The head of security for the hospital reported that only two keys were
missing. Although he could not tell if the keys had been stolen or lost, he
thought they were probably stolen. He emphasized that the missing keys
were "master keys" that could open the doors to all security wards where
the most dangerous criminals were housed. In his opinion, immediate
replacement of the locks on those doors was required.

The director of accounting estimated the cost of replacing the locks at
more than $5,000. She reminded the group that operating costs already
exceeded the hospital's operating budget by about 10 percent due to infla-
tion and other unexpected expenses, and that an emergency request for a
supplemental budget appropriation to cover the deficit had been sent to

the Department of Health and Rehabilitative Services the previous week. She concluded that no funds were available in the budget for replacing the locks, and an additional $5,000 request might jeopardize the request for supplementary operating funds already submitted. Besides, since it was early May, the hospital would begin operating under the budget for the next fiscal year in approximately 60 days. The locks could be replaced then and the costs charged against the new budget.

Another staff member reasoned aloud that if the keys had been lost, any person finding them would probably not know their purpose and that if the keys had been stolen, they probably would never be used in any unauthorized way.

Jackson thanked the staff members for their contributions, ended the meeting, and faced the decision. He reflected that behind the doors to the security wards were convicted first-degree murderers and sexual psychopaths, among others. He also remembered his impeccable 13-year record as an effective hospital administrator. The thought occurred to him that perhaps the most important action would be to find and place the blame upon the person who was responsible for the disappearance of the two keys.

As he continued his deliberation, Jackson realized that each staff member's suggestion reflected his or her individual profession or specialty. These divergent and contradictory recommendations, taken together, produced no solution. Jackson saw two critical requirements. He recognized an immediate need to decide upon and implement temporary procedures to guarantee containment of the mental patients. Moreover, he needed to develop an organizational response policy for future incidents that threatened to compromise the mental patient security system. Jackson didn't know how best to proceed. He was also concerned with ethical considerations.

CRITIQUES

ANDRÉ L. DELBECQ
Dean of The Leavey School
of Business and Administration
University of Santa Clara

If Mr. Jackson had had a managerially trained guardian angel on duty before his staff meeting, it might have whispered four aphorisms often found in management literature in his ear:

1. Remain problem centered and explore integrative combinations of alternative solutions.

2. Focus on system weaknesses, don't scapegoat individuals.
3. Confront difficulties, don't smooth them over or resort to authority.
4. Have policies in place for short-run safety emergencies.

Alas, the managerial angel must have been visiting a journal editor instead. Let's look at each of the four concerns.

Problem centeredness. Problem exploration, at best, was symptomatic. For example, the staff meeting did not explore how the keys might have been lost or stolen, whether there were different security needs between patients or wards, or the exact nature of public relations concerns. Similarly, giving round robin, off-the-cuff opinions does not constitute exploration of alternative solutions. The few proposed solutions were deeply embedded in subgroup biases. Security stressed security, Accounting stressed budgets, and Administration stressed public relations. In each instance, there was a single alternative suggested. Undoubtedly there are a variety of security options (such as changing some locks and increasing ward observation), budget options (such as cash flow and resource variations), and external relations options (such as contacting a limited number of outsiders).

Focusing on system weaknesses. The present tension, once a short-run solution is reached, offers an opportunity for reexamining security systems as a policy issue. Any tendency to scapegoat individuals will decrease attention to systemic weaknesses and increase information absorption. Unless a rule violation or serious negligence is involved, focusing on individuals is inappropriate.

Confronting difficulties. In this era of investigative journalism, one understands that smoothing over errors leads to later charges of an even more serious nature. Direct confrontation of the problem, sharing information with key authority figures, and admission of organizational failures indicate a manager's ability to confront a crisis. Benign neglect and negligence based on attempts to maintain illusions of omniscience are poor strategies for coping with system errors. A cover-up only exacerbates later suspicions that private ambition was placed over managerial responsibilities and, in this case, public trust and safety. Policies for coping with the media in a nonalarmist fashion and rehearsals for media interviews are often part of the "competency training" for top public administrators.

Emergency policies for public safety. Finally, in an emergency involving public safety, short-run coping procedures must be instituted even while intermediate and long-run solutions are explored. The early morning hours prior to the staff meeting were the time to respond with increased temporary security measures. Public trust should be based on well-organized policies for safety-related crises.

THOMAS A. NATIELLO
Professor of Management and
Health Administration
University of Miami

Any organization requires identification of its objectives, goals, priorities, and strategies. A state mental hospital is no exception. Important actions in any situation must be based on these criteria. Jackson, the administrator, and his staff must understand the reasons for the organization's existence, at least within the realm of security and responsibility for dangerous criminals and the system that discharges this responsibility.

Assigning individual responsibility for the missing keys would have a lower initial priority than maintaining institutional security. Hopefully, additional security systems would be available to prevent the keys from being used in a destructive manner. Systems did not exist for constant control of security keys. It is clear that a review of security procedures is necessary.

There is, however, a deeper implication in the apparent inadequacy of the administrator and the department heads involved to act decisively and effectively. The organizational environment seems to be one of reluctant innovation and extreme personal caution with little feedback to the administrator or staff; each individual considers only his or her point of view within the structure, which indicates a divergence of individual goals between each of the functional areas. The assistant administrator's suggestion of confidentiality among the staff, the director of accounting's concern about costs and the possible jeopardy of other funding requests, and the administrator's concern with his impeccable 13-year record and assignment of blame all indicate a lack of understanding organizational priorities and departmental responsibilities. The head of security, after recommending the replacement of all locks, appears to have no further responsibility for future actions. He has abdicated this responsibility, as it seems everyone else has, to the administrator, who will make the decision.

Often, organizations use approaches that allow individual goals to replace the organization's goals. Organization leaders should act not to avoid blame but to find solutions and set up effective systems in the best interests of the organization. The organization must also have a means of external communication, particularly with the Department of Health and Rehabilitative Services. Easy communication, rather than an adversary relationship, should provide information to aid decisions in such circumstances. Therefore, expenditures are required, because the loss of the keys should be considered in terms of their contribution to organizational effectiveness and the institution's maintenance of societal requirements.

Furthermore, the administrator should analyze the organizational systems within the hospital. Excessive reliance on individuals behaving normally in unusual situations rather than developing the systems necessary to meet contingencies in a more positive manner is a dangerous approach to an organization's high-priority requirements. There should be some means to constantly review the organization's readiness to act effectively in crisis situations.

The administrator must develop an understanding of the critical variables associated with his institution. Identifying these variables will help him develop appropriate organizational systems for their support, helping him to control the situation within the organization with a sensitivity to the external environment.

But what to do now? The administrator must take some action, even if the decision is to do nothing. A problem-solving decision structure could be useful, such as Kepner-Tregoe's decision-making procedure, which lends itself to risk-cost analysis.

The lost key incident can be analyzed in terms of the problems it has caused and the resultant risk to hospital personnel, patients, the community, and the organization. The risk and cost of alternative feasible solutions can be compared. Immediate action can then be taken to intervene in situations that result in a threat to life, morally and ethically undesirable situations, or prevention of the successful discharge of the hospital's responsibilities in its role as an agent of the state.

A careful analysis of the incident provides information for decisions about organizational and individual responsibilities, control processes, and ethical considerations.

First steps in applying the Kepner-Tregoe problem-solving procedure might involve developing a decision matrix that considers direct and indirect costs and policy implications relating to the state mental hospital's goals and objectives. This would be useful in determining priorities and courses of action. This suggested cost matrix could be constructed in the following format:

Costs Attributed to the Loss of Keys Matrix

Persons Affected	Direct Costs	Indirect Costs	Policy Issues
Victims	Physical and emotional injury	Negative attitudes toward hospital	Nonachievement of mandate of hospital

The development of a decision-making process that supports an organization's mandate via goals and objectives implemented through policy determination and application is a powerful tool for decision making and setting priorities that rises above the restricted perceptions of individuals in the organization.

OBSERVATIONS

Managers who have staffs and those who encourage subordinates to participate in problem-solving and decision-making processes can expect to receive contradictory advice and recommendations. Individuals tend to view decision problems from the perspective of their training and experience in their specialty or profession. Subordinates' recommendations, therefore, often reflect the goals for their part of the "big picture." Managers should be aware of this subgroup/specialty bias in recommendations and remember the organization's overall goals. The manager needs to consider integrative combinations of options and to decide upon policy and action in the best interests of the whole organization. Doing this is difficult, as illustrated by Mr. Jackson. This responsibility contributes to feelings of managerial "isolation," reflected in statements such as "It's lonely at the top" and "I don't have anyone that I can talk with." Managers sometimes engage consultants for assistance in examining problems from the managerial point of view, and to reduce their sense of organizational "isolation."

DISCUSSION ITEMS

1. Evaluate the recommendations that various staff members of the state mental hospital made at their meeting.
2. Who, if anyone, should be blamed for allowing the keys to be unaccounted for? What penalties would you consider appropriate?
3. What is the most immediate responsibility of the hospital administrator? Why? What is involved in using the Kepner-Tregoe technique suggested by Professor Natiello?

SUGGESTED READINGS

BOOKS

Arnold, Hugh J., and Daniel C. Feldman. *Organizational Behavior.* New York: McGraw-Hill, 1986, chap. 14.

Callahan, Robert E.; C. Patrick Fleenor; and Harry Knudson. *Understanding Organizational Behavior.* Columbus, Ohio: Charles E. Merrill Publishing, 1986, chap. 7.

Davis, Keith, and John W. Newstrom. *Human Behavior at Work*. 7th ed. New York: McGraw-Hill, 1985, chaps. 3, 13.

Donnelly, James H.; James L. Gibson; and John M. Ivancevich. *Fundamentals of Management*. 6th ed. Plano, Tex.: Business Publications, 1987, chap. 17.

French, Wendell L. *The Personnel Management Process*. 6th ed. Boston: Houghton Mifflin, 1987, chaps. 7, 13.

Griffin, Ricky W. *Management*. 2nd ed. Boston: Houghton Mifflin, 1987, chaps. 7, 17.

Heneman, Herbert G.; Donald P. Schwab; John A. Fossum; and Lee D. Dyer. *Personnel/Human Resource Management*. 3rd ed. Homewood, Ill.: Richard D. Irwin, 1986, chaps. 3, 12.

Megginson, Leon C. *Personnel Management: A Human Resources Approach*. 5th ed. Homewood, Ill.: Richard D. Irwin, 1985, chaps. 8, 11.

Rue, Leslie W., and Lloyd L. Byars. *Management: Theory and Application*. 4th ed. Homewood, Ill.: Richard D. Irwin, 1986, chaps. 4, 21.

Schermerhorn, John R. *Management for Productivity*. 2nd ed. New York: John Wiley & Sons, 1986, chap. 3.

JOURNALS

Agor, Weston H. "How Top Executives Use Their Intuition to Make Important Decisions." *Business Horizons* 29, no. 1 (January–February 1986), pp. 49–53.

Altier, William J. "Objectivity: The Critical Element." *Business Horizons* 25, no. 6 (November–December 1982), pp. 19, 20.

Bennis, Warren. "The Four Competencies of Leadership." *Training and Development Journal* 38, no. 8 (August 1984), pp. 14–19.

Cohen, Allan R. "Crisis Management: How to Turn Disasters into Advantages." *Management Review* 71, no. 8 (August 1982), pp. 27, 28, 37–40.

Ellis, R. Jeffrey. "Responsive Managing: Getting on with the Job." *Management Review* 72, no. 1 (January 1983), pp. 59, 60.

Gillett, Darwin. "Better QCs: A Need for More Manager Action." *Management Review* 72, no. 1 (January 1983), pp. 19–25.

Huber, George P., and André Delbecq. "Guidelines for Combining the Judgments of Individual Members in Decision Conferences." *Academy of Management Journal* 15, no. 2 (June 1972), pp. 161–74.

Kleinschrod, Walter A. "Thinking Like a Crook." *Administrative Management* 48, no. 1 (January 1987), p. 62.

Kreck, Lothar A. "A New Approach to Problem Solving." *Advancement Management Journal* 46, no. 3 (Summer 1981), pp. 19–22.

Rahim, M. Afzalur. "A Strategy for Managing Conflict in Complex Organizations." *Human Relations* 38, no. 1 (January 1985), pp. 88–89.

Tjosvold, Dean. "Effects of Crisis Orientation on Managers' Approach to Controversy in Decision Making." *Academy of Management Journal* 27, no. 1 (March 1984), pp. 130–38.

Weick, Karl E. "Organizational Culture as a Source of High Reliability." *California Management Review* 29, no. 2 (Winter 1987), pp. 112–27.

Wilmotte, Raymond M.; Phillip I. Morgan; and H. Kent Baker. "Using the Brain as a Model to Increase Rationality in Organizational Decision Making." *Management Review* 73, no. 2 (February 1984), pp. 62–65.

WHAT THIS INCIDENT IS ABOUT:
A classical organization problem of authority and
responsibility commonly found in hospitals is
identified in this incident and leads to further
examination of such topics as grievance handling,
organizing, policy formulation, policy implementation, procedures, and decision making.

8

Dual lines of authority

INCIDENT

James A. Grover, retired land developer and financier, is president of
the Chiefland Memorial Hospital Board of Trustees. Chiefland Memorial is
a 200-bed voluntary, short-term general hospital serving an area of approximately 50,000 persons. Grover has just begun a meeting with the hospital
administrator, Edward M. Hoffman. The purpose of the meeting is to seek
an acceptable solution to an apparent conflict-of-authority problem within
the hospital between Hoffman and the chief of surgery, Dr. Lacy Young.

The problem was brought to Grover's attention by Young during a golf
match between the two men. Young had challenged Grover to the golf
match at the Chiefland Golf and Country Club, but it was only an excuse
for Young to discuss a hospital problem with Grover.

The problem that concerned Young involved the operating room supervisor, Ms. Geraldine Werther. Werther, a registered nurse, schedules the
hospital's operating suite according to policies that she "believes" were
established by the hospital's administration. One source of irritation to the
surgeons is her attitude of maximum utilization for the hospital's operating
rooms to reduce hospital costs. She therefore schedules operations so that
idle time is minimized. Surgeons complain that the operative schedule
often does not permit them sufficient time to complete a surgical procedure in the manner they think desirable. All too often, there is insufficient
time between operations for effective preparation of the operating room for
the next procedure. Such scheduling, the surgical staff maintains, contributes to low-quality patient care. Furthermore, some surgeons have complained that Werther shows favoritism in her scheduling, allowing some
doctors more use of the operating suite than others.

70

The situation reached a crisis when Young, following an explosive confrontation with Werther, told her he was firing her. Werther then made an appeal to the hospital administrator, who in turn informed Young that discharge of nurses was an administrative prerogative. In effect, Young was told he did not have the authority to fire Werther. But Young asserted that he did have authority over any issue affecting medical practice and good patient care in Chiefland Hospital. He considered this a medical problem and threatened to take the matter to the hospital's board of trustees.

When Grover and Hoffman met, Hoffman explained his position on the problem. He stressed the point that a hospital administrator is legally responsible for patient care in the hospital. He also contended that quality patient care cannot be achieved unless the board of trustees authorizes the administrator to make decisions, develop programs, formulate policies, and implement procedures. While listening to Hoffman, Grover recalled the belligerent position taken by Young, who contended that surgical and medical doctors holding staff privileges at Chiefland would never allow a "layman" to make decisions impinging on medical practice. Young also had said that Hoffman should be told to restrict his activities to fund-raising, financing, maintenance, and housekeeping—administrative problems rather than medical problems. Young had then requested that Grover clarify in a definitive manner the lines of authority at Chiefland Memorial.

As Grover ended his meeting with Hoffman, the severity of the problem was unmistakably clear to him, but the solution remained quite unclear. Grover knew a decision was required—and soon. He also recognized that the policies Werther professed to follow were only implied policies that had never been fully articulated, formally adopted by board action, or communicated to employees. He also intended to correct that situation.

CRITIQUES

DAVID B. STARKWEATHER
Professor of Hospital
Administration
University of California, Berkeley

Given the basic organizational characteristics of hospitals, this situation is quite plausible: a power structure shared by professionals invoking the authority of scientific knowledge, administrators invoking the authority of office, and a board with the appearance of ultimate power but no practical way of acting on that power. The situation is also typical of most organizational conflict in that there are two elements inextricably entwined: a substantive, immediate issue and a larger, long-run power play. Any attempts at resolution must deal with both issues.

As for the immediate problem, management should *attempt to bring increased rationality* to the situation. Consider the following:

1. Werther's statement that she is operating within policies that she "believes" to have been established by the hospital's administration suggests that there is imprecision in hospital policies in need of clarification.
2. The allegation by surgeons that there is insufficient time to complete operations is a serious clinical matter that should be referred to the medical staff's surgical department for review and comment to Hoffman. Likewise, the charge that scheduling practices "contribute to low-quality patient care" should be carefully investigated and documented (if possible).
3. Even the charge of favoritism is subject to objective analysis.

As for the larger question of organizational power, management should aim to clarify authority and make it operative. That large gray zone in hospitals between medical and administrative jurisdictions is: (1) sometimes a no-man's-land left to nurses, and (2) more commonly a constantly shifting battlefield where both physician and administrator try to redefine organizational prerogatives into their own spheres. The contest goes on constantly and cannot be eliminated altogether. Yet, it is important to clarify authority as much as possible although it may be necessary to have a few remaining vague areas. There is a place in organizational dynamics for tacit agreement to avoid formal precision on a few points, because forcing the issue too far would negatively affect desired organizational relationships.

The confusion over authority between Hoffman and Chiefland's board must be clarified before the confusion between Hoffman and Young and the others can be addressed. Features of the case that make this apparent include: (1) conducting essential hospital business on the golf course, (2) Young's categorical statement that he has authority over any activity at Chiefland affecting medical practice, as if virtually all activities of a hospital administrator didn't already have that effect, and (3) Grover's recollection that physicians had previously prescribed a narrow maintenance function for the administrator, without apparent further clarification by the board when Hoffman was appointed.

In the last paragraph of the incident it is unclear as to who will make the required decision; yet the way seems clear for Hoffman to take the initiative. He should do so in the following way:

1. Propose a statement for board action that would both establish his management authorities and make clear his responsibility for Werther's employment.
2. Schedule a meeting with Young, or with the chief of surgery and the chief of staff, at which he should outline and seek agreement on a

method of inquiry into the charges of Werther's contribution to declining quality. This method should start by putting Young's complaints in a written memorandum to Hoffman.

3. Indicate to Werther his sole authority for her employment. (If this is not sustained by the board, Hoffman should resign, as there is no real opportunity for him at Chiefland without this recognition.)

4. Undertake a careful review of the scheduling practices regarding operating room use, preferably in concert with the chief of surgery or another respected surgeon acceptable to both the chief and Hoffman. Any favoritism should be corrected immediately through new scheduling procedures.

5. Finally, having taken this initiative, Hoffman should: (1) locate a friend, in or out of the hospital, with whom he can personally discuss the whole matter, and (2) maintain his sense of perspective about the whole situation regardless of the outcome.

STUART A. WESBURY, JR.
President, American College of Healthcare
Executives

This incident describes a classic problem in hospital administration. Conflicts involving the board of trustees, medical staff, and administrator are common and an inherent characteristic of the division of authority in a hospital. However, the seriousness of the situation described in this incident indicates that the problem is somewhat out of control.

Two basic issues must be addressed. First, Hoffman should begin a thorough investigation of the specific operating room incident to find a satisfactory resolution of the scheduling problem. Secondly, immediate steps must be taken with representatives of the board and the administrator to come to an understanding as to the administrator's role in managing the affairs of the institution. No order of priority is intended by the sequencing of these two steps. In fact, both should be started immediately and carried on concurrently.

Any attempt to identify the specific problem involved carries back to the occasion of Hoffman's appointment as administrator. Why was there not a better clarification of roles at that time? The fault lies both with the board and with the administrator. If an understanding had been reached and made part of the institution's operational policies, the operating room scheduling issue would never have been blown out of proportion. This mistake must be rectified by carefully examining the problem and developing clear-cut policies and job descriptions regarding operating authority. The medical staff must be involved in this process so that the problem's resolution can be communicated effectively to and understood by all parties involved. Hoffman's integrity as an administrator is certainly an issue that will pervade all discussions. It is implied that other serious problems exist similar to the operating room situation, which makes one feel that Hoffman has not been very effective in clarifying the authority issue from his point of view. Very simply stated, can he survive as an administrator?

Much time could be spent in discussing ways to rectify the operating room scheduling problem. The "real facts" of the case are not fully known. In fact, the incident's description indicates that nothing seems to be in writing and that the nurse follows policies that she "believes" have been established by the hospital's administration. This is not an insurmountable problem if only the parties involved will sit down and begin working on it. The board should not be involved in the process until there is a proposed policy to discuss and approve. That is, Werther, Hoffman, and Young (or appropriate representatives) should deal with the problem before the board gets involved. Board members cannot and should not be a part of such problem-solving activities.

In the incident description, Hoffman was reported as stating that he is legally responsible for patient care in the hospital. This is not literally true. The responsibility for patient care rests with the board. The board, through its delegation of authority, will place a great deal of this responsibility upon the administrator. However, again we are faced with the need to clarify this issue to the mutual satisfaction of the board, the medical staff, and the administrator.

In summary, the two primary problems of delegation of authority and the specific operating room scheduling policy must be dealt with immediately and simultaneously. This action should assure everyone involved that there is interest in resolving these current issues and in establishing long-range policies and practices that will prevent the recurrence of such problems.

OBSERVATIONS

The American Management Association has issued what it calls the "Ten Commandments of Good Organization." The issues in this incident illustrate that at least half of the commandments would be difficult, if not impossible, to follow in a typical community hospital. It is a pattern of a dual pyramid, with the administration hierarchy and the medical staff hierarchy existing side by side. This organizational structure differs substantially from the bureaucratic model of other large-scale organizations, and it is responsible for producing many conflicts of jurisdiction.

In this incident, someone who might be considered as a person outside the organization, a physician practicing surgery in the community, is attempting to exercise authority over employees of the organization. Is this an infringement on the administrator's prerogatives? Due to the organizational characteristics of the dual hierarchy in hospitals, Dr. Wesbury describes it as a classical and common problem in hospital administration, with no easy solutions. There are other unique organizations, such as specialized research groups, in which variations from the bureaucratic model also create complex problems for management. Professor Starkweather suggests the problems cannot be eliminated altogether, but they can be reduced through efforts to clarify authority and responsibility relationships and to formulate and implement policies that will provide guidance to all parties involved.

DISCUSSION ITEMS

1. Professor Starkweather suggests that the way seems open for Mr. Hoffman to take the initiative, and he indicates the approach that should be taken to combat the problem. What is your evaluation of Professor Starkweather's recommended approach?
2. Recognizing that no policy, or even an implied policy, may be mistakenly perceived as a policy, Mr. Grover realizes he must write a policy for formal adoption by the hospital's board that will clarify the division of authority existing in the hospital. Write a policy statement that will achieve that purpose.
3. What steps, in addition to formulating a policy, should Grover take regarding the incident at Chiefland Memorial Hospital? Why? How can the policy that you write for Grover be implemented?

SUGGESTED READINGS

BOOKS

Arnold, Hugh J., and Daniel C. Feldman. *Organizational Behavior*. New York: McGraw-Hill, 1986, chaps. 9, 10, 13.

Callahan, Robert E.; C. Patrick Fleenor; and Harry Knudson. *Understanding Organizational Behavior*. Columbus, Ohio: Charles E. Merrill Publishing, 1986, chap. 9.

Davis, Keith, and John W. Newstrom. *Human Behavior at Work*. 7th ed. New York: McGraw-Hill, 1985, chaps. 5, 13–15.

Donnelly, James H.; James L. Gibson; and John M. Ivancevich. *Fundamentals of Management*. 6th ed. Plano, Tex.: Business Publications, 1987, chaps. 6–8, 14, 22.

French, Wendell L. *The Personnel Management Process*. 6th ed. Boston: Houghton Mifflin, 1987, chaps. 5, 8–10, 14.

Griffin, Ricky W. *Management*. 2nd ed. Boston: Houghton Mifflin, 1987, chaps. 3, 4, 9–12, 17–19.

Harvey, Donald F. *Business Policy and Strategic Management*. Columbus, Ohio: Charles E. Merrill Publishing, 1982, chaps. 1–3, 8.

Heneman, Herbert G.; Donald P. Schwab; John A. Fossum; and Lee D. Dyer. *Personnel/Human Resource Management*. 3rd ed. Homewood, Ill.: Richard D. Irwin, 1986, chaps. 18–20.

Hershey, Nathan. *Hospital-Physician Relationships*. Rockville, Md.: Aspen Systems Corp., 1982.

Megginson, Leon C. *Personnel Management: A Human Resources Approach*. 5th ed. Homewood, Ill.: Richard D. Irwin, 1985, chaps. 2, 11, 12.

Rubright, Robert. *Persuading Physicians: A Guide for Hospital Executives*. Rockville, Md.: Aspen Systems Corp., 1983.

Rue, Leslie W., and Lloyd L. Byars. *Management: Theory and Application*. 4th ed. Homewood, Ill.: Richard D. Irwin, 1986, chaps. 4, 8–12, 14–17.

Schermerhorn, John R. *Management for Productivity*. 2nd ed. New York: John Wiley & Sons, 1986, chaps. 6–8, 20.

Shultz, Rockwell, and Alton Johnson. *Management of Hospitals*. New York: McGraw-Hill, 1983, chaps. 1–5.

JOURNALS

Astley, W. G., and P. S. Sachdeva. "Structural Sources of Intraorganizational Power." *Academy of Management Review* 9, no. 1 (January 1984), pp. 104–13.

Briscoe, D. K. "Organizational Design: Dealing with the Human Constraint." *California Management Review* 23, no. 1 (Fall 1980), pp. 71–80.

Cobb, A. T. "Political Diagnosis: Applications in Organizational Development." *Academy of Management Review* 11, no. 3 (July 1986), pp. 482–96.

Gray, Barbara, and S. S. Ariss. "Politics and Strategic Change across Organizational Life Cycles." *Academy of Management Review* 10, no. 4 (October 1985), pp. 707–23.

Joyce, W. F. "Matrix Organization: A Social Experiment." *Academy of Management Journal* 29, no. 3 (September 1986), pp. 536–61.

Macher, Ken. "The Politics of Organizations." *Personnel Journal* 65, no. 2 (February 1986), pp. 80–84.

Mahmoudi, H., and G. Miller. "A Causal Model of Hospital Structure." *Group and Organization Studies* 10, no. 2 (June 1985), pp. 209–23.

Marcus, Alfred A. "Professional Autonomy as a Basis of Conflict in an Organization." *Human Resource Management* 24, no. 4 (Fall 1985), pp. 311–28.

Mintzberg, Henry. "Organization Design: Fashion or Fit?" *Harvard Business Review* 59, no. 1 (January-February 1981), pp. 103–16.

―――. "Power and Organization Life Cycles." *Academy of Management Review* 9, no. 2 (April 1984), pp. 207–24.

Pavett, C. M., and A. W. Lau. "Managerial Work: The Influence of Hierarchical

Level and Functional Speciality." *Academy of Management Journal* 26, no. 1 (March 1983), pp. 170–77.

Penley, L. E., and B. Hawkins. "Studying Interpersonal Communication in Organizations: A Leadership Application." *Academy of Management Journal* 28, no. 2 (June 1985), pp. 309–26.

Rizzo, John R.; Robert J. House; and Sidney J. Lirtzman. "Role Conflict and Ambiguity in Complex Organizations." *Administrative Science Quarterly* 15, no. 2 (June 1970), pp. 150–63.

Stybel, L. J.; Robin Cooper; and Maryanne Peabody. "Planning Executive Dismissals: How to Fire a Friend." *California Management Review* 24, no. 3 (Spring 1982), pp. 73–80.

WHAT THIS INCIDENT IS ABOUT:
Leadership styles, contingency management, and
management development are all topics raised by
this incident involving a manager seeking answers to
the question of what constitutes an effective style of
leadership.

9

Effective leadership

INCIDENT

Dr. Sam Perkins, a graduate of the Harvard University College of
Medicine, was engaged in the private practice of internal medicine for 12
years. Fourteen months ago, he was persuaded by the governor to give up
private practice to be director of the State Division of Human Services.

After one year as director, Perkins recognized he had made little progress in reducing the considerable inefficiency in the Division of Human
Services. Employee morale and effectiveness seemed even lower than
when he assumed the position. He realized his past training and experiences were of a clinical nature with little exposure to effective leadership
techniques. Perkins decided to research literature published on the subject
of leadership available to him at a local university.

Perkins soon realized that management scholars are divided on the
question of what constitutes effective leadership. Some feel that leaders are
born with certain identifiable personality traits that make them effective
leaders. Others feel a leader can learn to be effective by treating subordinates with a personal and considerate approach and by giving particular
attention to the subordinate's need for good working conditions. Still
others emphasize the importance of developing a style of leadership characterized by either authoritarian, democratic, or laissez-faire approaches.
Perkins was confused further when he learned there is a growing number
of scholars who advocate that effective leadership is contingent on the
situation, and a proper response to the question of what constitutes effective leadership is that it "depends on the situation."

Since a state university was located nearby, Perkins contacted its College of Business Administration dean. The dean referred him to the director of the college's Management Center, Professor Joel McCann. Discus-

sions between Perkins and McCann resulted in a tentative agreement that the Management Center would organize a series of leadership training sessions for the State Division of Human Services. Before agreeing on the price tag for the leadership conference, Perkins asked McCann to prepare a proposal reflecting his thoughts on the following:

1. How will the question of what constitutes effective leadership be answered during the conference?
2. How will the lack of congruence among leadership researchers be resolved or reconciled?
3. What will be the specific subject content of the conference?
4. Who will the instructors be?
5. What will be the conference's duration?
6. How can the conference's effectiveness be evaluated?
7. What policies should the State Division of Human Services adopt regarding who the conference participants should be and how they should be selected? How can these policies be best implemented?

CRITIQUES

ELMER H. BURACK
Professor of Management
University of Illinois—Chicago

The fact that Dr. Perkins has turned to somebody, presumably an authority on leadership, may be a more important leadership fact than any referred to in the incident. Leadership's major challenge invariably involves introducing or managing change—helping people to change, changing situations to remove blockages, or paving the way to new performance levels. But regardless of the circumstances, change is impossible unless the principal involved in this case, Dr. Perkins, recognizes the need for change. On the other hand, there are no guarantees that effective changes will occur even if the nature of the situation and need for involvement of the "leader" is recognized by the leader. The causal factors may lie completely outside of the scope of his influence, and conditions may worsen because of organizational matters beyond the leader's control. Thus, two initial lessons are to be learned here: (1) the leader recognizes that change has occurred (he is the new head), and (2) the leader recognizes that problems (Division of Human Services inefficiencies) involve him. The personal leadership issues are addressed by Perkins' initiatives; he has taken specific steps to build organizational leadership skills via the conference. No corrections are possible without satisfying these minimal requirements. The next steps raise the question, "Does Perkins want to change or introduce change?" Let's assume Perkins wants to do so. Then the individual leadership question is, "Can he acquire the needed skills to become an 'effective' leader?" Research and our experiences indicate that Perkins can probably improve his interactions with others, including employees. In other words, leadership performance can be improved by those formal leaders who understand leadership situations, who demonstrate greater understanding of other viewpoints, and who vary their approach based on the situation. Modern leadership development approaches also recognize that knowing what to do often isn't enough. Supervisors and managers, as leaders, need help implementing new, effective behaviors. "Behavioral modeling" provides hands-on skills for approaches which in the past were merely described.

A reality that must be dealt with is that *high* levels of effective leadership are probably not reachable through these approaches. To an important extent, various features of the individual may or may not be well-suited to particular situations. The famous Management Progress Study at AT&T suggested that certain early behavior indicators, such as performance in school and independence, may give clues to these abilities. In the Management Progress Study and in subsequent studies, leadership and broader management abilities have been judged through systematic observation of applicants by trained panels of experts plus performance on various tests.

Promising new developments in leadership development have focused on defining those specific leader behaviors that define success for their job-related responsibilities. Thus the emphasis is on "what" the leader has to do in order to be considered successful in a responsibility area. Consequently Perkins will have to be clear as to what he *expects* from his division heads *and* they in turn, of section heads in DHS.

Summarizing the observations, it appears that:

1. Particular managerial or leadership needs emerge from a specific situation involving individuals, groups, work, and organizations.
2. Individual change or improvement requires recognition of this need — in this example, securing needed leadership qualities.
3. People must be able to change to acquire needed skills and outlooks.
4. Successful leadership is increasingly defined in terms of what the person has to do in order to be judged "acceptable" or "successful."
5. Various leadership characteristics can be learned.
6. High levels of leadership effectiveness probably reflect innate talents and abilities.

Dr. Perkins' conference requires critical review in light of factors already developed.

1. Will the organization environments of the manager/leaders be changed or supportive even if they have acquired some new skills? Has Perkins established as yet a climate that will be seen as supportive of leadership

actions? Closely allied with this point, are policies regarding such areas as rewards and employee influence sufficiently defined so that the role of DHS administrators and supervisors will be seen as unambiguous?

2. Will the conference format, regardless of "theories" discussed, do any more than increase cognitive awareness? Will managers develop any new hands-on skills, which will be supported and reinforced after the conference?

3. Conference results need to be viewed in an expanded model that accounts for both the (1) effectiveness and (2) efficiency of participants back in their organizational units. Thus, judging participant performances will have to take account of conventional efficiency appraisals as well as the much more difficult effectiveness measures involving subordinates and clients.

DENNIS F. RAY
Professor and Head of Management
Mississippi State University

The underlying problem in this incident is a situation that often plagues managers, especially those with a specialized or technical background. This is the lack of a basic understanding of the management function and the lack of basic managerial skills.

In this instance, Dr. Perkins has raised the issue of leadership style as the basic root of his difficulties. Although leadership does play a vital role in managerial effectiveness, it is clearly not the only factor. It will be necessary for Perkins to carefully examine his qualifications and his performance in other areas of importance to a manager. One classification of these other areas is the basic functions of management—planning, organizing, staffing, directing, and controlling. Besides leadership skills, a manager's success is also influenced by performances in these other functional areas.

Nevertheless, this particular incident emphasizes the issue of reconciling various leadership theories that often appear to be inconsistent. The leadership theories that support the personal-traits concept do not effectively delineate or identify a basic list of traits. Even after some traits have been identified, it then becomes a question of whether or not these traits really were a part of the individual's makeup at the time of birth or have been acquired through experiences. By the time the individual is in a managerial role, it is almost impossible to separate characteristics that were original traits from those that have been acquired. Whether the traits were present at birth or acquired later, there appears to be some justification for believing that certain traits might contribute to the individual's effectiveness as a leader. Temperament traits could be an example.

The characterizing of leadership as either authoritarian, democratic, or laissez-faire is only a classification of leadership styles. The more important issue seems to arise out of the controversy as to which one of these particular leadership styles is the most effective. Research has shown that either of the three listed categories might very well be effective in a particular situation.

The contingency approach to explain effective leadership is a likely outgrowth of the controversy over various theories concerning leadership effectiveness. Many writers on the subject seem to have come to the conclusion that the answer to this leadership dilemma is dependent on contingencies in the situation. Some of these contingencies would include types of individuals involved (skilled, nonskilled, professional), types of jobs being performed (routine tasks or research and development activities), or the leadership skills possessed by the manager. These are just a few of the contingencies that can influence leadership effectiveness.

Also, it would be important to inform Perkins of the previously mentioned considerations. Especially, Perkins should get involved in some evaluation process to assess his own leadership style. He would likely discover some attitudes that have influenced his leadership effectiveness and would better understand the factors influencing this effectiveness. It is imperative that he consider a much broader approach to his problem; that is, consideration should also be given to developing skills in other management functions. Perkins' problems are more likely to be solved when he reaches a higher level of competence in all management skills, not just in his concern for leadership. Since other individuals in the Division of Human Services come from technical backgrounds, they are probably experiencing similar problems. Therefore, the tentative agreement with Professor McCann, director of the college's Management Center, to organize a series of training sessions on the subject of leadership should be explored fully. All management and supervisory personnel in the Division of Human Services should be involved in this program. These training plans should be considered in conjunction with other strategic plans and then integrated into the division's master plan to help ensure overall effectiveness.

OBSERVATIONS

In this incident, Dr. Perkins sees leadership style as the root of his problem and indicates he is having difficulty reconciling the various leadership theories, which are often inconsistent. He is not alone in this dilemma, because researchers and practitioners alike have been wrestling with this issue for centuries. No other subject in the professional management literature has probably received as much attention as the subject of leadership. Professors Ray and Burack offer much to enlighten someone like Perkins regarding this issue. They both allude to situational or contingency approaches of leadership as the best means of explaining what years of research have provided about leadership. An excellent discussion of that approach is provided in "Strategic Selection: Matching Executives to Business Conditions," by Marc Gerstein and Heather Reisman. Both are members of the firm Gerstein, Reisman & Associates, and their thesis is that each business situation requires that executives have a specific set of management skills and characteristics to make the business successful. As businesses adapt their strategies and organizational structures to a changing environment, this set of managerial characteristics must also change. Thus, the authors contend that executive selection should be linked to strategy. In other words, some people are better at beginning an operation, some people are better at squeezing the most out of them once they are running, and some people are better at fixing them when they go wrong.

It is interesting that the concept of matching individuals with specific positional requirements has been around for years in manual and technical jobs. But in our quest to isolate a group of traits found in all good managers, or to find one style of leadership characterizing all successful leaders, we have been slow to extend this concept to managerial jobs.

DISCUSSION ITEMS

1. In this incident, Dr. Perkins has asked Professor McCann to prepare a proposal that will provide a response to seven questions relative to a leadership conference. Prepare a proposal reflecting your thoughts with regard to the seven questions.
2. What is the status of research on the question of what constitutes effective leadership?
3. Professor Ray states that Dr. Perkins should get involved in some evaluation process to assess his leadership style. How can he best do this?

SUGGESTED READINGS

BOOKS

Arnold, Hugh J., and Daniel C. Feldman. *Organizational Behavior*. New York: McGraw-Hill, 1986, chaps. 2–5.

Bennis, Warren, and Burt Nanus. *Leaders: The Strategies for Taking Charge*. New York: Harper & Row, 1985, pp. 1–244.

Callahan, Robert E.; C. Patrick Fleenor; and Harry Knudson. *Understanding Organizational Behavior*. Columbus, Ohio: Charles E. Merrill Publishing, 1986, chap. 5.

Davis, Keith, and John W. Newstrom. *Human Behavior at Work*. 7th ed. New York: McGraw-Hill, 1985, chaps. 1–3, 5, 8, 22.

Donnelly, James H.; James L. Gibson; and John M. Ivancevich. *Fundamentals of Management*. 6th ed. Plano, Tex.: Business Publications, 1987, chaps. 10–12.

French, Wendell L. *The Personnel Management Process*. 6th ed. Boston: Houghton Mifflin, 1987, chaps. 6, 7, 13.

Griffin, Ricky W. *Management*. 2nd ed. Boston: Houghton Mifflin, 1987, chaps. 1, 2, 13–16.

Heneman, Herbert G.; Donald P. Schwab; John A. Fossum; and Lee D. Dyer. *Personnel/Human Resource Management*. 3rd ed. Homewood, Ill.: Richard D. Irwin, 1986, chaps. 3, 4.

Megginson, Leon C. *Personnel Management: A Human Resources Approach*. 5th ed. Homewood, Ill.: Richard D. Irwin, 1985, chaps. 10–14.

Peters, Thomas J., and Robert H. Waterman. *In Search of Excellence: Lessons from America's Best-Run Companies*. New York: Harper & Row, 1982, pp. 1–325.

Rue, Leslie W., and Lloyd L. Byars. *Management: Theory and Application*. 4th ed. Homewood, Ill.: Richard D. Irwin, 1986, chaps. 2, 13–16, 19.

Schermerhorn, John R. *Management for Productivity*. 2nd ed. New York: John Wiley & Sons, 1986, chaps. 10–13.

Wall, Jim. *Leading*. Lexington, Mass.: D. C. Heath, 1986.

JOURNALS

Barnes, L. B., and M. P. Kriger. "The Hidden Side of Organizational Leadership." *Sloan Management Review* 28, no. 1 (Fall 1986), pp. 15–25.

Bass, Bernard. "Leadership: Good, Better, Best." *Organizational Dynamics* 13, no. 1 (Winter 1985), pp. 26–40.

Brush, Donald, and Lyle Schoenfeldt. "Identifying Managerial Potential." *Personnel* 57, no. 3 (May-June 1980), pp. 71–72.

Burke, W. W. "Leadership: Is There One Best Approach?" *Management Review* 69, no. 11 (November 1980), pp. 54–56.

Davis, T. R., and Fred Luthans. "Leadership Reexamined: A Behavioral Approach." *Academy of Management Review* 4, no. 2 (April 1979), pp. 237–48.

Dienesch, R. M., and R. C. Liden. "Leader-Member Exchange Model of Leadership." *Academy of Management Review* 11, no. 3 (July 1986), pp. 618–34.

Gerstein, Marc, and Heather Reisman. "Strategic Selection: Matching Executives to Business Conditions." *Sloan Management Review* 24, no. 2 (Winter 1983), pp. 33–37.

Graeff, Claude L. "The Situational Leadership Theory: A Critical Review." *Academy of Management Review* 8, no. 2 (April 1983), pp. 258–91.

Hoffman, F. O. "The Hierarchy of Training Objectives." *Personnel* 62, no. 8 (August 1985), pp. 12–16.

Howard, Ann, and James Wilson. "Leadership in a Declining Work Ethic." *California Management Review* 24, no. 4 (Summer 1982), pp. 33–46.

Katz, Robert. "Skills of an Effective Administrator." *Harvard Business Review* 52, no. 5 (September-October 1974), pp. 90–102.

Kiechel, Walter. "Wanted: Corporate Leaders." *Fortune* 107, no. 7 (May 30, 1983), pp. 135–40.

Scroll, R. W., and W. W. Brownell. "Let Management Development Score for Your Organization." *Personnel Journal* 62, no. 6 (June 1983), pp. 486–91.

Sinetar, M. "Developing Leadership Potential." *Personnel Journal* 60, no. 3 (March 1981), pp. 193–96.

Smith, J. E.; K. P. Carson; and R. A. Alexander. "Leadership: It Can Make a Difference." *Academy of Management Journal* 27, no. 4 (December 1984), pp. 765–76.

WHAT THIS INCIDENT IS ABOUT:
This incident addresses the specific and growing
problem of alcoholism and drug abuse among employees. An underlying issue here is the economic
responsibility a firm has to its owners versus the
social responsibility it has to its employees.

10

Employee complaint

INCIDENT

James Sikes, a recent graduate of a New England university with a
major in marketing, applied for a sales position with a firm producing fabri-
cated aluminum. In offering Sikes the position, the sales manager made it
clear that an essential feature of the job involved entertaining purchasing
agents and that a certain amount of social drinking was necessary. Sikes
assured the sales manager that he was a moderate imbiber with no moral or
religious prejudices against drinking.

During the next three years, Sikes became a successful salesman and on
two occasions received an award for being salesman of the month. He
found, however, that he had a problem resulting from the necessity of
entertaining customers at least two or three times a week. He felt he was
becoming an alcoholic, since he had recently been overindulging when not
entertaining customers. The problem worsened until he found himself
constantly inebriated and unable to conduct business.

Sikes was sent, at company expense, to an alcoholic rehabilitation
center, from which he was discharged after six weeks of rest and recuperation. Only two weeks after Sikes had returned to his duties, he was arrested in a local night club and charged with drunkenness and assault. The
assault victim was a customer whom Sikes had taken to the club to discuss
a sale.

Company officials took an extremely dim view of the incident and fired
Sikes. Shortly thereafter an attorney representing Sikes informed the president of the company, Mr. Joyce, that Sikes intended to file suit against the
company. Sikes felt the company was liable since his alcoholism was a
result of his employment. He contended that drinking was a requirement
of his job, and therefore alcoholism represented an occupational hazard.

Joyce appointed a committee to recommend a managerial response to the threatened lawsuit. In recognition of national trends toward increased employee alcohol and drug abuse, Joyce further instructed the committee to consider what policies should be adopted to guide company officials faced with similar situations, and how such policies could best be implemented.

CRITIQUES

WALTER T. GREANEY, JR.
Professor of Management
Boston College

Two issues are involved in the Sikes case: First, has the employer any legal liability to this employee? Second, what policy can be adopted in the future to benefit the company and its sales force?

Legal responsibility grounded on the allegation of an occupational hazard can be easily defended by the firm. Sikes had been informed of the demands of his position. Moreover, it is common knowledge that social drinking is often a useful adjunct to the talents of salespersons. The company's payment for the rehabilitation period was a voluntary act from which an admission of legal responsibility cannot be inferred. Sikes had an obligation to limit his drinking to a reasonable amount so that it would not interfere with his job. As an alternative, Sikes might have attempted to handle his work without drinking or make a provision that he quietly be served a soft drink. He has not done anything on his own to help himself. An organization such as Alcoholics Anonymous might have been very helpful.

Sikes does not appear to have the strength of character required to perform his job. All sales effort is not tied to social drinking and he should seek more suitable employment. He is a recent university graduate and undoubtedly could quickly get another job. After a short training period, he should be a success. Sales ability is an individualistic talent that is not weakened by a change of employers.

The firm must look beyond the particular problem with Sikes. To offer him a different type of job in the company might add frustration to his present difficulties and cause another problem for the firm. To seek a legal victory as the final solution would not solve the problem either. The firm must try to avoid such problems in the future. To this end, its hiring policy should require extensive investigation of a potential salesperson's social adjustment. In the Sikes case, this would involve his family situation and his work and school histories with special emphasis on his adjustment to stress situations. As for particular aspects of alcoholism, the firm can contact various universities that have been conducting research on this problem, in order to set up procedures for prehiring or early discovery and for periodic checks.

KARL O. MANN
Professor of Industrial Relations
Rider College

The discharge of an employee has frequently been compared to capital punishment. It is the most severe type of disciplinary action and, as such, should only be used in extreme situations where the facts fully justify it. In this case, the legal liability of the company with respect to James Sikes can of course be decided only by the courts. However, from the view of human resource management, which seeks to improve employer-employee relations, company officials should not have fired Sikes when they learned that he had been arrested in a local night club and charged with drunkenness and assault.

It cannot be assumed that the basic reason of Sikes's alcoholism was the social drinking required by his job, although it was probably a contributing and precipitating factor. Psychological research indicates that alcoholism is often caused by such factors as insecurity, personal problems, inability to cope with the environment, and lack of self-discipline. However, the company made no effort to find out what factors other than the job contributed to Sikes becoming an alcoholic. His six-week stay at an alcoholic rehabilitation center was probably sufficient for the "rest and recuperation" he needed, but it could not be expected to determine and eliminate the underlying causes of his alcoholism. Yet, the company allowed Sikes to return to work without requiring further treatment and without even giving him a warning. In fact, he was permitted to continue in his old job which required social drinking, although it is generally recognized that the arresting of alcoholism demands total abstention from alcohol and that even a single drink may precipitate a return to this condition. Under these circumstances, the company was, at least to some extent, responsible for the incident at the night club and therefore should not have fired Sikes.

This incident might have been avoided if company officials had taken preventive action. For example, Sikes could have been required to submit to further treatment after returning from the alcoholic rehabilitation center. Furthermore, he could have been transferred to a job that did not require drinking. And he could have been warned about the consequences of unacceptable behavior in the future.

The primary reason for the company's failure to act along these lines was that it had established neither a sound disciplinary policy nor effective alcoholism and drug abuse policies. Under the circumstances, Mr. Joyce was correct in appointing a committee to develop such policies for the guidance of company officials who might be faced with similar situations in the future. In formulating these policies, the committee should (1) determine the various types of unacceptable employee behavior, especially those involving the use of alcohol and drugs; (2) decide how the company ought to react if such unacceptable behavior does take place; (3) identify possible preventive measures which might be instituted, such as testing for alcohol and drug abuse; and (4) investigate the legal aspects involved, i.e., the extent to which any proposed policies may be affected by federal and state laws as well as court decisions, including those that deal with the issue of employment-at-will.

However, Mr. Joyce should not have instructed the committee to recommend a response to the threatened lawsuit by Sikes. Such a response is not a managerial but a legal matter and, therefore, should be based primarily on the recommendations of the company's attorney. Nor should he have requested the committee to suggest how the policies could best be implemented. Inasmuch as these are essentially personnel policies, Mr. Joyce should have instructed the company's personnel department to develop specific procedures that would clearly indicate the specific steps to be taken in the future by all company officials in order to ensure the effective implementation of the policies.

OBSERVATIONS

Professors Keith Davis and John Newstrom, authors of *Human Behavior at Work*, estimate that between 5 and 10 percent of all employees are alcoholics and that they cost employers more than $10 billion annually in absenteeism, poor work, lost productivity, and related costs. While the job environment may contribute to an employee's alcoholism, the employee's personal habits and problems are also major contributors. That is the essence of this incident: To what extent have job requirements caused James Sikes to become an alcoholic, and to what degree should his employer assume responsibility? There are many employee programs that treat alcoholism as an illness and provide both medical and psychological support for alcoholics regardless of the causes.

In this incident an employee has become an alcoholic, allegedly due to the demands of the job. Professor Greaney appears to think the action that was taken against Sikes was justified due to his lack of strength of character required to perform the job and because he had an obligation to limit his drinking to a reasonable amount. Professor Mann, on the other hand, seems to think that company officials should not have fired Sikes and that the company's legal liability is uncertain because it must be established by the courts. Thus, in this incident, as is the case with many incidents in this book, there are two opposite views expressed by the critique writers. The suggested readings will be valuable in assisting each reader to formulate his or her own views.

DISCUSSION ITEMS

1. Evaluate Mr. Joyce's wisdom in appointing a committee to recommend action regarding James Sikes. What would you like to see the committee recommend? Why?
2. Professor Mann states that a primary reason for the failure of Sikes's employer to act responsibly was that effective policies dealing with alcoholism and drug abuse had not been established. He also indicates certain considerations that such policies should include. Incorporate those considerations into a well-articulated policy addressing alcohol and drug abuse that could be adopted by this firm.
3. What are the factors that would dictate a company's liability in terms of occupational hazards? Do you know of any legislation or any court decisions relating to this incident?

SUGGESTED READINGS

BOOKS

Arnold, Hugh J., and Daniel C. Feldman. *Organizational Behavior*. New York: McGraw-Hill, 1986, chap. 16.

Callahan, Robert E.; C. Patrick Fleenor; and Harry Knudson. *Understanding Organizational Behavior*. Columbus, Ohio: Charles E. Merrill Publishing, 1986, chaps. 10, 12.

Collins, Eliza C. *The Executive Dilemma: Handling People Problems*. New York: John Wiley & Sons, 1985, pp. 1–586.

Davis, Keith, and John W. Newstrom. *Human Behavior at Work*. 7th ed. New York: McGraw-Hill, 1985, chaps. 16, 21.

Donnelly, James H.; James L. Gibson; and John M. Ivancevich. *Fundamentals of Management*. 6th ed. Plano, Tex.: Business Publications, 1987, chaps. 8, 20.

DuBrin, Andrew J. *Managerial Deviance: How to Deal with Problem People in Key Jobs*. New York: Mason/Charter, 1976.

Freeman, R. Edward. *Strategic Management: A Stakeholder Approach*. Hagerstown, Md.: Ballinger Publishing Co., 1984, pp. 1–250.

French, Wendell L. *The Personnel Management Process*. 6th ed. Boston: Houghton Mifflin, 1987, chaps. 8, 14, 19, 26.

Griffin, Ricky W. *Management*. 2nd ed. Boston: Houghton Mifflin, 1987, chaps. 3, 10, 21.

Heneman, Herbert G.; Donald P. Schwab; John A. Fossum; and Lee D. Dyer. *Personnel/Human Resource Management*. 3rd ed. Homewood, Ill.: Richard D. Irwin, 1986, chaps. 2, 5, 20.

Megginson, Leon C. *Personnel Management: A Human Resources Approach*. 5th ed. Homewood, Ill.: Richard D. Irwin, 1985, chaps. 12–14.

Rue, Leslie W., and Lloyd L. Byars. *Management: Theory and Application*. 4th ed. Homewood, Ill.: Richard D. Irwin, 1986, chaps. 3, 16, 18, 19.

Schermerhorn, John R. *Management for Productivity*. 2nd ed. New York: John Wiley & Sons, 1986, chaps. 17, 20, 21.

JOURNALS

Bensinger, Peter B. "Drugs in the Workplace." *Harvard Business Review* 60, no. 6 (November-December 1982), pp. 48–60.

Bhagat, Rabi S. "Effects of Stressful Life Events on Individual Performance Effectiveness and Work Adjustment Processes within Organizational Settings." *Academy of Management Review* 8, no. 4 (October 1983), pp. 600–671.

Cairo, Peter. "Counseling in Industry: A Selected Review of the Literature." *Personnel Psychology* 36, no. 1 (Spring 1983), pp. 1–18.

Camisa, Kenneth P. "How Alcoholism Treatment Pays for Itself." *Advanced Management Journal* 47, no. 1 (Winter 1982), pp. 53–56.

Edwards, Mark R., and J. Ruth Sproull. "Confronting Alcoholism through Team Evaluation." *Business Horizons* 29, no. 3 (May-June 1986), pp. 78–83.

Hilaski, H. J. "Understanding Statistics on Occupational Illnesses." *Monthly Labor Review* (March 1981), pp. 25–29.

Ivancevich, J. M.; M. T. Matteson; and C. Preston. "Occupational Stress, Type A Behavior, and Physical Well-Being." *Academy of Management Journal* 25, no. 2 (June 1982), pp. 373–91.

Johnson, Theresa. "Laws Prohibiting Employment Discrimination against the Alcoholic and the Drug Addict." *Labor Law Journal* 36, no. 9 (September 1985), pp. 702–6.

Klein, Alfred. "Employees under the Influence—Outside the Law?" *Personnel Journal* 65, no. 9 (September 1986), pp. 57–71.

Levison, H. "When Executives Burn Out." *Harvard Business Review* 59, no. 3 (May-June 1981), pp. 72–81.

Masi, Dale. "Company Responses to Drug Abuse from AMA's Nationwide Survey." *Personnel* 64, no. 3 (March 1987), pp. 40–46.

Pati, G. C., and J. I. Adkins. "The Employer's Role in Alcohol Assistance." *Personnel Journal* 62, no. 7 (July 1983), pp. 568–72.

Schreier, James W. "A Survey of Drug Abuse in Organizations." *Personnel Journal* 62, no. 6 (June 1983), pp. 478–84.

Susser, Peter. "Legal Issues Raised by Drugs in the Workplace." *Labor Law Journal* 36, no. 1 (January 1985), pp. 42–54.

Tersine, R. J., and James Hazeldine. "Alcoholism: A Productivity Hangover." *Business Horizons* 25, no. 6 (November-December 1982), pp. 68–72.

WHAT THIS INCIDENT IS ABOUT:
A company decides to relocate because of high labor costs and other considerations. Its alleged involvement in employee raiding raises the issue of corporate social responsibility and the concept of stakeholder analysis.

11

Employee raiding

INCIDENT

The Litson Cotton Yarn Manufacturing Company, located in Murray, New Jersey, decided, as a result of increasing labor costs, to relocate their plant in Fairlee, a southern community of 4,200. Plant construction was started, and a personnel office was opened in the State Employment Office, located in Fairlee.

Because of poor personnel practices in the other three textile mills located within a 50-mile radius of Fairlee, the Litson Company found it was receiving applications from some of the most highly skilled and best-trained textile operators in the state. After receiving applications from approximately 500 people, employment was offered to 260 male and female applicants. It was decided that these employees would be placed immediately on the payroll with instructions to await final installation of machinery expected within the following six weeks.

The managers of the three other textile companies, faced with resignations from their most efficient and best-trained employees, approached the Litson managers with the complaint that their labor force was being "raided." They registered a strong protest to cease such practices and demanded an immediate cancellation of the employment of 260 people hired by Litson.

The Litson managers discussed the ethical and moral considerations involved in offering employment to the 260 people. It was clear that Litson faced a tight labor market in Fairlee, and the Litson management thought that if the 260 employees were discharged, the company faced cancellation of their plans and large construction losses. It was felt, in addition, that the Litson management was obligated to the 260 employees who had resigned their previous employment in favor of Litson.

92

The dilemma facing Litson managers was compounded when the manager of one community plant reminded Litson that his plant was part of a nationwide chain supplied with cotton yarn from Litson. It was inferred that attempts to continue operations in Fairlee by Litson could result in cancellation of orders and a possible loss to Litson of an approximate 18-percent market share. It was also suggested to Litson managers that action taken by the nationwide textile chain could result in cancellation of orders from other textile companies friendly to them. The Litson president held an urgent meeting of his top subordinates to: (1) decide what to do about the situation in Fairlee, (2) formulate a written policy statement indicating Litson's position regarding employee raiding, and (3) develop a plan for implementing the policy.

CRITIQUES

THOMAS Q. GILSON
Arbitrator and Lecturer in Industrial Relations
University of Hawaii

The Litson managers face the question of whether they are prepared to retreat from the demand for cancelling the employment of 260 people. This demand is supported by the implied threat by a rival company's manager of a boycott that might seriously hurt Litson's business. Furthermore, the three companies who made the demand would certainly do anything in their power to undermine Litson's position in the community.

On the other hand, several considerations suggest "holding the line." First, the employees were hired in the open market. They evidently chose to apply at Litson because of unfavorable personnel practices at their former employers. Litson may have failed to make an adequate survey of community practices, but they certainly did nothing unethical. Second, Litson had created an obligation to the employees. Unless they were prepared to pull out completely, this obligation should be fulfilled. If the employment of the 260 was canceled, Litson could expect to attract only marginal workers and to suffer from a seriously damaged local image.

Third, to pull out completely appears to entail serious losses. On the other hand, if they stay, there is the threatened boycott. Litson should not be stampeded by the suggestion of one other manager. The idea that companies friendly to his company might cancel orders is certainly far-fetched in today's purchasing, where price, quality, and service are the primary determinants. Even the loss of his own company's orders may be questioned. Thus, a certain and substantial loss must be balanced against an uncertain one, a loss that appears considerably exaggerated, although it should not be completely discounted.

In weighing the considerations, those on the side of turning down the demand are preponderant on both business and moral bases. This decision is made despite the poor policies evident in the fact that the problem arose. A more gradual approach, an adequate survey of other employers' personnel policies, and work with other employers are all suggested by this case.

Assuming that the Litson Company decided to stay in Fairlee and continue the employment of the 260 employees, there remain some major policy questions that are pointed out in the case.

There was no evidence that the company had surveyed other area companies' personnel policies and practices before they relocated. Favoritism, arbitrary actions, and poor organization may have accounted for some of the applications. But it also appears that wages, fringe benefits, and similar policies account for much of the Litson Company's attractiveness. The company should consider if it is a more effective policy to fit its personnel policies reasonably close to those of existing companies, both for community relationships and long-range competitiveness.

Secondly, the policy of hiring a large number of employees on a standby basis appears questionable. Aside from the cost, the problem of starting a large group at once is almost insurmountable. Furthermore, the impact on other employers, as in this case, is much greater. A more gradual start-up would appear preferable from cost, technical, and strategic standpoints.

A third question raised by the case is the relation of the company to existing institutions in the community. The company evidently did not find out other companies' reactions until after employment had begun. Furthermore, even though Litson used the State Employment Office for hiring, it apparently did not check out the possible implications of Litson policies or of employing large numbers of people from other firms. The State Employment Office could undoubtedly have provided help on both questions if asked.

Next, the Litson Company should consider carefully what actions to take now or in the future faced with threats such as those in this case. Even if new policies were effectively applied, such a question might arise again. Therefore, the company should consider its position vis-à-vis such a threat.

Finally, the company should consider how it may offset any damage that has been done locally. Some revision of policies and efforts to develop cooperative relations may be in order.

JOHN H. JAMES
Associate Professor of Management
University of Florida

Litson Cotton Yarn Manufacturing Company has emerged as the preferred employer of at least 500 textile worker job applicants, most of whom were employed by three other textile companies in the area. Reasons for Litson's bonanza of job applicants appear to include a combination of poor personnel practice records in the other three mills and applicant expectations that Litson's personnel policies will be significantly better.

Litson's success in attracting job applicants and subsequent decision to hire 260 of them generated charges of "employee raiding" by the local textile companies who lost trained and experienced employees. "Raiding," or wholesale hiring of the human resources from other companies, is regarded as an unacceptable practice in most settings. For one company to intentionally decimate the valued employees of another firm is considered socially irresponsible behavior. But did the management of Litson *intend* to raid, or is the company simply the beneficiary of workers exercising the freedom to change employers? Regardless of Litson's intent, the other companies believe they were raided and have demanded that Litson cancel employment contracts with "raided" workers, backed by heavy pressure.

The best course for Litson is to propose a negotiated settlement of the "raiding" dispute. Even if Litson's original strategy had been to staff the Fairlee plant as fully as possible by "raiding" employees from other firms, this becomes a crucial time for strategy modification. Litson has the disputed 260 workers on the payroll and legally can keep all of them. From this position of strength, Litson's proposal for negotiations, where some of these workers will be lost, is likely to be viewed by the other textile firms as being "reasonable" and "socially responsible."

Consider other advantages of negotiating the issue: (1) it gives Litson an opportunity to assume a leadership role benefiting textile workers, competing companies, and the community; (2) it should defuse the threatened cancellation of orders from Litson, thereby eliminating potential loss of a major market segment; (3) it could cause improvements in personnel practices in the other textile mills; and (4) it allows Litson to enhance its local reputation and to save some money at the same time. In negotiations, if Litson agrees to release half of the 260 disputed workers, it will save the wages of 130 released workers for the six-week period. At an assumed wage of $350 per week, a total of $273,000 is saved for the period. To summarize, the balance of advantages and disadvantages of Litson seeking a negotiated settlement or holding what they have favors negotiation.

The relevant result produced by the negotiation process will be an agreement by Litson to release a number of workers. Since Litson has the workers and can keep them all if it wishes, Litson can control this agreement. From the information available, what percent of the 260 workers should be released? Whatever the negotiated percent becomes, a plan is required for determining which workers will be released and reemployed by their original employers. Not an easy thing to do. Some options are:

1. Let the other textile companies bid for the return of their workers by offering inducements such as improved wages, working terms and

conditions of employment, or improved personnel practices. By making the old jobs sufficiently attractive, the required number of workers will voluntarily return.
2. Let the former employees of each company decide which of them will return and which will continue with Litson.
3. Use a random drawing.
4. Let Litson select the cadre of workers it needs and release others.

Should the other firms refuse to negotiate their difference with Litson, then Litson should keep the 260 employees on its payroll without apology and proceed with its plans.

OBSERVATIONS

Litson Company's action to relocate because of high labor costs, its alleged involvement in employee raiding, and the possibility of canceling an offer of employment to 260 area workers raise issues of corporate social responsibility and questions regarding the degree to which Litson's management has considered its noneconomic goals.

A company's economic goals are those goals relating to such objectives as survival, growth, and profitability. Not so readily acknowledged and articulated, however, are noneconomic, or social, goals that reflect the notion that a firm has responsibilities other than to its owners. Consideration of noneconomic goals introduces two concepts that are receiving increased attention in management literature—"stakeholders" and "corporate social responsibility."

Professor R. Edward Freeman, whose book entitled *Strategic Management—A Stakeholder Approach* appears on the suggested reading list and whose critique appears for another incident in this book, defines a stakeholder as any group or individual who can affect, or is affected by, the achievement of a corporation's purpose. Stakeholders may include owners (stockholders), creditors, employees, suppliers, governments, unions, customers, competitors, environmentalists, communities, and the public. Because the firm's actions have an impact on one or more of the stakeholders, they have claims against the company and justifiable reason to expect the firm to act responsibly toward them and the satisfaction of their claims. The firm's willingness to consider how its action affects stakeholders and its ability to act responsibly and constructively toward stakeholders are indications of the firm's sense of corporate responsibility. If Litson's management had paid more attention to its actions toward former and present employees, its competitors, and the communities where it locates, the difficulties might have been avoided.

DISCUSSION ITEMS

1. What action should be taken by Litson Company management? Support your position. Do you think a stakeholder analysis prior to the relocation decision might have led to a different set of decisions? Elaborate.
2. While the Litson Company may be guilty of faulty planning, as suggested by the critique writers, do you think it engaged in any unethical, immoral, or illegal employment practices? Do you think it acted in a socially irresponsible manner? Defend your responses.
3. Professor Gilson states that the Litson Company should consider whether it is a more effective policy to fit its personnel practices reasonably close to those of existing companies. Do you agree or disagree? Why? Formulate an employment policy that could be used by a company moving into a new community.

SUGGESTED READINGS

BOOKS

Arnold, Hugh J., and Daniel C. Feldman. *Organizational Behavior.* New York: McGraw-Hill, 1986, chap. 6.

Callahan, Robert E.; C. Patrick Fleenor; and Harry Knudson. *Understanding Organizational Behavior.* Columbus, Ohio: Charles E. Merrill Publishing, 1986, chap. 16.

Davis, Keith, and John W. Newstrom. *Human Behavior at Work.* 7th ed. New York: McGraw-Hill, 1985, chap. 22.

Donnelly, James H.; James L. Gibson; and John M. Ivancevich. *Fundamentals of Management.* 6th ed. Plano, Tex.: Business Publications, 1987, chaps. 1–4, 9, 19, 20.

Freeman, R. Edward. *Strategic Management: A Stakeholder Approach.* Hagerstown, Md.: Ballinger Publishing Co., 1984, chap. 4.

French, Wendell L. *The Personnel Management Process.* 6th ed. Boston: Houghton Mifflin, 1987, chaps. 11, 16–18.

Griffin, Ricky W. *Management.* 2nd ed. Boston: Houghton Mifflin, 1987, chaps. 3, 4–8, 10, 21–23.

Heneman, Herbert G.; Donald P. Schwab; John A. Fossum; and Lee D. Dyer. *Personnel/Human Resource Management.* 3rd ed. Homewood, Ill.: Richard D. Irwin, 1986, chap. 7.

Levin, Dick. *The Executive's Illustrated Primer of Long-Range Planning.* Englewood Cliffs, N.J.: Prentice-Hall, 1981.

Megginson, Leon C. *Personnel Management: A Human Resources Approach.* 5th ed. Homewood, Ill.: Richard D. Irwin, 1985, chaps. 5, 6.

Rue, Leslie W., and Lloyd L. Byars. *Management: Theory and Application.* 4th ed. Homewood, Ill.: Richard D. Irwin, 1986, chaps. 3, 4–7, 20, 21.

Schermerhorn, John R. *Management for Productivity.* 2nd ed. New York: John Wiley & Sons, 1986, chaps. 4, 5.

JOURNALS

Angle, Harold; Charles Manz; and Andrew Van de Ven. "Integrating Human Resource Management and Corporate Strategy." *Human Resource Management* 24, no. 2 (Spring 1985), pp. 51–68.

Baley, Sandra. "Recruitment: The Legalities of Hiring in the 80s." *Personnel Journal* 64, no. 11 (November 1985), pp. 112–15.

Bork, R. H. "Modern Values and Social Responsibility." *MSU Business Topics* 28, no. 2 (Spring 1980), pp. 5–17.

Boulton, W. R.; W. M. Lindsay; S. G. Franklin; and L. W. Rue. "Strategic Planning: Determining the Impact of Environmental Characteristics and Uncertainty." *Academy of Management Journal* 25, no. 3 (September 1982), pp. 500–599.

Carroll, Archie B. "When Business Closes Down: Social Responsibilities and Management Actions." *California Management Review* 21, no. 2 (Winter 1984), pp. 125–39.

Dennis, D. L. "Evaluating Corporate Recruitment Efforts." *Personnel Administrator* 30, no. 1 (January 1985), pp. 21–26.

Ebert, R. J., and Everette Adam. "The Human Factor in Facilities Location Planning." *Business Horizons* 20, no. 6 (November 1977), pp. 35–42.

Edwards, Cathy. "Aggressive Recruitment: The Lessons of High-Tech Hiring." *Personnel Journal* 65, no. 1 (January 1986), pp. 40–48.

Felsten, Gary J. "Current Considerations in Plant Shutdowns and Relocations." *Personnel Journal* 60, no. 5 (May 1981), pp. 369–72.

Gridley, J. D. "Who Will Be Where When? Forecast the Easy Way." *Personnel Journal* 65, no. 5 (May 1986), pp. 50–58.

Nutt, Paul C. "Implementation Approaches for Project Planning." *Academy of Management Review* 8, no. 4 (October 1983), pp. 600–611.

Pakchar, Paul. "Effective Manpower Planning." *Personnel Journal* 62, no. 10 (October 1983), pp. 826–30.

Stone, T. H., and Jack Fiorito. "A Perceived Uncertainty Model of Human Forecasting Technique Use." *Academy of Management Review* 11, no. 3 (July 1986), pp. 635–42.

Winfield, F. E. "The Changing Face of Corporate Relocation." *Personnel* 63, no. 1 (January 1986), pp. 33–40.

Yoder, Dale, and P. D. Staudohar. "Management and Public Policy in Plant Closure." *Sloan Management Review* 26, no. 4 (Summer 1985), pp. 45–57.

WHAT THIS INCIDENT IS ABOUT:
Wives are fuming about the presence of a female
firefighter in the fire station's dormitory—affirmative action and equal employment policies not-
withstanding. This incident involves external
pressure groups, social change, and organizational
constraints.

12

Equal employment reaction

INCIDENT

Pleasantville, a southeastern city of 100,000 residents, earned the cov-
eted designation of "All-American City" last year as a progressive munici-
pality. Among other notable accomplishments, the city has established
human rights councils and has supported affirmative action and equal
employment opportunity programs. In fact, the first female firefighter ever
to complete training in the city recently has been assigned to duty at Fire
Station No. 5. Rookie firefighter Nancy Williams was welcomed for duty as
a fully qualified combat firefighter by Fire Chief Dunmore.

The firefighters' work schedule of 24 hours on duty followed by 48 hours
off duty required them to eat and sleep at the fire station. Station living
facilities, designed for males only, included an open bay with closely
spaced single beds, one toilet, a large unpartitioned shower room, and a
common kitchen for cooking and eating. The only private bedroom was
assigned to and occupied by the shift lieutenant. To accommodate Williams' presence, a shower schedule was arranged to afford her solitary
showering privileges, and most of the men voluntarily began wearing
bathrobes over their underwear, which they usually slept in.

This system worked well and seemed satisfactory until the firefighters'
wives began to complain bitterly that they didn't want another woman
living with their husbands under the conditions at Fire Station No. 5. It's
only a matter of time until some romance blossoms, they argued. Besides
that, the wives insisted, under intimate living conditions, the presence of
Williams infringed upon their husbands' right to privacy. These complaints
and others became front page news in the local press. Neither the hus-

bands nor Williams commented publicly on the issue. In rapid succession, the wives banded together and hired a prominent lawyer, who implied that legal action was being considered; the city manager (see organization chart, Figure 1) stated publicly that the fire chief ran the fire department and was solely responsible for resolving the issue; and the city commissioners declared the problem beyond their jurisdiction under the city manager form of government.

Realizing that he had been tossed the ball but not knowing what to do with it, the chief pondered his options, which included, but were not limited to: reassigning Williams to the fire departments' Administration and Fire Prevention unit, where she would have day-shift duty only; moving the shift lieutenant out of his private bedroom and assigning it to the female rookie; meeting personally with the wives and assuring them their complaints were unfounded; suspending Williams from duty, with

FIGURE 1
Fire Department Organization

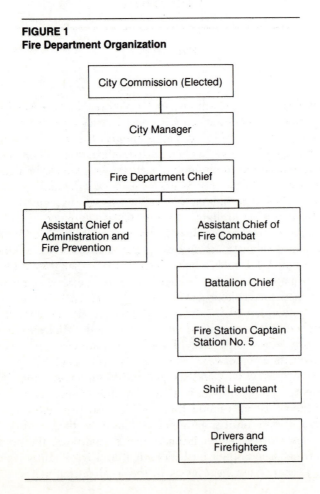

pay, until the furor blew over; seeking a solution through the local firefighter's union; doing nothing; or doing whatever would best protect his position as fire chief.

As several wives began picketing Fire Station No. 5, Chief Dunmore felt increased pressure for an immediate decision and action.

CRITIQUES

W. JACK DUNCAN
Professor of Management and Associate Dean of
the Graduate School of Management
University of Alabama—Birmingham

Chief Dunmore has a management problem that is not going away. Therefore, inaction is not an option. The city commission is quite correct in refusing to intervene in the issue since at this point it is administrative in character. The commission, as the elected, policymaking unit, has apparently established the policy of equal employment opportunity. The implementation of the policy is the city manager's job and, on matters relating specifically to the fire department, the fire chief's job. The city manager is not likely to be able to "wash his or her hands" of the problem so easily, since the solution has implications beyond the fire department.

Rather than take a legalistic or moralistic view, this critique will concentrate on the managerial issues. This is the only practical approach, since Williams' employment is legal and to dismiss or reassign her because of her sex would be illegal. Moreover, Pleasantville, as an "All-American" city, has its reputation on the line. Unless it is capable of solving this problem in a just manner, it hardly deserves such a designation.

One effective managerial view of this problem is from the perspective of planned organizational change. Anytime there is a deliberate attempt to do things in a different manner, the manager is faced with performing the role of change agent. That is, the policy statement has been made and the manager is responsible for implementing the policy. Thus, a change is required, and the manager is responsible for achieving desired results.

Many years ago, Kurt Lewin, a social psychologist, proposed a framework for viewing the dynamic aspects of planned change in his book *Field Theory in Social Science* (Harper & Row, 1951). This approach has been called "force field" analysis, because it conceptualizes change as a series of conflicting forces.

For example, the current problem regarding a female combat firefighter in Pleasantville is in a state of "quasi equilibrium" and is balanced by driving forces encouraging the breakdown of traditional attitudes about male occupations. There are also constraining forces trying to keep employment conditions as they are. Let us look at this problem with the aid of force field analysis.

The current state of affairs is confusion and uncertainty. The city is committed to equal employment opportunity—even affirmative action. No doubt many of the wives who object to female firefighters are committed, in principle, to this worthy goal. What they are experiencing is the discomfort of change when it affects them personally. Now, to apply Lewin's framework we illustrate both the driving and constraining forces at work:

Driving Forces

1. City commitment to equal employment opportunity and affirmative action.
2. Availability of a qualified female combat firefighter.
3. Apparent willingness of male firefighters to cooperate with and even facilitate the change.
4. Likely history of male/female assignments in other departments, such as patrol car assignments in the police department.

Constraining Forces

1. Traditional attitudes about male/female occupations.
2. Fear of legal action by the wives as evidenced by their threat of attorney involvement.
3. Design of physical facilities that support maintenance of traditional attitudes.
4. Desire of higher administration to delegate the problem to the chief when the implications transcend the fire department.

The strategies available to the city manager and the fire chief include increasing the driving forces, reducing the constraining forces, or a combination of both. This can be done in several ways.

First, it is important that the city manager and the fire chief determine exactly how committed the policymakers (city commissioners) are to equal employment and affirmative action. Assuming the commitment is genuine, the managers must act with conviction rather than defensiveness.

It is unrealistic to think that defensive actions like reassigning Williams to "nonline duty," giving her the lieutenant's private room, being frightened by threats of a lawyer, or waiting for the union to become foolish enough to get involved in the issue will be successful. The assignment of a trained combat firefighter to administrative or preventive duties will not work. Providing a female combat firefighter with the lieutenant's private quarters is sure to result in complaints, if not legal action, of reverse discrimination. Why should the union get involved in such a touchy issue? If the wives want to hire a lawyer, they should be informed that future negotiations will have to be conducted with the city attorney for the protection of the city manager and the fire chief. The counterthreat of removing the direct interaction should make the wives think twice before reducing the interaction to such formality.

The offensive should be taken by carefully explaining to the wives that their concerns are understood and that every reasonable precaution will be taken to maintain the privacy of male and female firefighters. It is likely that minor construction could provide more privacy than the open sleeping bays with relatively small expenditures. A commitment to planning future facilities so as to provide significantly more privacy for all firefighters regardless of sex might convince the wives that the city understands their fears and is responding to them in good faith.

The fire chief and the city manager obviously cannot guarantee that an affair will not take place. Neither can the police chief or any other manager. The responsible administrative personnel can assure the wives, however, that they expect the highest of behavior standards from all employees and will do all they can to ensure such behavior is reinforced while any "violations" are discouraged. This case provides an illustration of the "cutting edge" of implementing socially sensitive programs. The long-range good promised by such policies often involves short-range adjustments in attitudes and traditional prejudices. This provides the major challenge to the manager as an agent of change.

The policy has been established. The failure appears to be in the communication of the policy to departmental heads. With the city committed to equal employment opportunity, the city manager and the fire chief must implement the nuts and bolts of the policy. In doing so, they should be sensitive with regard to the wives' concerns. However, the wives should not be allowed to run the fire department's hiring policies any more than they should be allowed to establish policies on how to fight a chemical fire. In the future, the commission should be more careful to provide explicit policy guidelines to assist managers in implementing desired policies.

ROSEMARY PLEDGER
Former Dean of the School of Business and
Public Administration
University of Houston—Clear Lake

The basic issue this incident forces us to consider is commitment to equality in hiring policies and the acceptance of women in nontraditional job roles. Pertinent questions to be asked are: (1) Who sets organizational policies? (2) Who should be supporting whom in this situation? (3) What is the fire department's position on human rights? Once the overall question of commitment to equality is resolved, what to do immediately becomes more straightforward.

Is this organization committed to full integration of qualified people and to equal treatment of qualified employees whatever their sex? If the answer is yes, and in today's enlightened social climate that would seem a rational answer, then the other problems become somewhat simpler. Once the decision is made, the rest is execution.

Obviously, Ms. Williams should not be suspended with pay. No, Williams, a fully qualified combat firefighter, should not be reassigned to the fire department's Administration and Fire Prevention Unit. In fact, with the commitment decision made, the options no longer revolve strictly around what to do with Williams.

A broader, problem-solving approach is needed. An approach is needed that considers the impact of any decision on the organization's internal climate, as well as its immediate and future legal position. The rationale for this approach can be found in a number of relevant organizational or management theories such as systems theory and decision theory. The basic point, however, is to avoid treating symptoms and start identifying the fundamental issues so that viable long-term solutions can be found.

In this case, a number of alternatives are available and can be implemented rather quickly. For example: (1) providing separate sleeping quarters for all the firefighters, men and women; (2) actively recruiting more women firefighters; and (3) arranging informal meetings between the various levels of employees and their immediate supervisors to discuss this problem as well as others.

Would any of these alternatives be too costly? Are they impractical? Do they compound the problem? Not if commitment to equality is the goal. Present societal norms dictate separate bathrooms and sleeping quarters for the two sexes. However, since the present quarters were built when women were not considered equal members of the work force, we have a dilemma. Can we use cost as an excuse to perpetuate an outdated system? If our basic goal is equality, what is our next step?

Currently, no one in Fire Station No. 5 has any privacy. Partitioned sleeping areas and other arrangements for privacy may have been a very real need for the firefighters before Williams arrived on the scene. Private sleeping quarters for all firefighters then is one step toward improving conditions for both sexes.

Another strategy the chief could pursue is to hire more qualified women as soon as possible. Such a move would diffuse some of the attention and pressure being focused on Williams. Of course, this kind of reasoning causes the politically astute manager to simply shake his or her head. So, pragmatically speaking, what can be done during the next few working days? For one thing, Williams may have to stay in the shift lieutenant's bedroom (without the shift lieutenant, of course). However, the fire chief must make it clear that this is a temporary solution, both for his own credibility and to protect the lieutenant's earned status. Also tied to the issue of Williams and other women who will be hired is the anger of the wives.

A strategy that is always an option is not to do anything. This strategy may be used regarding the wives. Chief Dunmore is not likely to accomplish anything by assuring the wives that their fears are unfounded. In fact, meeting with the wives would probably compound the issues and would set a poor precedent for solving future problems. This case is a management-employee problem and should be resolved internally.

Finally, the last alternative discussed here is the more complex issue of communication. Informal meetings between various levels of the hierarchy would facilitate discussion of the immediate problem as well as other issues. Almost every organization needs to improve communication flow, both upwards and downwards. For managers, staying in touch with all levels of the organization is a form of preventive maintenance which means fewer surprises in terms of employee problems, concerns, and complaints. Furthermore, better decisions can be made with better data.

To conclude, in a committed organization the city manager and commissioners would be providing positive support for the fire chief's position. In this instance, however, Chief Dunmore himself must make his decisions.

OBSERVATIONS

Female entry into nontraditional jobs creates complexities that cannot always be anticipated or easily handled. Where unexpected problems arise, untested, risky, and creative action may be required for acceptable solutions. Uncertain conditions and transitional periods tend to produce stress for all concerned. Chief Dunmore is particularly challenged: due to the major source of his crisis (wives) being outside his organization and beyond his administrative control, due to the "public" nature of picketing and press releases, and due to threatened legal action against him and his organization. Environmental considerations loom large in this situation.

Professor Duncan views this problem from the managerial perspective of planned organizational change. He uses force field analysis to produce a structure of driving forces for change and constraining forces inhibiting change. Professor Pledger draws upon systems theory for a problem-solving approach broad enough to handle the internal and external factors in this incident. Both recognize a need for the policymakers to determine just how committed they are to equal employment and human rights.

DISCUSSION ITEMS

1. Identify advantages and disadvantages of each of the options available to Chief Dunmore.

2. What action would you recommend be taken by Chief Dunmore? Explain your recommendation.
3. Justify or challenge the action by the city commission and the city manager in telling the chief that only he had authority to deal with the issue.

SUGGESTED READINGS

BOOKS

Arnold, Hugh J., and Daniel C. Feldman. *Organizational Behavior.* New York: McGraw-Hill, 1986, chap. 5, pp. 223–29, 436, 440.

Callahan, Robert E.; C. Patrick Fleenor; and Harry Knudson. *Understanding Organizational Behavior.* Columbus, Ohio: Charles E. Merrill Publishing, 1986, chap. 11.

Davis, Keith, and John W. Newstrom. *Human Behavior at Work.* 7th ed. New York: McGraw-Hill, 1985, chaps. 11, 18.

Donnelly, James H.; James L. Gibson; and John M. Ivancevich. *Fundamentals of Management.* 6th ed. Plano, Tex.: Business Publications, 1987, pp. 740–45.

French, Wendell L. *The Personnel Management Process.* 6th ed. Boston: Houghton Mifflin, 1987, chaps. 8, 13.

Griffin, Ricky W. *Management.* 2nd ed. Boston: Houghton Mifflin, 1987, chap. 12, pp. 645–47.

Heneman, Herbert G.; Donald P. Schwab; John A. Fossum; and Lee D. Dyer. *Personnel/Human Resource Management.* 3rd ed. Homewood, Ill.: Richard D. Irwin, 1986, chap. 2, pp. 206–10.

Megginson, Leon C. *Personnel Management: A Human Resources Approach.* 5th ed. Homewood, Ill.: Richard D. Irwin, 1985, chap. 4.

Rue, Leslie W., and Lloyd L. Byars. *Management: Theory and Application.* 4th ed. Homewood, Ill.: Richard D. Irwin, 1986, chaps. 10, 16.

Schermerhorn, John R. *Management for Productivity.* 2nd ed. New York: John Wiley & Sons, 1986, chap. 3.

JOURNALS

Anthony, William, and Marshall Bowen. "Affirmative Action: Problems and Promises." *Personnel Journal* 56, no. 12 (December 1977), pp. 616–21.

Baron, Alma S. "What Men Are Saying about Women in Business." *Business Horizons* 25, no. 1 (January-February 1982), pp. 10–14.

Brief, Arthur P. "How to Manage Managerial Stress." *Personnel* 57, no. 5 (September-October 1980), pp. 25–30.

Chapman, Elwood. "Essence of Leadership: The Condensed Version." *Training* 21, no. 7 (July 1984), pp. 12–14.

Gilbreath, Jerri D. "Sex Discrimination and Title VII of the Civil Rights Act." *Personnel Journal* 56, no. 1 (January 1977), pp. 23–26.

Ivancevich, John M.; Michael T. Matteson; and Edward P. Richards, III. "Who's

Liable for Stress on the Job?" *Harvard Business Review* 64, (March-April 1985), pp. 60–71.

Kotter, John P., and Leonard A. Schlesinger. "Choosing Strategies for Change." *Harvard Business Review* 57, no. 2 (March-April 1979), p. 106.

Levinson, Robert E. "How to Conquer the Panic of Change." *Management Review* 66, no. 7 (July 1977), pp. 20–24.

Maclagan, P. W. "The Concept of Responsibility: Some Implications for Organization Behavior and Development." *Journal of Management Studies* 20, no. 3 (May-June 1983), pp. 411–23.

St. John, Walter D. "You Are What You Communicate." *Personnel Journal* 64, no. 10 (October 1985), pp. 40–43.

Sarkesian, Sam C. "Leadership and Management Revisited." *Bureaucrat* 14, no. 4 (April 1985), pp. 20–24.

Stillman, Nina G. "Conflict! Equal Employment versus Occupational Health." *Advanced Management Journal* 46, no. 2 (Spring 1981), pp. 16–23.

Weiss, Alan Jay. "How to Influence People Outside Your Control." *Supervisory Management* 22, no. 12 (December 1977), pp. 2–9.

Woodrum, Robert L. "Sexual Harassment: New Concern about an Old Problem." *Advanced Management Journal* 46, no. 1 (Winter 1981), pp. 20–26.

WHAT THIS INCIDENT IS ABOUT:
This incident calls attention to a major problem that
has been described as the "gendergap" issue of the
future. It is the politically charged issue of requiring
equal pay for dissimilar jobs of comparable value. It
involves a consideration of such topics as pay equity,
job evalution, methods of conducting comparable
worth studies, and options for implementing study
results.

13

Equal pay for comparable worth

INCIDENT

Only a few days after taking over as director of the Upstate Rehabilitation Facility, Dr. Cynthia Heron met her first management challenge. It
came in the form of an anonymous letter from an unidentified department
head indicating that women holding full-time administrative jobs in the
facility received less than two thirds as much pay as their male counter-
parts. The author of the letter stated that proof of this assertion could be
found in the wage differentials existing between the facility's department
heads. This, according to the letter, was only one example of sex discrimination in the facility, but one that Heron was requested to investigate and
correct.

Heron knew that federal law clearly prescribes that workers in the same
job cannot be paid differently because of their race or sex, a concept known
as *equal pay* for *equal work*. However, the author of the anonymous letter
also said there were several instances in which federal court judges have
ruled that *equal pay* must be given for *comparable worth*. This was a
different issue, and Heron was unsure that she, or anyone else, had the
ability to calculate the relative *worth* of disparate jobs and then adjust
wages to equitably reflect those determinations. She decided that she
should first review personnel records to determine the validity of charges
made in the letter. The review resulted in a lot of information about the
facility's major departments and the heads of those departments. In particular, she was interested to find the following:

DIRECTOR OF FISCAL AFFAIRS: Male, responsible for 38 employees, age 43, Certified Public Accountant, 12 years seniority, salary of $43,600.

DIRECTOR OF DIETARY SERVICES: Female, responsible for 53 employees, age 56, high school graduate, 30 years seniority, salary of $27,000.

DIRECTOR OF PERSONNEL: Male, responsible for 6 employees, age 36, college degree, 4 years seniority, salary of $38,500.

DIRECTOR OF HOUSEKEEPING: Male, responsible for 44 employees, age 54, high school graduate, 26 years seniority, salary of $32,000.

DIRECTOR OF NURSING SERVICES: Female, responsible for 202 employees, age 32, master's degree, 8 years seniority, salary of $28,500.

DIRECTOR OF PHARMACY: Male, responsible for 15 employees, age 27, pharmacy college graduate, 1 year seniority, salary of $34,000.

Records provided additional information about these and other positions in the facility, but Heron had already seen enough to convince her that she faced a complex problem. Before responding to the letter, she knew all dimensions of the problem must be examined and that an equitable compensation plan would have to be developed, that policies would have to be formulated to guide the behavior of those responsible for implementing the plan, and that a procedure would have to be adopted for adjusting existing wages and salaries in accordance with the established plan.

CRITIQUES

MAX L. DENSMORE
Professor of Business Administration
Grand Valley State College

Dr. Heron has moved into an organizational vacuum in terms of specific knowledge concerning personnel relationships, organizational conflicts, and ambiguities of policies, perceptions, and degree of dissatisfaction affecting performance. The anonymous letter may portend greater problems, and Dr. Heron has many unanswered questions. What is the general state of the organization's health and overall performance level of the facility? She must quickly become aware of both the organization's climate and its culture.

Specifically, Dr. Heron needs to determine what exact policies govern operation, both the existing long-term strategic plans and the policies guiding short-term implementation. She also needs to review position descriptions and the match between personnel qualifications and the stated job requirements. She might request her director of personnel to compare the Upstate Rehabilitation Facility data on salaries, education, and seniority levels with similar regional and national institutions. The director should then be better able to judge if institutionalized discrimination exists, whether it be racial, sexual, or pay related. More particularly, she can also determine if the salary level of the disgruntled, anonymous department head is within reasonable parameters of existing policy or if the pay issue is a mask for other morale problems.

Since the equality of pay for comparable worth question is so great, Dr. Heron should have a feel for what she *can* do, what she *wants* to do, and what she *must* do. Any significant policy change will probably require board action because of budgetary implications. If rapid increases are extended to long-tenured but underpaid department heads, then those who "lose" will likely view the situation as reverse discrimination. At best, she has a delicate problem; and unless handled carefully, Dr. Heron faces a no-win situation with all the attendant morale problems in all departments. The question of comparability of worth between departments must be addressed, although the investigation's results are likely to be imprecise.

If the current policies are reasonable and defensible, aside from the salary levels, she can deal directly with the individual department head. However, if the policies are incoherent and/or not defensible, Dr. Heron has a different set of circumstances. She must establish policies, set priorities, and institute a set of procedures first to implement the new policies and second to correct, as equitably as possible, past abuses. One would expect considerable turmoil if the entire organizational structure and all significant positions are reviewed and questioned. Prudent administration would involve all key managers in seeking solutions. Defensively, the director should be sensitive to the veiled threat of legal action by the unhappy department head.

As the chief administrator for the Upstate Rehabilitation Facility, Dr. Heron cannot become overly focused on any one individual. But it is most assuredly her responsibility to create or adjust the organizational structure to ensure that prescribed organizational procedures operate in meeting facility goals. Also, assigning key tasks and maintaining behavioral relationships through delegation are her ultimate responsibilities. And here, the perceived equity of salaries must be considered a prime motivational factor. She must strive to maximize overall quality of care within the constraints of budgets and efficiency. At the same time, the facility's administration must be both ethical and legal: not an easy task, especially if she has inherited years of questionable management.

CYNTHIA V. FUKAMI
Associate Professor of Management
University of Denver

This incident describes a health care facility that is facing one of an organization's most difficult human resource issues—how to fairly compensate its staff. In addressing the question of fair compensation, this facility also seems to be facing a broader societal concern called "comparable worth." Many experts have predicted that comparable worth will be the next equal opportunity battleground, as we move through the 1980s and 1990s.

Dr. Heron's compensation problem can be examined from two perspectives—external equity and internal equity. The external equity issue is whether or not the market is a fair source of compensation levels. The internal equity issue is whether or not the pay differentials within the facility are based on valid differences in the relative worth of these positions to the facility. Each of these perspectives involves a policy decision for Heron to assist Upstate Rehabilitation Facility in achieving its strategic goals, and will be discussed in turn.

One way for Heron to examine her pay structure is to assess its external equity. This analysis would basically involve a comparison of the facility's present wage structure with the "market" wage structure, and could be accomplished by conducting a wage and salary survey. Several issues must be dealt with in making this market comparison. First, Heron must determine who is included in her market—competitors, geographic region, etc. Second, market wages are assumed to reflect the marginal productivity that each employee contributes, yet there is really no way to directly measure this contribution. Third, for any position, a company will typically find a range of market rates that reflects factors other than marginal productivity, such as competition, the firm's financial condition, or the firm's strategic objectives. Finally, pay based on the market may mirror and perpetuate any discrimination on nonperformance factors, such as race or gender. This last issue has led to the quest for comparable worth. The market typically offers lower wages for jobs held predominantly by women than for jobs held predominantly by men. Proponents of comparable worth argue that the only way to reduce this earnings gap is to pay employees based on internal rather than external equity.

Internal equity in compensation suggests that we should offer equal pay levels for jobs of equal worth and differential pay levels for jobs of unequal worth. Heron might determine the worth, or value, of the positions in question by conducting a job evaluation study. A job evaluation examines the critical factors present in each job—*what* is to be done, *how* it is to be done, and *why* it is to be done. The job evaluation process enables the company to identify the amount that each position contributes to overall company effectiveness. Once the value or worth of each position is determined, the facility can then establish a pay system that links compensation to the value of each position.

Is there internal or external equity in the pay system at Upstate? It is difficult, if not impossible, to determine the equity of the system from the job titles and demographic information provided. Heron simply does not have the information to make this determination at this point. There are a few clues in the incident, however, that indicate the pay system may not have internal equity. For example, the "female" jobs are receiving lower wages that the "male" jobs. Whether or not this wage gap reflects inequity, however, is a more complex question. One way to address this question is to determine whether these wage differences are the result of relative worth to the facility (personnel is more important than nursing services). A job evaluation study will help Heron determine the level of the inequity, if any.

One additional concern that a job evaluation study will raise is how to adjust present wages to correspond to wages suggested by the evaluation. Typically, such studies will find that some positions are paid more than they are worth, and others are paid less than they are worth. In this case, the job evaluation study may determine that the director of nursing services is being paid too little, while the director of personnel is being paid too much. Heron would then be faced with the decision of whether to lower the pay of the personnel director or to raise the pay for the director of nursing services. Either decision may prove costly. People will probably resist having their pay cut, yet raising underpaid salaries will impose significant labor costs in an industry suffering from high labor costs. She may be able to lessen the impact of that decision by allowing attrition to take care of some of these problem areas. For example, the directors of dietary services and housekeeping seem to be nearing retirement, so Upstate may be able to readjust those salaries through replacement. Any decision that Heron makes must be based on the policies and strategic objectives of Upstate.

Ironically, equal employment legislation and related arguments for extending that legislation to include comparable worth seek actions which make good management sense—compensate people based on their value or contribution to the organization's performance. However, determining a job's worth is not devoid of value judgment. Upstate's management must decide on a policy of whether they would rather make the judgment of value internally or have the market make that judgment externally. In either case, Heron has some work to do before she can be assured of equity in the Upstate Rehabilitation Facility's pay structure.

OBSERVATIONS

Professor Fukami makes a point in her critique that is generally agreed on: the comparable worth issue will be the next equal opportunity battleground. At issue is the fact that in spite of federally mandated laws requiring equal pay for equal work, working women still earn only about 60 cents for every dollar earned by men. Studies show that female-dominated jobs, traditionally held by women, tend to pay less than male-dominated jobs, generally held by men, even though they may demand the same level of skills, knowledge, and responsibliity. This has fueled the vastly more complex issue of equal pay for comparable worth as opposed to equal pay for equal work.

Employers with policies calling for pay equity are now faced with implementing strategies designed to calculate the worth of dissimilar jobs and to adjust compensation accordingly. There are some who doubt we possess scientific methods capable of quantitatively determining the value of dissimilar jobs. Others believe we do. Two articles from the suggested reading list, written by Judy B. Fulghum, recommend various approaches, guidelines, and procedural steps for conducting comparable worth studies.

An additional issue is finding the resources necessary to achieve pay equity based on comparable worth. It has been estimated that it would have cost the state of Washington $400 million or more to implement recommendations that were made several years ago regarding pay equity based on comparable worth.

DISCUSSION ITEMS

1. Why is the issue of equal pay for comparable *worth* more complex than the issue of equal pay for equal *work*? Do you think we possess the means for determining the value, or worth, of dissimilar jobs? If so, what is it?
2. Professor Densmore states that unless Dr. Heron is careful, she faces a no-win situation. What should she decide, and how should she proceed?
3. Do you think the government and the courts have the right to mandate that employers calculate the relative worth of disparate jobs and then require them to adjust compensation rates to reflect those determinations? Write a policy statement for the Upstate Rehabilitation Facility that you think would meet any such mandate. Develop a strategy for implementing your policy.

SUGGESTED READINGS

BOOKS

Arnold, Hugh J., and Daniel C. Feldman. *Organizational Behavior.* New York: McGraw-Hill, 1986, chap. 12.

Callahan, Robert E.; C. Patrick Fleenor; and Harry Knudson. *Understanding Organizational Behavior.* Columbus, Ohio: Charles E. Merrill Publishing, 1986, chap. 10.

Davis, Keith, and John W. Newstrom. *Human Behavior at Work.* 7th ed. New York: McGraw-Hill, 1985, chap. 7.

Donnelly, James H.; James L. Gibson; and John M. Ivancevich. *Fundamentals of Management.* 6th ed. Plano, Tex.: Business Publications, 1987, chaps. 9, 23.

French, Wendell L. *The Personnel Management Process.* 6th ed. Boston: Houghton Mifflin, 1987, chaps. 10, 19–21.

Griffin, Ricky W. *Management.* 2nd ed. Boston: Houghton Mifflin, 1987, chap. 21.

Henderson, R. I. *Compensation Management: Rewarding Performance.* 4th ed. Reston, Va.: Reston Publishing, 1985.

Heneman, Herbert G.; Donald P. Schwab; John A. Fossum; and Lee D. Dyer. *Personnel Human Resource Management.* 3rd ed. Homewood, Ill.: Richard D. Irwin, 1986, chaps. 13–15.

Hoffman, W. M., and Jennifer Mills. *Business Ethics.* New York: McGraw-Hill, 1984, chap. 9.

Megginson, Leon C. *Personnel Management: A Human Resources Approach.* 5th ed. Homewood, Ill.: Richard D. Irwin, 1985, chaps. 4, 15–17.

Remick, Helen. *A Review of Comparable Worth and Wage Discrimination.* Philadelphia: Temple University Press, 1984.

Rue, Leslie W., and Lloyd L. Byars. *Management: Theory and Application.* 4th ed. Homewood, Ill.: Richard D. Irwin, 1986, chaps. 7, 18.

Schermerhorn, John R. *Management for Productivity.* 2nd ed. New York: John Wiley & Sons, 1986, chaps. 9, 14, 21.

JOURNALS

Abbasi, S. H.; Kenneth W. Holliman; and J. H. Murrey. "Comparable Worth: Should You Reexamine Your Compensation Program?" *Advanced Management Journal* 57, no. 2 (Spring 1986), pp. 26–35.

Bell, C. S. "Comparable Worth: How Do We Know It Will Work?" *Monthly Labor Review* 108, no. 12 (December 1985), pp. 5–12.

Birnbaum, M. H. "Perceived Equity of Salary Policies." *Journal of Applied Psychology* 68, no. 2 (February 1983), pp. 45–59.

Bovarnick, Murray E. "Comparable Worth: Is It the Answer?" *Management Review* 74, no. 9 (September 1985), pp. 40–43.

Bruning, N. S., and Robert A. Snyder. "Sex and Position as Predictors of Organizational Commitment." *Academy of Management Journal* 26, no. 3 (September 1983), pp. 485–91.

Carter, Michael F. "Comparable Worth: An Idea Whose Time Has Come?" *Personnel Journal* 60, no. 10 (October 1981), pp. 792–94.

Cooper, Elizabeth A., and Gerald V. Barrett. "Equal Pay and Gender: Implications of Court Cases for Personnel Practices." *Academy of Management Review* 9, no. 1 (January 1984), pp. 84–94.

Emig, M. F. "Job Evaluation: The Next Generation." *Personnel Journal* 65, no. 11 (November 1986), pp. 52–55.

Fulghum, Judy B. "The Employer's Liabilities under Comparable Worth." *Personnel Journal* 62, no. 5 (May 1983), pp. 400–404.

————. "The Newest Balancing Act: A Comparable Worth Study." *Personnel Journal* 63, no. 1 (January 1984), pp. 32–38.

Grams, Robert, and D. P. Schwab. "An Investigation of Systematic Gender-Related Error in Job Evaluation." *Academy of Management Journal* 28, no. 2 (June 1985), pp. 279–90.

Hoffman, C. C., and K. P. Hoffman. "Does Comparable Worth Obscure the Real Issues?" *Personnel Journal* 66, no. 1 (January 1987), pp. 82–95.

Mahoney, Thomas A. "Approaches to the Definition of Comparable Worth." *Academy of Management Review* 8, no. 1 (January 1983), pp. 14–22.

Remick, H. "The Comparable Worth Controversy." *Public Personnel Management Journal* 10, no. 4 (Winter 1981), pp. 371–83.

Rosen, Benson; Sara Rynes; and T. A. Mahoney. "Compensation, Jobs, and Gender." *Harvard Business Review* 61, no. 4 (July-August 1983), pp. 170–90.

WHAT THIS INCIDENT IS ABOUT:
Unacceptable group performance is the major issue
in this incident. It leads to a consideration of such
issues and topics as diagnosis of causes of poor group
performance, execution of control systems, decisions
relating to dishonesty, and the role of personal
values.

14

False reports

INCIDENT

Max Baxter, sales manager of the Solem Pharmaceutical Company, had just completed a two-week trip of auditing customer accounts and prospective accounts in the southeastern states. His primary intention was to follow up on prospective accounts contacted by sales staff members during the past six months. Company policy dictated that each salesperson was to call on a certain number of prospective clients and accounts—a monthly quota based on population growth in the sales area. Prospective clients and accounts were usually physicians, pharmacies, and drug departments in retail stores.

To his amazement, Baxter discovered that almost all the so-called prospective accounts were fictitious. The salespeople had obviously turned in falsely documented field reports and expense statements. Company salespeople had actually called on only 3 of 22 reported prospects. Thus, Baxter surmised that salespeople had falsely claimed approximately 85 percent of the goodwill contacts. Further study showed that the entire sales force of 20 persons had followed this general practice and that not one had a clean record.

Baxter decided that immediate action was mandatory, although the salespeople were experienced senior individuals. Angry as he was, he would have preferred dismissing or demoting them. But he was responsible for sales and realized that replacing the staff would seriously cripple the coming year's sales program. He was also confronted with the question of whether employee dishonesty could be rationalized because of his predecessor's ineffective implementation of policies.

CRITIQUES

JAMES H. DAVIS
Professor Emeritus of Business Administration
Ohio State University

Mr. Baxter was correct in believing that immediate action was mandatory, but firing the salespeople was hardly the proper course. The basic fault lay with the supervisor, not the supervised.

In the first place, it is apparent that the goodwill call reports had not even been checked, let alone used. Once the salespeople discovered this fact, inaccurate and incomplete reports were virtually assured. Furthermore, since all of the salespeople were making similar false reports, this lack of control had undoubtedly existed for many years.

The second aspect of the problem—that of falsifying expense records —is hardly commendable, but it is certainly understandable. Once this kind of practice begins, it is apt to spread until it becomes an acceptable and uniform method of obtaining additional compensation. Many of the people may have been told, and believed, that management approved of it as a means of providing extra, tax-free income. They certainly had been given no reason for disbelief.

Any kind of retaliation was of course out of the question if Baxter wanted to keep his sales force intact. His "mandatory action" should have been aimed at preventing similar occurrences in the future, not punishing the salespeople for past errors. He had already made a good start. Word of his trip, and its results, was undoubtedly spreading among the salespeople even as he considered his next move. If he next made it clear that such follow-up on prospective accounts was to be made a regular part of his schedule, false reporting should stop overnight. The salespeople might even start reporting real prospects.

It is surprising that Baxter was amazed at what he found. He should have known, before he left the office, that his predecessor's policies were not being implemented.

FRANK P. NUMER
Professor of Business
Administration
Robert Morris College

These false reports constitute fraudulent conduct—downright dishonesty—on the part of the Solem Pharmaceutical Company sales personnel. *They should be summarily dismissed.* Perhaps a rash decision, but in lieu of

Watergate, bribery scandals in high places, and a generally low regard for top officials by the American public, strong action is required. The salespeople represent the company and, in many cases, are the only direct contacts between the company and the customers. What a tarnished image these unethical salespeople present!

Baxter did not wish to cripple the sales program by a wholesale dismissal, but he must look at both the long-range sales program and the immediacy of the present. It will be to Baxter's advantage to recruit new sales personnel at once and start anew. He must have a first-rate sales team in order to succeed, and first-rate qualities would include loyalty and integrity.

This deplorable situation could have been avoided, however, if the company had instituted a more alert follow-up sales program on the prospective accounts. The sending of a "welcome aboard" letter together with printed sales promotion literature would be a means of such control. Further, the cost department, through a ferreting-out technique, could have established the trend of such fraudulent conduct on the part of the salespeople, although the basic lack of supervisory follow-up must be placed on the shoulders of the sales manager, Baxter. His delay of six months before instituting a follow-up program indicates a certain question about his judgment. The fact that all salespeople participated in this devious scheme indicates the laxity of the company management in its control procedures.

In the future, all prospective accounts submitted by the sales personnel should be sent specific literature with a direct reference to the name of the salesperson who had submitted the account. The follow-up cycle should be reduced to either 30 days or perhaps 90 days at the most. Since "honesty is the best policy," it must be vividly demonstrated to the sales personnel of the Solem Pharmaceutical Company through immediate wholesale dismissals.

OBSERVATIONS

In this incident, a sales manager has discovered that all his salespeople are guilty of turning in false field reports and expense accounts. The sales manager must determine why this is the case, decide what to do about it, and implement controls to prevent repetition.

It is interesting to note that in this incident, as is true in many of the incidents included in this book, two well-known management scholars differ markedly about what action Baxter should take. It again illustrates that there may not be one "right" action, and that decisions of this type are based on one's own perceptions, philosophies, or personal value system.

Most of the organizational research regarding employee performance has focused on unsatisfactory performance of individual employees. The unsatisfactory performance of an entire work force, such as in this incident, poses unique problems that are not encountered in cases of individual poor performance. The author of one of the suggested readings, Karen Brown, notes that one problem involves *diagnosis* of group poor performance. Supervisors themselves are judged on the overall performance of their employees. The poor performance of an individual employee will reflect far less on the supervisor than will a group's poor performance. As a result, the supervisor's ability to make an objective diagnosis is crucial. Baxter must be conscious of the distinction between individual and group performance and then accurately diagnose its causes and implications for Solem Pharmaceutical.

DISCUSSION ITEMS

1. Professor Numer thinks that immediate wholesale dismissals will vividly demonstrate that "honesty is the best policy." Is this an example of the "end justifying the means?" Elaborate.
2. If you were Baxter, what would you decide to do about the false reports? Why?
3. What methods would you employ to diagnose the causes for the dishonesty at Solem Pharmaceutical Company? Formulate a policy to prevent similar occurrences and state how you would implement that policy.

SUGGESTED READINGS

BOOKS

Arnold, Hugh J., and Daniel C. Feldman. *Organizational Behavior*. New York: McGraw-Hill, 1986, chap. 11.

Callahan, Robert E.; C. Patrick Fleenor; and Harry Knudson. *Understanding Organizational Behavior*. Columbus, Ohio: Charles E. Merrill Publishing, 1986, chaps. 7, 10, 11.

Davis, Keith, and John W. Newstrom. *Human Behavior at Work*. 7th ed. New York: McGraw-Hill, 1985, chaps. 4, 5, 8, 10, 11.

Donnelly, James H.; James L. Gibson; and John M. Ivancevich. *Fundamentals of Management*. 6th ed. Plano, Tex.: Business Publications, 1987, chaps. 8, 19, 20.

French, Wendell L. *The Personnel Management Process*. 6th ed. Boston: Houghton Mifflin, 1987, chaps. 6–9, 13–15, 18, 21.

Goodman, Paul S. *Designing Effective Work Groups.* San Francisco: Jossey-Bass, 1986.

Griffin, Ricky W. *Management.* 2nd ed. Boston: Houghton Mifflin, 1987, chaps. 3–7, 15, 17, 18.

Heneman, Herbert G.; Donald P. Schwab; John A. Fossum; and Lee D. Dyer. *Personnel/Human Resource Management.* 3rd ed. Homewood, Ill.: Richard D. Irwin, 1986, chaps. 3, 4, 18, 19.

Laczinak, Gene R. *Marketing Ethics: Guidelines for Managers.* Lexington, Mass.: D. C. Heath, 1985, pp. 1–208.

McFarland, Dalton E. *Management and Society.* Englewood Cliffs, N.J.: Prentice-Hall, 1982, chaps. 8, 9.

Megginson, Leon C. *Personnel Management: A Human Resources Approach.* 5th ed. Homewood, Ill.: Richard D. Irwin, 1985, chaps. 12, 16.

Rue, Leslie W., and Lloyd L. Byars. *Management: Theory and Application.* 4th ed. Homewood, Ill.: Richard D. Irwin, 1986, chaps. 3, 4–7, 11, 20, 21.

Schermerhorn, John R. *Management for Productivity.* 2nd ed. New York: John Wiley & Sons, 1986, chaps. 14–16, 20.

JOURNALS

Barkman, D. F. "Team Discipline: Put Performance on the Line." *Personnel Journal* 66, no. 3 (March 1987), pp. 58–63.

Beck, A. C., and E. D. Hillmar. "What Managers Can Do to Turn around Negative Attitudes in an Organization." *Management Review* 73, no. 1 (January 1984), pp. 22–25.

Beyer, J. M., and H. M. Trice. "A Field Study of the Use and Perceived Effects of Discipline in Controlling Work Performance." *Academy of Management Journal* 27, no. 4 (December 1984), pp. 743–64.

Bhagat, R. S. "Conditions under which Stronger Job Performance-Job Satisfaction Relationships May Be Observed." *Academy of Management Journal* 25, no. 4 (December 1982), pp. 772–89.

Brown, Karen A. "Explaining Group Poor Performance." *Academy of Management Review* 9, no. 1 (January 1984), pp. 54–61.

Discenza, Richard, and Howard Smith. "Is Employee Discipline Obsolete?" *Personnel Administrator* 30, no. 6 (June 1985), pp. 175–86.

Feldman, Daniel C. "The Development and Enforcement of Group Norms." *Academy of Management Review* 9, no. 1 (January 1984), pp. 47–53.

Geis, A. A. "Making Merit Pay Work." *Personnel* 64, no. 1 (January 1987), pp. 52–60.

Grant, P. C. "Why Employee Motivation Has Declined in America." *Personnel Journal* 61, no. 12 (December 1982), pp. 905–9.

Kanter, R. M. "From Status to Contribution: Some Organizational Implications for Changing Basis for Pay." *Personnel* 64, no. 1 (January 1987), pp. 12–37.

McClelland, D. C. "How Motives, Skills, and Values Determine What People Do." *American Psychologist* 40, no. 7 (July 1985), pp. 812–25.

Merchant, K. A. "The Control Function of Management." *Sloan Management Review* 23, no. 4 (Summer 1982), pp. 43–55.

Mills, P. K. "Self-Management: Its Control and Relationship to Other Organizational Properties." *Academy of Management Review* 8, no. 3 (July 1983), pp. 445–53.

Rowland, D. C., and Bob Greene. "Incentive Pay: Productivity's Own Reward." *Personnel Journal* 66, no. 3 (March 1987), pp. 48–57.

Schermerhorn, John R. "Team Development for High-Performance Management." *Training and Development Journal* 40, no. 11 (November 1986), pp. 38–41.

Sussman, Mario, and Robert P. Vecchio. "A Social Influence Interpretation of Worker Motivation." *Academy of Management Review* 7, no. 2 (April 1982), pp. 177–86.

WHAT THIS INCIDENT IS ABOUT:
The appropriate action to take when policies are
violated, or not followed completely, is the central
issue in this incident. It allows for an examination of
associated topics such as how flexible should policies
be, and how can they be effectively communicated
and implemented.

15

Heroic banker

INCIDENT

At noon one day, Jack Harvey, a teller in a local suburban bank, was
suddenly confronted by a man with a pistol, who demanded all the cur-
rency in the teller's cage. Harvey complied and put the money in a paper
bag. The bandit left unobtrusively through the front door, jumped in a car,
and drove away. Harvey immediately sounded the alarm, ran to his own
car, and pursued the bandit. Driving at high speed, he overtook the
bandit, forced him to a stop, and chased him on foot until overtaking him.
A struggle ensued in which Harvey was shot in the leg, but he successfully
detained the bandit until the local police arrived.

The local press gave Harvey wide coverage for his heroism. He also
received recognition from various individuals and groups for his bravery.
The bank officials, however, had mixed emotions about the incident. The
bank had a long-standing policy that a teller, when confronted with an
attempted robbery, was to fully comply with the demands, so as not to
endanger employees and customers. The policy further stated that tellers
were to give the alarm only when it was safe to do so, to await action by
police and insurance agents and that any bank employee who failed to
follow this procedure would be immediately discharged.

The bank president felt that Harvey, by violating a written and well-
understood policy, should be discharged. The personnel director urged
that his bravery, devotion to duty, and loyalty to the bank should mitigate
his policy infraction. The director of public relations reminded the president that the public might view Harvey's discharge with misgivings since
he, after all, had protected their deposits. The training director said that a

dangerous precedent would be established if a policy exemption were permitted. The president was faced with a decisional dilemma.

CRITIQUES

WILLIAM M. FOX
Professor of Industrial Relations
and Management
University of Florida

Policies are not ends in themselves, but rather means for achieving organizational objectives. Two bank objectives relevant to this case are keeping employees and customers safe in the event of attempted robbery, and safeguarding customers' deposits. Did Jack Harvey violate stated policy in any significant way, as he understood it?

He fully complied with the robber's demands, and did not endanger employees and customers. It appears also that he *did not* sound the alarm until it was safe to do so. Evidently, then, his only violation had to do with that part of the policy statement requiring that he "await action by police and insurance agents."

It could well be that his behavior constituted an unnecessary risk to his person and should be discouraged by the bank in view of modern theft insurance coverage. It is possible that the bank would face uncovered liability and poor publicity were one of its tellers killed in such an action. Certainly, the values of such heroism to the bank and the community that prevailed in frontier days before theft insurance are only symbolic today.

To the extent that such underlying reasons for the last part of the policy statement had not been communicated to employees, it is plausible to assume that Harvey and others felt he was sincerely pursuing the goals of the bank while scrupulously observing the "important" part of the policy.

It would be better if the policy statement had read that "any bank employee who fails to follow this procedure will be *subject* to immediate discharge." This would publicly acknowledge the need for "breathing room" for situations such as the present one. Actually, assuming Harvey's ignorance of the reasons for the last part of the policy, he showed intelligent initiative on the bank's behalf—an admirable quality for the management to reward and nurture.

The purpose of disciplinary action is to influence the future behavior of organizational personnel along desired lines. If the above assumptions are valid (we need more information about how the policy was explained and Harvey's understanding of it), then commendation of Harvey's intelligent initiative "within the framework of understanding" he had at the time would be in order, as well as a clear explanation to Harvey and others about why this type of action in the future would not be necessary and might prove quite disadvantageous to the bank. This approach would stand a much better chance of achieving future policy compliance while, at the same time, conserving and strengthening present harmonious relations.

If officials determined that Harvey had endangered himself despite clear understanding of the policy's reasons against such action, then different issues would be before us. Was Harvey an immature, publicity-seeking grandstander, or was this behavior inconsistent with his usual past behavior? Is Harvey ill? If so, understanding and professional attention are needed, not disciplinary action. Whatever the case, apparently no one reserved judgment and invited Harvey to discuss the matter.

With regard to the training director's position, it seems that the undesirable precedent would be for management to make the decision without due regard to anything but the fact that a "literal" breach of policy has occurred. Any organization that commands and expects nothing more than robotlike compliance with its policies, regardless of the circumstances, is doomed to mediocrity or failure.

J. CLIFTON WILLIAMS
Professor
of Management
Baylor University

From the bank's perspective, Jack Harvey behaved irrationally and emotionally—contrary to his own best interests and the best interests of the bank. Major consideration should be given to preventing such incidents in the future. That objective should be made explicit and kept in mind as a more immediate objective is achieved: charting a course of action that will satisfy the demands of the present situation.

Harvey's hot pursuit was indeed in violation of bank policy and was certainly unwise. After all, he did get shot in the leg, and his actions could have been even more tragic. He could have been killed or have caused extensive property damage and the death or injury of innocent bystanders. Therefore, the seriousness of the offense should not be underemphasized. On the other hand, it is unreasonable to expect that people in organizations should always behave rationally. Some senior loan officers of the world's most prestigious banks recently proved that in their rush to make high-interest loans to a host of small oil-producing countries in Central and South America. By remembering that good employees sometimes make mistakes, perhaps we can avoid the legalistic reactions that often characterize mechanistic organizations with a rational model of human nature.

Often, decisions must be made that fail to produce the desirable outcomes of a theoretically ideal solution. Nevertheless, it is useful to state what the desirable outcomes are. In this situation, the solution: (1) must be acceptable to the bank president, since he is presumably the final authority in the matter, (2) should be fair to Harvey, (3) should appear fair to bank officers, other employees, and the various bank publics who know about the event and will know the outcome, and (4) should prevent recurrence of the event. Having decided on these outcomes, the decision makers will chart a course for subsequent steps in problem solving.

In exploring possible courses of action, the bank's long-standing policy about employee behavior during robberies should be carefully reviewed. The probability is high that the policy will be reaffirmed, perhaps with even more emphasis than before. However, since bank robberies occur infrequently and Harvey's reaction is likely to occur even less frequently, it is probable that the enforcement of this policy has never been tested. Management should therefore take a close look at its general policy enforcement. If policy violations have occasionally gone unpunished, that fact would argue for using this incident as an occasion for strengthening this and other bank policies—emphasizing their purpose and, in effect, issuing a warning that future enforcement will be swift and certain. The training director's belief that a dangerous precedent would be established if *any* policy exception is permitted is unfounded. Surely failure to enforce this policy to the letter would not be the first time a bank policy exception has been made, nor would it have to be a precedent, dangerous or otherwise.

One major consideration in arriving at the final decision concerns the nature of the organization—whether, when the chips are down, allowance can be made for nonrational human qualities—those that might produce a rare act of ill-advised loyalty. Assuming that the bank president and other bank officers have led with an expertise that has produced in Harvey and others a strong loyalty and identification with the bank, the decision makers surely will not want to undermine those qualities by deciding this issue impersonally and legalistically.

Before a final decision is reached, input should be obtained from other key bank officers. In the final analysis, the directors of personnel and public relations should marshal their arguments in support of the following action, which assumes that Harvey is a reasonably mature and respected employee rather than an impulsive and irresponsible publicity seeker. Some degree of consensus can probably be achieved for this action:

1. Sincerely praise Harvey for his good intentions and pay his medical bills and his salary while he recuperates. Make it clear, however, that: (1) his actions are in no sense condoned, and (2) in the future, the policy will be enforced.
2. With minimum fanfare, the president should inform the other employees of his actions, fully explaining his support for the stated policy and his intent to enforce it in the future.
3. The occasion should be used to review and clarify related policies.

Additional employee education about the reasons for selected policies may be in order.

4. The president may also use the event to express appreciation for the many other bank employees whose actions show their dedication and loyalty to the bank. He should give specific examples of a more accept-able type, without casting aspersions on Harvey's motives. In this way, the event can be used to reinforce desirable attributes of the organiza-tion.

Incidents such as this one often evoke dramatic responses—the kind that make headlines and prompt newspaper readers to write letters to the editor. Statements from the bank to the news media should be written in factual but essentially bland prose that only the most imaginative reporter could use to stir significant interest. Since the bandit's trial will be forth-coming, management actions concerning the incident, certainly all press releases, should be cleared through the bank's attorneys. As soon as possi-ble, the issue should be allowed to die a natural death.

OBSERVATIONS

In this incident, a teller in a local bank violated a policy that called for the employee's immediate discharge for noncompliance. He acted in what one critique writer describes as an irrational and emotional manner, but succeeded in apprehending a robber, was hospitalized by an injury suf-fered in the fracas, and was praised as a hero by the local press. When a group of top managers attending a management development program was given this incident and asked what they would do if they were the bank president, the responses split into thirds. One group favored some form of reward ranging from monetary compensation to letters of commendation. Another group favored some form of disciplinary action ranging from immediate termination or suspension for a few days to verbal reprimands. The third group's responses included, "commend him and then slap his hand."

This incident, as is true of all the incidents in this book, is based on a disguised actual situation, and readers always want to know what the bank president actually did, as if that might represent some form of "right answer." What actually happened was that the bank president kept stalling until no decision was made. A well-reasoned decision to "do nothing" might have been an appropriate response, but to take no action because of pure procrastination was definitely not the correct decision.

DISCUSSION ITEMS

1. Both Professors Fox and Williams appropriately focus most of their attention in their critiques on this incident's policy implications. Revise the policy as you think it should have been stated and then discuss specific steps for implementing your policy.
2. What action should the bank president take regarding Jack Harvey? Be specific in indicating your recommendations. Justify your views.
3. Does Harvey's behavior suggest irrationality? If so, is it excusable or should it be dealt with? If not, how do you explain it? Elaborate.

SUGGESTED READINGS

BOOKS

Arnold, Hugh J., and Daniel C. Feldman. *Organizational Behavior.* New York: McGraw-Hill, 1986, chap. 6

Callahan, Robert E.; C. Patrick Fleenor; and Harry Knudson. *Understanding Organizational Behavior.* Columbus, Ohio: Charles E. Merrill Publishing, 1986, chaps. 4, 7, 12.

Davis, Keith, and John W. Newstrom. *Human Behavior at Work.* 7th ed. New York: McGraw-Hill, 1985, chaps. 16, 20.

Donnelly, James H.; James L. Gibson; and John M. Ivancevich. *Fundamentals of Management.* 6th ed. Plano, Tex.: Business Publications, 1987, chaps. 13, 16.

French, Wendell L. *The Personnel Management Process.* 6th ed. Boston: Houghton Mifflin, 1987, chaps. 8, 26.

Griffin, Ricky W. *Management.* 2nd ed. Boston: Houghton Mifflin, 1987, chaps. 7, 16, 19.

Heneman, Herbert G.; Donald P. Schwab; John A. Fossum; and Lee D. Dyer. *Personnel Human Resource Management.* 3rd ed. Homewood, Ill.: Richard D. Irwin, 1986, chaps. 11, 12.

Megginson, Leon C. *Personnel Management: A Human Resources Approach.* 5th ed. Homewood, Ill.: Richard D. Irwin, 1985, chap. 12.

Myers, D. W. *Employee Problem Prevention and Counseling: A Guide for Professionals.* Westport, Conn.: Quorum Publishing Co., 1985, pp. 1–388.

Pearce, John A., and Richard B. Robinson. *Formulation and Implementation of Competitive Strategy.* 3rd ed. Homewood, Ill.: Richard D. Irwin, Inc., 1986, chaps. 1–12.

Rue, Leslie W., and Lloyd L. Byars. *Management: Theory and Application.* 4th ed. Homewood, Ill.: Richard D. Irwin, 1986, chaps. 5, 16, 17.

Schermerhorn, John R. *Management for Productivity*. 2nd ed. New York: John Wiley & Sons, 1986, chaps. 3, 4, 8.

Thompson, Arthur A., and A. J. Strickland. *Strategy Formulation and Implementation*. 3rd ed. Plano, Tex.: Business Publications, 1986, chaps. 1–9.

JOURNALS

Asherman, I. G. "The Corrective Discipline Process." *Personnel Journal* 61, no. 7 (July 1982), pp. 529–31.

Bloom, Stuart P. "Policy and Procedure Statements that Communicate." *Personnel Journal* 62, no. 9 (September 1983), pp. 711–18.

Bowen, Michael. "The Escalation Phenomenon Reconsidered: Decision Dilemmas or Decision Errors?" *Academy of Management Review* 12, no. 1 (January 1987), pp. 52–66.

Cosier, Richard A., and Thomas L. Ruble. "Research on Conflict-Handling Behavior." *Academy of Management Journal* 24, no. 4 (December 1981), pp. 816–31.

Gaines, Jeannie, and John M. Jermier. "Emotional Exhaustion in a High-Stress Organization." *Academy of Management Journal* 26, no. 4 (December 1983), pp. 567–86.

Glicken, Morley D. "A Counseling Approach to Employee Burnout." *Personnel Journal* 62, no. 3 (March 1983), pp. 222–28.

Gorlin, Harriet. "An Overview of Corporate Personnel Practices." *Personnel Journal* 61, no. 2 (February 1982), pp. 125–30.

Leap, T. L., and M. D. Crino. "How to Deal with Bizarre Employee Behavior." *Harvard Business Review* 64, no. 3 (May-June 1986), pp. 18–25.

Logan, G. M. "Loyalty and a Sense of Purpose." *California Management Review* 27, no. 1 (Fall 1984), pp. 149–56.

Matteson, M. T., and J. M. Ivancevich. "The How, What, and Why of Stress Management Training." *Personnel Journal* 61, no. 10 (October 1982), pp. 768–74.

Parasuraman, Saroj, and J. A. Alutto. "Sources and Outcomes of Stress in Organizational Settings." *Academy of Management Journal* 27, no. 2 (June 1984), pp. 330–50.

Rafaeli, Anat, and R. I. Sutton. "Expression of Emotion as Part of the Work Role." *Academy of Management Review* 12, no. 1 (January 1987), pp. 23–37.

Schwartz, Howard S. "Job Involvement as Obsession-Compulsion." *Academy of Management Review* 7, no. 3 (July 1982), pp. 429–32.

Smith, Terry. "Developing a Policy Manual." *Personnel Journal* 61, no. 6 (June 1982), pp. 446–49.

Spruell, Geraldine. "Work Fever." *Training and Development Journal* 41, no. 1 (January 1987), pp. 41–45.

Stoner, C. R., and F. L. Fry. "Developing a Corporate Policy for Managing Stress." *Personnel* 60, no. 3 (May-June 1983), pp. 66–76.

WHAT THIS INCIDENT IS ABOUT:
Policy on illegal drugs, including testing for illegal
drugs, is implemented to protect the health, safety,
and productivity of the work force. Employee resists
policy and asserts rights of the individual worker.

16

Illegal drug policy

INCIDENT

Dan Fillmore stepped back from the machine he was repairing and tried to clear his head. He felt hot and dizzy. His stomach felt turbulent. The next thing he knew, his supervisor was bent over him, fanning him with a cap and asking what was wrong. Dan tried to stand and admitted that he didn't feel well.

Company policy required that anyone having a medical problem at work be given a standard series of laboratory tests. In keeping with this policy, Dan was taken to the infirmary and given the required tests, including a routine test for evidence of illegal drug use.

When Dan returned to work, he learned that the tests had revealed traces of methadone in his system and that shop management was alarmed, even though the amount of the drug in Dan's system was quite far below addictive levels.

Dan's supervisor met with administrators from the personnel and safety departments. Together they decided that Dan should be assigned temporarily to a drug rehabilitation program, for which all expenses would be paid by the company. Dan would continue to draw his regular paycheck and would return to his job after successfully completing the program. These provisions followed those of the labor contract.

Dan could not believe what was happening to him. He refused to accept the test results as valid and was unwilling to enter the drug rehabilitation program.

The personnel director, upon learning of Dan's resistance to the implementation of the company drug policy, began to examine and compare the

129

advantages and disadvantages of optional policies for dealing with drugs. He considered the following drug policies:

a. Hiring undercover narcotics agents to work in the plant. These agents would spy on regular workers and develop evidence on drug and drug dealing. A program of testing for illegal drug use would not then be necessary. The U.S. Attorney General had endorsed worker surveillance at work, in locker rooms, in parking lots, and even in nearby taverns. His views also embraced the philosophy of a former director of the Drug Enforcement Administration who emphasized that drug testing and the use of sanctions against drug users are an essential part of the message that illegal drug abuse will not be tolerated.

b. Establishing a program of urine testing for illegal drug use which included testing both job applicants and current employees. Reliable published reports indicated that 25 percent of U.S. corporations have a policy of testing for illegal drug use.

c. Adopting a "passive policy" toward illegal drug use. This policy would leave the matter of illegal drug use and abuse to local law enforcement agencies. This policy would be inexpensive and would avoid problems of company enforcement.

The personnel director faced the problem of effectively implementing the decision regarding Dan Fillmore. He also needed to formulate a company policy on illegal drug use.

CRITIQUES

LYNN H. PETERS
Professor of Management
San Diego State University

The Dan Fillmore case takes place in an employment setting and is an inquiry into several of the most troubling dilemmas in American life: the use and abuse of controlled substances and the relationship between the employment situation and private lives.

Let us first consider what rights and responsibilities each of the parties brings to the employment contract. The employer clearly has the right to effective, efficient, and safe performance of tasks assigned within the worker's competence. (Note that, as in this case, determination of competence may be affected by a labor contract.) Effective and efficient performance includes avoidance of tardiness and absenteeism. The employer also had the right to expect that employees will not act in such a manner so as to endanger themselves or others. Clearly, the employer has the responsibility to provide safe working conditions and the tools and materials necessary for the employee to meet work expectations.

What the employer does *not* have as a right in the employment contract is the control of the private life of the employee, so long as that private life does not negatively affect the economic interests of the employer. Additionally, ethicists and the courts are increasingly coming to include personal privacy in such things as dress, nonparticipation in group social activities, sexual preference, substance abuse, etc., where they do not interfere with the rights of others in the work situation. To put it another way, it is the employer's responsibility to respect employees' legal and ethical rights to privacy, in its various manifestations.

Nowadays it is agreed that employees have the right to safe working conditions, the corollary of the employer's responsibility. As indicated above, they also have the right to privacy where that right demonstrably does not interfere with their employment responsibility. That latter responsibility is the corollary of the employer's right to work performance as well as the avoidance of behaviors dangerous to self or others.

Of course, circumstances beyond the reasonable control of the parties (illness, floods, accidents, etc.) may temporarily or permanently alter the balance of rights and responsibilities.

I trust that no one is surprised or disturbed at a discussion that includes employees' rights. The fabric of American law no longer ends at the entrance to the work place.

	Rights	Responsibilities
Employer	1. Effective, efficient task performance. 2. Safe work place.	1. Employee privacy. 2. Safe work place.
Employee	1. Privacy. 2. Safe work place.	1. Effective, efficient task performance. 2. Safe work place.

Let us consider the ethical principles which may serve as guides to the balance between employer and employee rights.

The first question is whether in fact, in this instance, the rights of the employer have been violated and, if so, what is the cause.

A careful reading of the case gives no real indication as to the cause of Dan's inability to perform his duties satisfactorily. He became ill; the evidence available provides no necessary causal connection between the illness and behaviors that would have incapacitated him to perform his responsibilities. That is, there is no proof that he intentionally violated the rights of the employer. In fact, knowing what we do about the validity and reliability of substance testing, there should immediately have been a back-up test performed to verify the results of the first test.

What to do about Dan Fillmore? Clearly there is employment contract language available for guidance *if* the tests were accurate. Given the problems involved with the testing errors in this instance, and no evidence of earlier or associated substance problems, let it go.

Now to the general question of policy, always bearing in mind the presence of a union contract with relevant language. Let us consider possible actions by the employer not in some sort of a vacuum, but in response to a *need*. There is no indication that a needs assessment has been done in this instance, no study that showed an indication of reported usage on the job by the work force, decline in productivity, or a deviation in turnover, absenteeism, or tardiness from what is the norm for the labor market. The personnel director's first job is to find out if something is broken before he rushes out to fix it. Depending on what he finds, and only then, is he in a position to recommend policy. Put another way, are the rights of the employer being violated, to what degree, and what are the ethical and legal constraints on his ability to restore those rights?

If the plant is being operated by a bunch of zonked-out loonies, or if he ascribes to the philosophy of General Motors (who also hired surveillance on Ralph Nader when he criticized one of its cars), then clearly option (*a*) is likely to land him and the company in enough trouble to justify a very large personnel office and legal staff.

If the plant is essentially "clean" with little or no evidence of substance abuse on the basis of the various measures, then clearly alternative (*c*) is in order. This choice not only avoids problems, but saves money.

If there is evidence that there is substance abuse occurring in the plant, and *if* this substance abuse can be shown to be interfering with the rights of the employers and/or other employees, then the employees' rights to privacy must be reconsidered. Which employees? All employees, or those who indicate by their actions that they are involved in substance abuse? The easy route is to say "all employees," and then engage in some form of random testing [option (b)]. Privacy is then interfered with, both for those who have violated their responsibility and for those who have not. It seems to me that one's rights should be limited or abrogated only where there is cause, and that cause in this circumstance would be the violation of the rights of another, the employer, and perhaps other employees, if safety is involved. Because there is evidence that substance abuse does in fact reduce performance capacity, the testing approach most likely to meet both performance and ethical concerns is testing for cause; that is, of those individuals whose work behavior is of the kind associated with substance abuse.

In closing, I must touch on the invasion of the privacy of personal lives of employees, and this goes back to the collapse of Dan Fillmore. If it were established that there was a causal relationship between his collapse and the presence of a controlled substance in his blood, then let the machinery go into action. The public announcement of the results of the testing, without the evidence of such a causal relationship, is a glaring invasion of privacy. In short, probable cause as a reason for testing (which his collapse provided) needs to be followed by an indication of sufficient controlled substance in his system to allow the reasonable (statistically available) inference that the presence of the substance caused his collapse, and therefore the violation of the rights of the employer. No other circumstance justifies the invasion of Fillmore's, or anyone else's, rights to privacy as a condition of employment in a situation such as this.

MARILYN TAYLOR
Associate Professor of Strategic Management
University of Kansas

The incident with Dan Fillmore has opened a critical area for the company. Indeed drug abuse may be the leading health hazard in the workplace today. Estimates of the cost of drug abuse in the workplace range up to $100 billion yearly in the United States. Moreover drug abusers are known to incur three times as many work-related accidents as non-drug users. Small wonder that the number of *Fortune* 500 companies with drug testing programs has increased from about 3 percent in 1982 to over 30 percent in 1987! The company's current policy of routinely including drug testing during examination following a work-related health or accident incident is very much in line with current practice. Two major questions need to be answered in this incident:

1. Is the recommendation by Dan's supervisor and the personnel and safety departments appropriate?
2. What is the appropriate policy for future action for the company?

With regard to the first question, their response may well be inappropriate. In the first place there is no evidence as to *why* Dan was found to have methadone in his bloodstream or whether the dizziness episode was indeed connected to the methadone level. Methadone is used for treatment of substance abusers to mitigate the effects of withdrawal. Dan may already be in or have completed a voluntary program. If indeed Dan is or has been an addict, was the addiction from recreational use of drugs or from becoming hooked while under medical treatment for another condition? Further, was the dizziness an isolated incident? If Dan has had similar incidents in the past, the company is within its legal rights to reassign him, require him to enter a drug treatment program as a condition of keeping his job (and monitor his progress through use of drug tests), or dismiss him from the company. These actions, however, are subject to the conditions of the union contract. Moreover, the costs of each alternative have to be weighed carefully. Conditions of required treatment in many U.S. companies include continuity of salary and payment for treatment, although the latter may be covered under the company's health policy. Further, "cure" rates for such treatment programs are not high.

If Dan has had a past problem with drugs, has been through a treatment program, and is currently free of recreational drug use, then the personnel director must treat him as a handicapped person. Dan can be removed from the job if he is unable to adequately perform the job or if he poses a threat to maintaining a safe work environment for other workers as required under OSHA laws.

Further, we do not know the kind of test used that identified the methadone in Dan's bloodstream. Currently used tests are not reliable. Of special concern are the tests used by many laboratories, especially urinalysis tests, which have given many false positives, that is the tests have indicated the presence of drugs when none existed. Second, many tests do not indicate the level of drugs in the bloodstream or if the positive reading is triggered by a commonly available over-the-counter formulation such as a cold remedy! At the very least the personnel director should ask for a second test for Dan.

What should be the company's policy regarding testing for drug use? The policy must reflect the company's estimate of the level of drug use and its impact on the workplace in the form of reduced productivity, product quality, accident rate, damage and theft of equipment, and absenteeism. Certainly under the circumstances where drug use is fairly high and where drug pushing may be an on-premise problem, the company needs to take stronger steps than when occasional recreational use of drugs has not interfered with job performance. Indeed, under current interpretation of the Constitution by the courts, the employer has no right to fire or discipline for recreational use of drugs off work premises unless the drug use inhibits the employee's ability to perform the job or the employee's behavior renders the workplace unsafe for other workers.

Assuming that the company ascertains that drug use currently has a significant but moderate effect in the workplace, the company should choose the second alternative being considered by the personnel director, that is, testing job applicants and all current employees. Testing of all current employees may be implemented with routine yearly physicals if the latter are already part of the company's program. Such procedures must be approved by the union. Random testing of employees is not appropriate. It would seem that the company might take a phased approach including the following steps:

1. Educational program informing employees of the risks of drug use and the availability of the company's programs for help. Note that the company's policy concerning available programs for help must be clearly documented and applied evenly to all employees.

2. Training of supervisors to recognize symptoms of drug toxification.
3. Careful documentation of drug incidents. (Note: care must be given to keep such information confidential.)

If incidents in the workplace are at a frequency level to cause concern, periodic drug testing of all employees may be warranted. Random testing of employees as a method of deterrence and detection has not been viewed favorably by the courts. Currently, however, the situation does not require premise surveillance for drug pushers.

Overall Dan's dizziness appears to be an isolated incident not thoroughly investigated by the personnel and safety departments. Indeed, one wonders if Dan might have grounds for suing. If Dan can demonstrate that (1) he is not a user of drug substances, that is, that the test was a false positive, and any information that he gave the company was ignored in the investigation, or (2) he is a past user of drugs, has undergone treatment, and the fainting spell was not connected with his past use of drugs or to the treatment, or (3) the company did not treat the information confidentially, or (4) he was treated differently when he fainted/blacked out than were other employees incurring similar incidents, he will have the basis for a suit. Moreover, the grounds for suit may be exacerbated by the conditions of the union contract. The personnel director must more thoroughly investigate the incident with Dan before making a final decision.

OBSERVATIONS

While politicians declare "War on Drugs," employers initiate drug testing of employees and the legal system advances Fourth Amendment protections against unreasonable search and seizure. Many employers have concluded that the problems of illegal drug abuse require action. As an illustration, Amoco Corporation has begun a drug and alcohol testing program for its 40,000 U.S. employees that includes urinalysis testing and allows search of a worker's personal belongings if managers have "reasonable cause" to believe the worker is under the influence of drugs or alcohol. Another example is provided by Smith Barney, which has strengthened its policy on illegal drug use to require most of its staff to undergo urine tests. A Smith Barney spokesman was quoted as saying that it did not intend to intrude on personal lives of employees, but that it could not ignore any situation in which drugs might hurt the company's reputation. Refusal to submit to a urinalysis test is grounds for immediate termination under their policy. The interaction between efforts by employers to control illegal drug use and abuse and efforts by employees to preserve their individual rights provides fertile grounds for discussion.

DISCUSSION ITEMS

1. Explain why the drug policy of some companies requires mandatory drug testing of job applicants, but not of current employees?
2. Discuss the potential liability of the company in a case involving injury to an innocent employee caused by the action of a fellow worker who was proved by urinalysis to have been under the influence of illegal drugs at the time of the accident.
3. What safeguards of employee rights would you prefer to find in your present or future employer's policy on the use of illegal drugs? Explain.

SUGGESTED READINGS

BOOKS

Arnold, Hugh J., and Daniel C. Feldman. *Organizational Behavior.* New York: McGraw-Hill, 1986, chap. 2.

Callahan, Robert E.; C. Patrick Fleenor; and Harry Knudson. *Understanding Organizational Behavior.* Columbus, Ohio: Charles E. Merrill Publishing, 1986, chap. 2.

Davis, Keith, and John W. Newstrom. *Human Behavior at Work.* 7th ed. New York: McGraw-Hill, 1985, chap. 16.

Donnelly, James H.; James L. Gibson; and John M. Ivancevich. *Fundamentals of Management.* 6th ed. Plano, Tex.: Business Publications, 1987, pp. 663–67.

French, Wendell L. *The Personnel Management Process.* 6th ed. Boston: Houghton Mifflin, 1987, chaps. 8, 12.

Griffin, Ricky W. *Management.* 2nd ed. Boston: Houghton Mifflin, 1987, chap. 21.

Heneman, Herbert G.; Donald P. Schwab; John A. Fossum; and Lee D. Dyer. *Personnel/Human Resource Management.* 3rd ed. Homewood, Ill.: Richard D. Irwin, 1986, chaps. 9–11.

Megginson, Leon C. *Personnel Management: A Human Resources Approach.* 5th ed. Homewood, Ill.: Richard D. Irwin, 1985, chap. 7.

Rue, Leslie W., and Lloyd L. Byars. *Management: Theory and Application.* 4th ed. Homewood, Ill.: Richard D. Irwin, 1986, chap. 10.

Schermerhorn, John R. *Management for Productivity.* 2nd ed. New York: John Wiley & Sons, 1986, chaps. 9, 14.

JOURNALS

Bensinger, Ann, and Charles F. Pilkington. "Treating Chemically Dependent Employees in a Non-Hospital Setting." *Personnel Administrator* 30, no. 8 (August 1985), pp. 45–52.

Chapman, Fern Schumer. "The Ruckus over Medical Testing." *Fortune* 112, no. 9 (August 19, 1985), pp. 57–62.

"Companies Are Starting to Sniff Out Cocaine Users." *Business Week*, February 18, 1985, p. 37.

"Drug Abuse at Nuclear Plants: The Alarms Are Ringing." *Business Week*, October 28, 1985, p. 35.

"Drug Tests: Legal Challenges." *Newsweek*, May 5, 1986, pp. 50, 52.

Flax, Steven. "The Executive Addict." *Fortune* 111, no. 7 (June 24, 1985), pp. 24–31.

Lyons, Paul V. "EAPs: The Only Real Cure for Substance Abuse." *Management Review* 76, no. 3 (March 1987), pp. 38–41.

Madigan, Robert M.; K Don Scott; Diana L. Deadrick; and Jill A. Stoddard. "Employee Testing: The U.S. Job Service Is Spearheading a Revolution." *Personnel Administrator* 31, no. 9 (September 1986), pp. 102–12.

Schachter, Victor, and Thomas E. Geidt. "Cracking Down on Drugs." *Across the Board* 22, no. 11 (November 1985), pp. 28–37.

Sellers, David. "Positive Results for Drug Test Sales." *Insight*, January 12, 1987, pp. 44, 45.

Starr, Larry M., and Steve Waymaster. "Coping with Medical Emergencies in the Workplace." *Personnel Administrator* 30, no. 10 (October 1985), pp. 21–36.

Thomas, Evan. "America's Crusade: What Is behind the Latest War on Drugs." *Time*, September 15, 1986, pp. 60–68.

"Treating the Reality of Drugs in the Workplace." *Risk Management*, May 1985, p. 74.

"Worker Drug Tests Spread Despite Deep Controversy." *Money* 14, no. 10 (October 1985), p. 13.

WHAT THIS INCIDENT IS ABOUT:
A number of issues such as introduction to change,
resistance to change, leadership, and adoption of
turnaround strategies are inherent in this incident.
The basic question is: How can painful and
necessary organizational changes be implemented
with maximum acceptance and minimum
disruption?

17

Implementing strategic change

INCIDENT

On October 15, 1987, James Fulmer, chief executive officer of Allied Industries, reviewed three notes he had exchanged with Frank Curtis, president of a company owned by Allied. The two men were going to meet in a few minutes to discuss problems that had recently surfaced. During the past decade, Allied had aggressively pursued a growth objective based on a conglomerate strategy of acquiring companies in distress. Chairman Fulmer's policy was to appoint a new chief operating officer for each acquisition with instructions to facilitate a turnaround. Mr. Fulmer reviewed two of the notes he wrote to Curtis.

DATE: January 15, 1986: Memorandum

TO: Frank Curtis, Director of Fiscal Affairs, Allied Industries

FROM: James Fulmer, Chairman, Allied Industries

SUBJECT: Your Appointment as President, Lee Medical Supplies

You are aware that Allied Industries recently acquired Lee Medical Supplies. Mr. John Lee, founder and president of the company, has agreed to retire, and in line with our earlier discussions, I am appointing you to replace him. Our acquisitions group will brief you on the company, but I want to warn you that Lee Medical Supplies has a history of mismanagement. As a distributor of medical items, the company's sales last year totaled approximately $300 million, with net earnings of only $12 million. Your job is to make company sales and profits compatible with Allied standards. You are reminded that it is my policy to call for an independent evaluation of company progress and your performance as president after 18 months.

DATE: September 10, 1987: Memorandum

TO: Frank Curtis, President, Lee Medical Supplies

FROM: James Fulmer, Chairman, Allied Industries

SUBJECT: Serious Problems at Lee Medical Supplies

In accord with corporate policy, consultants recently conducted an evaluation of Lee Medical Supplies. In a relatively short period of time, you have increased sales and profits to meet Allied's standards, but I am alarmed at other aspects of your performance, as revealed by the consultant's report. I am told that during the past 18 months, three of your nine vice presidents have resigned and that you have terminated four others. An opinion survey conducted by the consultants indicates that a low state of morale exists and that your managerial appointees are regarded by their subordinates as hard-nosed perfectionists obsessed with quotas and profits. Employees report that ruthless competition now exists between divisions, regions, and districts. They also note that the collegial, family-oriented atmosphere fostered by Mr. Lee has been replaced by a dog-eat-dog situation characterized by negative management attitudes toward employee feelings and needs. After you have studied the enclosed report from the consultants, we will meet to discuss their findings. I am particularly concerned with their final conclusion that "a form of corporate cancer seems to be spreading throughout Lee Medical Supplies."

As Chairman Fulmer prepared to read the third note, written by Frank Curtis, he reflected on his exit interview with the consultants. While Fulmer considered Curtis to be a financial expert and a turnaround specialist, his subordinates characterized Curtis as an autocrat, a hatchetman, and better suited to be a marine boot camp commander.

DATE: September 28, 1987: Memorandum

TO: Mr. James Fulmer

FROM: Mr. Frank Curtis

SUBJECT: The so-called "Serious Problems" at Lee Medical Supplies

I have received your memorandum dated September 10, 1987, and reviewed the consultant's report. When you appointed me to my present position, I was instructed to take over an unprofitable company and make it profitable. I have done so in 18 months, although I inherited a family-owned business that by your own admission had been mismanaged for years. I found a group of managers and salespeople with an average company tenure of 22 years. They believed their jobs were guaranteed for life. Mr. Lee had centralized all personnel decisions so that only he could terminate an employee. He tolerated mediocre performance. All employees were paid on a straight salary basis with seniority the sole criterion for advancement. Some emphasis was given to increasing sales each year, but none was given to reducing costs and increasing profits. Employees did indeed find the company a fun place to work, did express undying loyalty and love for Lee, and a feeling of being a part of a family did permeate the company. Such attitudes were, however, accompanied by mediocrity, incompetency, and poor performance.

I found it necessary to implement immediate strategic changes in five areas: the organization's structure, employee rewards and incentives, management information systems, allocation of resources, and managerial leadership style. As a result, sales areas were reorganized into divisions, regions, and districts. Managers that I felt were incompetent and/or lacking in commitment to my objectives and methods were replaced. Unproductive and mediocre employees were encouraged to find jobs elsewhere. Authority for staffing and compensation decisions was decentralized to units at the division, region, and district levels. Managers of those units were informed that along with their authority went responsibility for reducing costs, and increasing sales and profits. Each unit was established as a profit center. A new department was established and charged with reviewing performance of those units. Improved accounting and control systems were implemented. A management-by-objectives program was developed to establish standards and monitor performance. Performance appraisals are now required for all employees. To encourage more aggressive action, bonuses and incentives are offered to managers of units showing increased profits. A commission plan based on measurable sales and profit performances has replaced straight salaries. Resources are allocated to units based on their performance.

My own leadership style has probably represented the most traumatic change for employees. Internal competition is a formally mandated policy throughout the company. It has been responsible for much of the progress achieved to date. Progress, however, is never made without costs, and I recognize that employees are not having as much fun as in the past. I was employed to achieve results and not to ensure that employees remain secure and happy in their work. Don't let a few crybabies unable to adjust to changes lead you to believe that problems take precedence over profits. Does it mean that I am not people oriented if I believe it is unlikely that a spirit of aggressiveness and competitiveness can coexist with an atmosphere of cooperativeness and family orientation? Do you feel that we are obligated to employees because of past practices? Frankly, I thought I had your support to do whatever was necessary to get this company turned around. In our meeting, tell me if you think my approaches have been wrong, and if so, tell me what I should have done differently.

Just as Chairman Fulmer finished reviewing the third memorandum, his secretary informed him that Curtis had arrived for their scheduled meeting. He realized that he was undecided how to communicate to Curtis his ideas and beliefs regarding how changes in an organization can best be implemented. One thing he did know was that he didn't appreciate how Curtis expressed his views in his memorandum, but he recognized that he probably should set aside emotions and respond to the questions Curtis posed.

CRITIQUES

JOHN A. PEARCE II
Chairman of Management Department
George Mason University

The realistic situation depicted in this incident highlights three fundamental considerations in company management: (1) the sensitive—sometimes explosive—nature of organizational change, (2) the negative and positive effects of setting goals, and (3) the detrimental effects of excessive stress in the work environment.

Imagine the organizational culture and climate at Lee Medical Supplies in January 1986. Frank Curtis was responsible for creating a dramatically improved sales and profit profile. Lee executives were undoubtedly nervous and defensive about the company's poor past performance. All employees were probably concerned about the likelihood of dramatic changes in organizational roles, status, responsibilities, priorities, and even membership. The resulting high levels of uncertainty apparently led to substantial interpersonal conflict within the company. One idea to remember, therefore, is that people do not resist change. Rather, people resist the uncertainty associated with change. If Curtis's strategy was to get employees to produce more from less, and if he failed to create opportunities for the thoughtful expression of anxiety and concern, then employee resistance and alienation were predictable.

It is possible that Curtis overlooked the company's disruptive work environment because he was so focused on the assigned goal of increasing sales and profits.

Most employees really attempt to achieve what their superiors want. This is the key to understanding both the value and the curse of setting goals. In the absence of assigned goals, subordinates divide their energies to achieve what they guess will satisfy their supervisors' wishes and the company needs. Sometimes they guess correctly—we mistakenly call that high performance. Sometimes, though they work extremely hard, they guess somewhat incorrectly—we mistakenly call that average performance. Thus, to correct the problem of misdirected energies, managers need to independently or collaboratively specify and communicate goals to subordinates. When they do, however, these managers must be clear to their subordinates about the degree to which the stated goals are their only goals. Was Curtis to achieve "sales and profits compatible with Allied standards," at any cost? Or was it Fulmer's intention that Curtis recognize that goal as the top priority, while simultaneously achieving an improvement in employee satisfaction, morale, and organizational commitment?

Another undesirable consequence of the uncertainty associated with change, goal conflicts, and pressures to radically alter performance is stress. The negative physical and mental effects of stress are now so well recognized that a survey conducted by the publication *Working Woman* in June 1983 found that the factor most associated with job satisfaction was a "job without too much rush and stress." This finding was true for male and female blue-collar workers, managers, and professionals.

Consider the situation at Lee. Almost every fact provided suggests a stress-building pressure. Is it surprising that employees were fired, quit, became alienated, or behaved in uncharacteristic or inappropriate ways? While stress cannot and should not be eliminated, it should be controlled within tolerable nondysfunctional limits. Giving people achievable goals, understanding supervision, deserved rewards and recognitions, and reasons to believe in an improved future can all lead to substantial reductions in stress. Unfortunately, there is little indication that Curtis managed in a stress-reducing manner.

What should Fulmer do? First, he should recognize that he contributed greatly to the problem. His perhaps unjustifiably high expectations and single performance goal for Curtis are at the root of the problem. Second, he should share with Curtis the ideas expressed above. Third, he should work with Curtis to design a strategy that will enable Lee to sustain its high productivity gains while allowing for the elimination of negative behavioral consequences that developed during the 18-month transitional period.

A. J. STRICKLAND
Professor of Strategic Management
University of Alabama

The secret of effective management is consistency of purpose. The management of change is the most difficult task of all. When the objective changes, the style and strategy of management also must change. In this incident, the implementation of change is at issue.

James Fulmer, chairman of Allied Industries, was specific in his January 15 memo that Frank Curtis's task was "to increase company sales and profits compatible with Allied standards." In addition, Fulmer reminded Curtis that his performance as president would be reviewed in 18 months.

There appears to be good news and bad news. The good news is that Curtis accomplished exactly what he was asked to do in the time requested. The bad news is that Curtis took Fulmer's request too literally. The "real" request was to accomplish the objectives and keep employee morale positive at Lee Medical Supplies—a most difficult, yet typical, assignment for today's management.

In preparation for assuming leadership at Lee, Curtis should have considered the following:

1. Organization structure and management capability: What type of structure exists at Lee? Can the new strategy be implemented with this structure? Do the qualifications and experience of key managers complement managerial requirements for the chosen strategy?
2. Internal operations: Does Lee have the necessary resources to successfully implement its new strategy? To what extent are functional and operating strategies coordinated and compatible? Is the firm missing any distinctive competence?
3. Controls and performance appraisal: Are policies and control procedures adequate at Lee? Are there provisions to furnish managers with solid, pertinent, and timely information on the status of current operations? Have objectives and performance standards been made explicit, communicated, and agreed upon at each level in the management hierarchy? Is the reward structure conducive to accomplishing the new strategy and achieving the revised objectives?
4. Managerial leadership and effectiveness: Is top management's leadership style (Curtis and Fulmer) adequate for the Lee Medical Supplies situation? Do they have the right temperament and personality orientation to implement the strategy successfully?

Curtis would have been more successful had he requested a face-to-face meeting with Fulmer to discuss in detail the problems associated with implementing a turnaround strategy. Curtis should have first known his game plan for executing the changes he planned in detail; and second, Curtis should have predicted the Lee Medical Supplies management team's response to the new strategy and communicated the response to Fulmer before taking charge.

Fulmer, at the same time, should have expected that management morale at Lee would deteriorate with the new strategy. The fear of the unknown is enough to send management attitudes into wild gyrations. Fulmer, if concerned about morale and attitude, should have communicated his concerns up front.

OBSERVATIONS

Because management initiates change, it is responsible for implementing change successfully. Employees typically control the final success of any changes, and for that reason, employee support becomes a major goal during times of change. Any change is traumatic to employees, but perhaps never as much as when turnaround strategies are adopted and implemented. Such strategies are necessary when a business worth saving has fallen into disrepair and decline. The situation must be arrested and reversed as soon as possible, as is illustrated in this incident.

News reports have related similar difficulties that the Hyatt Corporation experienced in its takeover of bankrupt Braniff Airways, Inc. A major difficulty appears to have been that a serious schism developed between senior executives sent in from Hyatt to manage the new Braniff and managers remaining from the bankrupt predecessor. One insider was quoted as saying, "It's us versus them."

Both Professors Pearce and Strickland, who wrote critiques for this incident, have authored leading textbooks on the strategic management process. They contribute insightful comments on the issues reflected in this incident.

DISCUSSION ITEMS

1. Discuss the view expressed by Frank Curtis that it is unlikely that a spirit of aggressiveness and competitiveness can be introduced into an organization at the same time that an atmosphere of cooperation and family orientation is maintained.
2. What ideas and beliefs regarding how needed changes in an organization can best be implemented should Chairman Fulmer communicate to Curtis?
3. Design a strategy that will enable Lee Medical Supplies to sustain its high productivity gains while eliminating the negative behavioral consequences that developed during the 18-month transitional period.

SUGGESTED READINGS

BOOKS

Arnold, Hugh J., and Daniel C. Feldman. *Organizational Behavior*. New York: McGraw-Hill, 1986, chaps. 4, 7, 8, 10, 13, 17.

Callahan, Robert E.; C. Patrick Fleenor; and Harry Knudson. *Understanding Organizational Behavior*. Columbus, Ohio: Charles E. Merrill Publishing, 1986, chaps. 11–15.

Davis, Keith, and John W. Newstrom. *Human Behavior at Work*. 7th ed. New York: McGraw-Hill, 1985, chaps. 11, 13–15.

Donnelly, James H.; James L. Gibson; and John M. Ivancevich. *Fundamentals of*

Management. 6th ed. Plano, Tex.: Business Publications, 1987, chaps. 1–7, 10–12, 14, 23.

EDrucker, Peter F. *Innovation and Entrepreneurship.* New York: Harper & Row, 1985, pp. 1–277.

French, Wendell L. *The Personnel Management Process.* 6th ed. Boston: Houghton Mifflin, 1987, chaps. 6–8.

Griffin, Ricky W. *Management.* 2nd ed. Boston: Houghton Mifflin, 1987, chaps. 4–8, 13–15.

Heneman, Herbert G.; Donald P. Schwab; John A. Fossum; and Lee D. Dyer. *Personnel/Human Resource Management.* 3rd ed. Homewood, Ill.: Richard D. Irwin, 1986, chaps. 3–6, 13–15.

Kirkpatrick, D. L. *How to Manage Change Effectively.* San Francisco: Jossey-Bass, 1985, pp. 1–280.

Megginson, Leon C. *Personnel Management: A Human Resources Approach.* 5th ed. Homewood, Ill.: Richard D. Irwin, 1985, chaps. 10–12, 14, 16.

Odiorne, George S. *Strategic Management of Human Resources.* San Francisco: Jossey-Bass, 1984.

Pearce, John A., and Richard B. Robinson. *Formulation and Implementation of Competitive Strategy.* 3rd ed. Homewood, Ill.: Richard D. Irwin, 1986, chaps. 1–12.

Peters, Thomas J., and Robert H. Waterman. *In Search of Excellence: Lessons from America's Best-Run Companies.* New York: Harper & Row, 1982, pp. 1–325.

Rue, Leslie W., and Lloyd L. Byars. *Management: Theory and Application.* 4th ed. Homewood, Ill.: Richard D. Irwin, 1986, chaps. 5, 6, 8–11, 13–16, 19, 20.

Schermerhorn, John R. *Management for Productivity.* 2nd ed. New York: John Wiley & Sons, 1986, chaps. 5, 10–15, 17.

JOURNALS

Allen, M. P., and S. K. Panian. "Power, Performance, and Succession in the Large Corporation." *Administrative Science Quarterly* 27, no. 4 (December 1982), pp. 538–47.

Beer, M. "Performance Appraisal: Dilemmas and Possibilities." *Organizational Dynamics* 9, no. 3 (Winter 1981), pp. 24–36.

Calish, I. G., and Donald Gamache. "How to Overcome Resistance to Change." *Management Review* 6, no. 4 (October 1981), pp. 22–23.

Fisher, C. D. "On the Dubious Wisdom of Expecting Job Satisfaction to Correlate with Performance." *Academy of Management Review* 5, no. 4 (October 1980), pp. 607–12.

Hofer, C. W. "Turnaround Strategies." *The Journal of Business Strategy,* Summer 1980, pp. 19–31.

Latack, J. C., and J. B. Dozier. "After the Ax Falls: Job Loss as a Career Transition." *Academy of Management Review* 11, no. 2 (April 1986), pp. 375–92.

MacMillan, I. C., and Randall Schuler. "Gaining a Competitive Edge Through Human Resources." *Personnel* 62, no. 4 (April 1985), pp. 24–29.

Magnet, Myron. "Help! My Company Has Just Been Taken Over." *Fortune* 110, no. 1 (July 9, 1984), pp. 44–51.

————. "How Top Managers Make a Company's Toughest Decision." *Fortune* 111, no. 6 (March 18, 1985), pp. 52–57.

Midas, M. T., and W. B. Werther. "Productivity: The Missing Link in Corporate Strategy." *Management Review* 74, no. 3 (March 1985), pp. 44–47.

Moravec, M. "Performance Appraisal: A Human Resource Management System with Productivity Payoffs." *Management Review* 70, no. 3 (June 1981), pp. 51–54.

Muczyk, J. P., and R. E. Hastings. "In Defense of Enlightened Hardball Management." *Business Horizons* 28, no. 4 (July-August 1985), pp. 23–29.

Peters, Tom, and Nancy Austin. "A Passion for Excellence." *Fortune* 111, no. 10 (May 13, 1985), pp. 20–32.

Pringle, C. D., and J. G. Longnecker. "The Ethics of MBO." *Academy of Management Review* 7, no. 2 (April 1982), pp. 305–12.

Robino, David, and Kenneth DeMeuse. "Corporate Mergers and Acquisitions: Their Impact on HRM." *Personnel Administrator* 30, no. 11 (November 1985), pp. 33–44.

Staw, Barry. "Organizational Psychology and the Pursuit of the Happy/Productive Worker." *California Management Review* 28, no. 4 (Summer 1986), pp. 40–53.

WHAT THIS INCIDENT IS ABOUT:
Employees turn to union representation when
informal communication of their concerns is not only
ineffective, but is punished. The incident involves
leadership style in handling grievances, listening
and communication skills, problem recognition, and
policy implementation.

18

Indigenous leader

INCIDENT

At 4:45 P.M. on Friday, Mike Henry, an employee in the accounting
department, walked to the office of Herschel Jones, department head, and
asked to see him privately. Henry told Jones that he had been elected by
the other 75 accounting department employees to speak on their behalf
about company practices that they wished to have modified or eliminated.
One practice concerned the merit rating system, which the employees
thought was unfair, poorly used, and utilized as a reason for not paying
higher salaries. A second practice that was poorly accepted by the employees was the arbitrary way in which management determined employee
vacation time. Henry said one employee told him that last year she was
given two days' notice before she received her first week of vacation in
October and five days' notice before a second week of vacation in April.

Jones listened attentively and told Henry that since it was so late in the
day, he would consider these requests again early the next week. During
the next week, Henry noticed that Jones was out of town, and no action
was taken concerning his remarks. However, his fellow employees treated
him like a hero for representing them in front of Jones.

Upon receiving his paycheck on Friday afternoon, Henry was shocked
to find his discharge notice and two weeks of additional pay in his enve-
lope. Accounting department employees were shaken and dismayed. They
were convinced that drastic collective action was needed.

During the following week, Jones noticed an unusually high interaction
level among members of the department. On Thursday, he called into his
office two of the senior employees and told them he wanted to know what
was going on. They reluctantly reported that more than 70 percent of the

employees had signed "Authorization Cards" calling for a labor election to be held in order to unionize.

"Well, what do they hope to accomplish?" Jones exploded. The answer was short but not sweet: (1) to reinstate Henry, (2) to establish a formal grievance procedure, and (3) to change the unfair and arbitrary implementation of the merit rating policy and the vacation policy. Jones now saw the problems more clearly, but solutions remained elusive. He felt the clear and present danger of impending unionization as he searched for practical decisions, policy, and action that would adequately respond to employee grievances over personnel practices and satisfy organization requirements at the same time.

CRITIQUES

LAWRENCE L. SCHKADE
Professor of Information Systems and
Management Sciences
University of Texas at Arlington

The difficulty in this incident lies in the perceived insensitivity, lack of good faith, and poor judgment by management. As a consequence, an informal organization, which initially emerged to communicate employee displeasure with existing policies and practices, is in the early stages of changing into a formalized union organization.

Employees want a sense of security by knowing what to expect from management. Even consistent enforcement of stringent policies is generally more acceptable than the arbitrary application of lenient policies. Furthermore, there has been no apparent attempt to inform employees of the reasons for management decisions or to involve them in these decisions. Perhaps the clearest evidence that management can give of its desire to treat employees fairly lies in administering a sound wage structure. In this case, a merit rating system may have been instituted in good faith, but its application, coupled with other circumstances, has led employees to suspect management motives. Negative employee reaction can result in poor morale, reduced productivity, higher turnover, and increased costs.

The method for selecting vacation periods in this case reflects extremely poor planning by management and has precluded any real opportunity for the employee to plan a vacation—further evidence that management did not view employee feelings and desires as important.

Jones's actions are the exact opposite of good personnel administration. Although Jones listened to Henry as he presented the employees' complaints, there was no real communication or discussion. To the contrary,

Jones apparently saw the employee views as rebellious and insubordinate. The summary dismissal of Henry, the employee champion, was apparently a rejection of employee "impertinence" and intended to intimidate the group into continued submission.

The substantial vote in favor of a labor election suggests that unionization is likely unless management quickly adopts a new philosophy toward labor relations and effectively communicates the new policy to employees. It must be recognized that employees have personal desires and rights. Henry should be reinstated and his leadership abilities used in creating a positive relationship with the employees. A grievance procedure should be established to settle complaints and keep management apprised of employee feelings. Existing policies and practices should be reviewed, utilizing employee views and suggestions where appropriate. Employees should be kept informed about the decisions that affect them. Finally, management should make every attempt to deal fairly with employees to achieve and maintain honest, positive motivation. If management does not take these actions voluntarily, management will probably have to deal with an organized labor union. The resolution of the resulting conflict is likely to cause significantly reduced management prerogatives and a change in the atmosphere and balance of power between management and the employees.

It could be that the principal problem is Jones. It is possible that the simplest solution to this growing problem is replacing Jones with someone who has an enlightened management philosophy. If higher management is not aware of Jones's actions and the resulting desire for employees to organize for their own protection, management-employee conflict may be inevitable.

RALPH N. TRAXLER, JR.
Professor of Management
Savannah State College

Every organization has the right to set reasonable policies for evaluating personnel. Establishing vacation policies is also the prerogative of management. But the company that Mike Henry worked for had failed to do two things concerning these two matters that are basic in building a good relationship with employees. First, the evaluation and vacation policies had not been completely clear to the employees. Second, the employees did not seem to have anyone to go to when they had questions or complaints about these subjects. Anyone in the group represented by Henry should have felt free to talk with Jones before reaching the stage where an employee representative had to be "elected."

At the very least, Jones should have explained the reasons for these policies to Henry. There was no logical reason for Jones to refuse to discuss these issues. Evidently Jones was not sure why the policies existed or what the attitude of higher management would be toward either changing the policies or explaining them in more detail to employees. Since Jones probably knew he would be away the next week, he should have made a decision or explained to Henry why he would have to delay action.

Henry became a hero because he had the courage to talk to Jones. The fact that he became a "hero" indicates a poor relationship between employees and employer that was probably long-standing. This might also mean that other issues would develop into major problems as the employee group sought to gain its "rights" by sending representation to the boss. If there was no union in this organization, management was certainly building a wonderful foundation for an aggressive union organizer to start agitation.

Under these conditions, Henry's discharge was completely unjustified. At the very least, Jones should have faced Henry with some reason for his discharge. Jones seemed to believe that the easiest solution to this complaint was to dispose of the problem's source by discharging Henry. Now Henry was more than a hero; he was a martyr. The problem still existed, and the employees would undoubtedly take much more aggressive action to gain their rights in the future.

All policies must be made clear to all employees in writing. Management should make sure employees understand the policies. Finally, policies must be reviewed and updated on a regular basis and policy changes must be explained to all employees.

OBSERVATIONS

Because formal grievance procedures are found universally in union-management labor contracts, the usefulness of management voluntarily establishing *formal* grievance procedures in nonunion work settings often tends to be overlooked. Another reason for the absence of grievance procedures is that management may prefer to retain authority for dealing with employee requests and complaints. Such preferences, coupled with the lack of response to complaints seen as legitimate by subordinates, can lead to the type of dead end faced by Herschel Jones. His options are few, and all have disadvantages that dim his future as department head and any reputation he may have as a leader.

Other modern management techniques Jones could have used are employee participation, quality circles, and interactive communications. How would one rate Jones's leadership skills, his interpersonal skills, and his understanding of the "quality of work life" concepts? Professors Schkade and Traxler have critiqued this situation in realistic managerial terms, although their thoughtful guidance comes too late for Jones, but in time for the reader's attention and discussion.

DISCUSSION ITEMS

1. Recommend a plan for Mr. Jones; give its advantages and disadvantages; and state how it should be implemented.
2. If Henry is reinstated, as suggested by Professor Schkade, how can his leadership abilities be used in a positive manner?
3. Describe Jones's leadership style. Identify his serious leadership errors and discuss better leadership responses to the problems he faced.

SUGGESTED READINGS

Arnold, Hugh J., and Daniel C. Feldman. *Organizational Behavior*. New York: McGraw-Hill, 1986, chaps. 6, 8, 13, 14.

Callahan, Robert E.; C. Patrick Fleenor; and Harry Knudson. *Understanding Organizational Behavior*. Columbus, Ohio: Charles E. Merrill Publishing, 1986, chap. 6.

Davis, Keith, and John W. Newstrom. *Human Behavior at Work*. 7th ed. New York: McGraw-Hill, 1985, chaps. 10, 14.

Donnelly, James H.; James L. Gibson; and John M. Ivancevich. *Fundamentals of Management*. 6th ed. Plano, Tex.: Business Publications, 1987, chap. 12, pp. 347, 361–64.

French, Wendell L. *The Personnel Management Process*. 6th ed. Boston: Houghton Mifflin, 1987, chap. 27.

Griffin, Ricky W. *Management*. 2nd ed. Boston: Houghton Mifflin, 1987, chap. 15, pp. 670–75.

Heneman, Herbert G.; Donald P. Schwab; John A. Fossum; and Lee D. Dyer. *Personnel/Human Resource Management*. 3rd ed. Homewood, Ill.: Richard D. Irwin, 1986, chaps. 4, 6, 16.

Megginson, Leon C. *Personnel Management: A Human Resources Approach*. 5th ed. Homewood, Ill.: Richard D. Irwin, 1985, chap. 11.

Rue, Leslie W., and Lloyd L. Byars. *Management: Theory and Application*. 4th ed. Homewood, Ill.: Richard D. Irwin, 1986, chap. 15.

Schermerhorn, John R. *Management for Productivity*. 2nd ed. New York: John Wiley & Sons, 1986, chap. 13.

JOURNALS

Berke, Elaine I. "Keeping Newly Trained Supervisors from Going Back to Their Old Ways." *Management Review* 73, no. 2 (February 1984), pp. 14–16.

Bittel, Lester R., and Jack E. Ramsey. "The Limited Traditional World of Supervisors." *Harvard Business Review* 60, no. 4 (July-August 1982), pp. 26, 28, 30, 31, 36.

_____. "Misfit Supervisors—Bad Apples in the Managerial Barrel." *Management Review* 72, no. 2 (February 1983), pp. 8–13.

Boyle, Richard J. "Wrestling with Jellyfish." *Harvard Business Review* 62, no. 1 (January-February 1984), pp. 74–83.

Gelb, Betsy. "When and How to Use Outplacement." *Business Horizons* 29, no. 5 (September-October 1986), pp. 55–59.

Gould, Richard. "Are You Firing Talented Managers?" *Management Review* 76, no. 3 (March 1987), pp. 49–51.

Guest, Robert H. "Management Imperatives for the Year 2000." *California Management Review* 28, no. 4 (Summer 1986), pp. 62–70.

Harrison, J. Richard, and James G. Marsh. "Decision Making and Post-Decision Surprise." *Administrative Science Quarterly* 29, no. 1 (March 1984), pp. 26–42.

Hershey, Paul, and Kenneth H. Blanchard. "Leadership Styles: Attitudes and Behaviors." *Training and Development Journal* 36, no. 5 (May 1982), pp. 50–54.

Joiner, Charles W., Jr. "One Manager's Story of How He Made the Z Concept Work." *Management Review* 72, no. 5 (May 1983), pp. 48–53.

Kilgour, John C. "Union Organizing Activity among White-Collar Employees." *Personnel* 60, no. 2 (March-April 1983), pp. 18–27.

Payson, Martin F. "Audit Your Policies and Procedures before the Union Does." *Personnel Journal* 63, no. 1 (January 1984), pp. 48–53.

Powell, Jon T. "Listen Attentively to Solve Problems." *Personnel Journal* 62, no. 7 (July 1983), pp. 580, 582.

Spencer, Daniel G. "Employee Voice and Employee Retention." *Academy of Management Journal* 29, no. 3 (September 1986), pp. 488–502.

Tidwell, Gary L. "The Supervisor's Role in a Union Election." *Personnel Journal* 62, no. 8 (August 1983), pp. 640–45.

Vecchio, Robert. "Are You *In* or *Out* with Your Boss?" *Business Horizons* 29, no. 6 (November-December 1986), pp. 76–78.

WHAT THIS INCIDENT IS ABOUT:
The major issue is whether psychological tests,
especially the polygraph test, represent an intrusion
on the privacy of individuals required to take
them. The importance of effective communication
in gaining acceptance for such tests can also be
explored.

19

Invasion of privacy

INCIDENT

The following notice was posted on the bulletin board for the 20 employees of the Atkins Finance Agency:

> This company recently retained the services of Consultants, Inc., and they have recommended that we include the polygraph test in our selection program. Since this test will be a part of our employment program, we are also requiring all employees to take the test. You will be told the time and date of the test. Your usual cooperation will be appreciated.

Three days later, the following statement appeared, signed by 15 employees:

> We, the undersigned, do at this time serve notice to the president of Atkins Finance Agency that we consider the requirement that we take the polygraph test an invasion of our privacy, and therefore refuse to comply with the requirement.

The president immediately met with representatives of Consultants, Inc., to formulate a policy that would clearly state conditions under which the polygraph test would be required and to decide how such a policy could best be implemented in view of the extremely negative employee reaction.

CRITIQUES

ROBERT M. GUION
Professor of Psychology
Bowling Green State University

Both the author of the notice and his consultant betray their ignorance of sound personnel research as well as their lack of concern for people's feelings. The tone of the notice is almost military in its terseness; people employed in reasonably responsible positions are not likely to respond favorably to any such notice. The fact that a polygraph test is popularly known as a "lie detector" and that it was not so identified in the notice both add to the emotionality with which such an announcement would be greeted. One can only speculate; speculation, however, suggests a three-day period filled with much gossip, fear, emotion, and little work! My sympathies are entirely with the employees!

Psychological testing has been effective primarily where the tests measure aptitude or specific ability. Personality tests are seldom useful except for sales and some managerial jobs. The polygraph detects, instead of lies, an emotionality in response; it is properly classified in broad terms with personality measures. The prospects for its validity in this situation are dim.

In addition, personality testing offers another serious problem for the competent personnel research person: the lack of correspondence between "concurrent" and "predictive" validity. In a selection program, a person is hired because of an at least implicit prediction that he or she will do well on the job. A selection test is, therefore, valid in that test scores are correlated with some measure of on-the-job behavior. "Predictive" validity is determined by testing applicants and then waiting until they've held the job long enough to be evaluated. "Concurrent" validity is computed by using people whose job performance is already known. This incident is an example of attempted concurrent validity and clearly shows one of the dangers. Employees will not have the same motivation as applicants—a fact that can seriously distort personality test scores. When this happens, there is no way to use the concurrent validities as estimates of the *predictive* value of the test.

In short, the practice illustrated here can be condemned on purely technical grounds; it is a poor testing technique. The ethical aspects of the case also deserve some attention, but they are probably more obvious since they have been well-publicized in television news features. I would suggest as a generalization that personality probes may be ethically justified only in situations where it can be demonstrated that the information obtained helps the employer make more accurate predictions about an applicant's future work-related behavior. From this generalization, it follows that technically incompetent testing is unethical.

It is good, however, that the president is aware of the "negative employee reaction" and wants to formulate a policy. I would suspect, however, that the policy would need to be a much broader one than polygraph testing, and that the representatives of Consultants, Inc., may not be the ideal people to help develop a broad policy of personnel testing. The president would do well to seek information from a broader set of sources.

PHYLLIS G. HOLLAND
Associate Professor of Management
Valdosta State College

It is not unusual for employees to feel threatened by a new procedure, policy, or approach introduced by management. Nor is it unusual for employees' anxiety to produce a negative reaction. In this incident, management and consultants have displayed an unusual insensitivity to this phenomenon and have created a win-lose confrontation.

The use of polygraphs in selection has been and will probably continue to be the subject of debate and litigation. Generally, use of a polygraph must be announced and voluntary. The reliability of polygraph testing is in question because of the inaccuracy of the procedure and the ability of a practiced person to "fool" the machine. The validity of the test is also questionable. In selection, such a test may be used as a substitute for the verification of background. With current employees, it would seem that performance on the job would be of more interest than verifying experience, education, etc. It is not at all clear how this test would improve performance of current employees or how results from the administration of tests to current employees would aid in the selection of new employees.

Aside from questions about the choice of selection tools, this incident raises issues that relate to the introduction of any change in an organization. The company is a small one with ample opportunity for face-to-face contact, yet the announcement is posted on a bulletin board with no preparation or warning. Presented with an entrenched position, the employees respond by establishing a similar position. It will be difficult for either side to retreat without loss of face. One approach would have been to make the announcement in a meeting. This would have given employees an opportunity to react and management or the consultants could have responded to reactions. The reasons for this decision might have been so compelling that the employees would agree when they had been explained. On the other hand, a meeting would have given management a reading on employee reaction which might have required them to reevaluate the decision and its implementation.

An even better approach would have been to involve employees in the problem solving that led to the decision to use the polygraph. A better alternative for solving the problem might have surfaced. If not, at least those who participated would have an understanding of why the decision was made and might be able to share that understanding with other employees.

As in many management incidents, it is easy to see what should have been done. That knowledge is useful to avoid future mistakes, but it does not help repair current damage. The management of Atkins Finance Agency faces a situation in which three fourths of their employees have gone on record in public that they do not intend to comply with an organizational policy. Management, with Consultants, Inc., now has the task of clarifying and expanding the original announcement to end this impasse. It is possible to dismiss employees for noncompliance, of course, but that does not appear to be a desirable course of action.

It does not seem to be too late to involve employees in the process. To be useful, however, this involvement should be based on a sincere effort to get useful input, not on an attempt to manipulate. To achieve this, management will have to do a certain amount of backtracking. They must admit that the reaction is unexpected and that they are alarmed by it, and they should emphasize that they respect their employees' right to privacy. This situation must be converted from a win-lose to a win-win situation if possible. This will best be done by focusing on the problem that needs to be solved. They must be able to articulate the benefits that they expect to gain from this policy and demonstrate how this outweighs the employees' rights. My guess would be that a debate over these issues may make management realize that there may be other alternatives to solve whatever problem they are addressing with the polygraph.

In a small office where everyone knows everyone else well and interacts with them constantly, the realization by employees that management doesn't trust them could be highly disruptive. This lack of trust may become a self-fulfilling prophecy. The dangers seem to far outweigh any potential benefits. If specific employees are under suspicion, actions should be directed toward them if at all possible. Only if all employees are under suspicion and if in fact management doesn't trust any of them does this policy seem useful.

OBSERVATIONS

An article has appeared in many newspapers written by an Associated Press writer indicating that employers seeking the truth from workers and job applicants are wiring an increasing number of people to polygraphs, prompting a surge of lawsuits that one lawyer says threatens to become a tidal wave. The American Civil Liberties Union estimates the number of employment-related polygraph tests has increased to more than one million a year and the number of practicing polygraphers has more than doubled. The American Polygraph Association estimates there are more than 4,000 examiners in the United States. A large Florida-based drug firm requires its employees to take a polygraph test once every 18 months, except in states where such tests are prohibited by law. The company has its own polygraph units and examiners, who gave over 40,000 tests last year. Employees can be dismissed for refusing to take the test.

Statutes in many states restrict the use of polygraphs for job applicants or employees, although law enforcement and government agencies are often exempted. Over one fourth of the states have some kind of licensing laws for examiners. Adherents of the polygraph contend that in the hands of a trained examiner, the test is a reliable method of verifying résumé or job application information, keeping employees honest, and getting rid of employees who are not. Critics say the tests are intrusive and unreliable, they detect neither truth nor lies, and they insult the people taking them. They consider the polygraph test, as did the Atkins Finance Agency employees, an invasion of privacy.

DISCUSSION ITEMS

1. The polygraph test is thought to be morally indefensible by many persons. Do you agree or disagree? Why?
2. Professor Guion commends the president of Atkins Finance Agency for wanting to formulate a policy governing usage of the polygraph test. Develop a policy that would conform to Guion's suggestions.
3. How could the Atkins Finance Agency management have gained acceptance for their decision to require employees to take the polygraph test?

SUGGESTED READINGS

BOOKS

Arnold, Hugh J., and Daniel C. Feldman. *Organizational Behavior*. New York: McGraw-Hill, 1986, chap. 15.

Callahan, Robert E.; C. Patrick Fleenor; and Harry Knudson. *Understanding Organizational Behavior*. Columbus, Ohio: Charles E. Merrill Publishing, 1986, chap. 2.

Davis, Keith, and John W. Newstrom. *Human Behavior at Work*. 7th ed. New York: McGraw-Hill, 1985, chap. 16.

Donnelly, James H.; James L. Gibson; and John M. Ivancevich. *Fundamentals of Management*. 6th ed. Plano, Tex.: Business Publications, 1987, chap. 9.

French, Wendell L. *The Personnel Management Process*. 6th ed. Boston: Houghton Mifflin, 1987, chap. 12.

Griffin, Ricky W. *Management*. 2nd ed. Boston: Houghton Mifflin, 1987, chaps. 1, 15–19.

Heneman, Herbert G.; Donald P. Schwab; John A. Fossum; and Lee D. Dyer. *Personnel/Human Resource Management*. 3rd ed. Homewood, Ill.: Richard D. Irwin, 1986, chaps. 9, 10.

McCoy, Charles S. *Management of Values*. Hagerstown, Md.: Ballinger Publishing Co., 1985, chaps. 1–5.

Megginson, Leon C. *Personnel Management: A Human Resources Approach*. 5th ed. Homewood, Ill.: Richard D. Irwin, 1985, chaps. 7, 12, 20.

Miner, John B. *People Problems: The Executive Answer Book*. New York: Random House, 1985, pp. 1–320.

Rue, Leslie W., and Lloyd L. Byars. *Management: Theory and Application*. 4th ed. Homewood, Ill.: Richard D. Irwin, 1986, chaps. 3, 10, 15, 20.

Rue, Leslie, and Phyllis G. Holland. *Strategic Management: Concepts and Experiences*. New York: McGraw-Hill, 1986.

Schermerhorn, John R. *Management for Productivity*. 2nd ed. New York: John Wiley & Sons, 1986, chap. 9.

JOURNALS

Barland, G. H. "The Case for the Polygraph in Employment Screening." *Personnel Administrator* 30, no. 9 (September 1985), pp. 58–65.

Belt, John. "The Polygraph: A Questionable Personnel Tool." *Personnel Administrator* 28, no. 8 (August 1983), pp. 65–76.

Brenkert, G. G. "Privacy, Polygraphs, and Work." *Business and Professional Ethics Journal* 1, no. 1 (Fall 1981), pp. 19–35.

Caffarella, Rosemary S. "Managing Conflict: An Analytical Tool." *Training and Development Journal* 38, no. 2 (February 1984), pp. 34–38.

Erez, Miriam; P. C. Earley; and C. L. Hulin. "The Impact of Participation on Goal Acceptance and Performance." *Academy of Management Journal* 28, no. 1 (March 1985), pp. 50–66.

Ewing, David W. "How to Negotiate with Employer Objectors." *Harvard Business Review* 61, no. 1 (January-February 1983), pp. 103–10.

Gladstein, D. L., and N. P. Reilly. "Group Decision Making under Threat." *Academy of Management Journal* 28, no. 3 (September 1985), pp. 613–27.

Goddard, R. W. "How to Avoid Employee Complaints that Could Lead to Litigation." *Management Review* 73, no. 2 (February 1984), pp. 58–61.

Greenhalgh, Leonard. "Managing Conflict." *Sloan Management Review* 27, no. 4 (Summer 1986), pp. 45–51.

Harris, Donald. "A Matter of Privacy." *Personnel* 64, no. 2 (February 1987), pp. 34–43.

Hartsfield, W. E. "Polygraphs." *Labor Law Journal* 36, no. 11 (November 1985), pp. 817–33.

Ivancevich, J. M., and M. T. Matteson. "See You in Court: Employee Claims for Damages Add to the High Cost of Job Stress." *Management Review* 72, no. 11 (November 1983), pp. 9–13.

Kleinmuntz, Benjamin. "Lie Detectors Fail the Truth Test." *Harvard Business Review* 63, no. 4 (July-August 1985), pp. 36–43.

Lawsche, C. H. "A Simplified Approach to the Evaluation of Fairness in Employee Selection Procedures." *Personnel Psychology* 36, no. 3 (Autumn 1983), pp. 601–8.

Schein, Edgar H. "Coming to a New Awareness of Organizational Culture." *Sloan Management Review* 25, no. 2 (Winter 1984), pp. 3–15.

Yoder, Dale, and Paul Staudohar. "Testing and the EEO: Getting Down to Cases." *Personnel Administrator* 29, no. 2 (February 1984), pp. 67–74.

WHAT THIS INCIDENT IS ABOUT:
Secretive moonlighting leads to abrupt dismissal for
enterprising high-technology employees ready to
branch out but reluctant to abandon their job
security. The incident prompts company officials to
consider appropriate policies and objectives, ethics,
personal value structures, and responses to
provocation.

20

Moonlighting policy

INCIDENT

Five key employees of General Electronic's Silicon Valley plant, which
employs about 1,300 persons producing and assembling printed circuit
boards for computers and military equipment, were released in late January after company officials discovered they were starting their own business. A spokesman said the company learned of the group's activities on
Tuesday and terminated them on Thursday.

"Company policy does not allow employees to be involved in business
that could be in conflict or competition with General Electronic," said
Mark Stone, manager of central operations and acting vice president for
operations. He added that many of General Electronic's employees have
part-time jobs on the side, "but these five people did not ask us or do this
in the open. They chartered their company more than three months ago
under the name of Advanced Board Circuitries, Inc., with Dale Garfield
as president and the other four persons as officers or founders of the
company."

Upon being interviewed, Garfield, a six-year employee who was unit
manager of engineering and production of printed circuit boards at General
Electronic, said "self-preservation" kept the five employees from revealing their plans to General Electronic while they worked weekends and
evenings on the building that houses their embryonic company and while
installing equipment. He said it was the challenge as much as anything that
provided the drive to start their own company. "We have no animosity
toward General Electronic whatsoever. Every company has the prerogative
to set its own policies. We have no ax to grind," he stated emphatically.

Garfield said his group even hoped to have a working relationship with General Electronic, possibly supplying circuit boards to the plant's assembly lines. If this occurred, the new company would be more of a supplier than a competitor to General Electronic, he believed.

Stone was careful to point out that "there is nothing illegal here as far as we know and, as far as we can determine, no business was taken from General Electronic." He had never indicated any dissatisfaction with the on-the-job performance of any of the five former employees. "It is," added Stone, "an unpleasant situation. As a result, our president has given me two assignments. First, I am to review the circumstances surrounding the release of those former employees and decide either to rehire them or to confirm their release. Second, I am to review our employee 'moonlighting' policy and submit policy recommendations to the president along with procedures for implementation. The president has insisted that my decision and recommendations must be supportable, legally defensible, and ethically acceptable."

CRITIQUES

BERNARD J. BIENVENU
Professor Emeritus of Management and
Administrative Studies
University of Southwestern Louisiana

The wisdom of dismissing five key employees of General Electronic's Silicon Valley plant can be seriously questioned and could be symptomatic of a basic management philosophy that leaves much room for disagreement. It does not appear that the decision and its implications were well planned. In fact, the dismissal on Thursday after finding out about the "moonlighting" on Tuesday indicates rather hasty action. This kind of action is usually more emotional than logical and more likely to be damaging than beneficial to the organization. The action also raises the question of an organization's right to determine employee conduct on a 24-hour-a-day basis. Employees of any organization would resent this intrusion into their private lives.

The fired worker who stated that "self-preservation" kept them from revealing their plans to the company indicates a lack of trust in General Electronic by the employees and that they do not feel they can be honest with the management. This is bound to thwart the upward communication so vital to effective management. It also deprives the workers of concern for and a feeling of being part of the company, which are two essentials for good morale and productivity. The issues in this situation involve much more than fired employees. They strongly suggest that the management practices, such as the way workers are treated, are not in the best interests of any business. In other words, this incident is not simply a question of who was right or wrong and whether or not management was justified in its action.

Even from the short-term viewpoint and the decision itself, one can seriously question what the company hoped to gain by terminating five employees. They were viewed as key workers who saw themselves as contributing significantly to the Silicon Valley plant, and it would seem that the longer they remained on the payroll, the more the company would benefit. Also, these workers appear to have ambition, drive, and imagination, attributes that they would undoubtedly—although perhaps unconsciously—continue to contribute to their jobs as long as they remained with General Electronic. The company admits that nothing illegal was done by the employees and that they did not steal any General Electronic business. Their firm, Advanced Board Circuitries, Inc., even hoped to do business with General Electronic's Silicon Valley plant. It appears that the only reason for their dismissal was that "these five people did not ask us or do this in the open," particularly in view of Stone's admission that many General Electronic workers had part-time jobs on the side. There is little doubt that other company employees will be adversely affected in their attitude toward the company and their work and will strive to keep their outside activities secret from General Electronic. The incident ends with a hint that legal action against General Electronic may be forthcoming, and one can imagine that the company already regrets its decision. Strange, indeed, how an established free enterprise looks upon employees who give birth to another free enterprise.

The fact that General Electronic is reviewing the firings is symptomatic of decision making without an established framework for arriving at decisions. Whether or not the employees should be rehired is not the fundamental issue. General Electronic must develop basic policies to serve as guidelines for future deliberation and action on such matters. In fact, a review of the overall decision-making process is advisable; for this experience indicates that there could be problems in other areas of behavior and operations. Policy questions needing discussion are:

1. How should employee performance be judged? Are outside activities relevant in the evaluation process? If so, is General Electronic opening up a "can of worms"?
2. Does the company have the ethical and legal right to consider factors other than behavior and contribution at work?
3. Who has authority to fire when such action is based on factors other than productivity and performance at work?
4. What about decisions in other areas? Are they often made with such haste and belated regret? If so, does this indicate a lack of policy formulation, or perhaps managerial incompetence?

5. What can be done to keep such unpleasant situations from recurring?

MAX B. JONES
Professor of Management
Old Dominion University

First, let us consider some general observations concerning moonlighting and company policies to curb it. Employers often are unaware of how much moonlighting occurs and make little or no effort to control it unless a problem develops. When problems develop, most firms probably would prefer to handle moonlighting on an individual case approach rather than committing themselves to an inflexible policy.

A concerted effort to track down and make an example of moonlighting practices can have some serious, unsought consequences. An unexpected moonlighting crackdown may create a general attitude of suspicion and mistrust among employees. It may also make employees feel that management is overextending its influence into employees' private lives and their freedom to use their leisure time as they see fit. For these reasons, many firms do not care to formally publicize their policy on moonlighting—if they have a policy at all. Where firms do have a policy prohibiting moonlighting, the tendency is to restrict such a policy to situations where moonlighting: (1) adversely affects work performance or (2) involves a conflict of interest.

In this case, the management of General Electronic had discharged five employees who started their own business. Discharge is a severe penalty. The firm's management leaves itself open to a serious charge of being arbitrary and capricious when it takes such actions—unless its moonlighting policy is stated and has been communicated to the employees involved. Can management establish that its moonlighting policy was effectively communicated? If not, it could expect some difficulty, particularly if the five employees were represented by an organized employee association.

Apparently the five employees are not challenging the discharge, if Garfield's statements of "no animosity" and "no ax to grind" can be taken literally. It is Stone who sees the matter as "an unpleasant situation." Furthermore, there is no indication that these employees have, to date, damaged the firm or not performed as expected. For these reasons, management would do well to ask the following questions and possibly reconsider their position on moonlighting:

1. Can General Electronic afford to lose five employees with the ability and initiative to set up Advanced Board Circuitries, Inc.?
2. Garfield stated that it was the "challenge" as much as anything that led the five to start their own business. Why did General Electronic provide insufficient challenges to absorb their employees' energies?

3. Why did the five employees not find sufficient incentive to develop their ideas within the structure at General Electronic?

OBSERVATIONS

Companies are particularly challenged to find ways of satisfying employees' entrepreneurial needs within the scope of company operations. Still, an overly restrictive moonlighting policy will likely be counterproductive for the firm and may cause the loss of human resources (entrepreneurial capabilities) required for successfully operating in a highly competitive environment.

Is it reasonable to expect that one job will satisfy the economic and professional needs of individual employees? Some management theorists think not, and they explain that management should not be expected to provide jobs that satisfy the full range of human needs. These theorists suggest that employees rely on off-the-job pursuits to supply satisfactions that are missing from the primary job's activities and reward structure.

Moonlighting policy ideally seeks a balance between employee rights in using their time away from work as they wish and the necessity for the company to protect its interests. Therefore, the following policies could be considered for adoption and implementation: (1) the employee who has an outside job is expected to inform the company; (2) outside jobs must not interfere with the "regular" job; (3) the company reserves the right to review any jobs held by employees outside of working hours; and (4) the company reserves the right to insist upon the termination of outside activities that endanger company interests. The implications of these policies for both the employee and the company must be examined.

DISCUSSION ITEMS

1. Do you agree or disagree with Dale Garfield's statement that every company has the prerogative to manage as it sees fit? Explain.
2. Do employees generally have the right to engage in moonlighting? What constraints should reasonably be placed on this right, if it exists?
3. How would you respond to the three questions that Professor Jones indicates management should ask itself?

SUGGESTED READINGS

BOOKS

Arnold, Hugh J., and Daniel C. Feldman. *Organizational Behavior*. New York: McGraw-Hill, 1986, chaps. 4, 19.

Callahan, Robert E.; C. Patrick Fleenor; and Harry Knudson. *Understanding Organizational Behavior*. Columbus, Ohio: Charles E. Merrill Publishing, 1986, chap. 11.

Davis, Keith, and John W. Newstrom. *Human Behavior at Work*. 7th ed. New York: McGraw-Hill, 1985, chaps. 5, 13.

Donnelly, James H.; James L. Gibson; and John M. Ivancevich. *Fundamentals of Management*. 6th ed. Plano, Tex.: Business Publications, 1987, chap. 22.

Drucker, Peter F. *Innovation and Entrepreneurship*. New York: Harper & Row, 1985.

French, Wendell L. *The Personnel Management Process*. 6th ed. Boston: Houghton Mifflin, 1987, chaps. 6, 19.

Griffin, Ricky W. *Management*. 2nd ed. Boston: Houghton Mifflin, 1987, chap. 22, pp. 570–72.

Heneman, Herbert G.; Donald P. Schwab; John A. Fossum; and Lee D. Dyer. *Personnel/Human Resource Management*. 3rd ed. Homewood, Ill.: Richard D. Irwin, 1986, chaps. 11, 12, 14.

Megginson, Leon C. *Personnel Management: A Human Resources Approach*. 5th ed. Homewood, Ill.: Richard D. Irwin, 1985, chaps. 8, 9.

Rue, Leslie W., and Lloyd L. Byars. *Management: Theory and Application*. 4th ed. Homewood, Ill.: Richard D. Irwin, 1986, chap. 19.

Schermerhorn, John R. *Management for Productivity*. 2nd ed. New York: John Wiley & Sons, 1986, chap. 8.

JOURNALS

Baron, James N.; Alison Davis Blake; and William T. Bielby. "The Structure of Opportunity: How Promotion Ladders Vary within and among Organizations." *Administrative Science Quarterly* 31, no. 2 (June 1986), pp. 248–73.

Boyd, David P., and David E. Gumpert. "Coping with Entrepreneurial Stress." *Harvard Business Review* 61, no. 2 (March-April 1983), pp. 44–46.

Carlund, James W.; Frank Hoy; William R. Boulton; and JoAnn C. Carlund. "Differentiating Entrepreneurs from Small Business Owners." *Academy of Management Review* 9, no. 2 (April 1984), pp. 354–59.

Drucker, Peter F. "Our Entrepreneurial Economy." *Harvard Business Review* 62, no. 1 (January-February 1984), pp. 58–64.

Gumper, David E. "Probing the Venture Creation Process." *Harvard Business Review* 62, no. 2 (March-April 1984), pp. 22–24ff.

Imberman, Woodruff. "The Golden Nuggets on the Factory Floor." *Business Horizons* 29, no. 4 (July-August 1986), pp. 63–69.

Kets de Vries, Manfred F. R. "The Dark Side of Entrepreneurship." *Harvard Business Review* 63, no. 6 (November-December 1986), pp. 160–67.

Kierulff, Herbert E. "Finding and Keeping Corporate Entrepreneurs." *Business Horizons* 22, no. 1 (February 1979), pp. 6–15.

Lasden, Martin. "Moonlighting: A Double Standard?" *Computer Decisions* 15, no. 3 (March 1983), pp. 83–92.

Posner, Barry G.; James L. Hall; and Joseph W. Harder. "People Are Our Most Important Resources, But: Encouraging Employee Development." *Business Horizons* 29, no. 5 (September-October 1986), pp. 52–54.

Shays, E. Michael, and Frank de Chambeau. "Harnessing Entrepreneurial Energy within the Organization." *Management Review* 73, no. 9 (September 1984), pp. 17–20.

Sherman, Lee, and Dan Roman. "Planning for Success." *Managerial Planning* 32, no. 2 (September-October 1983), pp. 40–44.

Tack, William L. "Don't Ignore Seasoned Managers—The Case for Management Cycling." *Sloan Management Review* 27, no. 4 (Summer 1986), pp. 63–70.

VanGundy, Arthur G. "How to Establish a Creative Climate in the Work Group." *Management Review* 73, no. 8 (August 1984), pp. 24–28, 37, 38.

Youngblood, Stuart A., and Gary L. Tidwell. "Termination at Will: Some Changes in the Wind." *Personnel* 53, no. 3 (May-June 1981), pp. 22–33.

WHAT THIS INCIDENT IS ABOUT:
The practice of cost shifting in the hospital industry
provides a basis for considering the much broader
issue of ethics in decision making, policy
formulation, and policy implementation.

21

Moral question

INCIDENT

The 12-member board of trustees of Salem County Hospital met to consider a proposal made by the hospital's chief executive officer (CEO) to stop providing specialty and technical training programs for clinical personnel such as laboratory technicians, licensed practical nurses, and radiological technicians.

The CEO emphasized that the trend is for hospitals to stop providing training programs for such personnel. Instead, the trend is toward locating these programs in community colleges. A significant cost increase for such training has caused the trend. To provide such training activities, general hospital funds derived from patient charges or from funds appropriated for patient care must be diverted. At Salem County Hospital, it means each patient must pay an additional $9.10 for each day in the hospital.

The chief of the voluntary medical staff, who vehemently opposes the move, explained some of the benefits to be derived from continuation of the training. Most important, in his view, is the retention of trainees. With the serious shortage of paramedical personnel, both nationally and locally, he considers this an inappropriate time to stop training. In addition, trainees render a service to the hospital when they are being trained. Lastly, he feels a health care facility such as Salem, a 200-bed nonprofit and county-owned general hospital, has an educational responsibility to the community.

The CEO made a final plea that in view of steadily increasing hospital costs and corresponding patient charges, continuing the training could not be justified. In his opinion, it was a moral consideration: It is not equitable to require a patient to bear the burden of training paramedical personnel. He also asked the board to consider a much broader issue under increasing scrutiny by provider and consumer groups. That issue involved apparent board acceptance of policies that supported increasing patient charges for services to more than the cost of delivering those services in order to offset costs incurred in other areas. The board must decide what action to take.

CRITIQUES

ROBERT BOISSONEAU
Professor of Health Services Administration
Arizona State University

The board finds itself with several important unanswered questions, such as:

1. What effect will discontinuing technical training programs have on the supply of technicians?
2. Has the administrator approached a college to assume responsibility for these programs?
3. Has the administrator discussed this issue with others in the hospital?
4. Is cost the only important consideration?
5. Are there other funding sources for the training programs?
6. Is it reasonable to reduce this complex issue to a moral question?

Based on what is known about this incident, the administrator has not given the board a comprehensive report. It does need one.

The key element is to determine whether eliminating training programs will reduce the supply of technicians. The modern hospital must have trained technicians to function successfully.

It is important to know if other area institutions train these technicians. If they do, and Salem County Hospital can employ adequate numbers, there may be no problem.

If there are no other training programs that could supply technicians, the administrator is obliged to approach an appropriate college requesting that the college assume responsibility for the training program. It is likely that a community with a 200-bed general hospital would have such a college.

In communicating with others, such as the chief of the medical staff, the administrator would want to explain the trend of locating training programs in educational institutions. While the hospital may want to offer its facilities for the clinical portion of the training program, it can no longer provide blanket educational opportunities because of changing expectations regarding cost control. The development of an agreement with a college for the use of the hospital's clinical facilities could be an important recruiting device and might be income producing for the hospital.

The importance of the cost factor cannot be denied. Hospital administrators are under fire from every direction to control costs. The $9.10 charge per patient per day amounts to more than $450,000 a year based on 50,000 patient days, a reasonable number for a 200-bed facility.

If a relationship with an appropriate college is not developed, the administrator would want to explore other funding sources. Since the chief of the medical staff is so interested, he may want to have the medical staff assume part or all the financial responsibility for the training program by assessing each physician's professional fee account. After all, the trainees serve physicians as well as the hospital.

However, to base the entire decision on the moral issue of unfair charges is too simplistic. The patient care and training components must also be considered.

Finally, by the very nature of moral questions, some people have a different view. There is no question that thousands of health care providers are charging people who are sick for the training of health care personnel. Possibly more important is that millions are accepting those charges with hardly a question.

JAMES O. HEPNER
Professor and Director of the
Health Administration Program
Washington University in St. Louis

The Salem County Hospital trustees should approve the proposal made by the hospital's CEO to terminate the specialty training programs for laboratory technicians, licensed practical nurses, and radiological technicians.

It is traditional for hospital patients to pay additional fees to support training programs in teaching hospitals affiliated with medical schools. The cost per patient day in teaching hospitals is substantially higher because of educational programs, primarily for medical students, interns, and residents. It is inappropriate for a 200-bed community hospital to carry the primary load for training programs. The hospital is too small to completely support such training and a community college may be willing to assume this responsibility. The rationale for supporting the CEO's proposal goes beyond that of a moral question where patients must pay an additional $9.10 per day to support the training programs. There is a serious question regarding the quality of such hospital training programs because of the inability of hospitals to attract full-time certified faculty who will devote their entire efforts to education as opposed to patient service. The community college would have a broader base and greater potential for attracting qualified faculty.

In terms of quality, the didactic aspects of the training could be handled at the community college. However, it is extremely important that the students be offered clinical exposure, which might be completed at the community hospital. This way the cost to the hospital would be less, the quality of education would be higher, and the hospital would still retain many of the best graduates to work in the clinical laboratories, the X-ray department, and the nursing divisions.

There have been serious questions raised by various third-party payors of hospital care regarding their responsibility for supporting training programs at the insured patient's expense. Therefore, various hospital insurance plans have eliminated training expense from their reimbursement formulas. This means that training expenses must be borne by "full pay" patients, that is, those who do not have insurance or who pay the full billed charges. There is also a question of future reimbursement of such educational costs now that the government's Diagnostic Related Groups (DRG) plan is fully implemented for Medicare patients.

By dividing appropriate responsibility for didactic and clinical education between a community college and the hospital, one point of opposition to closing the training program made by the chief of the voluntary medical staff would be resolved. Furthermore, the physician's concern regarding the hospital's education responsibility to the community would be met. However, the doctor is in error favoring the service that the trainees could render to the hospital during training. Accreditation bodies such as the American Medical Association and the National League of Nursing, who are concerned with the quality of allied health and nursing education, vehemently oppose using students as "cheap labor" for the benefit of the hospital or the medical staff. In fact, they make a strong distinction between education and service starting with undergraduate and graduate education, where medical students, interns, and residents complete their clinical training in a teaching hospital.

In conclusion, if the board of trustees approves the CEO's proposal, it is important that the CEO have a detailed plan to transfer the didactic responsibility for education to a community college and work out arrangements for clinical training within the hospital. In transferring the primary responsibility for education to a community college, the hospital staff, medical staff, program alumni, and students in training must be informed, and their cooperation must be sought in supporting the change before the plan is implemented.

OBSERVATIONS

This incident employs a rather specific question as a vehicle for consideration of the much broader issue of ethics, and the importance of recognizing our changing beliefs and values in formulating and implementing policies that will offer a more equitable way of life for people in the future. The specific issue faced by decision makers in this incident is whether or not education is an acceptable goal for a hospital. The much broader issue involves the equity of requiring a hospitalized person to bear the cost of that education.

Several years ago an article appeared in many newspapers written by a Pulitzer Prize-winning columnist entitled "Ripping off Those Sick Suckers." The opening sentence asked the reader what industry systematically rips off people when they are ill and flat on their backs. The answer was the hospital industry. To disguise the rip-off, it is called "cost shifting." It happens when one patient cannot pay his or her bills and the loss is shifted to another patient. It happens when costs incurred from providing educational programs are shifted to the patient. Since most patients have insurance, that means higher premiums for all of us. It helps explain why a single aspirin in a hospital may cost as much as three dollars.

Both Professors Boissoneau and Hepner have experience as hospital administrators. In their critiques they too decry the practice of cost shifting, but they recognize there are no easy solutions and few acceptable alternatives. Boissoneau raises an interesting philosophical issue when he asserts that there are millions of people accepting charges resulting from cost shifting with hardly a question.

DISCUSSION ITEMS

1. Do you agree or disagree with the CEO of Salem County Hospital that it is not equitable to require a hospitalized person to bear the burden of training specialty and technical personnel? Discuss your position based on the suggested journal articles on morals and ethics as references.
2. Write a critique that reflects the relevant issues revealed by your examination of this incident and its critiques. Be sure to make a decision regarding what should be done about continuing specialty and technical training at Salem County Hospital. You should also include a policy statement that reflects Salem County Hospital's mission as it relates to specialty and technical training for clinical personnel.
3. Are nonprofit organizations faced with the same primary goals and objectives as profit-oriented organizations? How would Salem County Hospital's goals and objectives be affected if it were a proprietary (for-profit) hospital, as opposed to the voluntary hospital (nonprofit) that it is now?

SUGGESTED READINGS

BOOKS

Arnold, Hugh J., and Daniel C. Feldman. *Organizational Behavior*. New York: McGraw-Hill, 1986, chaps. 18, 19.

Beck, Donald F. *Principles of Reimbursement in Health Care*. Rockville, Md.: Aspen Systems Corp., 1983.

Callahan, Robert E.; C. Patrick Fleenor; and Harry Knudson. *Understanding Organizational Behavior*. Columbus, Ohio: Charles E. Merrill Publishing, 1986, chap. 5.

Davis, Keith, and John W. Newstrom. *Human Behavior at Work*. 7th ed. New York: McGraw-Hill, 1985, chap. 12.

Donnelly, James H.; James L. Gibson; and John M. Ivancevich. *Fundamentals of Management*. 6th ed. Plano, Tex.: Business Publications, 1987, chaps. 11, 18, 20.

French, Wendell L. *The Personnel Management Process*. 6th ed. Boston: Houghton Mifflin, 1987, chaps. 16–18.

Griffin, Ricky W. *Management*. 2nd ed. Boston: Houghton Mifflin, 1987, chap. 21.

Heneman, Herbert G.; Donald P. Schwab; John A. Fossum; and Lee D. Dyer. *Personnel/Human Resource Management*. 3rd ed. Homewood, Ill.: Richard D. Irwin, 1986, chap. 12.

Hoffman, W. M., and Jennifer Moore. *Business Ethics*. New York: McGraw-Hill, 1984, chap. 9.

Megginson, Leon C. *Personnel Management: A Human Resources Approach*. 5th ed. Homewood, Ill.: Richard D. Irwin, 1985, chap. 8.

Miller, Murray. *Unequal Care: A Case Study of Interorganizational Relations in Health Care*. New York: Columbia University Press, 1980.

Rue, Leslie W., and Lloyd L. Byars. *Management: Theory and Application*. 4th ed. Homewood, Ill.: Richard D. Irwin, 1986, chaps. 3, 9, 19.

Schermerhorn, John R. *Management for Productivity*. 2nd ed. New York: John Wiley & Sons, 1986, chap. 20.

JOURNALS

Brady, F. N. "A Janus-Headed Model of Ethical Theory: Looking Two Ways at Business/Society Issues." *Academy of Management Review* 10, no. 3 (July 1985), pp. 568–76.

Donaldson, Gordon. "Financial Goals and Strategic Consequences." *Harvard Business Review* 63, no. 3 (May-June 1985), pp. 57–66.

Egdahl, Richard H. "Should We Shrink the Health Care System?" *Harvard Business Review* 62, no. 1 (January-February 1984), pp. 125–32.

Fottler, M. D., and J. A. Lanning. "A Comprehensive Incentive Approach to Employee Health Care Cost Containment." *California Management Review* 29, no. 2 (Fall 1986), pp. 75–93.

Gellerman, S. W. "Why 'Good' Managers Make Bad Ethical Choices." *Harvard Business Review* 64, no. 4 (July-August 1986), pp. 85–90.

Goodpaster, Kenneth E., and John B. Matthews. "Can a Corporation Have a Conscience?" *Harvard Business Review* 60, no. 1 (January-February 1982), p. 133.

Jansen, Erick, and Mary Ann Von Glinow. "Ethical Ambivalence and Organizational Reward Systems." *Academy of Management Review* 10, no. 4 (October 1985), pp. 814–22.

Johnson, Harold. "Ethics and the Executive." *Business Horizons* 24, no. 3 (May-June 1981), pp. 53–59.

Larson, K. P. "Why Health Care Costs Keep Rising." *Personnel Journal* 63, no. 3 (March 1984), pp. 68–74.

Mills, P. K., and Dennis Moberg. "Perspectives on the Technology of Service Operations." *Academy of Management Review* 7, no. 3 (July 1982), pp. 467–78.

Nash, Laura L. "Ethics without the Sermon." *Harvard Business Review* 59, no. 6 (November-December 1981), pp. 79–90.

Saul, G. K. "Business Ethics: Where Are We Going?" *Academy of Management Review* 6, no. 2 (April 1981), pp. 269–76.

Sherwin, Douglas. "The Ethical Roots of the Business System." *Harvard Business Review* 61, no. 6 (November-December 1983), pp. 183–92.

Wartick, S. L., and P. L. Cochran. "The Evolution of the Corporate Social Performance Model." *Academy of Management Review* 10, no. 4 (October 1985), pp. 758–69.

White, Louis P., and Kevin C. Wooten. "Ethical Dilemmas in Various Stages of Organizational Development." *Academy of Management Review* 8, no. 4 (October 1983), pp. 690–97.

WHAT THIS INCIDENT IS ABOUT:
Wage complaints preface a life-and-death work
stoppage by public beach lifeguards frustrated by
their attempts to navigate bureaucratic waters
successfully. The incident involves motivation and
compensation issues, upward communication,
bureaucracy, and group action.

22

Perceived pay inequity

INCIDENT

The Atlantic County Division of Beach Safety employs 100 trained
lifeguards during the summer months on the county's ocean beaches. The
lifeguard corps is mainly comprised of young college-age males and females
who are strong swimmers and have completed specific courses in swimming, water safety, and lifesaving. Officials in the Division of Beach Safety
are proud of the beach patrol, as it was ranked second in the nation on
quality of its performance.

Last summer, however, the lifeguards exhibited a lack of motivation and
complained about the terms of their employment and working conditions
but continued to work effectively. Their discontent centered on the issue of
inadequate wages. Compared with other ocean lifeguards, they were
receiving one to three dollars less per hour. Compared with other Atlantic
County employees, the lifeguards were the lowest workers on the pay
scale. Entry-level secretaries, for example, received higher pay than the
lifeguards.

To reasonably resolve their pay problem, the lifeguards met with their
immediate supervisors and were told, "We can do nothing about your low
pay. The Division of Beach Safety sets your wage rates, not us. We have
many applicants for lifeguard jobs, and jobs are scarce in the summer. You
are lucky to have your jobs; don't rock the boat. If you still want to try and
do something about your pay, see the head of the Division of Beach Safety
or the head of the Department of Public Safety."

After appropriate appointments had been arranged, the head officials of
beach safety and public safety, accompanied by staff members, came to a
lifeguard meeting at the main lifeguard station. In reply to demands for
increased pay, Sally Wingate, head of the Department of Public Safety,

FIGURE 1
County Government Organization

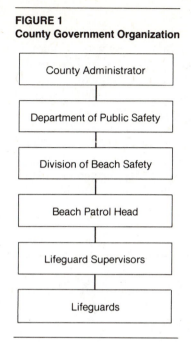

stated, "There's nothing I can do to alter the adopted budget. Remember that volunteer lifeguards originally did your jobs. Being a lifeguard puts you where the action is and it doesn't hurt your tan, either! After all, we do pay minimum wages. You'll have to see the county administrator about any budget changes."

At a meeting the following week, the county administrator, Roy Hamilton, heard about the lifeguards' request for increased pay and responded, "This years' county budget has been completed and approved. Unfortunately, we were constrained by the tax dollars available. Funds were sufficient to support raises for most other employees. Have a good summer."

Events moved swiftly. Feeling frustrated, rebuffed, and unappreciated, even though their daily work involved life-and-death situations, the lifeguards sought legal advice, learned that they could strike without breaking the state law (because they were not unionized), and decided to "go public" with their grievance. The strike was set for Saturday on the Fourth of July weekend, the busiest day of the year. Area newspapers and television and radio stations were informed about the strike.

On the designated strike day, all lifeguards showed up at the main lifeguard station. More than 75 percent of them supported the strike and remained in front of the main station, refusing to go to appropriate guard stations along the beach. People began to fill the beaches and the water.

The probability of accidental injury and drowning increased steadily along the crowded, unguarded ocean shore.

As the danger increased, two lifeguard supervisors contacted Bill King, chairman of Atlantic County's board of commissioners, who sensed both the immediate dangers and the long-run organization implications.

King instructed Hamilton to decide on prompt action for restoring safety to the county's public beaches, and to develop some specific policy and procedure recommendations dealing with relevant underlying issues such as personnel policy and operational policy. Hamilton knew that he must decide and act quickly on the critical beach safety problem. He also knew that afterwards he must develop recommendations for compensation policy and grievance handling procedures, among others, for the next meeting of the county commissioners.

CRITIQUES

FRED LUTHANS
Professor of Management
University of Nebraska at Lincoln

This incident has several interesting aspects for motivation and human-resource management. First, it should be recognized that there is a problem here. A majority of the lifeguards feel they are underpaid and have become so frustrated that they are willing to strike with the risk of someone drowning. How did they get to this point? Is pay really that important to them? How did the various levels of supervision handle the lifeguards' grievances?

Employee motivation problems, such as the one in the incident, can be analyzed from an internal or external perspective. From an internal approach, the lifeguards' expectancies for equitable pay are not being met. This imbalance between their perceived equitable reward and their actual reward has led to considerable dissatisfaction. The managerial solution is to either change the lifeguards' perceptions of equitable pay or to increase the actual pay in line with their current perceptions. The supervisors' attempts at doing this have failed. Supervisors tried to convince the lifeguards that: "You are lucky to have your job"; or "Being a lifeguard puts you where the action is and it doesn't hurt your tan either." They also said that since the budget was set, there was no way that wages could be increased. In other words, an internal approach can readily explain the problem but very few, if any, solutions are offered.

An external approach would concentrate on the environmental contingencies affecting observable behaviors in this incident. Instead of analyzing unobservable expectancies, perceptions, attitudes, and satisfactions, studying the antecedents and especially the consequences of observable behaviors is more important. The consequence of the lifeguards' exemplary performance is their supervisor telling them they are lucky to have jobs and there is no way they will receive more money. The supervisors' words and refusal to do anything is a punishing consequence for the lifeguards' desirable performance. The supervisors' refusal eventually led to the lifeguards walking off the job. Pay is an important consequence for these young people, but it is not the only means of rewarding their efforts. The supervisors could have been more sympathetic toward the lifeguards' request for more pay. The supervisors could have pointed to other contingent consequences of the lifeguards' good performance besides the pay, such as the lifeguards' fine record in saving lives or providing alternative rewards such as more days off or a choice of assignment/location. The supervisors could also provide feedback concerning the lifeguards' job performance (for example, absenteeism, tardiness, staying at assigned posts, compliments and complaints from patrons, saving swimmers, following procedures, socializing on the job, and so forth) and recognition for attaining mutually determined goals. In other words, the supervisors could have handled the guards much differently. They could possibly have prevented the problem by providing more nonfinancial rewards for effective job behaviors, and once the problem arose, they could have reacted differently. Again, there is no intention of implying that pay is not important. Pay is very important as to how long the lifeguards stay at their jobs. In the long run, at least, higher wages will have to occur. But for day-to-day job behaviors, feedback and social rewards are critical to the lifeguards' effective performance.

It is appropriate that the chairman of Atlantic County's board of commissioners has asked Roy Hamilton to develop some specific policies. Such policies can help prevent the current serious problems. In particular, policies and procedures are useful behavior guidelines; they also are useful cues for the lifeguards' behavior. Importantly, however, unless the reward systems are in place, these policies become meaningless and can even backfire, leading to more problems. The challenge facing Hamilton is to develop an equitable compensation plan and make sure his supervisors are providing contingent reinforcement (attention and feedback) for desirable lifeguard behavior.

VIDA SCARPELLO
Associate Professor of Management
University of Georgia

The Perceived Pay Inequity incident is an example of management at its worst. County mangement is grossly negligent in its major responsibility of ensuring public safety on the county beaches. It doesn't even have an emergency plan to handle the potential safety problems that could arise from a work stoppage by its beach patrol. Because management neglects its major service responsibility, it is not surprising that it also fails to listen and deal with employee concerns when those concerns are formally voiced up the chain of command.

The Perceived Pay Inequity incident centers around the supposed discontent of lifeguards with their pay rates. Several factors suggest that the actual problem may be quite different. Research on equity theory shows that people compare their job inputs and outcomes to the inputs and outcomes of similarly skilled individuals and individuals whose jobs place them in close contact with them, such as their supervisors and other people who perform similar work in higher or lower ranked jobs. Perceptions of being underpaid motivate individuals to try to balance their job inputs with the outcomes they receive from their jobs so that their input/outcome ratios equal the input/outcome ratios of individuals with whom they compare their job inputs and outcomes. Thus, perceptions of being underpaid lead employees to do such things as decrease their quality and/or quantity of work, take excessively long work breaks, increase their absences from work, quit their jobs, or attempt to unionize.

In evaluating this situation, I assume that the lifeguards, like other employees, are rational human beings. Thus the work stoppage is not a random emotionally based event. Yet, the lifeguards did not seem to behave in a rational manner. For example, why did they compare their pay to county secretretaries? It is highly unusual for part-time employees in one job classification, such as lifeguard, to compare their pay rates to full-time employees in an unrelated job classification, such as secretary. Why didn't members of such an elite and high-performing group as the Atlantic County beach patrol apply for higher paying lifeguard positions on other ocean beaches? The case implies that such other positions were not available within commuting distance from home. The local labor market appears tight, i.e., there are more lifeguard applicants than jobs. Given this situation it seems that the $1 to $3 per hour higher pay rate is not a realistic expectation. Finally, why were the lifeguards unwilling to recognize budget constraints? Were they promised a pay increase? Again, there is no indication that they expected to get a pay increase.

The beach patrol's professionalism and commitment to work is evident by its rank of second in the nation on the quality of its performance. They complained about their low wages. Yet, the case provides little evidence to suggest that pay inequity was the cause of the work stoppage. A skilled investigator may discover that the cause of the work stoppage may have been the way management treated their lifeguards and the way it responded to their pay grievance.

Besides complaining about their pay, the lifeguards had complained about the terms of their employment and the working conditions. Reading between the lines suggests that the source for those complaints may be the management structure. The "pay" issue was the vehicle for bringing forth the sum total of various frustrations with terms and conditions of employment. After all, it is socially acceptable to voice dissatisfaction with pay. We all do this at times. It is not socially acceptable, however, to complain about one's boss to his or her face or to complain about management's failure to listen to one's concerns.

The lifeguards first voiced their pay complaints to their immediate supervisor whose basic response was to tell them they could be easily substituted by other job applicants. Furthermore, if they wanted to complain, they should complain to the head of the Division of Beach Safety or the head of the Department of Public Safety. The head of public safety also told them they were replaceable and suggested that they see the county administrator about changing the payroll budget. The county administrator informed them that the county had used the available money to grant pay raises to most other county employees.

Nobody in county government showed any interest in finding out what the actual problems were, nor acknowledged the beach patrol's outstanding performance record. It is therefore not at all surprising that "feeling frustrated, rebuffed, and unappreciated," the lifeguards decided to strike their employer. If they were to balance their job inputs (i.e., having to deal with ineffective management) with their job outcomes, the way to do it was to strike for more pay. Another way of saying it is: "This job is not worth it unless we get paid for putting up with this management."

The incident ends with Bill King, chairman of Atlantic County's board of commissioners instructing Hamilton, the county administrator, to take prompt action to restore safety to the county's public beaches and to develop some specific policy and procedure recommendations dealing with relevant *underlying* issues such as personnel policy and operational policy. It is this writer's opinion that those instructions cannot be accomplished by a county administrator who has not exhibited the managerial competence in dealing with a major service responsibility area of his job, i.e., public safety, and in diagnosing and effectively dealing with formally voiced employee concerns.

OBSERVATIONS

Many factors enter into decisions on employee pay adjustment including: merit, seniority, available funds for raises, and supply and demand of relevant labor. In this case, however, none of these factors seem important to administrators who appear to have arbitrarily neglected lifeguards but have given raises to other county employees. No wonder the lifeguards are frustrated, dissatisfied, and relentless in pursuing recognition and pay raises. The "comparable worth" concept might be appropriately applied in their behalf since their supervisors have not used standard methods for determining eligibility for pay raises, such as job descriptions and performance evaluations.

Professors Luthans and Scarpello apply behavioral theory and organizational concepts such as perceptions, expectancies, equity, feedback, and terms and conditions of employment in discussing the incident.

DISCUSSION ITEMS

1. Evaluate the options open to county officials when the lifeguards refused to assume their stations on the beach.
2. As public employees, were the lifeguards justified in jeopardizing the lives of innocent citizens via a strike to increase their pay? Explain.
3. Critique the attitudes and actions of supervisors and other county officials.

SUGGESTED READINGS

BOOKS

Arnold, Hugh J., and Daniel C. Feldman. *Organizational Behavior*. New York: McGraw-Hill, 1986, chap. 12.

Callahan, Robert E.; C. Patrick Fleenor; and Harry Knudson. *Understanding Organizational Behavior*. Columbus, Ohio: Charles E. Merrill Publishing, 1986, chaps. 4, 10.

Davis, Keith, and John W. Newstrom. *Human Behavior at Work*. 7th ed. New York: McGraw-Hill, 1985, part 2, chap. 20.

Donnelly, James H.; James L. Gibson; and John M. Ivancevich. *Fundamentals of Management*. 6th ed. Plano, Tex.: Business Publications, 1987, part 3.

French, Wendell L. *The Personnel Management Process*. 6th ed. Boston: Houghton Mifflin, 1987, chaps. 8, 19, 21.

Griffin, Ricky W. *Management*. 2nd ed. Boston: Houghton Mifflin, 1987, chap. 13, pp. 666–70.

Heneman, Herbert G.; Donald P. Schwab; John A. Fossum; and Lee D. Dyer. *Personnel/Human Resource Management*. 3rd ed. Homewood, Ill.: Richard D. Irwin, 1986, chap. 13.

Megginson, Leon C. *Personnel Management: A Human Resources Approach*. 5th ed. Homewood, Ill.: Richard D. Irwin, 1985, chaps. 15, 16.

Rue, Leslie W., and Lloyd L. Byars. *Management: Theory and Application*. 4th ed. Homewood, Ill.: Richard D. Irwin, 1986, chap. 17.

Schermerhorn, John R. *Management for Productivity*. 2nd ed. New York: John Wiley & Sons, 1986, chap. 12.

JOURNALS

Baird, Lloyd. "Managing Dissatisfaction." *Personnel* 58, no. 3 (May-June 1983), pp. 12–21.

Bisesi, Michael. "Strategies for Successful Leadership in Changing Times." *Sloan Management Review* 25, no. 1 (Fall 1983), pp. 61–64.

Cosier, Richard A., and Dan R. Dalton. "Equity Theory and Time: A Reformulation." *Academy of Management Review* 8, no. 2 (April 1983), pp. 311–19.

Imberman, Woodruff. "How to Enjoy NOT Having to Strike." *Management Review* 70, no. 9 (September 1981), pp. 43–47.

Lasden, Martin. "Facing Down Groupthink." *Computer Decisions* 18, no. 5 (May 6, 1986), pp. 52–56.

Lawler, Edward E., III, and Gerald E. Ledford, Jr. "Skill-Based Pay: A Concept That's Catching On." *Management Review* 76, no. 2 (February 1987), pp. 46–51.

Mahoney, Thomas A. "Approaches to the Definition of Comparable Worth." *Academy of Management Review* 8, no. 1 (January 1983), pp. 14–21.

Panken, Peter M. "What Every Company Should Have: A Formal Employee Complaint Procedure." *Management Review* 73, no. 1 (January 1984), pp. 42–45.

Renken, Henry J. "Employee Incentives." *Advanced Management Journal* (Spring 1984), pp. 8–12.

St. John, Walter D. "Successful Communications between Supervisors and Employees." *Personnel Journal* 62, no. 1 (January 1983), pp. 71–77.

Schein, Edgar H. "Coming to a New Awareness of Organizational Culture." *Sloan Management Review* 25, no. 2 (Winter 1984), pp. 3–16.

Shotshat, H. M., and Bong-Gon P. Shin. "Organizational Communications: A Key to Successful Strategic Planning." *Management Planning* 30, no. 2 (September-October 1981), pp. 37–40.

Tannenbaum, Arnold S., and Walter J. Kuleck, Jr. "The Effect on Organization Members of Discrepancy between Perceived and Preferred Reward Implicit in Work." *Human Relations* 31, no. 9 (September 1978), pp. 809–21.

Tharpe, Charles G. "Linking Annual Incentive and Individual Performance." *Personnel Administrator* 31, no. 1 (January 1986), pp. 85–90.

WHAT THIS INCIDENT IS ABOUT:
Performance appraisal leaves both superior and
subordinate dissatisfied with each other and with the
process. Misaligned expectations, faulty actions, and
misunderstandings doom the performance appraisal
interview.

23

Performance appraisal
policy

INCIDENT

Scottie Jenkins sat in the interview room awaiting the arrival of his
supervisor, Clinton Raleigh. His performance appraisal interview was
scheduled for 2:00 P.M., but Scottie had come 10 minutes early. He always
tried to be on time.

Scottie liked working at the regional headquarters of Planetwide Insurance Company and had made good job advancement. Now, after working
as a senior clerk in the staff services department for a year under Clinton's
supervision, Scottie expected to be appraised as "above average" or possibly as "excellent." He thought that "outstanding" was beyond reach at this
time. Under two previous supervisors at Planetwide he had been rated
"outstanding" once and "excellent" once.

The job description for Scottie's senior clerk position included three
main areas of performance: mail room, inventory property records, and the
computerized insurance data system. Scottie shared duties with seven
other senior clerks, all of whom reported directly to Clinton. He felt that
he had mastered the mail room. He could handle the details and complexities of both incoming and outgoing mail. Rarely did he make a mistake.
Moreover, he handled the inventory property records accurately and
efficiently. Scottie had not yet been assigned to work with the computerized insurance data system and therefore had not learned it. He knew that
he had done everything asked of him by his supervisor during the rating
period, including special projects not included in his job description. He
had received no complaints about his performance.

As Clinton walked the hall toward the conference room, he recalled that he had evaluated Scottie's job performance as "average." Scottie had the least seniority of any employee in the department and Clinton wanted to leave some room for improvement. Because of his personal bias, Clinton also did not want to rate Scottie equal to others in the department with more seniority than he had. Clinton was disappointed that Scottie could not use the computerized record system and that he had not indicated an interest in learning. Besides, other senior clerks in the department were proficient at operating the computerized data system and there was no need at present to train Scottie. Clinton's practice as a supervisor was to assign people to duties they could do best. The department ran well that way.

As Clinton entered the room, he began the interview by stating in a tired sounding voice, "Scottie, in our company 'performance appraisal' means the systematic and regular evaluation of an individual's job performance and potential for development." The performance appraisal interview followed this opening statement and included the following significant exchanges.

CLINTON:

Now, Scottie, if you will sign your performance appraisal form right here at the bottom, we can get on with the interview.

SCOTTIE:

If you don't mind, I would rather sign after I have read the appraisal and we have discussed it.

CLINTON:

You'll notice that your overall rating is "average." That's how the numbers worked out.

SCOTTIE:

[*with astonishment*] "Average." How can you rate me that low? My work before always has been rated "above average."

CLINTON:

[*with defensiveness and increased volume*] Are you questioning my evaluation of your work? What gives you the right to judge me?

SCOTTIE:

I'm saying I don't understand your low rating of my job performance.

CLINTON:

Well, for one thing, you don't know anything about the computerized insurance data system and you have showed no initiative or interest in learning it.

SCOTTIE:

[*decidedly defensive*] I did everything you asked me to do, Clinton, and I did it well. I even asked you why the others were always working at the computers, and you told me that my turn would come later. Please show me your explanation and documentation for rating me so low.

CLINTON:

[*with firmness and authority*] I am your supervisor. You work for me. I observe your work. I judge your work. I make out your performance appraisal just like I do the others. You are the only one to complain.

SCOTTIE:

What does this do to my raise?

CLINTON:

Everybody gets 1 percent across the board. Your average job performance does not qualify you for any merit raise money.

SCOTTIE:

[*with mixed anger, anxiety, and resignation*] This is just not fair. I know my work is better than half the others in the department.

CLINTON:

It isn't your job to rate the performance of your fellow workers. That's my job. We don't seem to be getting anywhere. If you'll sign and date this to indicate that we have had the required performance appraisal interview, we'll be through here.

SCOTTIE:

I'm not ready to sign anything yet.

CLINTON:

[*gathering up the papers and standing*] Well, its plain to me that you resent being rated as "average." You don't respect my judgment and you won't follow my instructions. Time to get back to work. [*Clinton departs.*]

Scottie now sat alone in the interview room. It seemed unreal to him. For the first time in his life he had been rated "average." This rating meant practically a zero raise. Little had been said about his strengths. No steps had been discussed for improving his future performance. Clinton had reacted defensively at his attempts to objectively discuss these issues. This performance appraisal interview unsettled him. He had worked hard and wanted to be successful. He liked his job and the company. Scottie considered his options, which included: (1) going over Clinton's head to his boss, or to the personnel department; (2) toughing it out for another year and hoping for a better performance appraisal next time; (3) seeking transfer to another department; and (4) leaving the company. What to do, he thought; there must be a better way. Scottie could not see a light at the end of the tunnel of options. All looked dark to him. Questions whirled uncontrollably through Scottie's mind. I'm a good person, why did this happen to me? He felt discriminated against, dissatisfied, and organizationally doomed.

Unanswered questions troubled Clinton also as he reached his office still steaming over the unsatisfactory outcome of the performance appraisal interview. What does it take to be able to justify an "average" rating? Why did Scottie have such a bad attitude? What can I do to more skillfully communicate and gain acceptance, Clinton asked himself. Perhaps the company's policy requiring a formal rating at six-month intervals using a graphic rating scale and requiring a rating interview between the rater and ratee was somehow faulty? What operational policies would produce improved outcomes for the performance appraisal process and interview? What ethical considerations deserved attention?

CRITIQUES

R. DUANE IRELAND
Chairman, Department of Management
Baylor University

As we can see from this incident, a company's performance appraisal policy, and the manner in which that policy is implemented, can significantly impact an individual's level of productivity and attitude toward his/her job. Scottie and Clinton clearly approached this performance appraisal interview with vastly different assumptions. How could this happen?

It appears that a major problem area is that of communications. Scottie has received one "outstanding" and one "excellent" rating from each of his two previous supervisors. Because of these ratings, Scottie believes that his performances at Planetwide are quite consistent with supervisory expectations. Clinton, however, is judging Scottie by different standards. Scottie feels that he has more than adequately completed all assignments Clinton asked him to accept. Clinton's view is that Scottie should aggressively pursue additional assignments (such as learning how to work with the company's computerized insurance data system). These differences in perspectives regarding Scottie's work responsibilities should have been examined long before a performance rating was determined. Following a careful review of each employee's previous ratings and work assignments, Clinton should have communicated his expectations to each individual. At that time, the two parties could exchange their views. The outcome of such a session would be an agreement regarding the work-related and developmental responsibilities to be accepted by the subordinate and the superior, respectively. In this manner, the performance appraisal policy could be used as a developmental tool. Although Clinton implies that the interview is intended to be a developmental session, the manner in which he conducted the session is inconsistent with this suggestion. Clinton did not clearly specify the range of issues to be discussed during the interview. Even more damaging was the manner in which the session started. Asking Scottie to sign the performance appraisal form prior to examining its contents reflects several concerns. First, Clinton should understand the importance of the interview. Scottie enjoys working for Planetwide and appears to be an individual desiring to make important contributions to his employer. In this sense, Scottie seeks specific feedback through which he can grow and develop. A second concern is Clinton's apparent inability to effectively conduct the interview. As a supervisor, Clinton must develop the interpersonal skills necessary to communicate with his employees about issues as significant as performance ratings.

Clinton should also be sensitive enough to recognize that Scottie will not be receptive to an "average" rating when similar performances under two previous supervisors earned an "excellent" and an "outstanding" rating. Further, Clinton should understand that no individual, particularly one who believes that he has performed well enough to earn either an "above average" or possibly an "excellent" rating, will respond favorably when informed that his performance is only "average." Clinton may find it useful to visit with his superiors to evaluate the possibility of using a word other than "average" to denote acceptable performance. On the other hand, Scottie must understand that Clinton has expectations that differ from his previous supervisors. Open communication about these differences, followed with the setting of mutually agreed-upon performance objectives, is necessary to improve this situation and to result in a performance appraisal policy that is oriented to employee development.

As noted in the incident, the outcome of this interview was unsatisfactory to both Clinton and Scottie. At this point, Clinton should visit with the personnel department. Topics to be considered during discussions with these people include how other supervisors implement Planetwide's performance appraisal policy, how others conduct interviews, and a request for any additional information that could be of value to him. With this information, Clinton should examine Scottie's previous ratings, adjust his rating (if appropriate), and then conduct a second interview with Scottie. During the interview, each party's expectations should be discussed in order that mutually agreed-upon performance objectives might be established. Scottie should wait a reasonable period of time (two or three weeks). If Clinton does not request a second interview at the end of that time period, he should ask Clinton for another interview. If that request is denied, or Scottie is dissatisfied with the results from the second session, he should visit the personnel department to request information regarding Planetwide's performance appraisal policy. If he believes that Clinton has violated that policy, in terms of how his rating was prepared and/or how the appraisal interview was conducted, he should discuss his concerns with personnel department representatives.

STEPHEN P. ROBBINS
Professor of Management
San Diego State University

Whether Scottie received an overall performance rating of "average," "excellent," or "outstanding" is of minor importance in this incident. The real issue is the way Clinton mishandled the performance appraisal review. Given Clinton's behavior, should we be surprised by Scottie's response? Let's take a brief look at how a performance review *should* be done and compare it with Clinton's approach.

1. *Schedule the appraisal review in advance and be prepared.* While Clinton has scheduled the review in advance, his nonchalant style suggests he has put little time or thought into the review. After having worked with Scottie for a year, Clinton should have anticipated Scottie's reaction and planned a response.

2. *Put the employee at ease.* The performance review can be a traumatic experience for the best of employees. No one likes to hear criticism about his or her work. Given the fact that individuals tend to overrate themselves—approximately 60 percent of people place their own performance in the top 10 percent—managers need to create a supportive climate to lessen tensions and reduce the likelihood of confrontation. Clinton certainly failed at putting Scottie at ease.

3. *Obtain employee participation.* Effective performance reviews are characterized by high employee participation. The employee should be allowed to do the majority of the talking. In this case, Clinton sought to totally control the review session.

4. *Have the employee engage in self-evaluation.* Consistent with high participation, the employee should be encouraged to evaluate his or her own performance. In this way, the manager becomes a partner in helping the employee to be a better performer, rather than a "boss" looking for negatives to criticize. Again, Clinton made no effort to listen to what Scottie had to say.

5. *Use specific examples to support your ratings.* An employee's performance ratings should be documented with specific examples. Clinton did a poor job of supporting his rating of Scottie.

6. *Give positive as well as negative feedback.* Clinton has turned the performance review into a totally negative-feedback session. Research shows that areas of job performance that are most criticized are least likely to show improvement. Clinton should have provided more balanced feedback.

7. *Have the employee sum up the appraisal review.* As a review nears its conclusion, the employee should be encouraged to summarize the discussion that has taken place. This is to ensure clarity of communication

and bring closure to the interview. Clinton's authoritarian and defensive stance has essentially precluded this from occurring.

A final note: It's best for goal setting to precede the performance appraisal. Had Clinton and Scottie agreed on a set of specific, measurable, and verifiable goals six months ago—during the previous review session—Clinton would have had tangible standards against which to judge Scottie's job performance. A few years ago, a major hotel chain used the phrase, "the best surprise is no surprise," to describe its philosophy. That is also good advice for the development of an employee performance appraisal system. Employees should understand, in no uncertain terms, what is expected of them. They should additionally get ongoing, informal feedback from their boss so that the formal review is merely a summary and confirmation of facts they already know. Clinton did neither of these with Scottie.

In conclusion, Planetwide's appraisal policy—formal ratings every six months using a graphic rating scale with a follow-up interview—is probably satisfactory. Graphic rating scales, which rate employees on traits, are generally inferior to a behaviorally based or a goal-focused rating system, but they are widely used in practice and can be effective. The problem here does not seem to be with the company's policy but rather with Clinton's implementation of that policy.

OBSERVATIONS

Organizational managers make human resource decisions concerning pay, placement, promotion, development, and termination. Managers must continually remember these multiple uses of the appraisal system so the purpose of evaluating job performance does not overshadow the purpose of evaluating the potential for development. The quality of these decisions largely depends on the quality of the information generated by the performance appraisal system.

Regular and periodic performance evaluations occur for most employees at annual intervals, while six-month intervals are also often used. It is common practice for the employees new to an organization to be placed in a probationary or conditional work status for the first six months of employment, and to be formally evaluated by the immediate supervisor at the end of that period. Results of the performance appraisal process are typically fed back to the subordinate by means of a performance appraisal interview with the immediate superior. The effectiveness of the interview, the usefulness of the feedback, and the shaping of employee expectations depend crucially on the knowledge and skill of the supervisor conducting the interview. Supervisors must recognize the importance of working to improve their interpersonal and communication skills required for successfully implementing the performance appraisal process.

DISCUSSION QUESTIONS

1. Discuss ways in which the supervisor, Clinton Raleigh, could have improved his handling of the performance appraisal interview.
2. Do you believe that most supervisors do an effective job of appraising the job performance of their subordinates? On what evidence do you base your opinion?
3. How may a subordinate appropriately respond to a performance appraisal with which he/she disagrees? Explain the advantages and disadvantages of your recommendations.

SUGGESTED READINGS

BOOKS

Arnold, Hugh J., and Daniel C. Feldman. *Organizational Behavior*. New York: McGraw-Hill, 1986, chap. 11.

Bernardin, H. J., and R. W. Beatty. *Performance Appraisal*. Boston, Mass.: Kent, 1984.

Callahan, Robert E.; C. Patrick Fleenor; and Harry Knudson. *Understanding Organizational Behavior*. Columbus, Ohio: Charles E. Merrill Publishing, 1986, chap. 10.

Carroll, S. J., and C. E. Schneier. *Performance Appraisal and Review Systems*. Glenview, Ill.: Scott, Foresman, 1982.

Davis, Keith, and John W. Newstrom. *Human Behavior at Work*. 7th ed. New York: McGraw-Hill, 1985, chap. 7.

Donnelly, James H.; James L. Gibson; and John M. Ivancevich. *Fundamentals of Management*. 6th ed. Plano, Tex.: Business Publications, 1987, pp. 254–60.

French, Wendell L. *The Personnel Management Process*. 6th ed. Boston: Houghton Mifflin, 1987, chap. 15.

Griffin, Ricky W. *Management*. 2nd ed. Boston: Houghton Mifflin, 1987, pp. 662–66.

Heneman, Herbert G.; Donald P. Schwab; John A. Fossum; and Lee D. Dyer. *Personnel/Human Resource Management*. 3rd ed. Homewood, Ill.: Richard D. Irwin, 1986, chap. 5.

Latham, G. P., and K. N. Wexley. *Improving Productivity through Performance Appraisal*. Reading, Mass.: Addison-Wesley, 1981.

Megginson, Leon C. *Personnel Management: A Human Resources Approach*. 5th ed. Homewood, Ill.: Richard D. Irwin, 1985, chap. 14.

Rue, Leslie W., and Lloyd L. Byars. *Management: Theory and Application*. 4th ed. Homewood, Ill.: Richard D. Irwin, 1986, chap. 18.

Schermerhorn, John R. *Management for Productivity*. 2nd ed. New York: John Wiley & Sons, 1986, pp. 404–9.

JOURNALS

Bernardin, H. John, and Lawrence A. Klatt. "Managerial Appraisal Systems: Has Practice Caught up to the State of the Art?" *Personnel Administrator* 30, no. 11 (November 1985), pp. 79–86.

Brush, Donald H., and Lyle F. Schoenfeldt. "Performance Appraisal for the 80s." *Personnel Administrator* 27, no. 12 (December 1982), pp. 76–83.

Cederblom, D. "The Performance Appraisal Interview: A Review, Implications, and Suggestions." *Academy of Management Review* 7, no. 2 (April 1982), pp. 219–27.

Foegen, J. H. "The Case for Positive Documentation." *Business Horizons* 29, no. 5 (September-October 1986), pp. 60–62.

Henneman, R. L., and K. N. Wexley. "The Effects of Time Delay in Rating and Amount of Information Observed on Performance Rating Accuracy." *Academy of Management Journal* 26, no. 4 (December 1983), pp. 677–86.

Ivancevich, J. M. "Subordinates' Reactions to Performance Appraisal Interviews: A Test of Feedback and Goal-Setting Techniques." *Journal of Applied Psychology* 67, no. 5 (October 1982), pp. 581–87.

Jacobs, Rick, and Steven Kolowski. "A Closer Look at Halo Error in Performance Ratings." *Academy of Management Journal* 28, no. 1 (March 1985), pp. 201–12.

Kay, Emanuel; Herbert H. Meyer; and John R. P. French, Jr. "Effects of Threat in a Performance Appraisal Interview." *Journal of Applied Psychology* 49, no. 5 (October 1965), pp. 311–17.

Kingstrom, P. O., and L. E. Mainstone. "An Investigation of Rater-Ratee Acquaintance and Rater Bias." *Academy of Management Journal* 28, no. 3 (September 1985), pp. 641–53.

Reed, Paul R., and Mark J. Kroll. "A Two-Perspective Approach to Performance Appraisal." *Personnel* 62, no. 10 (October 1985), pp. 51–57.

Rice, Berkeley. "Performance Review: Examining the Eye of the Beholder." *Across the Board* 22, no. 12 (December 1985), pp. 24–32.

Shore, Lynn McFarlane, and George C. Thornton, III. "Effects of Gender on Self- and Supervisory Ratings." *Academy of Management Journal* 29, no. 1 (March 1986), pp. 115–29.

Smith, David E. "Training Programs for Performance Appraisal: A Review." *Academy of Management Review* 11, no. 1 (January 1986), pp. 22–40.

Thompson, Duane E., and Toni A. Thompson. "Task-Based Performance Appraisal for Blue-Collar Jobs: Evaluation of Race and Sex Effects." *Journal of Applied Psychology* 70, no. 4 (November 1985), pp. 747–53.

Woods, James G., and Theresa Dillion. "The Performance Review Approach to Improving Productivity." *Personnel* 62, no. 3 (March 1985), pp. 20–27.

WHAT THIS INCIDENT IS ABOUT:
Collective employee attitudes and legal issues can
be crucial factors in policy formulation and execution. A basic question of whether the ends justify
the means is evident in this incident.

24

Policy under pressure

INCIDENT

At the regular meeting of the National Office Managers Association,
Joan Smith, office manager of a local mortage company, asked the speaker,
a local psychological consultant, for advice on a problem that she faced at
work. The problem concerned a decision she had to make regarding one of
her employees, Joe Lamb, who had been with the company for eight years
as a clerk-typist, bookkeeper, and more recently as a chief file clerk. Lamb
was described as a mild-tempered, introverted bachelor of 43 with a good
employment record who usually preferred to keep to himself.

One evening after work, Lamb had dinner alone at a local restaurant
and went to a movie. Returning to his one-room apartment four blocks
away, he took a short-cut through a park, where a local policeman was
attracted by the shouts of a young woman who claimed she had been
attacked. Lamb was described as the assailant, arrested, and subsequently
brought to trial on a battery charge. In accordance with company policy,
which stated that "employees charged with felonies must be suspended
without pay pending resolution of the matter," Lamb was relieved of duties
soon after his arrest. The trial ended with a verdict of not guilty due to
insufficient evidence.

Smith reinstated Lamb immediately after the trial and requested the
finance department to pay him for his three-month absence. Shortly after
Lamb returned to work, Smith noticed that much antagonism was being
directed toward him by other employees. Many workers, male and female,
refused to associate with him, and several failed to coordinate their work
activities with the file department. Thus, office procedures were disrupted.
The matter culminated in a demand from some employees that Lamb be
transferred or discharged. They felt that Lamb was guilty of the crime, and
some women were fearful of him.

Smith talked with Lamb hoping to persuade him to resign voluntarily or to accept a transfer to another department. Lamb refused and implied that if he was discharged, he would bring charges against the company for damaging his reputation and jeopardizing his opportunity for employment elsewhere.

The consultant's opinion was that Lamb should have been discharged immediately after his arrest based on a suspicion of guilt. He also questioned the wisdom of a policy that calls for suspending persons suspected of committing felonies. His recommendation was that since Lamb had been reinstated, he should be transferred to a different department, even though such action could have undesirable consequences.

CRITIQUES

C. B. GAMBRELL, JR.
Dean, School of Engineering
Mercer University

The consultant's recommendation takes the path of least resistance. In this case, such a decision offers the advantages of placating the disturbance among the other office workers and avoiding the risk of damaging customer goodwill. However, there are serious disadvantages to this solution. There are no technical grounds for discharge, and management runs the risk of setting a precedent by supporting a breach of policy, and incurring a severe court investigation. It must be remembered that federal and many state and local regulations require that a due-process procedure be followed in discharging persons, especially employees who have successfully passed any required probationary period. Thus, if Lamb is discharged, he might sue for job retention and damages. If he succeeds, management's reputation would be marred, which could result in a severe loss of business and unfavorable statements by competitors and others familiar with the case. Although through adverse publicity some customer goodwill may be lost if he is retained, this would be minimal compared to what would result from Lamb's suit following his dismissal. Although retaining Lamb could impair office efficiency, it would uphold the torch of management integrity even though Lamb's success and chances for promotion within the department appear to have been irreparably damaged.

A tempting consideration is that Lamb should be transferred to another department, and that the incident should never be officially revealed to anyone other than the personnel director and Lamb's new superior. Should this transpire, Lamb might gain acceptance among his new associates, the workers in his former department would be partially satisfied, and management's integrity would be maintained. The risks that Lamb may not approve a transfer, or that he might have to be demoted and/or trained, are possibilities if this procedure is adopted.

It appears that Smith should do a more comprehensive job of working with Lamb to identify a change acceptable to him. If Lamb is in fact a mild and introverted person, he too feels pressure. Does Lamb really appreciate that there is a problem? What would he like to do? An attempt should be made to convince him that management cannot control the personal feelings of its employees. Management could, however, move him to another office a considerable distance away. The transfer alternative would work better if Lamb could be moved across the country and would agree to do so. But to take this approach as a solution obligates management to reoccurring personnel pressure of a similar nature for other employee disturbances.

Unfortunately, such a transfer may be seen as a "constructive discharge" by a court and could, therefore, wreak just as much legal havoc as if Lamb had been discharged. Second, Lamb's transfer at this time would constitute a de facto capitulation to a "policy-by-popular-demand" precedent. This would be unjust to Lamb and unwise as a basis for future management decisions. Third, Lamb's personal life history cannot be concealed from his associates in a new department—the ubiquitous "grapevine" will see to that. Lastly, Smith will get absolutely nowhere in verbally upholding the integrity of management's personnel decisions while in the same breath transferring Lamb on the basis of hearsay in the office and not on the basis of a guilty finding in the courts. Arbitrarily transferring Lamb to a nearby department will only move the problem and create others; it will not solve the problem.

A promising solution would be for Smith to try to keep Lamb in the office, while working to help his associates resolve their fear and resentment of him. First, she must have the solid support of top management for a policy that protects employees from adverse action without just cause and due process. If management is unwilling to commit to this policy, Smith has two choices: (1) Leave the company or (2) fire or transfer Lamb and prepare for a rash of adverse consequences. Given management backing for a policy of fairness, Smith can try to sell this eminently American idea of fairness to Lamb's associates, reminding them that this same policy would also protect them from unfair treatment in the future. That all employees—including Lamb—will be treated fairly should be made crystal clear to all concerned.

In discussions with Lamb's co-workers, especially those in informal leadership positions, Smith can make Lamb the fully competent employee he was before the incident by indicating a strong management position on sexual harassment of and by employees. For example, should Lamb (or anyone else) engage in sexual harassment of any kind on the job, management will take positive action for discharge. In the interim, there will be some friction and possibly some attrition; but the prize at stake—management's creditability and integrity—would be worth the cost. Without these assets, management is bankrupt.

For further consideration: First, what is the company policy with respect to employees' rights? If Smith can discern the answer to this question, she will also discover the proper course of action—at least from the company's viewpoint. The fact that the company suspends an employee suspected of a felony *without* pay implies probable guilt, which is perhaps punitive in itself. Why not suspend *with* pay? Is it company policy to presume guilt until innocence is proven? Regardless of what the company says its policy is, in handling Lamb's case the company will define what its policy really is. That definition has important implications for the company's future and for the long-run creditability of its managers.

Second, is there not also a moral or ethical consideration? With the current emphasis being placed on morality in business, almost all of the Lamb case rationales are based on keeping management and the company in a good position with respect to possible litigation or strength of policy or customer relations or whatever. No action seems to have been taken because it was the ethical or morally correct thing to do. Lamb was never guilty of anything even though he was accused, and it is important that the company not imply that he might have been even by implication. Certainly suspension without pay implies that if he is not in fact guilty, he must at least prove his innocence before coming back to work. This is not good practice. If suspension is thought to be either desirable or necessary, the company should at least pay him until the legal issues are resolved. This would go a long way toward not placing a stigma on Lamb that proved so troublesome upon his return from the suspension.

In a similar fashion, Smith's automatic reaction to employee unrest should have been an unqualified support of Lamb. After all, he did nothing wrong . . . he was acquitted! Anyone who is uncomfortable at working with him should be politely, but firmly, shown the door. Now the case arrived at this point eventually, but not because it was the correct thing to do but for political reasons. An important question to ask is, should things not be done for moral reasons in the workplace?

A. T. HOLLINGSWORTH
Professor of Management
Monmouth College

Joe Lamb's suspension was the correct action *if* Lamb was aware of the company's policy relating to the suspension of employees charged with felonies. Given such a policy, the consultant's advice that Lamb should have been dismissed immediately was incorrect. The consultant's questioning of the wisdom of such a policy is unfounded given today's legal environment. The present policy ensures due process for employees and protects their civil rights. This is extremely important in case the company is taken to court.

By reinstating Lamb with back pay, Smith has adhered to company policy. What does Smith do now? The alternatives are: firing, transferring, ignoring the situation, seeking voluntary resignation from Lamb, or keeping him in his present position.

Recently an attorney gave a group of business executives the following advice: "You may fire an individual for no reason, the wrong reason, or for the right reason, but you cannot fire an individual for an illegal reason." This is the initial question facing Smith: Can Lamb be fired legally? Yes, he can. The only way that the company can get into legal difficulty is if, when asked for references, they give the reason for the firing as Lamb's arrest. If, however, Lamb's performance deteriorates due to his inability to deal with other employees, he can be fired for poor performance of his duties.

However, simply because it is legal is not necessarily a good reason for firing an individual. It would set an undesirable precedent and could result in future Equal Employment Opportunity Commission (EEOC) problems if a similar occurrence happened and concerned an individual in another type of protected class. Lamb is in a protected class due to his age, but it is unlikely that age discrimination could be claimed in ths case. Voluntary resignation is out of the question based on Lamb's reaction to this suggestion. A transfer offers a possible solution, but is not the best answer from a managerial viewpoint.

Smith must initiate a solution. It is clear that the problem cannot be ignored since general performance will most likely deteriorate. Smith must make all employees aware, either in an open meeting or through personal conversations, that the only reasons for which individuals will be terminated will be related to job performance. Smith should inform the employees that Lamb's accusation and subsequent acquittal is not related to his job performance, and as long as his work is "acceptable," he will remain on the job. Smith should explain that this is the company policy and will be applied equally to *every* individual in the company. People are not required to like Lamb, only to perform needed job activities with him.

It is possible that ostracism would ultimately lead to Lamb's resignation and/or poor performance leading to dismissal, but the manager's position would be quite clear: The organization is interested in performance as a criterion of employment. This position would demonstrate to employees that Smith intends to keep this matter on an objective basis, not an emotive basis, and should minimize future problems.

The need for specific company policies and adherence to such policies is evident in this case. Such policies ensure that employees will not be treated capriciously by management. This should result in positive management-employee relations. These type policies are also necessary in an age where the courts are becoming more sympathetic toward employees that are discharged without due process. State laws and court decisions must also be considered.

OBSERVATIONS

This incident's critiques illustrate that there are certain factual premises and value premises that influence decisions of the kind facing Ms. Smith. One factual premise is the very real threat of legal action against the company if the decision is made to terminate, or even transfer, Joe Lamb. In the Social Issues section of the June 18, 1984, issue of *Business Week*, several incidents are related that illustrate the possibility that Smith's company would be liable for damages if she yields to the group pressure she faces. In New Jersey, a United Parcel Service of America, Inc., manager, who was fired on the grounds that he falsified records, sued UPS claiming that his extramarital affair with another UPS employee was the real reason for his dismissal. The manager's lover, who has since become his second wife, sued the company for invasion of privacy and harassment. In Michigan, a waiter at the Gandy Dancer, an Ann Arbor restaurant, was told he could quit, be transferred, or be fired if he married his fiancee, a waitress at the same establishment. The waiter quit, married, and sued his employer for discrimination based on marital status. He won reinstatement and back wages.

There are also value premises that Smith may consider relevant. She may believe that the end (tranquility and restored office efficiency) will justify the means (termination of an employee who was found not guilty of a crime). The decision will involve factual premises of a legal nature and Smith's personal value structure, code of ethics, feelings toward what might be considered the "easy way out," and, perhaps most importantly, her empathy toward Lamb.

DISCUSSION ITEMS

1. If you were Joan Smith, would you accept the consultant's recommendation to discharge Joe Lamb based on suspicion of guilt? Defend your position.
2. Suppose the following policy had been formally adopted in Smith's company: "It is the policy of this company to treat all employees fairly,

to respect their personal rights and dignity, and to ensure that no employee is unjustly denied any benefit of employment." Would it affect your position?

3. Professor Gambrell states that keeping Lamb will uphold the torch of management integrity. Do you agree this is worth the work disruption and negative attitudes that seem to be occurring in the company? How should Smith have planned for Lamb's return to work?

SUGGESTED READINGS

BOOKS

Arnold, Hugh J., and Daniel C. Feldman. *Organizational Behavior*. New York: McGraw-Hill, 1986, chaps. 7, 8.

Buchholz, Rogene A. *Business Environment and Public Policy*. Englewood Cliffs, N.J.: Prentice-Hall, 1982, chap. 14.

Callahan, Robert E.; C. Patrick Fleenor; and Harry Knudson. *Understanding Organizational Behavior*. Columbus, Ohio: Charles E. Merrill Publishing, 1986, chap. 6.

Davis, Keith, and John W. Newstrom. *Human Behavior at Work*. 7th ed. New York: McGraw-Hill, 1985, chaps. 8–12.

Donnelly, James H.; James L. Gibson; and John M. Ivancevich. *Fundamentals of Management*. 6th ed. Plano, Tex.: Business Publications, 1987, chaps. 11, 12.

French, Wendell L. *The Personnel Management Process*. 6th ed. Boston: Houghton Mifflin, 1987, chaps. 5, 8, 11, 27.

Griffin, Ricky W. *Management*. 2nd ed. Boston: Houghton Mifflin, 1987, chaps. 15, 16.

Heneman, Herbert G.; Donald P. Schwab; John A. Fossum; and Lee D. Dyer. *Personnel/Human Resource Management*. 3rd ed. Homewood, Ill.: Richard D. Irwin, 1986, chaps. 6, 11.

Hosmer, LaRue T. *The Ethics of Management*. Homewood, Ill.: Richard D. Irwin, 1987.

McFarland, Dalton E. *Management and Society*. Englewood Cliffs, N.J.: Prentice-Hall, 1982, chaps. 8, 9.

Megginson, Leon C. *Personnel Management: A Human Resources Approach*. 5th ed. Homewood, Ill.: Richard D. Irwin, 1985, chaps. 10–12.

Rue, Leslie W., and Lloyd L. Byars. *Management: Theory and Application*. 4th ed. Homewood, Ill.: Richard D. Irwin, 1986, chaps. 15, 16.

Schermerhorn, John R. *Management for Productivity*. 2nd ed. New York: John Wiley & Sons, 1986, chap. 13.

JOURNALS

Albanese, Robert, and David D. Van Fleet. "Rational Behavior in Groups: The Free-Riding Tendency." *Academy of Management Review* 10, no. 2 (April 1985), pp. 244–55.

Aram, J. D., and P. F. Jalispante. "An Evaluation of Organizational Due Process in the Resolution of Employee/Employer Conflict." *Academy of Management Review* 6, no. 1 (January 1981), pp. 197–204.

Brockner, Joel. "Improving the Performance of Low Self-Esteem Individuals." *Academy of Management Journal* 26, no. 4 (December 1983), pp. 642–56.

Cosier, Richard A., and Dan R. Dalton, "Equity Theory and Time: A Reformulation." *Academy of Management Review* 8, no. 2 (April 1983), pp. 311–19.

Einhorn, H. J., and R. M. Hogarth. "Decision Making: Going Forward in Reverse." *Harvard Business Review* 6, no. 1 (January-February 1987), pp. 66–70.

Farrell, Dan, and James C. Petersen. "Patterns of Political Behavior in Organizations." *Academy of Management Review* 7, no. 3 (July 1982), pp. 403–12.

Hatano, Daryl G. "Employee Rights and Corporate Restrictions: A Balancing of Liberties." *California Management Review* 24, no. 2 (Winter 1981), pp. 5–13.

Karp, H. B. "Working with Resistance." *Training and Development Journal* 38, no. 3 (March 1984), pp. 69–73.

Labovich, G. H. "Managing Conflict." *Business Horizons* 23, no. 3 (June 1980), pp. 31–37.

Matusewitch, Eric. "Employment Rights of Ex-Offenders." *Personnel Journal*, pp. 951–54.

Pulich, Marcia A. "Train First-Line Supervisors to Handle Discipline." *Personnel Journal* 62, no. 12 (December 1983), pp. 980–86.

Singh, J. V. "Performance, Slack, and Risk Taking in Organizational Decision Making." *Academy of Management Journal* 29, no. 3 (September 1986), pp. 562–85.

Stanley, John D. "Dissent in Organizations." *Academy of Management Review* 6, no. 1 (January 1981), pp. 13–19.

Taylor, Hugh R. "Power at Work." *Personnel Journal* 65, no. 4 (April 1986), pp. 42–49.

Trevino, L. K. "Ethical Decision Making in Organizations." *Academy of Management Review* 11, no. 3 (July 1986), pp. 601–17.

WHAT THIS INCIDENT IS ABOUT:
When the new supervisor improves production
dramatically at the expense of employee relations,
the plant must face rumblings of rebellion. The
incident calls for considering grievances, using
authority, gaining acceptance of change, generating
motivation, obtaining commitment, and linking
output with job satisfaction.

25

Production slowdown

INCIDENT

Frederick Woolsey had been made supervisor of a production line at
Metal Fabrication, Inc. The plant manager made him responsible for
operating the entire production line efficiently and effectively. Woolsey
supervised 6 foremen and 48 assembly line workers. His job was to keep
the assembly line going at the scheduled 71 units per hour.

When Woolsey took the supervisor's job two months previously, the
production line was losing 90 minutes of production a day. Line stoppages,
maintenance problems, absenteeism, and workers stopping the line for
repair were some causes of lost production. The 90-minute loss was approximately 20 percent of the daily operating schedule.

Woolsey reduced absenteeism and took other steps to prevent the loss
of scheduled production time. He kept the main line going even when
some feeder lines stopped. "The workers don't like it," said Woolsey.
"They resent working the required 7 hours and 45 minutes a day instead of
only 6 hours and 30 minutes."

The disgruntlement of the production line workers toward Woolsey
seemed to be centered in Robert Long and Vic Green. The complaints
against Woolsey were varied and included the following. Both Green and
Long said that Woolsey laid off workers for being two minutes late. They
also said that Woolsey had foremen picking up trash. Long said that
Woolsey had threatened him with an iron bar about eight inches long and
claimed that Woolsey was guilty of using "speed-up" tactics. As a result of
these events, the two filed a formal grievance targeting Woolsey.

The plant manager knew that Woolsey was the target of increasingly vitriolic verbal protests by Long and Green. Both were openly defiant and implied that they were ready to take matters into their own hands.

Confronted with this high and rising level of employee unrest, the plant manager reflected upon Woolsey's inability to achieve simultaneously adequate production and adequate behavioral relations with his workers. He wondered "Are these two goals necessarily incompatible? Does the problem lie with Woolsey, the assemblyline workers, or the situation?" More importantly, the plant manager knew that prompt decisions and actions were essential to defuse the explosive situation.

While action was immediately needed to extinguish the agitation among the assembly line workers, the plant manager wished to use Woolsey in a positive role, and he desired to maintain the improved production rates achieved under Woolsey's leadership. For the longer run, he reasoned that developing specific operational policies would be essential in areas such as supervisory training, introduction of change, team building, and other areas relevant to balancing supervisory concern for task performance with concern for behavioral relationships. Implementation of these policies would be difficult, and he knew it. As the plant manager pondered his plight, his stress increased. He was uncertain where to begin.

CRITIQUES

LYMAN W. PORTER
Professor, Graduate School of Management
University of California at Irvine

There are at least three salient points to examine with respect to this incident:

1. The supervisor, Woolsey, has failed to obtain the commitment of his subordinates to the goal of 71 units per hour. (Whether this is a realistic goal is a separate question.) There is no indication that the assembly line workers had any voice in formulating goals or in helping to determine how goals are to be reached. The situation appears to be a strictly "top down" type of operation, with subordinates given little credit for having ideas about planning how the production line should be operated. Indeed, Woolsey almost seems more interested in making sure no one misses a minute on the line than he does in reaching the 71-unit goal. (A case of the means becoming more important than the ends, or goal.) Woolsey is operating more like a watchdog than a facilitator.

2. Woolsey seems to lack the support of, and rapport with, the informal leadership structure existing among his subordinates (that is, Green and

Long, who, if not informal leaders, are at least vocal). Green and Long seem more upset at Woolsey than at having to produce 71 units per hour.

3. It is not clear how the assembly line workers see themselves benefiting from reaching the goal of 71 units (or any other particular goal, whether lower or higher than 71). Similarly, we do not know what they believe will happen if the line does not produce at precisely 71 units. In other words, the reward/punishment structure in this situation is unclear.

If improvements are to be made for both the company and the workers, it appears that the following steps need to occur:

1. An objective analysis should be used to determine if the goal of 71 units is feasible. If not, Woolsey should take the issue up with his superiors. In that way, he would demonstrate to his subordinates that he is as concerned with their welfare as he is with the company's welfare, and he would gain their increased confidence. If the goal is reasonable, then the employees should receive some opportunity to help determine how it is reached. The superior needs to try to gain subordinate acceptance of and commitment toward the goal.

2. The situation regarding the two apparent informal leaders is critical, and this issue probably needs to be addressed very soon. The goal would be to turn Green and Long's outspokenness into positive leadership acts among their peers. The plant manager needs to assess whether Green and Long are basically capable employees or whether they would be disruptive under almost any supervisor and any set of circumstances. If the former is the case, then the plant manager should encourage Woolsey to overcome the problem directly through discussion of Green and Long's complaints (assuming they are legitimate). If Woolsey would feel uncomfortable doing this alone, the plant manager could offer to sit in as a mediator. If problems persist, the manager will have to decide whether Green and Long should be transferred to a different supervisor or whether they should be separated. To reiterate, the goal would be to see if it is possible with reasonable effort to turn Green and Long into informal leadership assets rather than disaffected liabilities.

3. The reward structure needs to be clarified, so that the subordinates can feel some connection between their efforts and performance and the positive outcomes they can obtain if they meet the goal. Simply an opportunity to have some control over the variation in the day's work pace, as long as the goal of 71 units (or whatever goal is adopted) is reached, could be incentive for attaining the goal. An effective supervisor ought to think of other ways to link rewarding outcomes to adequate or outstanding performance.

4. For the longer run, the plant manager should consider providing additional supervisory training and development for Woolsey. He seems to have the potential to be an effective leader, and he already has achieved some definite results for the organization. However, his "style" is causing

some problems that may render his future efforts ineffective. Woolsey appears to be an excellent candidate for a supervisory development program.

WILLIAM B. WERTHER, JR.
Professor of Executive Management
University of Miami

Successful leaders achieve their organization's objectives while concurrently meeting the needs of their people. At best, Woolsey is only half successful, since he fails to meet the needs of his supervisors and workers.

The production employees developed an expectation of working ". . . only 6 hours and 30 minutes." Woolsey violated their expectations by demanding more. He upset supervisors, too, by making them pick up trash. Although the plant manager was pleased with the production gains, Woolsey focused too narrowly on the production goals without paying enough attention to behavioral relationships. Restated, Woolsey was "task oriented" without being sufficiently "people oriented." Production benefited at the expense of employee needs; Woolsey was, in effect, achieving production results by "consuming" the morale, motivation, teamwork, and goodwill of employees. Ultimately, the flow of grievances, turnover, and declining teamwork will affect production. Then, neither production nor people's goals are likely to be met.

What is to be done? The plant manager needs to intervene with Woolsey, positively reinforcing the production results while explaining the need to build, not destroy, the team spirit among supervisors and workers. It is important for the plant manager to begin with an acknowledgement of Woolsey's production results for two reasons. First, criticizing Woolsey's methods without recognizing the performance gains might send a mixed message. Woolsey might perceive that production results are suddenly less important than employee relations. Second, as a practical matter, criticizing Woolsey's methods without recognizing his results would likely lead to a blockage of the communication channel between Woolsey and the plant manager. Sensing a lack of appreciation for his "impressive" production gains, Woolsey might severely discount the plant manager's comments, thinking his boss had the wrong priorities or had gone "soft" on production goals. Since Woolsey has achieved production increases, he probably valued them. For the plant manager to ignore these gains might lead Woolsey to be defensive about any criticism of his methods. In short, the plant manager should follow the psychologist dictum, "Start where the patient is." Besides, the plant manager can begin the interventions on a positive note—Woolsey's production improvements.

Still, the employee relations issue must be addressed. Although the exact approach used by the plant manager with Woolsey will depend on personality variables and their past relationship, a defensive reaction is likely, even if the performance review discussion acknowledges Woolsey's production accomplishments. Specifically, the plant manager may want to talk about employee perceptions. Regardless of what Woolsey's behavior has been or what his goals were, Woolsey needs to understand his supervisors' and workers' perceptions. Rather than telling Woolsey what is happening to employee relations, the plant manager might want to solicit Woolsey's opinions first, venting some defensive behavior.

Armed with specific examples (e.g., the grievances), the plant manager needs to get Woolsey to see the impact of his approach on employee relations. Perhaps one successful strategy would be for Woolsey to describe what he imagines are the supervisors' and employees' feelings. Then, asking what is going to be done about those perceptions should lead Woolsey to the realization that he needs to do something different.

Through repeated coaching, the plant manager can guide Woolsey to handling tardiness, absenteeism, production delays, and other impediments to production in a more employee-centered manner. In the long term, Woolsey will need training in group dynamics, interpersonal relations, and team building. Perhaps the best long-term strategy is for Woolsey to become more participative in his decision making by involving supervisors (and employees) in the identification of production problems and the creation of feasible alternatives.

OBSERVATIONS

Discipline does not occupy a prominent place in motivation theory or practice. Typically, discipline is imposed for certain employee behaviors that violate prescribed rules, regulations, or procedures. Penalties for infractions are usually established in advance. Failing to work hard or steadily is generally considered an offense in need of attention. Frederick Woolsey, however, is applying discipline and other techniques as interventions to modify employee behavior toward achieving the prescribed 7 hours and 45 minutes of production each workday. The short-run results are mixed: production has increased markedly, but so has worker disgruntlement. The long-run issue may well be: "Who runs the production line, the foremen or the workers?" After all, it is not easy to get hourly employees to work more than they are accustomed to, as this incident illustrates. If it is felt that Woolsey's methods are not appropriate, one should examine popular motivational and leadership theories in search of guidance for Woolsey. He needs all the help he can get.

DISCUSSION ITEMS

1. How can employees have opportunities to react to the production goal of 71 units per hour and help determine how the goal is to be achieved?
2. What approaches would you recommend in seeking the cooperation of Green and Long, the two apparent informal leaders? Explain.
3. How might the reward/penalty structure be clarified so that the workers can see the connection between their efforts toward improved production and some positive outcomes for them in terms of rewards?

SUGGESTED READINGS

BOOKS

Arnold, Hugh J., and Daniel C. Feldman. *Organizational Behavior*. New York: McGraw-Hill, 1986, chaps. 3, 13.

Callahan, Robert E.; C. Patrick Fleenor; and Harry Knudson. *Understanding Organizational Behavior*. Columbus, Ohio: Charles E. Merrill Publishing, 1986, chap. 14.

Davis, Keith, and John W. Newstrom. *Human Behavior at Work*. 7th ed. New York: McGraw-Hill, 1985, chaps. 8, 9, 11.

Donnelly, James H.; James L. Gibson; and John M. Ivancevich. *Fundamentals of Management*. 6th ed. Plano, Tex.: Business Publications, 1987, chap. 3, pp. 746, 747.

French, Wendell L. *The Personnel Management Process*. 6th ed. Boston: Houghton Mifflin, 1987, chaps. 6, 8, 22.

Griffin, Ricky W. *Management*. 2nd ed. Boston: Houghton Mifflin, 1987, chap. 13, pp. 552–58.

Heneman, Herbert G.; Donald P. Schwab; John A. Fossum; and Lee D. Dyer. *Personnel/Human Resource Management*. 3rd ed. Homewood, Ill.: Richard D. Irwin, 1986, chaps. 3, 12, 13.

Megginson, Leon C. *Personnel Management: A Human Resources Approach*. 5th ed. Homewood, Ill.: Richard D. Irwin, 1985, chaps. 8, 11.

Rue, Leslie W., and Lloyd L. Byars. *Management: Theory and Application*. 4th ed. Homewood, Ill.: Richard D. Irwin, 1986, chap. 14.

Schermerhorn, John R. *Management for Productivity* 2nd ed. New York: John Wiley & Sons, 1986, chaps. 10–12.

JOURNALS

"Automakers Share Profits with Employees." *Monthly Labor Review* 108, no. 4 (April 1985), p. 61.

Barnard, Janet C. "Leadership Is a Survival Skill." *Administrative Management* 48, no. 1 (January 1987), pp. 56, 57.

Beary, Rodney F. "Discipline Policy—A Neglected Personnel Tool." *Administrative Management* 46, no. 11 (November 1985), pp. 21–24.

Beck, Arthur C., and Ellis D. Hillmar. "What Managers Can Do to Turn around Negative Attitudes in an Organization." *Management Review* 73, no. 1 (January 1984), pp. 22–25.

Cameron, Dan. "The When, Why, and How of Discipline." *Personnel Journal* 63, no. 7 (July 1984), pp. 37–39.

Debobes, Leo. "Psychological Factors in Accident Prevention." *Personnel Journal* 65, no. 1 (January 1986), pp. 34–48.

Deming, Donald D. "Reevaluating the Assembly Line." *Supervisory Management* 22, no. 9 (September 1977), pp. 2–7.

Fox, Harold W. "Eliciting Latent Productivity." *Business Horizons* 26, no. 6 (November-December 1983), pp. 37–45.

Geisler, Eliezer. "Artificial Management and the Artificial Manager." *Business Horizons* 29, no. 4 (July-August 1986), pp. 17–21.

Golembiewski, Robert T.; Carl W. Rothl; and David Sink. "Estimating the Success of OD Applications." *Training and Development Journal* 36, no. 4 (April 1982), pp. 86–94.

King, Albert S. "Barriers to Adapting Japanese Personnel Practices." *Advanced Management Journal* 48, no. 3 (Summer 1983), pp. 34–41.

Luthans, Fred, and Robert Krietner. "The Role of Punishment in Organizational Behavior Modification." *Public Personnel Management* 2, no. 3 (May-June 1973), pp. 156–61.

McGee, Philip H. "Management Training Not Enough." *Training* 21, no. 9 (September 1984), p. 122.

Muczyk, Jan P., and Robert E. Hastings. "In Defense of Enlightened Hardball Management." *Business Horizons* 28, no. 4 (July-August 1985), pp. 23–29.

Pryor, Frederic L. "Incentives in Manufacturing." *Monthly Labor Review* 107, no. 7 (July 1984), pp. 40–43.

Renken, Henry J. "An Employee-Incentive Program Can Be the Answer to Increased Productivity." *SAM Advanced Management Journal* 49, no. 2 (Spring 1984), pp. 8–12.

Sailer, Heather R.; John Schlacter; and Mark R. Edwards. "Stress: Causes, Consequences, and Coping Strategies." *Personnel* 59, no. 4 (July-August 1982), pp. 35–48.

WHAT THIS INCIDENT IS ABOUT:
Personal profits from government consulting work
are at issue when an enterprising author appears to
be "double-dipping" at the public trough. The
incident involves ethics, personal value structures,
consultant relations, entrepreneurship, and government affairs.

26

Public versus private interests

INCIDENT

While serving as educational consultant to the State Real Estate Board, Robin Rostow, professor of real estate at Keowee State University, discovered that applicants wishing to become registered state real estate agents were required to study a variety of topics, including the legal and financial aspects of real estate transactions, contracts, and calculations. Professor Rostow realized that no one source contained the required materials for the wide variety of real estate topics.

Because required materials were scattered among different sources and because of the location of applicants throughout the state, members of the State Real Estate Board faced the problem of assembling the required materials into study packets for distribution to applicants. This procedure was awkward, time-consuming to the board, and costly to the applicants.

Professor Rostow proposed a solution. He proposed to write a textbook tailored to the state board requirements. The real estate book would cover the required topics in sequence and with the emphasis preferred by the state board, so that it would meet their needs exactly. This one source of information could be reproduced in quantity and conveniently distributed to applicants. Moreover, it was proposed that each applicant be required to purchase the special text. Other advantages for the applicants were: (1) reduced cost, (2) increased convenience, and (3) improved preparation of the applicant and thus a reduced failure rate on the state real estate agent license examination.

The real estate board accepted the professor's proposal *in toto*. The book was written and published, and it served its intended purpose for three years. Then came the newspaper headline, PROF GIVES NO COMMENT TO PROBE INTO BOOK SALE, followed by the lead paragraph: "A Keowee State University professor whose state-commissioned book earned $300,000 for him and his wife would not comment Thursday on a planned investigation into the circumstances surrounding the preparation, publication, and sale of the book."

The newspaper account was based on the state auditor's report, which, in part, contained the following facts: The real estate board had retained Rostow as a consultant and paid him consulting fees to develop the book for them. After the book was written, however, Rostow retained the copyright and established the T-A-T Publishing Company to produce the book. During the three-year period covered by the auditor's report, Rostow received $10,000 in consulting fees from the State Real Estate Board and $105,000 in royalties from the book, while his wife received a $225,000 profit as publishing company president and treasurer. The auditor's report asserted that the real estate board could have published the textbook on its own at a savings for license applicants and as a source of funds for the real estate board. Moreover, board publication of the book would have lowered the price for applicants to $7.80 instead of $12.80, the actual selling price. The T-A-T Publishing Company was the sole publisher of the book, which was the company's sole product.

The members of the joint legislative auditing committee investigating the situation were outspoken in their concern. "I think they (the State Real Estate Board) gave away the public's assets," said State Representative Mary Krause, a member of the committee. During the ensuing discussion, the following questions were debated: Had anyone done anything ethically wrong here? Did the State Real Estate Board acceptably serve the public interest? If not, where had it failed? Had the public interest been served by the entrepreneurial action of Professor Rostow? What is an acceptable entrepreneurial role in government affairs, if any?

The auditing committee unanimously approved a motion that their staff investigate the profit made by Rostow and his wife in the publishing venture. As a policy guide for the auditing committee, moreover, the staff was instructed to develop drafts of policies distinguishing between public and private interests, with attention to the issues of professional ethical standards, conflicts of interest, collusion, and the acceptable allocation of risk and revenues between governmental agencies and suppliers of professional services.

Finally, the following motion was made: "That the legislative auditing board assert a claim for 50 percent of the profits realized by the T-A-T Publishing Company from the sale of the real estate book." As Krause sought guidance from her structure of personal values and from her sense of ethics, the call came to vote on the question and she remained undecided, without a clear notion of the right thing to do.

CRITIQUES

OGDEN H. HALL
Professor of Allied Health Auxiliaries
Louisiana State University Medical Center

Was Rostow hired as an "educational consultant" to develop instructional materials and methods for those applying for State Real Estate Board licenses? If so, it would seem that any materials produced would be the board's property, not the professor's. If the agreement between the parties is unclear on this point, the auditing committee would best serve the public interest by concentrating on what the board should do in the future.

In retrospect, is there any reason why the professor should be precluded from personal gain because he developed the materials? The board should resolve this question based on how the public interest can be served by T-A-T Publishing or by other alternatives. We must conclude from the information presented that there has been a significant improvement in the service rendered to applicants compared with previous alternatives. Whether Professor Rostow and his company offer the best approach remains untested and unproven

Two board actions are questionable. One is the requirement that applicants purchase Professor Rostow's book. Making the material conveniently available at a lower price is a distinct service. Requiring its use may suggest the possibility of a collusion. The other questionable action is retaining Professor Rostow as a consultant after publication of the book. If he was employed to provide services other than producing the materials, continuation of the relationshp could be desirable. If not, there is a strong implication of collusion.

The incident must also be examined from the perspective of Professor Rostow as a professional educator, applying professional education standards. The professor's principal allegiance must be to his academic affiliation. Typically, any extramural activities should contribute to his teaching and researching ability and/or provide a community service. There is nothing reported in the incident that could not conceivably raise his productivity in each of these categories. There is, however, a serious question arising from his entrepreneurial role.

With the required purchase of the book, T-A-T Publishing has a virtual monopoly. A pricing policy that would yield profits and royalties of the magnitude reported is exploitative. Also, his acceptance of royalties under the monopolistic arrangement has overtones of violating professional ethical standards. And if Rostow was paid by the board to prepare the materials, his rights to the property and any personal gains are questionable.

The auditing committee properly instructed its staff to investigate the profitability of publishing materials and selling them to license applicants. The inquiry should also cover board actions that resulted in profits accruing solely to the benefit of the Rostows. However, the committee should limit itself to fact-finding and not fault-finding. These facts should be used for recommending policy governing future board actions.

The board, like any other state agency, exists solely (at least in theory) to serve the public interest. The public includes prospective licensees and their future customers. But we must remember that the "public" is not too likely to be served (except by coercion) without the opportunity for individual entrepreneurs to serve their private interests. History suggests that the entrepreneurial Rostows have faired well by providing better service to the public represented by the board.

Unless the investigation reveals that the Rostows (and/or board members) have violated the law or the terms of their contract, it would be inappropriate to seek retribution. Far better that the legislative auditing committee and the board address formulating and implementing clear policies for future decisions. Only in this way can the board achieve equity in balancing the interest of its constituencies, both public and private.

DANIEL D. ROMAN
Professor Emeritus of Management Science
George Washington University

Rostow's finding that no single satisfactory source existed for the required study material was not very profound based on the information already available. As a consultant, he merely confirmed known facts. He was operating within ethical bounds when he suggested that a special text could be written to incorporate all required information. He would still not transcend an ethical position by suggesting that he could provide such a text to the state for additional consulting compensation. Rostow was guilty of poor judgment and questionable ethics, however, in establishing a conflict-of-interest situation when he proposed to be the author and recommended that the State Real Estate Board require each applicant to purchase the special text.

Rostow's recommendation for a single information source had merit, but the board could have considered some alternatives:

1. The board could refer to applicable material with applicants responsible for acquiring the information.
2. It could refer to applicable material and indicate its availability for a nominal fee.
3. It could commission Rostow to write a book for a consulting fee. This is a common governmental practice. The results of government-sponsored research are often offered to the public for a nominal sum.

4. If Rostow independently wrote a book, which would meet the board's requirements and be exclusive of the consulting arrangement, the board should, at most, include the book as a reference and not as required reading. Had the board done this, it would have avoided criticism for establishing Rostow in a monopolistic position. Rostow would then have had to assume the responsibility for the book's promotion and sale outside the auspices of state sponsorship. This is reasonable—to perceive a need and take an entrepreneurial position. It is compatible with free-enterprise doctrines.

5. A fifth possibility also might have been explored. If the board felt that such a book was essential and should be required of all applicants, it could have acquired ownership rights to the book and offered a royalty arrangement to the author.

6. A more normal governmental procedure, once there was a determination of need, would be the release of a Request for Proposal (RFP). The RFP would have solicited competitive bids relative to the project's content and price. Proposals submitted by qualified bidders could have been evaluated by an independent selection board. By following this procedure, the board would have shown neutrality and that they had operated within the boundaries of acceptable practice for this type of procurement.

Additionally, the issue of excessive profits would not be germane if the board had not established a captive market for the author.

In the academic profession, it is not unusual to publish for prestige. Often, academic publication affords little or no direct monetary returns. However, professional recognition, establishing expertise in a given area, and potential consulting fees may be inducements to undertake such ventures.

What constitutes excessive profits is a matter for conjecture where creative effort is involved. It is not unusual for authors of best selling books to enjoy financial returns in six figures. The price of the book in question is not unreasonable based on current textbook prices.

The board erred in not considering its alternatives. Additionally, the board should have obtained a legal opinion relative to the book's ownership rights since they had already paid Rostow a consulting fee for developing the project. The profit issue was incidental; the real problem was procedural.

Other significant policy issues are involved in this incident. If the consultant had provided the required material as part of the consulting engagement, the ethical question might not have arisen. There could have been subsequent questions about the consultant's qualifications. Policy should have been established whereby: (1) an impartial board could review recommendations entailing activities beyond the board's normal operational sphere; (2) after review board approval, the activity could be performed in-house or contracted out; and (3) consultants would be precluded from operating in a dual capacity as consultant and vendor. Another policy issue involves determining "reasonable" profit. In a competitive market, profit limitations may not be realistic considering degrees of risk. In a captive market, as in this case, the market is established, distribution costs are minimal, and risk is negligible. Policy should address the type and the extent of allowable compensation in return for providing goods and/or services in a controlled market.

OBSERVATIONS

While acting in the public interest, government agencies at national, state, and local levels regularly make decisions that provide opportunities for some and deny them for others. Real estate zoning boards provide an example. The value of property zoned for multifamily dwellings, allowing the construction of apartments and condominiums, is several times greater than the value of the same property zoned for single-family dwellings— due to the more intense economic use of the land. In this incident, opportunity arose for Professor Rostow because of decisions made by the State Real Estate Board. In the enterpreneurial tradition, he negotiated contract terms, provided services and products, and earned a profit.

The unexpected size of Rostow's profit motivated the board to raise several thorny public-interest issues including a belated claim for 50 percent of Rostow's profits. Professors Hall and Roman address the issues of public interest versus private interest with insight based on experience. The clarity and depth of their analyses provide a stimulating basis for discussing this incident.

DISCUSSION ITEMS

1. Are the issues in this incident mainly political, ethical, personal, organizational, or otherwise? Explain.
2. On what grounds would you justify preventing the professor (consultant) from realizing personal gain from the materials he created and developed?
3. Discuss the advantages and disadvantages of the enterpreneurial role in governmental affairs. Discuss conditions in which private activity can be joined beneficially with public activity.

SUGGESTED READINGS

BOOKS

Arnold, Hugh J., and Daniel C. Feldman. *Organizational Behavior*. New York: McGraw-Hill, 1986, chap. 14.

Callahan, Robert E.; C. Patrick Fleenor; and Harry Knudson. *Understanding Organizational Behavior*. Columbus, Ohio: Charles E. Merrill Publishing, 1986, chap. 7.

Davis, Keith, and John W. Newstrom. *Human Behavior at Work*. 7th ed. New York: McGraw-Hill, 1985, chap. 4.

Donnelly, James H.; James L. Gibson; and John M. Ivancevich. *Fundamentals of Management*. 6th ed. Plano, Tex.: Business Publications, 1987, chap. 13, pp. 27, 28.

French, Wendell L. *The Personnel Management Process*. 6th ed. Boston: Houghton Mifflin, 1987, chap. 8.

Griffin, Ricky W. *Management*. 2nd ed. Boston: Houghton Mifflin, 1987, chap. 3.

Heneman, Herbert G.; Donald P. Schwab; John A. Fossum; and Lee D. Dyer. *Personnel/Human Resource Management*. 3rd ed. Homewood, Ill.: Richard D. Irwin, 1986, chap. 4.

Megginson, Leon C. *Personnel Management: A Human Resources Approach*. 5th ed. Homewood, Ill.: Richard D. Irwin, 1985.

Rue, Leslie W., and Lloyd L. Byars. *Management: Theory and Application*. 4th ed. Homewood, Ill.: Richard D. Irwin, 1986, chap. 3.

Schermerhorn, John R. *Management for Productivity*. 2nd ed. New York: John Wiley & Sons, 1986, chap. 20.

JOURNALS

Benfari, Robert C.; Harry E. Wilkinson; and Charles D. Orth. "The Effective Use of Power." *Business Horizons* 29, no. 3 (May–June 1986), pp. 12–16.

Berger, P. "New Attack on the Legitimacy of Business." *Harvard Business Review* 59, no. 5 (September–October 1981), pp. 82–89.

Blieberg, Robert M. "Conflict of Interest in Business—Never More Dangerous than Now." *Business Horizons* 23, no. 4 (August 1980), pp. 67–73.

Brady, F. Neil. "Aesthetic Components of Management Ethics." *Academy of Management Review* 11, no. 2 (April 1986), pp. 337–44.

Fritsche, D. J., and H. Becker. "Linking Management Behavior to Ethical Philosophy: An Empirical Investigation." *Academy of Management Journal* 27, no. 1 (March 1984), pp. 166–75.

Gillis, J. G. "Legal Consequences of Unethical Conduct." *Financial Analysts Journal* 29, no. 11 (November 1973), pp. 12, 13.

Jones, D. "Confessions of a Consultant." *Management Review* 62, no. 6 (June 1973), pp. 42–44.

Lynn, Lawrence E., Jr. "Managing the Public's Business: Are Private-Sector Skills Appropriate?" *California Management Review* 26, no. 2 (Winter 1984), pp. 112–24.

Morgan, Lee L. "Business Ethics Start with the Individual." *Management Accounting* 58, no. 9 (March 1977), pp. 14, 60.

Ramamurt, Ravi. "Public Entrepreneurs: Who They Are and How They Operate." *California Management Review* 28, no. 3 (Spring 1986), pp. 142–58.

"The Tempest Raging over Profit-Minded Professors." *Business Week*, November 7, 1983, pp. 86, 87, 91.

Von Glinow, M. A., and Luke Novelli. "Ethical Standards within Organizational Behavior." *Academy of Management Journal* 25, no. 2 (June 1982), pp. 417–36.

Wartick, Steven L., and Robert E. Rude. "Issues Management: Corporate Fad or Corporate Function." *California Management Review* 29, no. 1 (Fall 1986), pp. 124–40.

WHAT THIS INCIDENT IS ABOUT:
When the plant manager abdicates his authority in a burst of enthusiasm for participative decision teams, he is dismayed by the results. The incident involves quality circles, productivity improvement, and the implementation of policy changes and decisions.

27

Quality circle consequence

INCIDENT

John Stevens, plant manager of the Fairlee Plant of Lockstead Corporation, which manufactures structural components for aircraft wings and bodies, became interested in using quality circles to improve performance in his plant. "Quality circles" was the name used to describe joint labor-supervision participation teams operating at the shop-floor level at Lockstead. Other companies called quality circles names such as "productivity groups," "people involvement programs," and "departmental teams." By whatever name, the purpose of quality circles was to improve the quality of manufacturing performance.

The subject of quality circles was a hot topic in the press. Stevens had seen books on Japanese management and productivity successes, which featured the use of quality circles. In these books, the slogan "None of us is as smart as all of us" was prominent.

Other books related quality circles to productivity gains. Articles on quality circles appeared often in trade journals and in business magazines, including *Business Week*.

Stevens also had a pamphlet from a management consulting firm announcing a "new and improved" training course for quality-circle leaders, scheduled consecutively in Birmingham, Alabama; Williamsburg, Virginia; and Orlando, Florida. Another consultant offered "A program that will teach your managers and supervisors how to increase productivity and efficiency without making costly investments . . . by focusing on techniques germane to the quality-circle process." Stevens was impressed enough to attend an advanced management seminar at a large midwestern university. A large part of the program concentrated on quality circles.

Professor Albert Mennon particularly impressed Stevens with his lectures on group discussion, team problem solving, and group decision making. Mennon convinced Stevens that employees meeting in quality-circle teams with adequate leaders could effectively consider problems and formulate quality decisions that would be acceptable to employees. The staff conducting this state-of-the-art seminar covered five areas, including: (1) training quality-circle members in the six-step problem sequence, (2) describing what leaders and facilitators should do during the quality-circle sessions, (3) planning and writing a policy guide, (4) developing an implementation plan, and (5) measuring quality-circle progress and success.

The potential benefits of a successfully implemented quality-circle program were expected to affect workers and the company. The list of such payoffs included improved job satisfaction, productivity improvements, efficiency gains, and better quality of performance and labor relations. It was expected, moreover, that a reduction would occur in such areas as grievance loads, absenteeism, and costs.

Returning to his plant after the seminar, Stevens decided to practice some of the principles he had learned. He called together the 25 employees of Department B and told them that production standards established several years ago were too low in view of the recent installation of automated equipment. He gave the workers the opportunity to discuss the mitigating circumstances and to decide among themselves, as a group, what their standards should be. On leaving the room, he believed that the workers would establish much higher standards than he would have dared propose.

After an hour of discussion, the group summoned Stevens and notified him that, contrary to his opinion, their decision was that the standards were already too high, and since they had been given the authority to establish their own standards, they were making a reduction of 10 percent. Stevens knew these standards were far too low to provide a fair profit on the owner's investment. Yet he believed his refusal to accept the group decision would be disastrous. Stevens thought of telephoning Professor Mennon for consultation about the quality-circle dilemma, but he chose to act on his own.

Options filled Stevens' mind: (1) He could accept the blame for the quality-circle experiment having gone awry and tell them to begin anew; (2) he could establish incentive pay adjustment linkage between the quality circle's decisions and productivity improvements; (3) he might even operate for a short while at a loss to prove that the original quality-circle decision had been unacceptable; and (4) he might abandon the participative team program. Stevens knows that he needs a decision, an operational policy for the quality-circle program, and an implementation plan.

CRITIQUES

STEPHEN G. FRANKLIN
Associate Professor of Business Administration
Emory University

First, let's discuss how John Stevens could have avoided this situation. Obviously, his intentions were noble, but his implementation lacked knowledgeable insight into the complexities of participative management or quality circles. When using quality circles or participative management techniques, two key concepts must always be kept in focus: accuracy and acceptance. We know from extensive research that group input improves accuracy of decisions by enlarging the resource base for more and better ideas. And, if properly implemented, participative group decisions can improve acceptance of new standards, systems, and ways of doing things because they become "our" ideas, "our" goals, and "our" strategies, rather than those of management.

Stevens should have met with small groups of employees (five to eight) and *explained* to them why the production standards were too low, rather than just *telling* them they were too low. This initial "divide and communicate" strategy is as effective as the militaristic "divide and conquer" strategy of old. *Then*, Stevens should have called a group meeting, briefly explained the reasons for low standards, and remained with the group to maintain the two-way communication channel, to exchange ideas, to air differences of opinion, and to provide reasons why certain actions could or could not be followed. Had he remained with the group, Stevens could have stated his opinion about the problem of production standards and what strategies should be pursued. He could have then asked the group members what they thought about following the approach he outlined. The ensuing discussion would shape a suggested course of action and represent both his and the group's opinions as to what should be done.

However, as the old saying goes, "hindsight is 20-20 vision." In light of the present situation, Stevens should call another meeting with the production employees of Department B and indicate that there is additional information concerning the subject of production standards that he wishes to discuss with them. He should gather all data dealing with the company's production standards, profits, continuity, and other significant data. He should assemble this data in some sort of visual format to increase effectiveness of presentation and to generate meaningful discussion. He should establish a format for the meeting something like the following:

1. Extend verbal appreciation for each member's interest and previous participation in discussing the subject matter.

2. Inform the employees that additional information vital to the modification of present production standards will be presented and discussed by everyone present.
3. Present the information in a candid, forthright manner using overhead transparencies or posterboard charts to display statistics visually.
4. Remain with the group, join in the discussion, and point the group in a direction that will establish a basis for the decision regarding the production standards to be adopted by the entire department.

The emphasis of the meeting should be the determination of direct labor cost goals, why such goals are necessary, and what assistance the group members can contribute in achieving them.

A key ingredient in the situation is for Stevens to provide effective leadership by offering a plan, giving reasons for the plan, and taking into account suggestions offered by the members who would be affected by the plan. This approach incorporates the manager's ideas, the group members' wishes, and the needs of the enterprise into an effective program.

It is quite possible that the employees are correct—the standards are too high. Errors in calculating the standards are possible, and the employees must be given an opportunity to present their reasons for reducing the standards.

Historical facts and experience are very important in determining the level of production standards adopted by Department B, and Stevens should abstain from forcing the decision unless the group absolutely cannot come to an agreeable resolution. It may take several weeks or possibly months for production events to demonstrate what standards should be, for they will be influenced by the verification of employee beliefs, the correctness of Stevens' statements, the extent of modifications required, and employees' full comprehension of the situation.

Finally, a student of management should understand that raising production standards is not a popular subject among employees. The naive, ineffective manager believes that an employee will accept increases in production standards without rational explanation. Regardless of the issue involved (survival, necessary returns to stockholders, regaining competitive position in the marketplace, or any number of managerial reasons), it must be explained to employees if they are to be considered as valuable human resources. It is quite obvious that John Stevens needs to spend more time to stay in touch with the attitudes, beliefs, perceptions, and misperceptions of Department B employees to effectively lead and supervise quality circles and participative management practices.

CHARLES R. KLASSON
Professor of Business Organization and Policy
University of Iowa

Here we witness the consequences of a manager's decision to implement a new management technique without due regard for the entire implementation process. John Stevens failed: (1) to understand how quality circles would change the basic work structure, and (2) to comprehend the complex organizational process associated with implementing this concept into work groups. The consequences are bad news for Stevens. He now has: (1) a hostile group of workers; (2) a work situation that will degenerate in terms of employee morale and productivity; (3) a negative group attitude toward quality circles; and (4) a slim chance of turning things around in the next 6 to 12 months, if at all. Next, let's consider where Stevens erred in his efforts to use the latest management technique as a means to improve his plant's performance.

The introduction of quality circles into a standard manufacturing operation, which probably uses a functional form, represents a major organizational change. Any major change requires a large degree of employee understanding. This, in turn, requires massive communication efforts to share reasons for the change, how such changes can be made without endangering job security, and how each employee can be directly involved in the entire process of change. Commitment to a decision is related to one's involvement in reaching a decision. It is predictable that employee resistance to structural changes will be high. To change work roles, formal patterns of authority and responsibility, work norms, value systems, and reward/penalty systems requires a great deal of educating and tender loving care. Even then, it remains a formidable task. Stevens failed to compare the Japanese work culture to the U.S. work culture. There are many major differences. To use the new "fad," much effort would be required from Stevens. The benefits could not be realized without a corresponding investment of time and energy on his part.

Stevens failed the course. The instructor provided the students with a list of activities associated with undertaking such a program within their own organizations. These included: (1) training quality-circle members in problem-solving exercises; (2) showing how quality-circle leaders should behave; (3) developing implementation plans; and (4) measuring the progress of quality-circle activities and performance. All of these principles were ignored by Stevens. He did not understand decision-making groups or how to create them in an effective manner.

By calling the Department B personnel together to announce that production standards set several years ago were too low, he announced his decision to change production standards. This decision obviated the need for a decision-making group. Stevens completely misused the concept. He did not have a quality circle; he had the same employees who were playing a new game with their boss. They would not set standards higher than present ones. On what grounds would they logically take such an action? If standards are to be set higher, then Stevens should be responsible for setting them.

Stevens blew his chance to use a valuable and appropriate management technique. His organization made aircraft parts, which suggests that the work force had skilled jobs with above-average qualifications. Employees could have been trained to assume more responsibility for group technology and work habits. They also probably would have enjoyed this revised work setting, which has existed in many other American high-technology firms (teams are not a new method of organizing work units). Stevens should forget the suggestion and now try to find a conventional means of improving work quality. To do otherwise would produce continued antagonism among workers with the attending reduced level of performance and productivity.

If Stevens could start all over, we could share with him some ideas about how to make quality circles work in his plant. An outside consultant might begin by explaining how the structure of work would need to change with this concept. To change the structure, one would explain the techniques for implementing such structural changes. The following steps could help:

1. Stevens could inform all plant supervisors about his experience and the ideas to which he was exposed.
2. Stevens could suggest that he felt the idea had merit and wanted the supervisors' assessment regarding usefulness of quality circles in the plant.
3. Stevens could request ideas about sending a group of supervisors to similar programs or sponsoring a quality-circle training program in the plant.
4. Stevens could have supervisors report about the overall merits of pursuing the quality-circle concept in the department on an experimental basis.
5. If positive feedback is obtained, Stevens could proceed with an appropriate training program for supervisors and production employees.
6. Stevens could implement the idea with the department for a mutually agreeable time and assess its merit for expansion or elimination.

This procedure permits employees to be involved in learning about the concept, trying it out, selling the merits to others, asking questions and raising concerns, and developing the idea to fit the unique characteristics of that department and company. Ample time needs to be granted for testing, developing, evaluating, selling, and learning the new skills and behaviors required to operate in a more group-oriented environment. More time would permit necessary changes to the plant's administrative systems and structures. All of this is necessary for the idea to produce the results promised by the consultants and the professor.

OBSERVATIONS

Quality circles have received a level of attention accorded few management techniques. As an integral part of the productive and successful Japanese management system, quality circles have been popularized for use in other settings, including the United States. Quality-circle techniques embrace elements of other, more traditional management concepts, such as participative management, group decision making, employee suggestion programs, and the task-force technique, all of which have earned recognition in management practice and theory.

In this incident, the failure of Stevens in using the quality-circle technique reminds us that even valuable management techniques may produce unwanted outcomes when misused. Professors Klasson and Franklin provide some useful ideas about making quality circles work.

DISCUSSION ITEMS

---

1. Discuss the advantages and disadvantages of continuing to use the quality-circle technique in the Fairlee plant.
2. Recommend a course of action for John Stevens now that his quality-circle experiment is in trouble. Explain your reasoning.
3. What would have been the appropriate procedure for Stevens to follow before, during, and after calling the 25 employees together for quality-circle interaction?

SUGGESTED READINGS

BOOKS

Arnold, Hugh J., and Daniel C. Feldman. *Organizational Behavior*. New York: McGraw-Hill, 1986, pp. 496–502.

Callahan, Robert E.; C. Patrick Fleenor; and Harry Knudson. *Understanding Organizational Behavior*. Columbus, Ohio: Charles E. Merrill Publishing, 1986, pp. 515–22, 532–34.

Davis, Keith, and John W. Newstrom. *Human Behavior at Work*. 7th ed. New York: McGraw-Hill, 1985, chap. 9, p. 198.

Donnelly, James H.; James L. Gibson; and John M. Ivancevich. *Fundamentals of Management*. 6th ed. Plano, Tex.: Business Publications, 1987, pp. 340–43.

French, Wendell L. *The Personnel Management Process*. 6th ed. Boston: Houghton Mifflin, 1987, chap. 27.

Griffin, Ricky W. *Management*. 2nd ed. Boston: Houghton Mifflin, 1987, pp. 563, 564.

Heneman, Herbert G.; Donald P. Schwab; John A. Fossum; and Lee D. Dyer. *Personnel/Human Resource Management*. 3rd ed. Homewood, Ill.: Richard D. Irwin, 1986, pp. 13, 629–35, 637–40.

Megginson, Leon C. *Personnel Management: A Human Resources Approach*. 5th ed. Homewood, Ill.: Richard D. Irwin, 1985, pp. 317–38.

Rue, Leslie W., and Lloyd L. Byars. *Management: Theory and Application*. 4th ed. Homewood, Ill.: Richard D. Irwin, 1986, chap. 12, p. 334.

Schermerhorn, John R. *Management for Productivity*. 2nd ed. New York: John Wiley & Sons, 1986, pp. 362, 363, 392, 393.

JOURNALS

Alexander, C. Phillip. "A Hidden Benefit of Quality Circles." *Personnel Journal* 63, no. 2 (February 1984), pp. 54–58.

Ambler, A. R., and M. H. Overholt. "Are Quality Circles Right for Your Company?" *Personnel Journal* 61, no. 11 (November 1982), pp. 829–31.

Ferris, Gerald R., and John A. Wagner III. "Quality's Circles in the United States: A Conceptual Reevaluation." *Journal of Applied Behavioral Science* 21, no. 5 (May 1985), pp. 155–67.

Jones, W. G. "Quality's Vicious Circles." *Management Today*, March 1983, pp. 97–102.

Klein, Gerald D. "Implementing Quality Circles: A Hard Look at Some of the Realities." *Personnel* 58, no. 6 (November-December 1981), pp. 11–20.

Klein, Janice A. "Why Supervisors Resist Employee Involvement." *Harvard Business Review* 62, no. 5 (September-October 1984), pp. 87–95.

Lawler, E. E., III, and S. A. Mohrman. "Quality Circles after the Fad." *Harvard Business Review* 63, no. 1 (January-February 1985), pp. 64–71.

Main, Jeremy. "The Trouble with Managing Japanese-Style." *Fortune* 109, no. 7 (April 2, 1984), pp. 50–56.

Munchus, George, III. "Employer-Employee-Based Quality Circles in Japan: Human Resources Policy Implications for American Firms." *Academy of Management Review* 8, no. 2 (April 1983), pp. 255–61.

Rowland, Alan D. "Combining Quality Circles and Work Simplification." *Training and Development Journal* 38, no. 1 (January 1984), pp. 90, 91.

Shea, Gregory P. "Quality Circles: The Danger of Bottled Change." *Sloan Management Review* 27, no. 3 (Spring 1986), pp. 33–46.

Smeltzer, Larry R., and Ben L. Kedia. "Knowing the Ropes: Organizational Requirements for Quality Circles." *Business Horizons* 28, no. 4 (July-August 1985), pp. 30–34.

Werther, William B. "Quality Circles: Key Executive Issues." *Journal of Contemporary Business* 11, no. 2 (February 1982), pp. 17–26.

Wood, Robert; Frank Hull; and Koya Aqumi. "Evaluating Quality Circles." *California Management Review* 24, no. 1 (Fall 1983), pp. 37–53.

WHAT THIS INCIDENT IS ABOUT:
Misguided subordinate practices threaten the
reputation of a respected firm in the absence of a
clearly defined operating policy. The incident
focuses on the authority-responsibility issues of
sharing responsibility, assuming responsibility for
the actions of subordinates, and the role of the board
of directors.

28

Questionable purchasing practices

INCIDENT

The Motton Electronics firm was widely respected in the industry as
being fair, dependable, and progressive. Cy Bennett, founder of the
company, was chairman of the board and majority stockholder. One of the
progressive practices of the company was to employ professional managers
as members of top management. Each had been carefully selected and
received an excellent salary for performing his or her job. None of the top
management group served on the board.

One month ago, Bennett reported to the board that he had facts to
prove that the director of purchasing for the company, Russell Hale, was
giving preferential treatment to certain vendors and, in turn, was receiving
merchandise and money for these favors. After the chairman presented the
evidence, the board formally condemned such purchasing practices by a
unanimous vote.

Immediately following this action, a vocal board member asserted that
he felt the chief executive officer was responsible for all employee behavior
on the job, that such administrative negligence should not be tolerated,
and that the board needed a policy on the issue. This statement triggered
an extensive discussion among the directors on topics such as shared
responsibility for subordinates' action, relevant duties of the board of directors, and related policy implications.

The meeting ended with a motion, unanimously supported, that Bennett: (1) decide on appropriate measures regarding the errant director of
purchasing, and (2) develop and implement a policy on shared responsibil-

ity. Bennett believed that his prompt action on these matters would be critical to managerial performance, to the firm's profitability, and to the value of his majority block of company stock.

CRITIQUES

SHEILA A. ADAMS
Associate Professor of Management and Marketing
University of North Carolina at Wilmington

The incident illustrates several important issues which may be classified into three main categories:

1. The question of appropriate behavior for purchasing directors vis-à-vis vendors.
2. The question of chief executive officers' responsibility.
3. The question of board members' responsibility.

The first category is the easiest to deal with. There are two schools of thought regarding purchasing agents' acceptance of gifts from vendors. One is that nothing should be accepted of greater than advertising value. For example, pens or calendars imprinted with a vendor company's name are easily identified as having advertising value. Anything beyond these (that is, liquor, airline tickets, tape recorders, and so forth) is taboo. The other school of thought advocates a policy that is simpler to implement and enforce: Accept nothing!

If Motton Electronics were operating under either policy and Bennett had evidence of Hale's acceptance of merchandise and money from vendors, there is no doubt that the director of purchasing should be fired. However, the facts do not present such a clear-cut case. The board voted to condemn the practices, which implies there was no clearly stated policy. In the absence of such a policy, appropriate action is less obvious.

Another aspect of the appropriateness of gift and favor exchange should be considered. Board members are rightly concerned about their purchasing director's questionable behavior. One must wonder if they are equally fastidious about the behavior of their *own* sales force. Executives often seem to advocate a double standard within their organizations. It is acceptable for their sales personnel to *give* gifts and favors to potential or actual customers. At the same time, it is unacceptable for their own purchasing department employees to *receive* gifts or favors from actual or would-be vendors. Such a stance makes a mockery of a company's claims of ethical conduct.

The second issue is the responsibility of the chief executive officer for subordinates' behavior. The facts indicate that the board has no policy on this issue. Therefore, some ambiguity exists at this level as well as at the purchasing director's level. However, it is generally accepted that the CEO is responsible for the selection, development, and motivation of the organization's members. It is his or her responsibility to set the tone for the company; to create, nurture, and, if necessary, change the organization's climate. This includes setting ethical and economic performance standards and ensuring that they are met. Just as a president is held responsible for a firm's unsatisfactory financial performance (or, conversely, an exceptionally good financial performance), he or she is also responsible for the integrity and ethics of the firm's employees. Subordinates who fail to live up to the firm's performance standards must be counseled, disciplined, and, if necessary, terminated. The president is accountable to the board, the stockholders, and the community for company and employee performance.

Finally, the third issue is that of board members' responsibility. One might say, "the buck stops here!" In the past, board membership was largely ceremonial and often directors knew little about what was happening in the organization. Duties involved hiring a president and approving documents prepared by corporate counsel. This was particularly true of outside directors with little or no ownership in the organization. In recent years, however, the role of board member has changed considerably. Heavily influenced by court decisions holding directors responsible for actions of corporate managers, board members have become more actively involved in monitoring management performance.

In the case of Motton Electronics, Cy Bennett, as founder, board chairman, and majority stockholder has a special responsibility. He should lead the board in establishing the firm's philosophy and appropriate goals and standards to guide the chief executive officer in policy formulation. It is then the CEO's responsibility to develop policy guidelines and ensure that all departments operate in accordance with them. Had Bennett, the board, and the CEO fulfilled their obligations in this respect, there would already be specific policies forbidding the acceptance of gifts or favors from vendors and Hale either would not have accepted such gifts or, if he violated the policy, should have been terminated.

The board's final motion is appropriate—insofar as it goes. Bennett must propose for board approval an explicit statement of the company's position with respect to appropriate behavior vis-à-vis suppliers (and, ideally, customers). There should also be an explicit statement of joint responsibility; however, the board members cannot absolve themselves of responsibility in these matters. Ultimate responsibility rests with the board.

Because of the apparent lack of explicit policy, the purchasing director probably should not be fired at this time. Even in the absence of such policies, however, professional managers should be expected to maintain high ethical standards. Therefore, Hale should be reprimanded and warned that any further such behavior will not be tolerated.

Once the board has adopted statements explaining the company's position with respect to standards of ethical behavior and the responsibility of managers for their subordinates' behavior, these positions must be clearly communicated to the organization's members. It is the board's responsibility to make its position clear to the president, and it is the president's responsibility to implement the board's policy. Ambiguity and double standards must be avoided.

ANNE SIGISMUND HUFF
Associate Professor of
Strategic Management
University of Illinois

How many people should be blamed for the purchasing director accepting kickbacks? The purchasing director almost certainly should be—because organizations need people, especially at the top, who feel responsible for their actions on behalf of the organization. The president of the company, as the director's immediate superior, probably should be blamed too—because those who delegate tasks should also monitor and evaluate how they are performed. Perhaps the board should be blamed as well, since it is ultimately responsible for the firm's activities; though the vocal board member may not be too happy to have his arguments turned against him.

The key problem with determining shared responsibility, however, is that delegating responsibility is a critical managerial task. Delegation is necessary to get work done; managers cannot do everything, or even review everything that must be done. To ask them to accept responsibility for all actions made by subordinates can be unfair and demotivating.

It is also important to realize that delegation accomplishes more than the organization's work. Delegation is a tool in developing new managers. Promising younger managers need to experience responsibility. They learn from being able to make mistakes. They will learn to act like managers faster, rather than mere employees, if they are confronted with the results of their choices. If the boss always takes the ultimate responsibility, the training can be seriously undermined.

On the other hand, supervisors cannot be entirely blameless. They will take the job of providing results for the company more seriously if they are held responsible for their units' overall results. They will take the job of developing managerial talent more seriously if the failures of their subordinates are also counted as their failures.

One of Cy Bennett's problems then is how to develop a policy on shared responsibility that will maximize the likelihood that *both* the supervising manager and the subordinate work hard to accomplish assigned tasks and also feel responsible to those around them. The policy also should emphasize that every employee should be oriented toward the company's welfare—not just self-interest.

Bennett's second problem is that the action he takes regarding the purchasing director will speak louder than any policy. Bennett can use this to his advantage, but only if his actions illustrate the general stance of the organization toward shared responsibility and ethical behavior.

If I were Bennett, I would emphasize the quality of the evaluation process in my overall policy on shared responsibility. The policy would say something like:

> Managers are ultimately responsible for their subordinates' activities. They therefore should ensure that they have adequate mechanisms for monitoring and evaluating subordinates' performance. When a subordinate acts in ways which damage the company or are otherwise inappropriate, the manager will be held responsible for the adequacy of the review process.

This policy assists in dealing with the immediate problem of disciplining the director of purchasing. But first Bennett must ask, "How should individuals who appear to have made a serious mistake be treated in this organization?" A "fair" company gives anyone suspected of erring the opportunity to respond to the evidence. It is always possible that all relevant facts are not known. The individual deserves a chance to present his or her side of the story *before* a decision is made about the appropriate response. (It is best, however, if minimal time is available to construct elaborate excuses and self-justification.)

In light of this policy on shared responsibility, board members should exercise their responsibility to review the actions of individuals who normally report to them. They should discuss the facts they have with the company president, who is presumably the individual to whom the purchasing director reports. The board should then give the purchasing director the opportunity to hear and elaborate on the facts held by the board, through a meeting with the president.

The incident suggests that new information will not be discovered in this process. Assuming this is true, I would consider firing the director of purchasing. Accepting kickbacks for preferred consideration of vendors is unlike any other mistakes made by managers. It is not merely an error of judgment, but it is a clear case of putting individual interests far above the interests of the organization. Companies must assume that individuals will, and should, consider their own interests in making decisions. But the company has the right to ask that the company's interests remain in the forefront. They must reward those who commit themselves to the company's interest, and punish those who do not.

Several considerations might change the recommendation to fire the director of purchasing. For example, perhaps this is a person who has been with the company for many years, and has served the company well during that time. A less drastic response might then be called for.

Bennett should remember, however, that this is the kind of dramatic incident that carries a strong message to members of the organization. How the incident is handled can convey three important messages:

1. This company holds managers responsible for the activities assigned to them.
2. Actions that disregard the best interest of the company will be strongly disciplined, with due respect to the rights of individuals involved to present the situation as they understood it.
3. Managers are responsible both for delegating responsibilities to their subordinates and for monitoring the performance of those responsibilities; instances of poor performance by a subordinate will trigger an evaluation of the monitoring mechanisms in use.

OBSERVATIONS

Boards of directors have far-reaching responsibilities. One board responsibility is to establish appropriate policies for governing the operation of the firm and the professional behavior of employees. In this case, actions by the board. Of the questions that arise, many relate to organization and organizationally between the board and the director of purchasing is the company president, whose responsibilities in the matter are being assessed by the board. Of the questions that arise, many relate to organization and behavioral theory. Has the board established and implemented policies that require ethical behavior? Has the board by its own behavior demonstrated support for its policies? Has the president used reasonable care in supervising the director of purchasing? Has the delegation process established relevant responsibility for the president and the errant director of purchasing? Did the board misjudge the president's ability to manage the firm in a "responsible" way? While answers to these questions are not made clear in the incident, it appears that the president made a misjudgment in placing confidence in the director of purchasing.

DISCUSSION ITEMS

1. How "responsible" is an executive for the actions of subordinates? Justify your position.

2. What is legally or ethically wrong with giving preferential treatment to selected vendors and receiving merchandise and money in return?
3. Draft a policy statement of the board's expectations regarding (1) ethical behavior and (2) the responsibility of superiors for the ethical behavior of their subordinates.

SUGGESTED READINGS

BOOKS

Arnold, Hugh J., and Daniel C. Feldman. *Organizational Behavior.* New York: McGraw-Hill, 1986, chap. 14.

Callahan, Robert E.; C. Patrick Fleenor; and Harry Knudson. *Understanding Organizational Behavior.* Columbus, Ohio: Charles E. Merrill Publishing, 1986, chaps. 7, 8.

Davis, Keith, and John W. Newstrom. *Human Behavior at Work.* 7th ed. New York: McGraw-Hill, 1985, chaps. 11, 16.

Donnelly, James H.; James L. Gibson; and John M. Ivancevich. *Fundamentals of Management.* 6th ed. Plano, Tex.: Business Publications, 1987, chap. 16.

French, Wendell L. *The Personnel Management Process.* 6th ed. Boston: Houghton Mifflin, 1987, chap. 7.

Griffin, Ricky W. *Management.* 2nd ed. Boston: Houghton Mifflin, 1987, chap. 3, pp. 80–86.

Heneman, Herbert G.; Donald P. Schwab; John A. Fossum; and Lee D. Dyer. *Personnel/Human Resource Management.* 3rd ed. Homewood, Ill.: Richard D. Irwin, 1986, chap. 12, pp. 364–69.

Megginson, Leon C. *Personnel Management: A Human Resources Approach.* 5th ed. Homewood, Ill.: Richard D. Irwin, 1985, chap. 12.

Rue, Leslie W., and Lloyd L. Byars. *Management: Theory and Application.* 4th ed. Homewood, Ill.: Richard D. Irwin, 1986, chap. 4.

Schermerhorn, John R. *Management for Productivity.* 2nd ed. New York: John Wiley & Sons, 1986, chap. 20.

JOURNALS

Andrews, Kenneth R. "Rigid Rules Will Not Make Good Boards." *Harvard Business Review* 60, no. 6 (November-December 1982), pp. 34–36, 38, 42–44.

Buchan, Bruce P. "Boards of Directors: Adversaries or Advisors." *California Management Review* 22, no. 2 (Winter 1981), pp. 31–39.

Carroll, Archie B. "Linking Business Ethics to Behavior in Organizations." *Advanced Management Journal* 46, no. 3 (Summer 1981), pp. 4–11ff.

Cullather, James L. "Musings II: Revisiting the *New Yorker*'s Business Ethics Cartoons." *Business Horizons* 29, no. 3 (May-June 1986), pp. 23–26.

Dayton, Kenneth N. "Corporate Governance: The Other Side of the Coin." *Harvard Business Review* 62, no. 1 (January-February 1984), pp. 34–37.

Ferguson, Charles R., and Roger Dickinson. "Critical Success Factors for Directors in the Eighties." *Business Horizons* 25, no. 3 (May-June 1986), pp. 14–18.

Fox, Harold W. "Quasi-Boards: Useful Small-Business Confidants." *Harvard Business Review* 60, no. 1 (January-February 1982), pp. 158, 162–65.

Harvey, Eric L. "Discipline versus Punishment." *Management Review* 76, no. 3 (March 1987), pp. 25–29.

Herzel, Leo; Richard W. Sherpro; and Leo Katz. "Next to Last Word on Endangered Directors." *Harvard Business Review* 65, no. 1 (January-February 1987), pp. 38, 42, 43.

Lagges, James G. "The Board of Directors: Boon or Bane for Stockholders and Management?" *Business Horizons* 25, no. 2 (March-April 1982), pp. 43–50.

Leana, Carrie R. "Predictors and Consequences of Delegation." *Academy of Management Journal* 29, no. 4 (December 1986), pp. 754–74.

McCanna, Walter F., and Thomas E. Comte. "The CEO Succession Dilemma: How Boards Function in Turnover at the Top." *Business Horizons* 29, no. 3 (May-June 1986), pp. 17–22.

Weber, James. "Institutionalizing Ethics into the Corporation." *MSU Business Topics* 29, no. 2 (Spring 1981), pp. 47-52.

Weihrich, Heinz. "How to Set Goals that Work for Your Company—And Improve the Bottom Line." *Management Review* 71, no. 2 (February 1982), pp. 60–65.

WHAT THIS INCIDENT IS ABOUT:
Employees face the threat of the unknown when
consultants arrive to study their performance. The
incident involves the process of successful change:
gaining acceptance, coordination, use of consultants,
attitudes, and morale.

29

Resistance to change

INCIDENT

As office manager of the Duncan Paper Products Corporation, Robert
Hale was responsible for the work of approximately 45 employees, of whom
26 were classified as either stenographers or file clerks. Acting under
instructions from the company president, he agreed to allow a team of
outside consultants to enter his realm of responsibility and make time and
systems-analysis studies in an effort to improve the efficiency and output of
his staff.

The consultants began by studying job descriptions, making observations, and recording each detail of the work of the stenographers and file
clerks. After three days, they indicated to Hale and his employees that
they were prepared to begin more detailed studies, observations, and
interviews on the following day.

The next morning, five employees participating in the study were
absent. On the following day, 10 employees were absent. Concerned, Hale
investigated the cause of the absenteeism by telephoning several absentees. Each employee related approximately the same story. Each was
nervous, tense, and tired after being viewed as a "guinea pig" for several
days. One stenographer told Hale that her physician had advised her to ask
for a leave of absence if working conditions were not improved.

Shortly after the telephone calls, the chief of the systems-analysis team
explained to Hale that if there were as many absences on the next day, his
team would have to drop the study and proceed to another department.
He said that a valid analysis would be impossible to conduct with 10 employees absent. Realizing that he would be held responsible for the failure of the systems analysis, Hale began to create and evaluate alternative
actions that would provide the conditions necessary for the study. He was

also concerned about implementing the procedural changes that he knew would be mandated after the study was completed. Hale was astute enough to realize that policies declared and orders issued are not always followed by instant compliance, even in the military, and that this wasn't a military situation.

CRITIQUES

ALAN C. FILLEY
Professor of Management
University of Wisconsin

An outside group of consultants has been imposed upon Hale and his subordinates. The result has been absenteeism, lower performance, and pressure on Hale to avoid displeasing his superior. The case may exemplify one of two common errors in the consulting process. First, top executives sometimes identify and attempt to solve the wrong problem. For example, the president might have discovered that profits were down, identifying the problem as a need for more productivity and the solution as a need for time and methods analysis. Second, consultants with fixed solutions some- times attempt to apply them universally. For example, the president may have obtained consultants whose chief skills are the ones employed here. After all, auditors will audit, surgeons will operate, and time-study special- ists will do time studies.

Assuming a legitimate need to increase productivity, the intervention process used by Duncan Paper Products has added a new problem. Now, the resistance to the consultants' study must be addressed. In addition, ways to increase output and efficiency must be found. The employee discomfort and resistance are understandable. They have been asked to cooperate in an activity that threatens familiar methods and that offers no evidence that any changes would be personally rewarding. The process has ignored the fact that an effective outcome for the company depends both on the solution's quality and its acceptability to those affected by it. Fur- thermore, neither we nor Hale and his employees know whether the consultants' product will be facts that Hale and his employees can use to develop improved work methods or whether the consultants will be impos- ing their own prescriptions upon Duncan Paper Products' employees.

It is time for Hale to gain necessary information and, hopefully, obtain agreements with the president and consultants about the change process. A promising approach would have the consultants provide data while work- ing with Hale and his employees to find ways to improve output and efficiency. Some companies faced with this kind of problem have been able to redesign jobs and work arrangements to increase both work satisfaction and productivity. Others have tied specific measures of efficiency to extrinsic rewards. Hale and the consultants should meet with his employees to describe the project's nature, the action to be taken, the cost of not proceeding, and the gains expected upon its completion. Even if these actions are not possible, Hale can at least demonstrate more initiative in dealing with both his subordinates and his superior. His subordinates expect him to represent their interests with the president. Hale can provide his subordinates with more information than he has to date. Also, Hale might alert management to the fact that actions creating dissatisfaction will generally result in greater absenteeism and turnover. If the employees lost during a mandatory work evaluation are already poor performers, then the results need not be bad. If the lost employees include top performers, then well-intended managerial actions will have resulted in negative consequences.

The case provides a nice example of the difference between the *process of change* and the *substance of change*. While the intended substance is not described in the case, it is reasonable to assume that the consultants know about the well-founded techniques for increasing productivity: clear goals, rewards for performance, avoidance of penalties, and improved work flow, to name a few. On the other hand, we do know about the process of change used here, and it is one that increases the odds of failure by substituting uncertainty and lack of control for work methods that are certain and, in that sense, rewarding.

JAMES P. LOGAN
Professor of Management
University of Arizona

This incident can be understood through the application of (1) four theoretical perspectives and (2) an administrative point of view. The theoretical perspectives should help the reader think about the incident and the administrative viewpoint should help one decide what action is most suitable. The four relevant theoretical perspectives are:

1. Problem and decision analysis.
2. Organizational development.
3. Organizational structure.
4. Leadership.

An early step in problem and decision analysis is the revelation of a gap between expected results and actual outcomes.[1] The gap becomes a devia-

---

[1]See Kepner and Tregoe, *The New Rational Manager*, (Princeton, N.J.: Princeton Research Press, 1981), chapters 2, 4.

tion statement specifying the extent of the deviation, what it is, and where and when it occurs. The deviation statement provides three more steps of the problem analysis—developing possible causes, testing for probable cause, and verification of the cause through logic and reality testing. When this is completed, the problem is known and can then be subjected to decision analysis.

In the incident of the absentee office force, a gap seems apparent to the president, who has hired consultants and imposed them on the office. More rational and useful behavior in problem and decision analysis would be for the president to ask Hale for an explanation of the results so that hypotheses could be set and an investigation started to pinpoint the problems that are hinted at by the existence of the gap. For example, do the expected results need modification? How much training has the office force had. Have revised procedures been put into practice? There is a large set of potential hypotheses that need at least cursory attention.

But, instead, the president has done what students often do: jumped to a conclusion before a thorough examination of the problem. His conclusion is that consultants are needed and that work-method analysis is called for. After examining this incident by problem analysis, we move on to questions of organizational development.

A basic tenet of the theory of organizational development is that effective organizations are built with information from people on the job and by soliciting recommendations from the line employees involved.[2] We see none of that here—only an imposition of "experts" by the president. One can readily predict that, in the absence of some unusual action by Hale, any new system developed by the consultants will be ineffective because the employees and Hale are not involved in their work and planning. On the contrary, the office employees are being repelled. Absenteeism is an early consequence of the consultant's work. The consultants are not gaining data. They are gaining behavioral responses that are dysfunctional for everyone in the incident—Hale, the employees, the consultants, and the president.

Theories of organizational structure explain, among other things, span of control, delegation of authority, and the position and use of staff. What is Hale's span of control? It appears that he has 45 employees reporting to him directly because no mention is made in the incident about supervisors or section heads in his department and because we find Mr. Hale phoning employees himself. A span this wide is highly unusual and is undoubtedly a direct contributor to the effectiveness and efficiency of the operations of the office and the office manager's work. Hale appears unable to delegate authority and responsibility to anyone else in his office. In this incident, we

---

[2]See Peters and Waterman, *In Search of Excellence* (New York: Harper & Row, 1982), chapter 8, "Productivity through People"; and Gene Bylinsky, "America's (10) Best-Managed Factories," *Fortune*, May 28, 1984, pp. 16–27.

substitute the use of outside experts for the use of staff, but the question of suitable behavior is the same. Effective staff experts do not impose a study on the line organization without carefully bringing the line manager(s) into the planning and operation of their expert work.

The final theoretical perspective is the role and performance of leaders. We see only a portion of the total ideas about leadership in this incident, but two points should be noted: (1) the leader's responsibility for output and (2) the leader's responsibility to act as a bridge between his or her unit and other units of an organization.[3] Bridging means protecting his or her unit and relating to other units. How does Hale fulfill these two parts of his role?

Effective executives demonstrate a viewpoint aimed toward output, results, and taking responsibility for moving their units toward their objectives. Peters and Waterman, in their well-known book about excellence in management, call this "a bias for action." We can test Hale's administrative viewpoint by asking four questions:

1. What are the present pressures on Hale?
2. What behavior on Hale's part contributed to the situation?
3. What does the incident reveal about the office's organization?
4. What might Hale reasonably do now?

Present pressures on Hale: Hale must now: (1) Maintain current output in the office; (2) find out what conditions would lead to the absentees' return; (3) find a way to have the systems-analysis work done soon; and (4) have an answer to these problems that will satisfy himself and the president.

With almost 20 percent of his stenographic and filing force absent, Hale has a major problem of work load and output. The easiest remedy would probably be to get the regular employees back to work. Hale knows why they are gone, but he does not know what would persuade them to return.

Further, Hale eventually has to see that the systems-analysis work is done to satisfy the president's desires. Postponement or proceeding at once will depend on talks with the chief of the systems team and the absentees. Hale's situation is complex enough that he has to respond to several forces.

Hale's behavior: The surprises about Hale's actions as an executive are: (1) Why does the president have to pressure Hale for a study? Is something remiss with office productivity? Or has Hale not educated him about the office's effectiveness? (2) Why has Hale taken three days to discover difficulties? On such a major project, it would seem that Hale would be acquainted with his workers' condition and the analysts' behavior at least twice each day. (3) Why did Hale not explain the project to his employees

---

[3]For a comprehensive review see R. M. Stogdill, *Handbook of Leadership* (Riverside, N.J.: Free Press, 1981).

and observe it from the beginning? As the key supervisor, Hale is considerably distant from the events.

Organization of the office: Are there other office supervisors and did they have roles in the incident? If Hale is attempting to manage the employees directly, he has too much work—as is shown by his lack of knowledge about the study and perhaps by the president's pressure. If Hale has other supervisors, he is not using them effectively. He makes the phone calls and notices the absences. He hears nothing through any supervisors. The organization influences the type of action suitable for Hale. For example, further information on inducing the employees to return to work should be obtained by the supervisors. Also, the problem of maintaining output should be worked out with the supervisors. If there are none, Hale has a question of organization, selection, and promotion.

What might Hale reasonably do now? First, talk to his supervisors, if he has any, for their help is important in getting the word out, in discovering why people are absent, and in getting the employees back to work in a proper atmosphere. Second, find out how the systems team operated so that he can judge whether the team's methods contributed to the problem. Finally, when he has the information, set up a program to restore output, restore the work force's confidence, and eventually finish the systems analysis. He might also be prepared to explain to the president what has happened and what the most reasonable next steps are.

Readers should check their thinking for any of the following common errors: (1) Concluding that the stenographers were "wrong" because they opposed change or because they stayed out sick when they really weren't. Did you blame the employees? (2) Concluding that the systems team was "wrong" because it was ineptly using time-study techniques. Did you blame "unfeeling engineers"? (3) Hale was wrong because he did not "correctly" prepare the employees for the study. Did you try to pin the whole thing down to some one error by Hale? (4) "Searching for a villain." Did you look for one person to blame everything on? (5) Substituting value judgments for investigation. Did you jump to conclusions that actions were "good" or "bad" when really Hale seems to be in need of more information rather than judgments? (6) Identification. Did you immediately think you were Hale, one of the stenographers, the chief analyst, or the president? You will learn most by looking at the incident from all of these viewpoints. Do not automatically identify with one.

OBSERVATIONS

In this incident, employee stress levels have risen, office production has declined, and workers are protesting via absenteeism. Stress affects health, productivity, and performance. The eclectic CAPE theory of stress has emerged from stress-related research. It suggests that one's sense of con-trol, *a*ppropriateness, *p*redictability, and *e*xpectations regarding a situation crucially affect one's stress level. In this incident, more than 20 percent of the office workers are absent from their jobs and symptoms of stress are being reported to Robert Hale, office manager. These employees appear to feel that they, and their office manager, are losing control of their work situation. In their view the consultants are inappropriate and threatening. Working conditions have become unstable and unpredictable. Moreover, the expectations of the office employees are not being satisfied.

Professor Logan's application of theoretical perspectives and an adminis-trative viewpoint to this incident deserves careful thought and rereading. Professor Filley's distinction between the process of change and the sub-stance of change brings attention to the incident's intervention process for analysis and discussion.

DISCUSSION ITEMS

1. What action do you think Hale should adopt? Justify your response.
2. Hale's subordinates appear to be exercising sanctions in the form of absenteeism. Examine how sanctions can be applied by both superiors and subordinates.
3. Assuming that the consultant's study will be completed and include recommendations for changes in office procedures, develop policies and procedures for implementing the changes.

SUGGESTED READINGS

BOOKS

Arnold, Hugh J., and Daniel C. Feldman. *Organizational Behavior*. New York: McGraw-Hill, 1986, chap. 7.

Ash, M. K. *Mary Kay on People Management*. New York: Warner Books, 1984.

Callahan, Robert E.; C. Patrick Fleenor; and Harry Knudson. *Understanding Organizational Behavior*. Columbus, Ohio: Charles E. Merrill Publishing, 1986, chaps. 6, 11.

Davis, Keith, and John W. Newstrom. *Human Behavior at Work*. 7th ed. New York: McGraw-Hill, 1985, chaps. 3, 11.

Donnelly, James H.; James L. Gibson; and John M. Ivancevich. *Fundamentals of Management*. 6th ed. Plano, Tex.: Business Publications, 1987, chaps. 11, 14.

French, Wendell L. *The Personnel Management Process.* 6th ed. Boston: Houghton Mifflin, 1987, chaps. 7, 9.

Griffin, Ricky W. *Management.* 2nd ed. Boston: Houghton Mifflin, 1987, pp. 192, 362–63.

Heneman, Herbert G.; Donald P. Schwab; John A. Fossum; and Lee D. Dyer. *Personnel/Human Resource Management.* 3rd ed. Homewood, Ill.: Richard D. Irwin, 1986, chaps. 6, 12, 18.

Megginson, Leon C. *Personnel Management: A Human Resources Approach.* 5th ed. Homewood, Ill.: Richard D. Irwin, 1985, chap. 10.

Rue, Leslie W., and Lloyd L. Byars. *Management: Theory and Application.* 4th ed. Homewood, Ill.: Richard D. Irwin, 1986, chap. 20.

Schermerhorn, John R. *Management for Productivity.* 2nd ed. New York: John Wiley & Sons, 1986, chaps. 8, 17.

JOURNALS

Connell, John J. "The Future Office: New Technologies, New Career Paths." *Personnel* 60, no. 4 (July-August 1983), pp. 23–32.

Davis, Tim R. V. "The Influence of the Physical Environment in Offices." *Academy of Management Review* 9, no. 2 (April 1984), pp. 271–83.

Dilts, David A., and Clarence R. Deitsch. "Absentee Workers Back on the Job: The Case of GM." *Business Horizons* 29, no. 2 (March-April 1986), pp. 46–51.

Erez, Miriam, and Frederick H. Kanfer. "The Role of Goal Setting and Task Performance." *Academy of Management Review* 8, no. 3 (July 1983), pp. 454–63.

Glicken, Morely D. "A Counseling Approach to Employee Burnout." *Personnel Journal* 62, no. 3 (March 1983), pp. 222–28.

Hansen, Theodore L., Jr. "Management's Impact on First-Line Supervisors' Effectiveness." *SAM Advanced Management Journal* 52, no. 1 (Winter 1987), pp. 41–45.

Hoffman, John J., Jr., and Charles J. Hobson. "Physical Fitness and Employee Effectiveness." *Personnel Administrator* 29, no. 4 (April 1984), pp. 101–13.

Ilgen, Daniel R., and John H. Hollenback. "The Role of Job Satisfaction in Absence Behavior." *Organizational Behavior and Human Performance* 19, no. 1 (June 1977), pp. 148–61.

Kinlaw, Dennis C., and Donna R. Christensen. "Confront—Don't Criticize—To Improve Performance." *Advanced Management Journal* 49, no. 1 (Winter 1984), pp. 56–58.

Levinson, Robert E. "How to Conquer the Panic of Change." *Management Review* 66, no. 7 (July 1977), pp. 20–24.

McPherson, Joseph. "Inspiring Creativity While 'Wandering Around.'" *International Management* 39, no. 4 (April 1984), p. 77.

Mischkind, Louis A. "No-Nonsense Surveys Improve Employee Morale." *Personnel Journal* 62, no. 11 (November 1983), pp. 906–14.

Oldham, Greg R., and Nancy L. Rotchford. "Relationships between Office Characteristics and Employee Reactions." *Administrative Science Quarterly* 28, no. 4 (December 1983), pp. 542–56.

Stanislao, Joseph, and Bettie C. Stanislao. "Dealing with Resistance to Change." *Business Horizons* 26, no. 4 (July-August 1983), pp. 74–78.

Weisz, William J. "Employee Involvement: How It Works at Motorola." *Personnel* 62, no. 2 (February 1985), pp. 29–30.

WHAT THIS INCIDENT IS ABOUT:
Job applicants who knowingly submit incorrect
information and false credentials raise several
significant issues in affected organizations. This
incident addresses the ethics and consequences of
such misrepresentation, methods of detection,
problems of late discovery, and associated policy
implications.

30

Résumé falsification

INCIDENT

Jonathon White, director of personnel for CBA, Inc., a middle-sized company that designs and manufactures electrical equipment, was personally responsible for the recruitment, selection, and hiring of professional employees. The company employs many types of engineers, but most of them are electrical engineers. White established three operating policies to assure consistent hiring decisions for professional employees: (1) The applicant's education and experience had to be in line with the stated job requirements. (2) Applicants were not to be hired into positions for which they were overqualified. (3) Information presented in support of the application had to be accurate and complete. This included information on the application blank, certificates, letters of recommendation, and personal interview comments.

Telephone checks were regularly made by White and his assistant to verify the accuracy and completeness of information supplied by applicants, but these checks were not always completed prior to the hiring of many individuals. On some occasions, a person may have worked several months for the company before routine checking would be completed. In some cases, discrepancies and apparently false information would be discovered. These falsifications included overstatement of previous salary, enhancement of previous responsibilities and/or position titles, and adjustments to educational records such as claims of degrees, certificates, or progam completions that never existed. Upon uncovering this sort of thing, White would write a statement detailing the infraction(s) and place it in the employee's personnel file.

White thought he had seen everything, but he had not. Today he had been stunned to learn that Walter Jackson had *understated* several items on his résumé when he applied for employment about a month ago. The facts surrounding this unique event are as follows.

Jackson was a trim, gray haired, 50-year-old man with three degrees in electrical engineering, including a Ph.D. He had, moreover, an outstanding employment record reflecting advancement and accomplishment while employed by several first-rate companies. Six months before applying to CBA, Inc., Jackson had been terminated by his former employer due to a severe funding cutback for the project to which he was assigned. Because the economy was in a lengthy recession, Jackson couldn't find a job to match his training and experience. When he heard that CBA, Inc., was hiring electrical engineers, Jackson desperately needed the job and decided to maximize his chances of being hired. He was afraid of being rejected for employment because he was overqualified. Jackson therefore reduced his indicated educational level from a Ph.D. to a master's degree and eliminated 10 years of employment experience from his résumé. He also lowered his listed age from 50 to 40 and dyed his gray hair brown. Then Jackson submitted his adjusted résumé to CBA, Inc., applied for employment, was hired, and has since worked quite successfully. Actually, his supervisor was so impressed with Jackson's talent for electrical design that he had written a letter of commendation for Jackson's personnel file.

Upon receiving these facts, White was dismayed. His personal value system wasn't structured to deal with this situation. He was unsure if reducing one's claimed qualifications was ethically as bad as expanding them. White was sure, however, that three things had to be done: (1) Specific decisions were needed on what to do about Jackson, his transgressions, and his continued employment. (2) A policy review of not hiring overqualified persons was needed, since Jackson was doing well and appeared to invalidate the concept. (3) Policy guidance was needed to handle employees whose credentials were discovered to be intentionally flawed. Perhaps criteria could be developed to gauge the seriousness of various kinds of false statements.

CRITIQUES

LINDA MCGEE CALVERT
Associate Professor of Management
University of Houston—Clear Lake

This case presents an interesting opportunity to test the limits of policy. White, the personnel director, has what appear to be reasonable policies and procedures for hiring decisions. However, the policies and procedures seem to have betrayed him in this case and so he may assume that they need to be revised. On the other hand, White may simply have some unrealistic expectations about what policies and procedures can do.

The particular procedures at fault seem to be those dealing with checking résumé information. The assumption is that if the information contains minor flaws, then the matter should be handled by a letter in the employee's file. However, if the information contains major falsifications, then the person can simply be fired. Furthermore, the policy about not hiring overqualified applicants seems reasonable since common sense would dictate that overqualified candidates will likely be unhappy or simply leave when they get a better position.

On the other hand, White's policies and procedures did not take into account an overqualified candidate who falsified the record in a major way for what might be considered defensible reasons and then turned out to be an excellent employee. Questions which arise are: Should White just go by the rules even in this case? In that case, he should simply fire Jackson. Or should White make an exception in this case? If so, he must then be concerned about consistency and what to do if this should happen again.

Did the policy fail to take into account this kind of situation? Apparently it did or White wouldn't be stunned and dismayed—he doesn't know what to do. If White is expecting that "good" policies and procedures will protect him in all cases, then he is expecting too much. Policies and procedures that are too comprehensive can be just as much of a problem as those that are too loose. However, White might expect to find something in the policy about how to handle exceptions. Apparently he does not. What White needs then is a policy that takes into account the likelihood of exceptions. He probably also needs to examine his assumptions about what policies can and cannot do.

Let's switch to the actual problem before considering policies and procedures further. Many people would probably consider that revising a résumé to adjust for being overqualified is a qualitatively different act than adjusting for being underqualified. An underqualified person may not, after all, have the skills needed for the job, whereas an overqualified person is more than qualified to do the job. And although an overqualified person may be taking the job as a stopgap measure, this is an assumption that could be applied to anyone seeking a job.

This question of overqualification deserves a closer look not only because organizations commonly use this as a criterion for turning down job applicants but also because the same dynamics, the same ways of thinking, can be found in a number of corporate decision processes. In other words, "common sense" and various stereotypes and myths, unsubstantiated by actual research, inform many corporate decisions. "Overqualified" is one of them. So what does "overqualified" mean to recruiters or managers? How do you measure overqualified? Is 25 years of experience a dead giveaway on overqualified, whereas 15 years of experience is okay or even good?

Is a Ph.D. overqualified because of his or her work in a specialized area or because he or she is the kind of person who would go out and earn a Ph.D.? In other words, is the overqualified label a job-related label or is it a judgment about the individual? Another way of testing this is to ask if a Ph.D. in political science is overqualified for a sales training job. Many employers would say yes, although the degree and the work are not really related. So overqualified is usually a judgment about the person. Such employers probably believe that Ph.D.s require more challenging work, more variety, or more prestigious work. That may or may not be true. Furthermore, these beliefs are generally not derived from tested theory or systematic observation.

We are talking then about assumptions as opposed to sure knowledge. We may even be talking about prejudice. Walter Jackson probably wasn't sure what CBA's policy was or what White might do, but his instincts told him to expect the worst. Most employers would assume that Jackson was taking this job as a stopgap measure and would surely switch as soon as he could. On the other hand, Jackson is 50 years old. Perhaps he is less interested in climbing the corporate ladder than in doing certain kinds of work that are satisfying to him. Perhaps he is more interested in a job in the same location than in a better job that would cause him to move.

Age, education, and experience are highly relevant factors in hiring someone, but so are work values, feelings about loyalty and commitment, outside interests, security needs, and concerns about family and friendships. Assuming that the person has the requisite skills, the real question is what kind of an employee will the person be, regardless of age, experience, and education. For instance, a person might choose and prosper in a less-challenging job because of life transitions or family considerations.

"Overqualified" applicants may force employers to consider different issues or to evaluate the potential employee somewhat differently than normal. Therefore, the employer needs to be clear about his or her assumptions or beliefs about education, experience, and age. By addressing actual concerns rather than acting on untested assumptions, the employer may gain a valuable employee with unexpected but useful capabilities.

However, Jackson, rather than hoping that an employer might listen, finds himself not only being concerned about being "overqualified" but also being concerned about age discrimination. Perhaps CBA does not want to hire older people. Jackson would know such a policy cannot be explicit but he knows such things happen nevertheless. He chooses not to trust the organization.

Now White, the personnel director, finds himself in an uncomfortable predicament. Here is a man who is overqualified but who is performing in a superior manner. What is White to do? In a philosophical sense, White is paying for the cumulative effects of stereotyping and prejudice that Jackson and others like him are trying to counteract. Jackson knows that with his education, experience, and age, he won't get the chance to explain anything about his job needs and aspirations.

White hasn't faced reality from Jackson's point of view and now he finds himself in a philosophical bind. His ethics probably say it is wrong to lie for any reason. Also, he is the company representative and company policy must be clear, fair, and followed. However, in this case, conventional wisdom about overqualification has been wrong. This lying isn't the same as some lying, or is it? The company needs for people to be honest on their résumés and there must be sanctions for those who are dishonest. On the other hand, the company is part of a system which has created for many people the sure knowledge that they will not be able to explain their intentions concerning work. They know that they will be judged by other factors. White has a dilemma but he is part of the system that created the dilemma.

White needs a company policy that will deal fairly and consistently with both practical and ethical issues. He needs to think about his company's ethical responsibilities and he needs to get others to do likewise. Then he needs to consider the procedures used to carry out the policy. Those procedures should support the letter and spirit of the policy and not create any additional problems.

Beginning with policy, let's consider what is needed. A policy is a guide for action that has both direct and indirect effects. A policy should, therefore, be specific enough so that clear procedures can be formulated but it must also be broad enough to allow for flexibility. Policies should not be viewed as mechanical decision rules designed to cover every case. Policies that attempt to remove all use of judgment rarely succeed, and where attempted, either they are too restrictive or they require more than their fair share of paperwork or both.

In this case, White probably needs a better policy. He may also need some changes in hiring procedures. However, if White is looking for protection from having to make tough judgments, then maybe he had better reconsider his career objectives. To construct a good policy, White needs to meet with the appropriate managers and carefully consider actual needs and concerns.

The policy should be examined for "best case" and "worst case" possibilities. In other words, as this policy is written, what is the best that we could expect and what is the worst? Such considerations could improve the policy or, at least, prepare people for possible problems. The "worst case" does not necessarily mean that the policy should be more restrictive, but it may mean that procedures should be set up to handle unusual cases.

In this particular case, the policy makers should look at the possibility of age discrimination as well as questioning their assumptions about the consequences of being "overqualified." No doubt other forms of discrimination should also be considered. This consideration should include not just the numbers, but subtle or indirect forms of discrimination which may be allowed or even encouraged under the policy.

In other words, companies should be explicit about their ethics but should also consider the indirect effects of their various policies and procedures. On the other hand, policies, procedures, and even statements of ethics will not eliminate discrimination if management does not stand behind and support the policies and statements. Nor can tough decisions in "gray" areas be delegated to policy. In the end, no policy, no procedure, no statement of ethics is more useful or ethical than the reasoned and ethical individual who is representing it at the moment.

And what should White do about Jackson? Now that's a good question.

RICHARD I. HARTMAN
Professor and Chairman of
Business Management and Administration
Bradley University

This incident raises a number of issues. Jonathon White, director of personnel, must develop a procedure that enables him and his assistant to verify the accuracy and completeness of applicant information *before* a job offer is extended. Had this system been operational, this incident would not have arisen.

Falsification of applicant-supplied information is falsification, regardless of whether it is overstatement or understatement of information. There is, however, a difference between deliberate and accidental falsification. Walter Jackson has deliberately falsified his record through acts of omission (Ph.D. degree and 10 years experience) and commission (lowering his age from 50 to 40).

It appears that White has not considered falsification of applicant-supplied information a serious matter, since his only action has been to place a statement detailing the infraction in the employee's personnel file. Some organizations view information falsification as a more serious matter. These organizations often require that the applicant sign a statement such as: "I declare each of the answers given to the questions on this application to be complete and true to the best of my knowledge, and that any material misrepresentation or omission may be cause for dismissal. I also authorize the investigation of all statements given in this application, including contacting former employers for reference verification." Some job applicants believe they have little to lose from falsification, since they would not receive job offers if they did not falsify applications.

Since CBA, Inc., has not dismissed employees in the past for falsification, Jackson should be retained as long as his performance is satisfactory. White should be consistent and place a statement detailing the infractions in Jackson's personnel file. In addition, White should discuss these infractions with Jackson and inform him of the seriousness of the situation. Jackson has already demonstrated his talent and could continue to be a valuable and stable worker. Jackson may be inclined to stay at CBA, Inc., because of his age and recent termination experience.

A review of the policy of not hiring overqualified persons is necessary. A more workable and realistic policy would require review of each over-qualified candidate. Undoubtedly, the firm would find it advantageous to hire some of these individuals. A blanket policy of not hiring overqualified persons causes a firm to eliminate good candidates, especially in periods of less than full employment.

CBA, Inc.'s, personnel department should develop a procedure for verifying applicant-supplied information prior to employment. The personnel department should inform job candidates that the application information will be verified. This may reduce the amount of deliberate information falsification. In checking employee information, the personnel department must not violate the Privacy Act, the Fair Credit Reporting Act, or Equal Employment Opportunity laws.

Developing criteria to gauge the degree of ethical seriousness of various false official statements is probably impractical. It would be better to evaluate the seriousness of false statements on an individual basis. Elimination from employment consideration is probably appropriate where an individual has grossly misrepresented factual information. Less serious action should be taken in cases of minor misrepresentation. Another important factor is the nature of the position's responsibilities. For example, it would not be prudent to hire a person who misrepresents applicant information for a position that involves fiduciary responsibility or organizational security.

OBSERVATIONS

The incidence of employee information falsification on application blanks is rapidly increasing, according to Thorndike-Deland, a personnel recruiting firm. They also report that small enhancements are turning into large lies. The most important underlying factor for falsification appears to be the difficulty in checking references. Personnel people fear libel suits and have become reluctant to provide work experience details for ex-employees. In his syndicated column "Management Corner," Larry Stessin, professor emeritus of Hofstra University, indicates that employee falsification typically falls into these categories: inflated educational background; false MBAs; nonexistent universities; and periods of unemployment described as "self-employed" or "consultant."

Falsification occurs in the reverse direction in this incident when Walter Jackson understates his education, work experience, and age on his application blank. Professors Calvert and Hartman present thorough analyses of issues in the incident. Both address issues raised by the "overqualified for the position" concept prevalent in personnel management and in certain theories of motivation and job satisfaction. They wisely leave the question of "What action should Jonathon White take now?" to readers.

DISCUSSION ITEMS

1. Discuss the advantages and disadvantages of using the "overqualified for the position" concept in selecting applicants for employment.
2. Now that Walter Jackson's application falsifications have been belatedly discovered, do you recommend his continued employment or discharge? Explain your position. If he is to be retained, would you recommend any form of penalty, sanction, or special condition such as probation? Explain.
3. Explain your preference for one of these policy statements: (a) "False official statements are all falsifications and should be treated alike," or (b) "Since the ethical seriousness of falsifications varies, each instance should be treated individually."

SUGGESTED READINGS

BOOKS

Arnold, Hugh J., and Daniel C. Feldman. *Organizational Behavior*. New York: McGraw-Hill, 1986, chap. 15.

Callahan, Robert E.; C. Patrick Fleenor; and Harry Knudson. *Understanding Organizational Behavior*. Columbus, Ohio: Charles E. Merrill Publishing, 1986, chaps. 2, 7.

Davis, Keith, and John W. Newstrom. *Human Behavior at Work*. 7th ed. New York: McGraw-Hill, 1985, chap. 16.

Donnelly, James H.; James L. Gibson; and John M. Ivancevich. *Fundamentals of Management*. 6th ed. Plano, Tex.: Business Publications, 1987, chap. 20, pp. 664–67.

French, Wendell L. *The Personnel Management Process*. 6th ed. Boston: Houghton Mifflin, 1987, chap. 16.

Griffin, Ricky W. *Management*. 2nd ed. Boston: Houghton Mifflin, 1987, chap. 21, pp. 93, 94.

Heneman, Herbert G.; Donald P. Schwab; John A. Fossum; and Lee D. Dyer. *Personnel/Human Resource Management*. 3rd ed. Homewood, Ill.: Richard D. Irwin, 1986, chap. 10.

Megginson, Leon C. *Personnel Management: A Human Resources Approach*. 5th ed. Homewood, Ill.: Richard D. Irwin, 1985, chaps. 5, 7.

Rue, Leslie W., and Lloyd L. Byars. *Management: Theory and Application*. 4th ed. Homewood, Ill.: Richard D. Irwin, 1986, chap. 3.

Schermerhorn, John R. *Management for Productivity*. 2nd ed. New York: John Wiley & Sons, 1986, chap. 20.

JOURNALS

Campbell, David N.; R. L. Fleming; and Richard C. Grote. "Discipline without Punishment—At Last." *Harvard Business Review* 63, no. 4 (July-August 1985), pp. 162–74.

Cohen, Yinon, and Jeffrey Pfeffer. "Organizational Hiring Standards." *Administrative Science Quarterly* 31, no. 1 (March 1986), pp. 1–24.

Cressey, D. R., and C. A. Moore. "Managerial Values and Corporate Codes of Ethics." *California Management Review* 25, no. 4, pp. 53–77.

Deland, Rawle. "Recruitment: Reference-Checking Methods." *Personnel Journal* 62, no. 6 (June 1983), pp. 458–63.

Drucker, P. E. "Ethical Chic." *Forbes*, September 14, 1981, pp. 160–73.

Foegen, J. H. "The Case for Positive Documentation." *Business Horizons* 29, no. 5 (September-October 1986), pp. 60–62.

Levine, Hermine Zagat. "Consensus: Recruitment and Selection Programs." *Personnel* 61, no. 1 (January-February 1984), pp. 4–10.

Long, John D. "The Responsibility of Schools of Business to Teach Ethics." *Business Horizons* 27, no. 2 (March-April 1984), pp. 2–4.

McCoy, Bowen H. "Applying the Art of Action-Oriented Decision Making to the Knotty Issues of Everyday Business Life . . . and Executive's Perspective on Ethics." *Management Review* 72, no. 7 (July 1983), pp. 20–24.

Metz, Edmund J. "Job Security: The Quality of Worklife Issue." *Managerial Planning* 31, no. 2 (September-October 1982), pp. 4–9.

Meyer, Richard W. "How to Read an Applicant's Résumé." *Administrative Management* 48, no. 2 (February 1987), p. 44.

"Recruitment: Evaluating Employment Applications." *Personnel Journal* 63, no. 1 (January 1984), pp. 22–24.

Vecchio, Robert P. "The Problem of Phoney Résumés: How to Spot a Ringer among the Applicants." *Personnel* 61, no. 2 (March-April 1984), pp. 22–27.

Wooten, Bob E., and Robert L. Laud. "The Specter of Malpractice: Are Personnel Managers Liable for Job-Related Actions?" *Personnel* 60, no. 6 (November-December 1983), pp. 53–58.

WHAT THIS INCIDENT IS ABOUT:
This incident illustrates how easily well-intentioned policies can lead to employee perceptions of unfair management practices and charges of discrimination.

31

Reverse discrimination

INCIDENT

At a meeting of all management personnel, the legal advisor to the Rampart Insurance Company spoke about employee discrimination, emphasizing subjects relating to female and minority group employees. Essentially the message was that there should be no discriminatory decisions by managers relating to the selection and hiring process, promotion policies, seniority, recognition, vacations, work loads, and so forth.

Company managers accepted the advice seriously, formally adopted a nondiscriminatory personnel policy, and under a climate established and implemented by the president, administered the policy vigorously. In some cases, women who had good performance records, equal seniority with men, and other minimal qualifications were promoted to supervisory positions, even though they might be married, have several children, and could not work overtime when needed. In other cases, employees who were classed as minority group members were purposely rated high on employee evaluation reports so forthcoming promotions could be justified.

After about a year, other nonmanagement employees gave signs that they were upset, dissatisfied, and angry about the new personnel policy. When no attention was given to their statements that *they* were now being discriminated against, and when no action came after they requested a hearing with the president, the informal leaders of the group posted a notice on all bulletin boards that read as follows:

> All employees who are dissatisfied with present management practices and who desire to meet and discuss the possibility of bringing a class-action suit against Rampart, please sign below.

Rampart's legal advisor was asked to appear at a hurriedly scheduled meeting of the company's management and specifically instructed to recommend a response to employee threats and suggest any needed revisions in the nondiscriminatory policy in view of recent legislation and court decisions.

CRITIQUES

SHEILA DAVIS
Assistant Professor of Organizational Behavior
Ohio State University

Employee dissatisfaction at Rampart suggests three basic issues:

1. How Rampart's management handled inferences about discrimination.
2. The charges of "reverse discrimination" by nonmanagement personnel.
3. The apparent need for an effective affirmative action program.

It is important to review the factors that led to the bulletin board notice and to consider the implications of each factor.

In the meeting with management, the company's legal advisor initiated discussion of employee discrimination. The message to management was a clear warning, but there was no clear objective, except intimidation. No definition of discrimination is produced, no statistics on the actual numbers of women or minority employees are provided, and no suggestions for corrective action are ever made. In the spirit of affirmative action and equal opportunity, the Rampart managers try to operationalize some "philosophy." However, because of a lack of clarity and direction from upper management, middle management attempts to implement this philosophy without specific guidelines. The manager who promoted women with qualifications similar to men was acting properly. If previous discrimination exists either in that department or in the entire company, promoting women even with minimal but equal qualifications is acceptable under the law. However, being married, having children, or having less flexibility concerning overtime cannot be used in considering promotions, since none of those factors are job-related.

It is not in the spirit of affirmative action to artificially inflate job ratings for purposes of promotion. In fact, supervisors' performance appraisal ratings should never be used alone in making promotion decisions. Such ratings are usually biased and should always be considered as part of an employee's total picture.

The second issue of reverse discrimination is clearly demonstrated by the anger and frustration of lower level employees. After requesting several meetings with the president and the management of Rampart, their understandable hostility could lead to threats of a lawsuit.

The Supreme Court, in a case involving the use of quotas in an on-the-job training program at a Kaiser Aluminum plant in Louisiana (*United Steelworkers* v. *Brian F. Weber et al.*, 1979), found that Kaiser was not discriminating against white employees because of past discrimination and because Kaiser was attempting to "eliminate manifest racial imbalances in traditionally segregated job categories" (*Chronicle of Higher Education*, July 2, 1979, 18, no. 17). However, no evidence is ever presented to suggest that Rampart is practicing discrimination. The women promoted are as minimally qualified as men who might be promoted. The courts have decided in past cases that when a seniority system is bona fide, it can be used as the basis for selection and promotion. Minority employees who are rated artificially high do not constitute a case of reverse discrimination, but rather they are examples of poor selection and promotion procedures.

If communication with employees had been consistently open and clear, the entire problem probably could have been eliminated. Little or no communication about the new policy was ever evident. In fact, nonmanagement personnel were denied access to information. It is little wonder that some employees resorted to charges of discrimination.

Now the question is what can be done to reestablish the trust and support needed between management and other employees to put an effective affirmative action plan in place?

The third issue is concerned with implementing an effective affirmative action plan for Rampart. Establishing such a plan may help alleviate some of the problems that have occurred.

1. Rampart's staff should be conversant in legal decisions and other policies that protect both the company and the concerned employees, such as women or minority employees.
2. Part of Rampart's responsibility to its employees is to establish and maintain a separate affirmative action office with a full-time coordinator. A "legal advisor" is not usually well-versed in current equal opportunity issues.
3. Rampart should establish, as one of the first priorities of the affirmative action office, a complete study of its selection, promotion, and retention policies. The company should also know how many women and minorities it employs.
4. Company policies regarding affirmative action should be given to each employee to protect both the employee and the company.
5. Training programs and promotional opportunities should be made available to women and minority employees as part of the affirmative action plan. It is typical to find women in dead-end jobs in many occupations. Promotional programs would help eliminate this problem, if it exists at Rampart.

Rampart employees are angry because they perceive company management as autocratic by excluding them from company policymaking. To help establish better communication with employees, discriminatory policies should be examined and poor communication should be improved. However, affirmative action still represents a threatening change for many employees and some will always resist efforts to improve the status of affected employees. The law only provides guidelines to assist companies in meeting goals in the spirit of equal opportunity; it cannot suggest strategies for dealing with problems. Rampart has the responsibility for finding effective solutions which protect all employees.

JOSEPH F. McGRAW
Dean, Division of Business Administration
Troy State University at Montgomery

Discrimination in any form, including reverse discrimination, is wrong. Rampart's president has clearly practiced discrimination. Perhaps some would even conclude that he is stupid and deserves the lawsuit he seems likely to get. I would hesitate to reach such a conclusion hastily based on so little evidence. Not too many stupid people get to occupy the president's office. Further, I've seen too many otherwise brilliant presidents make what appear on the surface to be questionable decisions in actions related to the 1964 Civil Rights Act. Why do they do it? All they need to do is obey the law. Isn't it just that simple? No! There is nothing simple about it. It is one thing to discuss these matters in the safety of the classroom. Applications in real life, however, often become entwined in a jungle of inconsistencies and contradictions.

Let's look first to the law. Just how clear is it? When he was U.S. Attorney General, Edward H. Levi expressed an opinion on the subject. He was quoted in the March 19, 1976, issue of *U.S. News & World Report* as saying:

> that if a person examined statutes banning discrimination, executive orders issued pursuant to them, and court rulings interpreting them, he would have a view of a madhouse. The resemblance between the statutes and court decisions would be purely coincidental—and usually there isn't any resemblance.

Well, if the law itself is fuzzy, perhaps the federal agency charged with enforcement of the act has shed some light on the subject. Not so, according to many who have dealt with the Equal Employment Opportunity Commission (EEOC). In fact, this has been a highly criticized agency. The December 1976 issue of *Fortune* contains a lengthy article on the EEOC, which claims the EEOC is among the most poorly run agencies in Washington. The article states,

> The view that the EEOC is badly run is not really controversial these days. Its critics have included the General Accounting Office, the investigative arm

of Congress, which recently found the agency to be minimal in its effectiveness. Its own internal audits have raised questions about the destruction and falsification of files, employees doing jobs for which they had never been properly trained, and friction between district and regional offices. More remarkable is the fact that the agency's employment standards and practices have led to well-documented charges that there is discrimination in the EEOC itself. The agency has shown itself to be susceptible to the very sort of prejudice for which it takes employers to court.

Have things improved in the 80s? I see no evidence of it.

It is not just the law and the EEOC that managers must contend with when fishing in these troubled waters. Many other groups and individuals bring pressure on managers that result in questionable decisions. A recent incident that occurred in a major southeastern city provides an example. A large high school selected the best qualified cheerleaders on the basis of a long-standing set of standards. As it turned out, all girls selected one year were white. This resulted in protests by black students. Immediately, a black state legislator threw himself into the incident. He demanded that cheerleaders be selected on the basis of race so that the team would be comprised of blacks and whites in the same ratio as the student body. The school was roughly 35 percent black. Newspapers gave his proposal wide publicity. Then he was advised that a majority of the football team was black. Should blacks be removed from it to make way for less competent white players? It was at this point that the legislator learned that these matters are not always simple. By now the situation was getting nasty. To avoid potential violence, the principal made a decision. All girls who tried out would be declared cheerleaders regardless of qualifications. The school had a large squad that year.

Did Rampart's president just wake up one morning and decide to implement so radical a departure from past practice? Or was he under pressure? What were his alternatives? Was he about to lose important contracts for lack of an affirmative action program? Had he been visited by EEOC representatives? Had a quota system been imposed? Was he so naive as to not know that his new program would demoralize his work force? We don't know the answer to these questions. We do, however, know that the woods are full of organizations that have placed incompetent people in leadership positions in the name of what is called, all too casually, "equal employment opportunity." When employees perceive that they have been discriminated against, the effects are deadly. Enthusiasm, loyalty, and performance are compromised and organizational effectiveness and efficiency suffer. I fully support the 1964 act and regard it as a milestone in American history. The implementation of the act, however, has been deplorable and has resulted in conditions just as "sick" as the ills the act was intended to cure. Perhaps one of the suits being processed as this is written will result in a reexamination of what is happening. If not, it will be a great pity, for the insanity has gone on too long.

OBSERVATIONS

Most moralists would readily acknowledge that since workers have the right to equal treatment, discrimination in hiring, firing, or promoting people based on characteristics unrelated to the job is unethical. From a legal point of view, the situation has not been so clear. If the Civil Rights Act of 1964 is taken literally, it seems to rule out any form of preferential treatment, yet the widespread use of goals or quotas to implement affirmative action means that reverse discrimination will inevitably occur against employees not included under the umbrella of affirmative action programs.

Rogene Buchholz, author of one of the books on the suggested reading list, states that reverse discrimination exists when a minority or a woman is as qualified as a white male and is given preference over the latter for a job or promotion. Reverse discrimination also occurs where quotas resulted in hiring minorities or women who are actually less qualified than white male applicants for the same position. While the practice was tolerated for a while, cases of reverse discrimination began to receive attention, and some courts have ruled that civil rights laws apply to whites as well as blacks and that preferential treatment is a violation of these laws. Until recently the Supreme Court chose to rule narrowly rather than broadly in such cases as the one involving Kaiser Aluminum and the Steelworkers Union, which Professor Davis refers to in her critique. However, during the last week of March 1987, after Professors Davis and McGraw wrote their critiques, the Supreme Court ruled 6 to 3 that women as well as blacks and other minorities can receive preferential treatment. In its April 6, 1987, issue *Time* magazine declared that after a decade of on-the-one-hand, on-the-other-hand rulings, the decision provides the clearest declaration yet on the role of affirmative action as a remedy for inequality in the American workplace.

DISCUSSION ITEMS

1. Review current legislation and court cases pertaining to nondiscriminatory employment and promotion practices with which managers must conform. What do you consider to be legal or illegal hiring and promotion practices? Evaluate Rampart Insurance Company policies and practices accordingly.
2. Does the implementation of vigorous affirmative action and equal employment opportunity programs inherently dictate that some employees will receive unfair and unequal treatment relating to selection, performance evaluation, and promotion? Defend your views.

3. Recommend the appropriate action for Rampart's management now that employees are threatening legal action.

SUGGESTED READINGS

BOOKS

Arnold, Hugh J., and Daniel C. Feldman. *Organizational Behavior*. New York: McGraw-Hill, 1986, chap. 15.

Buchholz, Rogene A. *Business Environment and Public Policy*. Englewood Cliffs, N.J.: Prentice-Hall, 1982, chap. 14.

Callahan, Robert E.; C. Patrick Fleenor; and Harry Knudson. *Understanding Organizational Behavior*. Columbus, Ohio: Charles E. Merrill Publishing, 1986, chap. 6.

Davis, Keith, and John W. Newstrom. *Human Behavior at Work*. 7th ed. New York: McGraw-Hill, 1985, chaps. 16, 18.

DeGeorge, Richard T. *Business Ethics*. New York: MacMillan, 1982, chap. 10.

Donnelly, James H.; James L. Gibson; and John M. Ivancevich. *Fundamentals of Management*. 6th ed. Plano, Tex.: Business Publications, 1987, chap. 9.

French, Wendell L. *The Personnel Management Process*. 6th ed. Boston: Houghton Mifflin, 1987, chaps. 8, 10–14.

Griffin, Ricky W. *Management*. 2nd ed. Boston: Houghton Mifflin, 1987, chap. 21.

Heneman, Herbert G.; Donald P. Schwab; John A. Fossum; and Lee D. Dyer. *Personnel/Human Resource Management*. 3rd ed. Homewood, Ill.: Richard D. Irwin, 1986, chap. 2.

McFarland, Dalton E. *Management and Society*. Englewood Cliffs, N.J.: Prentice-Hall, 1982, chap. 14.

Megginson, Leon C. *Personnel Management: A Human Resources Approach*. 5th ed. Homewood, Ill.: Richard D. Irwin, 1985, chap. 4.

Robertson, Cliff. *Staying out of Court: A Manager's Guide to Employment Law*. Lexington, Mass.: D. C. Heath, 1985, pp. 1–177.

Rue, Leslie W., and Lloyd L. Byars. *Management: Theory and Application*. 4th ed. Homewood, Ill.: Richard D. Irwin, 1986, chap. 10.

Schermerhorn, John R. *Management for Productivity*. 2nd ed. New York: John Wiley & Sons, 1986, chap. 9.

JOURNALS

Barclay, Lizabeth. "Social Learning Theory: A Framework for Discrimination Research." *Academy of Management Review* 7, no. 4 (October 1982), pp. 587–94.

Bell, James D.; James Castagnera; and Jane Young. "Employment References: Do You Know the Law?" *Personnel Journal* 63, no. 2 (February 1984), pp. 32–36.

Brady, F. N. "Aesthetic Components of Management Ethics." *Academy of Management Review* 11, no. 2 (April 1986), pp. 337–44.

Greenhalgh, Leonard, and Zehava Rosenblatt. "Job Insecurity: Toward Conceptual Clarity." *Academy of Management Review* 9, no. 3 (July 1984), pp. 438–49.

Greenlaw, Paul. "Affirmative Action or Reverse Discrimination." *Personnel Journal* 64, no. 9 (September 1985), pp. 84–86.

Hart, Ann W. "Intent versus Effect: Title VII Case Law that Could Affect You." *Personnel Journal* 63, no. 3 (March 1984), pp. 50–58.

Ledvinka, James, and Vida Scarpello. "Surviving an EEO Lawsuit." *Advanced Management Journal* 47, no. 3 (Summer 1982), pp. 23–30.

Leigh, David. "Business Planning Is People Planning." *Personnel Journal* 64, no. 5 (May 1984), pp. 44–54.

Magnus, Margaret. "Is Your Recruitment All It Can Be?" *Personnel Journal* 66, no. 2 (February 1987), pp. 54–63.

McFeeley, N. D. "*Weber* v. Affirmative Action?" *Personnel* 57, no. 1 (January 1980), pp. 38–51.

Pascale, Richard. "Fitting New Employees into the Company Culture." *Fortune* 110, no. 3 (May 28, 1984), pp. 28–42.

Robertson, D. E., and R. D. Johnson. "Reverse Discrimination: Did *Weber* Decide the Issue?" *Labor Law Journal* 31, no. 11 (November 1980), pp. 693–99.

Spence, Janet. "Achievement American Style: The Rewards and Costs of Individualism." *American Psychologist* 40, no. 12 (December 1985), pp. 1285–95.

Steinberg, Harvey. "Where Law and Personnel Practices Collide: The At-Will Employment Crossroad." *Personnel* 62, no. 6 (June 1985), pp. 37–43.

Vernon-Gerstenfeld, Susan, and Edmund Burke. "Affirmative Action in Nine Large Companies." *Personnel* 62, no. 4 (April 1985), pp. 54–60.

WHAT THIS INCIDENT IS ABOUT:
Industrial robots offer the potential to improve
manufacturing performance and to decrease
manufacturing employment. Accordingly, labor
unions desire to bargain decisions on the use of
robotic technology, on advance notice, on retraining
for displaced workers, and for spread-the-work
programs, which are all related to traditional
management rights.

32

Robot repercussion

INCIDENT

Victor Principal, vice president of industrial relations for General Manufacturing, Inc., sat in his office reviewing the list of benefits the company expected to realize from increasing its use of industrial robots. In a
few minutes, he would walk down to the labor-management conference
room for a meeting with Ralph McIntosh, president of the labor union local
representing most of the company's industrial employees. The purpose of
this meeting would be to informally exchange views and positions preliminary to the opening of formal contract negotiations later in the month,
which would focus on the use of computer-integrated robotic systems and
the resulting impact on employment, workers, and jobs.

Both Principal and McIntosh had access to similar information flows
relevant to industrial robots, including the following. Unlike single-task
machines, installed in earlier stages of automation, robots can be programmed to do one job and then reprogrammed to do another one. The
pioneering generation of robots is mainly programmed to load machines,
weld, forge, spray paint, handle materials, and inspect auto bodies. The
latest generation of robots includes vision-controlled robots, which enable
the machines to approximate the human ability to recognize and size up
objects, using laser-beam patterns recorded by television cameras and
transmitted to "smart" computers. The computer software interprets and
manipulates the images relayed by the camera in a "smart" or artificially
intelligent way.

Experts concluded that the impact of robot installation on employment
would be profound, although the extent of the worker replacement was not

255

clear. The conclusion was inescapable that robot usage had the capacity to increase manufacturing performance and to decrease manufacturing employment.

Principal walked down to the conference room. Finding McIntosh already there, and after exchanging appropriate greetings, Principal stated the company's position regarding installation of industrial robots. "The company needs the cooperation of the union and our workers. We don't wish to be perceived as callously exchanging human workers for robots." Principal then listed the major advantages associated with robots: (1) improved quality of product due to the accuracy of robots; (2) reduced operating costs, as the per-hour operational cost of robots was about one third of the per-hour cost of wages and benefits paid to an average employee; (3) reliability improvements, as robots work tirelessly and don't require behavioral support; (4) greater manufacturing flexibility, since robots are readily reprogrammable for different jobs. Principal concluded that these robot advantages would make the company more competitive, which would allow the company to grow and increase its work force.

McIntosh's response was direct and strong. "We aren't Luddites racing around ruining machines. We know it's necessary to increase productivity and that robotic technology is here. But we can't give the company a blank check. We need safeguards and protection." McIntosh continued, "We intend to bargain for the following contract provisions: (1) establishment of labor-management committees to negotiate *in advance* about the labor impact of robotic technology and, of equal importance, to have a voice in deciding how and whether it should be used; (2) rights to advanced notice about installation of new technology; (3) retraining rights for workers displaced, to include retraining for new positions in the plant, the community, or other company plants; (4) work to be spread among workers by use of a four-day work week or other acceptable plan as an alternative to reducing the work force." McIntosh's final sentence summed up the union's position. "We in the union believe that the company is giving our jobs to robots in order to reduce the labor force."

Their meeting ended amiably, but Principal and McIntosh each knew that much hard bargaining lay ahead. As Principal returned to his office, the two opposing positions were obvious. On his yellow tablet, Principal listed the requirements as he saw them: (1) a clearly stated overall policy was needed to guide negotiation decisions and actions; (2) it was critical to decide on a company position regarding each of the union's announced demands and concerns; (3) an implementation plan must be developed.

As Principal considered these challenges, he idly contemplated a robot possessing artificial intelligence and vision capability that could help him in this work. Immediately a danger alarm sounded in his mind. A robot so constructed might be more than helpful and might take over this and other important aspects of *his* job. Slightly chagrined, Principal returned to his task, needing help—but not from any "smart" robot.

CRITIQUES

CYRIL C. LING
Professor of Management
University of Wisconsin—Whitewater

In his capacity as vice president of industrial relations at General Manu-facturing, Victor Principal has broader responsibilities than he is contem-plating over his yellow tablet. His chief executive officer expects him to contribute to setting the firm's direction. Such participation may be, on the one hand, full and deep involvement with other members of the top management team in developing corporate strategy; on the other hand, he will likely be asked, at the very least, for his informed judgment and analy-sis in his specialized area. Whatever strategic planning characterizes Gen-eral Manufacturing, Principal is faced with three important and complex challenges:

1. He must prepare and present a strategy on robotics to the senior man-agement team.
2. He must negotiate a labor agreement based on and consistent with that strategy.
3. He must implement the strategy in General Manufacturing plants once negotiations are concluded.

If management's strategy or Principal's leadership should be in error at any point, a fourth challenge can quickly present itself—a labor dispute. A strike, grievance, or unfair labor practice charge does not eliminate the three basic tasks facing Principal, but any one of them could alter strategic considerations and will certainly make completion of these responsibilities more difficult.

To prepare a strategy Principal must understand the goals and objec-tives that are of overriding interest to senior management and the compa-ny's board of directors. Most likely lower production costs and improve-ment in long-run competitive position are central to the firm's goals.

Principal also needs to assess the values and attitudes of his company's senior management—he needs to accurately determine the principles that will guide their thinking and the extent of their application. Will the company agree to protect current workers from displacement? Will senior management share decision making on robotics applications? General Manufacturing appears to be an automotive-related business, one of our nation's older industries and a volume-driven business where production economies are essential to survival. The result is that management will likely agree to provide retraining and some protection for workers, but they will probably not agree to spreading work or sharing decision making on a matter so close to the firm's ability to survive.

Principal must also consider what the environment will hold for his company and what relationship will exist between environmental forces and the agreement he is about to negotiate. He must also remember that while the labor contract will have a life of two or three years, the principles it is based upon and the precedents it creates can live long after the contract expires.

He needs to forecast the economic environment and its impacts: What, for example, will happen to wage rates, and what does that mean for the economies assumed to be associated with further robotics applications? The social environment must also be studied: Are there any discernible public attitudes forming about robotics? Are those attitudes positive or negative? How are these attitudes related to foreign competition?

In the political arena, are patterns of judgment beginning to form in Congress about robotics or the potential displacement of employees? Is protective legislation possible? What is the probability of such legislation being passed? What direction does public opinion seem to be taking? The technological environment, too, is important for Principal to consider. He needs to know the direction and pace of robotics technology to avoid making proposals which may soon be unworkable or even disadvantageous to the firm.

Principal should turn to another clean sheet in his yellow tablet as he recognizes that the internal strengths and weaknesses of General Manufacturing will have a significant effect on the type of robotics strategy the firm can develop and on how that strategy can be implemented. Strong management, especially at lower levels of the organization, will be needed to supervise conversion to automatic systems and the attendant human problems. The firm will also require a financial plan that supports the strategy and considerable resources to make the capital commitment required by the new equipment.

Once senior management has settled on their overall corporate strategy, the place of robots in that strategy—likely a very central place—and the role of the firm's industrial relations function in managing the strategy, Principal's second major challenge is to plan and implement the negotiating tactics the strategy requires. This involves determining the firm's position, what it will negotiate, the sequencing of negotiations and related matters, and the prediction of the positions taken by the union and ways the company desires to respond. Negotiations will occur in an environment defined by both parties and their estimates of what is important to the other party together with price estimates the other is willing to accept.

When negotiations are completed, Principal still has the sizable task of implementing the company's strategy and the new labor agreement. The tone of the negotiating sessions, the demeanors of both parties, and whether or not a labor dispute occurred will all color the background against which implementation will happen. Nonetheless, policies need to be revised or developed, procedures spelled out, and information and control systems created and modified to make the new robotics system work. If, for example, the new labor-management committee desired by the union has been created in the new contract, poilicies are needed to determine which issues go to the committee; procedures will be required to specify how the committee is to take action; information systems may be needed to provide the committee data; and a budget will be needed to indicate the extent of the support made available.

As Principal ponders these complex tasks, he might recall that more than a quarter-century ago Walter Reuther, then UAW president, was taken on a tour of a newly automated auto plant. When the company's president extolled the new automatic machines, Reuther quickly asked: "How many cars will they buy?"

SHARON TUCKER
Principal Consultant
Hay Management Consultants

The fundamental problem confronting Victor Principal is that General Manufacturing, Inc., wants to implement an organizational change that will benefit the company economically while harming the workers economically, a dilemma increasingly affecting the industrial sector. Both Principal and McIntosh believe that "robot usage has the capacity to increase manufacturing performance and to decrease manufacturing employment." In addition, Principal himself experienced a personal threat as he imagined being replaced by a robot. He did not want help from any "smart" robot. People generally want to feel pride in their work, and being replaced by a robot can be demeaning. In later negotiations, he may be able to use his personal concerns about robots in his job to understand more fully how threatened the employees feel.

Given the conflicting goals of managers and workers, managers might be tempted to use their authority and simply mandate the use of robots. However, organizations do not actually change just because managers say they should change. The result of using authority to mandate a change is likely to cause resistance from workers in the form of a strike, sabotage, or other forms of withholding high-quality work. On the other hand, research on organizational change indicates that change can be implemented in a manner acceptable to both parties. This requires that managers recognize that a real conflict of interest exists and that employee interests are legitimate.

A useful model of introducing workable changes in organizations was developed by David Nadler. Applying his model to this situation, it appears that McIntosh's suggestions are actually very good for implementing a change that is acceptable to both labor and management. First of all, it is important for an organization to show its members that there is a real need for change. It is apparent that McIntosh's readings have helped him conclude that robotics are inevitable, and that the union must participate in the transition to robotic technology. This acceptance of the need for change is a critical first step in implementing any change. Second, McIntosh argues for the establishment of labor-management committees to negotiate the use of robots. This is probably the most important step in gaining the workers' commitment. If workers participate in making a decision to use a robot, then that decision is their own and not imposed on them. When the decision is their own, employees are less likely to resist. The cost to management is that when labor is involved in a decision, it is unlikely that the outcome will be exactly what management first had in mind. On the other hand, without that input, it is likely that few managers' decisions will be implemented. For the use of this joint committee not to rebound as a negative factor, boundaries on authority must be clearly defined and announced to all participants at the start of their deliberations. The third step necessary in motivating the change and in reducing resistance to the change is to provide a reward system consistent with the new technology. In this case, one reward might be simply keeping one's job. In addition, there may be ways to phase in new, technically advanced job positions, giving those jobs to current workers who can quickly learn to work with the new technology. Finally, workers are much more likely to accept a change if it is implemented slowly—so that each employee can absorb the full meaning of the change. General Manufacturing should consider a long lead time for introducing the robots into the production process, allowing the workers to gradually adapt to the robots.

Once workers have accepted the need for the change and are not resistant to making the change, they still need a structure and a process for actually making the change. To cooperate with the change, workers will need to be retrained. Again, this is one of McIntosh's suggestions. While it costs the company some money for training, it also ensures that workers have the skills to work successfully with the new technology. Furthermore, it is helpful to set up a process of frequent feedback from different levels of employees who are affected by the change. This both allows for information from the floor to help the company adjust the new technology for maximum usefulness, and gives employees continuing input, which maintains their commitment to the change. In order to keep that feedback coming, General Manufacturing will need to appoint a committee or an individual to oversee the change process, ensuring that everything runs smoothly.

Finally, there are many people who have an interest in the use of robotics at General Manufacturing. Principal will need to be in touch with all different groups, from the finance people to the production managers to

the union. Principal recognizes the need to manage the power relationships with the union, but he will need to include the interests of other
groups in the organization to have a stable and workable solution with the
union.

If Principal is able to: (1) motivate the change with the workers, (2)
provide the training and the transition processes necessary for workers to
actually make the change, and (3) meet the needs of powerful groups in the
organization who have an interest in the change to robotics, then he has a
good chance of making a workable change in the organization. However,
the issue of displaced workers still remains. It seems likely that labor-
management committees may be able to minimize the amount of displacement that occurs as a result of the change, particularly if the change is
phased in slowly. Depending on the turnover rate, attrition may be a
better way to reduce the labor force than layoffs, because layoffs have such
dramatically negative effects on employee morale. Another alternative,
depending on conditions in the surrounding labor market, might be an
outplacement program, perhaps with subsidized payments for some period
of time for workers who take wage cuts when they accept new jobs. Because a positive relationship with labor is so critical to quality and productivity in manufacturing, it is in the organization's best interest to find ways
to meet some of the displaced workers' needs. Many companies are retraining displaced workers for employment outside of their companies and
are spreading the work around instead of laying off employees. Both of
these strategies seem reasonable compared to the cost of hostile relations
between the union and management over the long term.

In sum, General Manufacturing is faced with a situation where it needs
employee support. Without a solid commitment from labor, there is a
possibility that employees will refuse to do an adequate job of implementing the new robotic technology, thus negating its possible efficiency.
As a result, the organization may need to pay serious attention to meeting
the needs of its workers, as it tries to meet its own needs for improving
efficiency through robotics.

OBSERVATIONS

Support from labor is essential for successful manufacturing operations,
even in technologically advanced organizations. This crucial point, emphasized by both Professor Ling and Ms. Tucker, provides a basic criterion for
Victor Principal and others who evaluate proposed decisions and policies.
Decisions about issues to accept as negotiable and nonnegotiable, and how
hard to bargain once negotiations are underway, are complex and challeng-

ing. Successful implementation of strategies and policies poses another formidable challenge.

Modern labor-management relations function within a complex structure of labor laws designed to reflect political realities and to sustain an acceptable balance among the interests of labor, management, and the public. Technological advances, such as the use of robotics, apparently have the potential to generate unacceptable unemployment levels. Labor legislation may be generated, therefore, to protect jobs and the legitimate interests of workers in selected industries.

DISCUSSION ITEMS

---

1. "Management has both the right and obligation to install technologically advanced production equipment, including robots, to achieve desired and competitive levels of quality and efficiency of production." Do you agree or disagree with this statement? Explain your position.
2. From the company's viewpoint, discuss the advantages and disadvantages of the union's proposal to "spread the work" among the present work force rather than to reduce the size of the work force.
3. Considering the institutional purpose in society of management and unions, respectively, which do you believe is in the stronger position to bargain the issues raised in this incident? Explain your position.

SUGGESTED READINGS

BOOKS

Arnold, Hugh J., and Daniel C. Feldman. *Organizational Behavior*. New York: McGraw-Hill, 1986, chap. 10.

Callahan, Robert E.; C. Patrick Fleenor; and Harry Knudson. *Understanding Organizational Behavior*. Columbus, Ohio: Charles E. Merrill Publishing, 1986, chap. 13.

Davis, Keith, and John W. Newstrom. *Human Behavior at Work*. 7th ed. New York: McGraw-Hill, 1985, chap. 17.

Donnelly, James H.; James L. Gibson; and John M. Ivancevich. *Fundamentals of Management*. 6th ed. Plano, Tex.: Business Publications, 1987, chap. 14.

French, Wendell L. *The Personnel Management Process*. 6th ed. Boston: Houghton Mifflin, 1987, chaps. 16, 22, 24.

Griffin, Ricky W. *Management*. 2nd ed. Boston: Houghton Mifflin, 1987, chaps. 4, 12.

Heneman, Herbert G.; Donald P. Schwab; John A. Fossum; and Lee D. Dyer. *Personnel/Human Resource Management.* 3rd ed. Homewood, Ill.: Richard D. Irwin, 1986, chaps. 16, 17.

Megginson, Leon C. *Personnel Management: A Human Resources Approach.* 5th ed. Homewood, Ill.: Richard D. Irwin, 1985, chaps. 3, 18, 19.

Rue, Leslie W., and Lloyd L. Byars. *Management: Theory and Application.* 4th ed. Homewood, Ill.: Richard D. Irwin, 1986, chap. 16.

Schermerhorn, John R. *Management for Productivity.* 2nd ed. New York: John Wiley & Sons, 1986, chap. 18.

JOURNALS

Argote, Linda; Paul Goodman; and David Schkade. "The Human Side of Robots: How Workers React to a Robot." *Sloan Management Review* 24, no. 3 (Spring 1983), pp. 31–41.

Beary, Rodney. "Know Your Labor Climate before Contract Negotiations Begin." *Personnel Journal* 63, no. 3 (March 1984), pp. 26, 27.

Bleicher, Knut; Frank Bleicher; and Herbert Paul. "Managerial Frameworks for Innovative Responses in High-Tech Organizations." *Business Horizons* 26, no. 6 (November-December 1983), pp. 69–78.

Chaison, Gary N., and Mark S. Plovnick. "Is There a New Collective Bargaining?" *California Management Review* 28, no. 4 (Summer 1986), pp. 54–61.

Hawver, Dennis A. "Plan before Negotiating . . . and Increase Your Power of Persuasion." *Management Review* 73, no. 2 (February 1984), pp. 46–48.

Knod, Edward M., Jr.; Jerry L. Wall; John P. Daniels; Hugh M. Shane; and Theodore A. Wernimont. "Robotics: Challenges for the Human Resources Manager." *Business Horizons* 27, no. 2 (March-April 1984), pp. 38–46.

Lambrinos, James, and William G. Johnson. "Robots Reduce the High Cost of Illness and Injury." *Harvard Business Review* 62, no. 3 (May-June 1984), pp. 24–28.

McDermott, Kevin. "Exploring Job Guarantees." *Advanced Management Journal* 48, no. 1 (Winter 1983), pp. 4–11.

Mitchell, Roger H., and Vincent A. Mabert. "Robotics for Smaller Manufacturers: Myths and Realities." *Business Horizons* 29, no. 4 (July-August 1986), pp. 9–16.

Mooney, Marta. "Let's Use Job Security as a Productivity Builder." *Personnel Administrator* 29, no. 1 (January 1984), pp. 38–42.

Nierenberg, Gerald I. "Negotiating Strategies and Counter Strategies: How to Develop Win/Win Techniques." *Management Review* 72, no. 2 (February 1983), pp. 48, 49.

Perry, Lee Tom. "Cutbacks, Layoffs, and Other Obscenities: Making Human Resource Decisions." *Business Horizons* 28, no. 4 (July-August 1985), pp. 68–75.

Raskin, A. H. "Can Management and Labor Really Become Partners?" *Across the Board* 19, no. 7 (July-August 1982), pp. 12–16.

Scobel, Donald N. "Business and Labor—From Adversaries to Allies." *Harvard Business Review* 60, no. 6 (November-December 1982), pp. 129–36.

Whaley, George L. "The Impact of Robotics Technology upon Human Resource Management." *Personnel Administrator* 27, no. 9 (September 1982), p. 61.

WHAT THIS INCIDENT IS ABOUT:
Managers face complex challenges as victims of
job-induced stress and mental-stress injuries
become nonproductive and are upheld in their
claims for compensation.

33

Stress management

INCIDENT

On Monday morning, Chief of Police Abercrombie arrived at the station
in good spirits. He intended to conclude his review of the proposed budget
for the training and special programs department before presenting it to
the city commission at a meeting that afternoon. As he leafed through the
morning newspaper prior to beginning work, a boldfaced headline on page
B-3 caught his eye: "Officer Fired over Shooting Gets Life Pension."
Puzzled, he quickly read the article and learned the following details about
the incident which occurred in a nearby city.

> Policeman Richard Grim, 31, who was suspended and then fired over a
> shooting incident involving his girlfriend and another police officer, has been
> granted a lifetime pension because of work-related stress. The police pension
> board agreed with a psychologist that Grim suffered a permanent disability
> because of stress on the job. The board granted Grim a medical-disability
> retirement equal to 80 percent of his pay. Six months earlier in late January,
> Grim went to Reserve Officer Debbie Sue Partridge's home while on duty
> about 3:30 A.M. He found Ms. Partridge and fellow officer Frank Carroll
> together. The two men fought briefly, then Grim shot out all the windows of
> Carroll's pick-up truck after threatening his life.
>
> During its review, the pension board found that in the months before the
> shooting, Grim had told his supervisors that he was under extreme stress
> because of depression over a recent divorce, pressure from working five years
> on the night shift, and grief over his brother's death in a fiery traffic accident.
>
> Policeman Grim had an exemplary career in his 7½ years with the police
> force. He had earned marks of "excellent" from his supervisors in the police
> dog-handling unit and was considered a prime candidate for promotion.

As Chief Abercrombie pondered the facts of this critical incident, he
recalled that stress in the workplace was a widely recognized issue for

management attention. He had read an article in *Business Week* titled "Stress Claims Are Making Business Jumpy," which reported that all but nine states now pay compensation for job-related stress problems. A variety of examples were included. Also he remembered that the newspaper *USA Today* had devoted a full page to a special report on the world of work dealing with stress on the job, including reference to one organization that gave workers three "stress leave days" a year and offered stress management seminars. He realized that if management was to be held responsible for preventing stress to build up to critical levels among subordinates, management guidance would be needed. Timely and appropriate intervention would be difficult to achieve.

The chief decided to enter a specific budget request to support stress management training. In support of this program, he needs to develop a stress management policy, procedures, and implementation plan. Chief Abercrombie is open to relevant recommendations for formulating useful operational policies for management training and guidance to avoid the escalation of stress to nonproductive levels among members of the organization.

CRITIQUES

TERRY L. LEAP
Professor of Management
Clemson University

Officer Grim's situation is unfortunate and probably could have been prevented through an employer- or community-sponsored stress management program. Stress can have both positive and negative effects; a certain level of stress keeps us alert and active at work, but too much stress can have a number of adverse consequences, an extreme example being the violent episode involving Officer Grim. The potentially destructive effects of high stress levels on employees have prompted management to take a more active role with this problem, and Chief of Police Abercrombie is about to add his organization to the growing list of those with stress management programs.

People have varying tolerances for stressful situations and episodes; some can endure large amounts of stress for extended periods of time while others have a much lower tolerance for stressful events. Another problem is that individuals can silently endure stress in their personal and work lives without displaying danger signals that would be noticed by supervisors, family, or friends. Although Officer Grim's reaction was bizarre and violent, the more typical reactions to stress include excessive smoking, alcohol and drug abuse, accident proneness, appetite disorders, headaches, mild depression, and loss of enthusiasm for work and family. Eventually these symptoms damage the employee's job performance and personal life. Chief Abercrombie realizes, much to his dismay, that the case described in the morning newspaper has irreparably damaged the career of a promising young police officer, not to mention the disability pension costs incurred by the taxpayers and the loss of public confidence in the police force.

Chief Abercrombie should be advised that an effective stress management program consists of three basic components: (1) a screening program to identify employees who may be experiencing high levels of stress, (2) individual treatments or methods for managing stress, and (3) an assessment to identify sources of stress within the organization. A number of tests such as the Workaholic Questionnaire and the State-Trait Anxiety Inventory are available to help employees diagnose problems before they become severe. Periodic physical examinations can also be used to detect signs of stress in employees. Blood pressure, muscle tension, hormone levels, and cholesterol levels are used in stress assessments and can be incorporated into routine physical examinations. Stress programs often help alleviate employee problems through managing personal perceptions of stress, lifestyle management, relaxation training, medical care, and psychotherapy. It is possible that the shooting incident involving Officer Grim could have been avoided if professional counseling had been available. Stress management programs should also examine jobs, work routines, and policies to determine whether organizational sources of stress can be eliminated. Police work, by nature, is stressful. However, methods such as task redesign, flexible working schedules, career development programs, social support, and team building have been used to reduce work-related stress.

The budget request by Chief Abercrombie to establish a stress management program is money well spent. A program containing the components described here may pay for itself many times over if future episodes such as the one involving Richard Grim are avoided. Police officers who experience stress levels that are significantly lower than those faced by Officer Grim will also benefit from a well-designed and professionally run stress management program.

MARK J. MARTINKO
Professor of Management
Florida State University

Police Chief Abercrombie's action is commendable in that it recognizes and emphasizes the potential of stress-related problems in his organization. However, it is not clear that throwing dollars at the problem for training will result in its resolution. Since there is no current litigation pending against Chief Abercrombie's organization, he has time to make a more thorough diagnosis of the situation before committing resources and taking action.

Before proceeding, Police Chief Abercrombie first needs to determine and establish the nature and extent of stress-related problems within his organization. There are a number of paper and pencil tests as well as physical and psychophysiological measures designed to assess stress within individuals and organizations. Oftentimes measures of stress may accompany routine physicals. Medical professionals as well as professionals in the health care industry should be consulted in order to determine the most reasonable diagnostic process. Because stress programs have become somewhat faddish, Chief Abercrombie is strongly urged to get the advice of several competent professionals so that his resources are not wasted on unnecessary testing and treatment.

Once there has been a determination of the general nature and extent of stress within the organization, the chief needs to establish the objectives of his stress-management program. There are a variety of tenable objectives, not all of which are complementary. For example, one possible objective is to demonstrate organizational responsibility in order to reduce the possibility of a lawsuit. If this were the chief's objective, his action plans would probably include seeking legal advice and making sure that his program is highly visible. Another potential objective is to *improve* the fitness and capabilities of his force, suggesting a proactive rather than a reactive approach. In this case, action plans might include physical fitness training, diet planning, and other forms of physical regimen. A third potential objective might be concerned with the identification and rehabilitation of specific individuals who display stress-related symptoms. If this were the case, the program could include mandatory drug screening and early detection training for alcohol abuse. Regardless of which objective, combination, or set of objectives is eventually agreed upon, it is clear that the action plans and the eventual outcomes of the program will differ depending on the objectives identified.

The process by which the chief proceeds to establish the program objectives should also be considered carefully. Several factors suggest that a participative/team-building policy-formulation strategy will be most effective. First, because many stress-related symptoms such as alcohol and drug abuse have negative social connotations, the identification of these symptoms will only be effective if there is voluntary cooperation within the organization. Involving its members in the policy formulation process will facilitate the development of the support, commitment, and understanding which will undoubtedly be necessary for voluntary cooperation. Second, the development of the program may cut across a variety of functional areas. Although the case suggests that the program be centered in the training and development area, other areas of the organization might also be integrally involved. Potential program components could include a variety of activities such as medical diagnoses, psychological counseling, job-redesign, and a variety of reporting, feedback, and detection systems. At present, there is no clear evidence that there is a training or "knowledge" problem regarding stress in the organization. The inclusion of representatives from the various functional areas in the organization would focus maximum resources and information on the problem. Thus, for example, representatives from the benefits and insurance section may have knowledge that many of the components of stress-related diagnostic and treatment programs can be fully reimbursed under the current insurance program. Similarly, representatives from the various groups of office workers, officers, sergeants, dispatchers, lieutenants, and detectives may already be able to identify key areas where stress is occurring. With participation from these various parts of the organization, knowledge regarding this complex problem will be more readily available and the final quality of the program will be enhanced. Finally, in order for the program to be implemented effectively, knowledge and communication regarding the program are essential. A fully participative policy-formulation process is probably the most effective way to begin communication regarding the nature, intent, and mechanics of the program.

In summary, Chief Abercrombie is probably premature in committing funds for training in stress management. His first concerns should focus on determining the nature and severity of the problem and coordinating his resources so that he has maximum information and cooperation for the development and implementation of the program.

OBSERVATIONS

Job-induced stress claims by employees are making managers jumpy. Job-stress claims began as a trickle in the 1970s and have steadily expanded the liability of the workers' compensation system. Compensation is paid by 80 percent of the 50 states for job-related emotional problems blamed on stress, according to a *Business Week* article. As stress-related liability increases, so does the insurance premium paid by companies for workers' compensation insurance coverage. Employers themselves feel the stress of coping with current stress claims and avoiding future ones.

Episodes of nervous breakdown, depression, loss of motivation, reduced productivity, and unacceptable behavior are increasingly being blamed on stress arising from employment. Moreover, such claims have been recognized as legitimate by courts, by the National Institute for Occupational Safety and Health, and by state workers' compensation boards. Fashionable terms such as *techno-stress*, *excess-stress*, or simply *stress* are used by some in referring to mental-stress injuries.

Dr. Hans Selye popularized the view that stress could be either positive or negative, either productive or nonproductive. He posited that eustress (good stress) was stress that motivated productive behavior. Bad stress was seen as stress that diminished an individual's capacity to perform. Therefore, according to him, it follows that as a goal, the elimination of all stress is neither useful nor desirable.

One's definition of stress is important to thinking clearly about it. Some define stress as the force or stimulus acting on an individual. Others define stress as the response, physiological or psychological, of an individual to an external situation or event. A combination of these two definitions produces a preferred definition of stress as being the consequence of the interaction between the force of stimulus and the response of the person. Applying this definition, then, job stress is seen as resulting from the worker's response to conditions in the work environment. This interactive definition of stress helps explain that of two workers exposed to the same work environment, one may develop symptoms of stress while the other may not.

Modern management recognizes the positive values of improving the quality of work life in contemporary organizations. Managers can attempt to reduce the stress-generating tendency of the work environment. Far less accessible, however, are the means for predicting and controlling worker response to the work environment. Work-related stress remains a challenge for employer and employee alike.

DISCUSSION ITEMS

1. Since job stress arises from interaction between the job holder and the work setting, who shall be held responsible for stress problems, the employer or the employee, or both in some combination? Explain your position.
2. Do you agree that workers who are not able to cope with ordinary stress levels at work deserve to receive compensation? Why or why not?
3. Formulate an operational policy for reducing stress in the workplace. Discuss its implementation.

SUGGESTED READINGS

BOOKS

Arnold, Hugh J., and Daniel C. Feldman. *Organizational Behavior*. New York: McGraw-Hill, 1986, chap. 16.

Callahan, Robert E.; C. Patrick Fleenor; and Harry Knudson. *Understanding Organizational Behavior*. Columbus, Ohio: Charles E. Merrill Publishing, 1986, chap. 12.

Davis, Keith, and John W. Newstrom. *Human Behavior at Work*. 7th ed. New York: McGraw-Hill, 1985, chap. 21.

Donnelly, James H.; James L. Gibson; and John M. Ivancevich. *Fundamentals of Management*. 6th ed. Plano, Tex.: Business Publications, 1987, chap. 14.

Fielding, Jonathan E. *Corporate Health Management*. Reading, Mass.: Addison-Wesley, 1984.

French, Wendell L. *The Personnel Management Process*. 6th ed. Boston: Houghton Mifflin, 1987, pp. 594–96.

Griffin, Ricky W. *Management*. 2nd ed. Boston: Houghton Mifflin, 1987, chap. 10.

Heneman, Herbert G.; Donald P. Schwab; John A. Fossum; and Lee D. Dyer. *Personnel/Human Resource Management*. 3rd ed. Homewood, Ill.: Richard D. Irwin, 1986, pp. 699, 702–5.

Matteson, Michael T., and John M. Ivancevich. *Managing Job Stress and Health*. New York: Free Press, 1982.

Megginson, Leon C. *Personnel Management: A Human Resources Approach*. 5th ed. Homewood, Ill.: Richard D. Irwin, 1985, pp. 208, 209, 372, 404–6.

Quick, James C., and Jonathan D. Quick. *Organizational Stress and Preventive Management*. New York: McGraw-Hill, 1984.

Rue, Leslie W., and Lloyd L. Byars. *Management: Theory and Application*. 4th ed. Homewood, Ill.: Richard D. Irwin, 1986, chap. 16.

Schermerhorn, John R. *Management for Productivity*. 2nd ed. New York: John Wiley & Sons, 1986, pp. 635–41.

Selye, Hans. *The Stress of Life*. Rev. ed. New York: McGraw-Hill, 1976.

JOURNALS

Bhagat, Rabi S.; Sara J. McQuaid; Hal Lindholm; and James Seqovis. "Total Life Stress: A Multimethod Validation of the Construct and Its Effects on Organizationally Valued Outcomes and Withdrawal Behaviors." *Journal of Applied Psychology* 70, no. 1 (February 1985), pp. 202–14.

Bowers, David G. "What Would Make 11,500 People Quit Their Jobs?" *Organizational Dynamics*, Winter 1983, pp. 5–19.

Dobbin, Murial. "Is the Daily Grind Wearing You Down?" *U.S. News and World Report*, March 24, 1986, p. 43.

Foegen, J. H. "Quiet Please!" *SAM Advanced Management Journal* 52, no. 1 (Winter 1987), pp. 17–19.

Friend, Kenneth E. "Stress and Performance: Effects of Subjective Work Load and Time Urgency." *Personnel Psychology*, Autumn 1982, pp. 623–33.

Good, Roger K. "Employee Assistance." *Personnel Journal* 65, no. 2 (February 1986), pp. 96–101.

Hendrix, William H.; Nestor K. Ovalle; and George R. Troxler. "Behavioral and Physiological Consequence of Stress and Its Antecedent Factors." *Journal of Applied Psychology* 70, no. 1 (February 1985), pp. 188–201.

King, Resa. "Stress Claims Are Making Business Jumpy." *Business Week*, October 14, 1986, p. 152.

Krietner, Robert. "Personal Wellness: It's Just Good Business." *Business Horizons* 25, no. 3 (May-June 1982), pp. 28–35.

Matteson, Michael T., and John M. Ivancevich. "The How, What, and Why of Stress Management Training." *Personnel Journal* 61, no. 10 (October 1982), pp. 768–74.

McQuade, Walter. "Easing Tensions between Man and Machine." *Fortune* 109, no. 6 (March 19, 1984), pp. 58–66.

Pesci, Michael. "Stress Management: Separating Myth from Reality." *Personnel Administrator* 27, no. 1 (January 1982), pp. 57–67.

Quick, James C., and Jonathan D. Quick. "How Good Working Relationships Can Help Relieve Pressures on the Job." *Management Review* 7, no. 5 (May 1984), pp. 43–45.

Sailor, Heather R.; John Schlacter; and Mark R. Edwards. "Stress: Causes, Consequences, and Coping Strategies." *Personnel* 59, no. 4 (July-August 1982), pp. 35–48.

Solomon, Barbara Anne. "Consensus on Wellness Programs." *Personnel* 62, no. 11 (November 1985), pp. 67–72.

WHAT THIS INCIDENT IS ABOUT:
Gifts from friendly businesses cause a minor scandal
in the public sector. The incident focuses upon
ethical considerations, personal value structures,
extralegal activity, and the importance of
organizational policy.

34

Stringless gift?

INCIDENT

One of the charges leveled against Hugh Springfield last month when he was dismissed from his state job of beverage control agent was the charge of "gift taking." His attorney won Springfield's reinstatement after a brief hearing in which he established that both the executive director of the Department of Business Regulation, which oversees the Beverage Department, and the director of the State Highway Patrol had accepted gifts from commercial firms and others.

The business regulation director said that originally he saw nothing wrong in accepting gifts from businesses under his regulation but that they had become "a public embarrassment." He admitted that he had received free motel rooms and other gifts from businesses regulated by his department.

Col. Rutledge Seashore, the highway patrol director, acknowledged that he had received gift certificates from a grocery chain at Christmas for several years. "I see nothing wrong with it," said Seashore, who last year admitted to receiving nearly $1,000 in cash and other gifts from troopers under his command in appreciation for a pay raise that he had won for them. "We don't do anything for the donors and I don't intend to stop my men from accepting gifts from friendly businesses," Seashore emphatically announced. "They're underpaid as it is."

As Springfield was drinking his second cup of coffee before leaving home for his first day back at work in his reinstated job, he scanned the newspaper, a leading one in the state. His eye focused on the editorial. It said, in part:

> It is human to feel kindly toward someone who has done you a favor. A
> psychological thread attaches to the gift. As the gifts are repeated, the

threads twine into a string. One day the giver pulls the string and asks for just a small favor in return—can the beneficiary refuse? There is also the matter of public confidence. Say a public official is absolutely incorruptible. But it becomes known that he takes a handout here, and a handout there, from those who come under the authority of his office. Who is going to believe that he is dealing impartially with the gift givers?

During the 20-minute drive to his office, Springfield reflected on the rapid-fire events in which he had been a central figure: dismissal from his job, the legal hearing, revelation of gift taking on a scale greater than he had previously imagined, reinstatement, the thought-provoking editorial. While trying to organize his thoughts and derive a personal policy regarding gifts, other questions came to mind. What was the essential difference between gifts, bribes, kickbacks, and graft? Where was the problem in accepting gifts if the public interest did not suffer? Was there a distinguishable line between acceptable and unacceptable gifts? Was it acceptable for persons highly placed in the organization to receive large gifts? What was the clue to gift acceptability—size, frequency, source, or recipient? Springfield was still uncertain as he parked his car and headed toward the elevator that would take him to his familiar office and surroundings.

As he walked through the office door, Springfield was greeted by a person well-known to him as a holder of a beverage license in the area under his official jurisdiction. The license holder said, "Welcome, Hugh. Here's a little something to help you forget your worries of the last few days—a country-cured 12-pound ham!"

Taken by surprise and faced with the choice of either accepting or rejecting the gift, Hugh felt trapped. Potential consequences and policy implications of his options flashed through his mind. Speechless, Hugh was desperate for relevant policy guidance. He wanted to do the right thing.

CRITIQUES

WILLIAM C. FREDERICK
Professor of Business Administration
University of Pittsburgh

Hugh Springfield's ethical dilemma is a perfect example of what is known in management theory as a policy vacuum. Here is an employee who does his job well, who wants to do the right thing, and who had just been through a traumatic test of his personal and professional integrity —but who still lacks strong guidance from his employer about how to handle gifts.

No wonder Springfield is confused. He is getting mixed signals from his work environment. If he looks toward his own boss (the one who tried to fire him), he sees someone who has admitted accepting gifts. If he looks toward the highway patrol, he knows that the officers regularly take favors from various businesses and that they return part of their salaries to *their* boss, who won a pay raise for them. No one seems to feel guilty about this behavior. The only reason given by Springfield's boss for trying to stop the practice is that it was publicly embarrassing. Springfield might conclude from that comment that under-the-table gifts are all right to accept if the public never knows about them.

In the absence of any clear policy guidance from his own department, Springfield is reduced to two other sources, one internal and one external. The external source is the newspaper editorial, which at least raises some ethical issues for him to consider. It states that gifts forge a bond of obligation that is difficult to ignore in a showdown. ("If I take the ham from this guy, could I crack down on him if he violates the state's liquor-licensing code?") The internal source is Springfield's personal code of ethics. By "wanting to do the right thing," Springfield might find the inner strength to cope with the friendly gesture from a client without offending him, while maintaining ethical standards for the Beverage Department.

This leave-it-up-to-Hugh approach causes two kinds of problems that most managers would want to avoid: It throws the entire ethical burden on the individual employee, and it leaves the employer especially vulnerable to unethical acts that might be committed by employees. If Springfield's ethics prove to be weak, he might accept the ham from this client, a Thanksgiving turkey from another, a personal computer from the next one, and so on until the Beverage Department has a real public scandal on its hands.

Now put yourself in the position of the executive director of the Department of Business Regulation. What can you do to reduce the pressure your employees feel concerning gifts? How can you safeguard the department against charges of graft and corruption?

Might you undertake a four-part plan, which would include the following components?

1. Issue a clear policy statement regarding the acceptance of gifts by department employees.
2. Follow up the policy statement with a more detailed code of ethical conduct that would specify the differences between trivial gifts, bribes, kickbacks, and graft. It would also define the situations where it would be improper to accept gifts of any kind.
3. Communicate the new policy and the ethics code to all persons in contact with the department (potential givers and receivers of gifts) who might be affected by these new guidelines.
4. Provide for periodic audits of employee behavior, perhaps as part of each employee's annual performance appraisal, to ensure enforcement of the ethics code.

Taking these steps—that is, formulating and implementing a policy—will enable Beverage Department employees to make decisions on a professional and not a personal basis. Refusing gifts, or having them prohibited by law or a departmental policy, is one way to clear the decision process of subjective considerations of friendship. This puts decision making on a more rational, objective basis.

Such an officially sanctioned management policy also helps the organization—whether a regulatory agency or a private business—to maintain an image of public confidence and trustworthiness. The policy and the code of conduct are important symbols of integrity, giving strong guidance to employees and bolstering the public's confidence that standards of ethical conduct are of top importance to the organization and its leaders.

MARY ANN VON GLINOW
Associate Professor of Management
and Organization
University of Southern California

Gift giving, and taking, is part of every culture on this earth (see Reardon citation on Suggested Book list). There are many reasons why this is true, however. Gifts can say things that we cannot. For example, a gift can say "thank you" or express feelings of sorrow. Gifts engender feelings of gratitude, thankfulness, and affection. On the other hand, some gifts can evoke an obligation.

Gift giving is generally categorized into four major types—expressive, normative, strategic, and ulterior motivated (Reardon). Expressive gifts are gifts that "come from the heart" with no expectation that a return gift is necessary. The normative gift is given because it is expected. For example, the Christmas gift is a normative gift. The reason for the normative gift is that if it weren't given, the recipient would probably feel hurt. The strategic gift is most frequently given for strategic reasons—to position oneself to get something in return. In general, most business gifts are of this type. Strategic gifts create the impression that something should be given in return. The final category, the ulterior-motivated gift, is given for the sole reason of obligating the receiver. There is nothing subtle about this gift, and the receiver knows what the gift giver wants in return. Some might call this a bribe; however, in many cultures, these ulterior-motivated gifts are part of the culture of "doing business." According to Reardon and others who study gift giving, we should always be aware that there are at least two parties that help interpret the message of the gift, and therefore there may be some misinterpretations. The donor may have meant the gift to be a strategic gift, while the receiver interprets it as an expressive gift. Hence the need for clarity on the intentionality of gifts, since misunderstandings abound in almost all cultures.

Hugh Springfield needs that clarity now, since there is virtually no policy guidance on gift giving and taking in the Department of Beverage Control. It is equally likely that very few governmental units or even private companies have detailed policy guidance with respect to gift giving and taking despite the fact that those four categories of gifts are commonplace in almost all countries. Nevertheless, Hugh Springfield needs an answer—what should he do?

In the immediate context of his being dismissed from his job, the legal hearing, the revelation of gift giving and taking on a larger scale, his subsequent reinstatement, and the editorial that had preoccupied him, his immediate response should be to thank the giver for the "country-cured 12-pound ham" and tell him that under the circumstances, he cannot accept the ham. Hopefully Hugh will be able to do this with tact and finesse, so that the giver doesn't feel badly rejected. Hugh should then proceed to investigate the giving of gifts, with an eye toward developing for himself and others the "relevant policy guidance" he so desperately seeks. Hugh should array the four categories of gifts, and note that with respect to any other category other than expressive, gifts would most likely be inappropriate, and taking them would engender concern on the part of the workers in that department. The policy would discuss when and under what conditions strategic gifts would be appropriate. Normative and ulterior motivated are either irrelevant or inappropriate, respectively. It is clear to me, however, that absent any policy such as the one identified earlier, Hugh and others like him will continue to face personal dilemmas when expressive or strategic gifts are given. Such a policy can be a welcome stance for all of us, particularly when the gifts have left us with some sense of obligation.

OBSERVATIONS

Definition of ethical behavior for organization members is difficult. Many organizations have not faced up to the task; but the issue of taking and giving gifts appears frequently in different settings. Examples are provided by business gifts to customers and gifts to police officers patrolling business districts. Gift taking, in the eyes of onlookers, appears to lack propriety even if the gift giver receives no benefit. As a form of "side payment," gifts typically are neither reported nor accounted for in business and professional transactions. Organizations need to provide employees with policy guidelines on side payments and other ethical issues.

These issues are receiving attention from business schools, consultants, and practicing managers. The December 1983 issue of *Managing Ethics*, the newsletter of the Center for Private and Public Ethics at Arizona State University, highlighted results of their *Making Ethics Work* seminar as follows: 70 percent of the participants noted a change in their attitudes about ethics. One participant noted, "It increased my belief in the possibilities of ethical conduct. I will attempt to instill ethics into almost every corner of my organization."

A 1987 article, "A CEO Looks at Ethics," *Business Horizons*, by Vernon R. Loucks, Jr., reminds us that ethical issues are both timely and timeless. Loucks recommends four principles for ethical management: (1) hire the right people, people with principles; (2) set standards more than rules; (3) don't let yourself get isolated; and (4) most importantly, let your ethical example at all times be absolutely impeccable.

In his critique, Professor Frederick analyzes the ethical issues of this incident and he promotes developing an organizational code of ethics. Professor Van Glinow in her critique describes four major types of gift giving and observes that the message of a gift may be subject to misinterpretation.

DISCUSSION ITEMS

1. What is the basis of gift acceptability—is it size, frequency, source, recipient, or something else?
2. What ethical principles are likely to be violated by gift taking?
3. In developing a detailed code of ethical conduct for an organization, would you seek input from the employees concerning ethical guidelines? Why or why not?

SUGGESTED READINGS

BOOKS

Arnold, Hugh J., and Daniel C. Feldman. *Organizational Behavior*. New York: McGraw-Hill, 1986, chaps. 2, 3.

Callahan, Robert E.; C. Patrick Fleenor; and Harry Knudson. *Understanding Organizational Behavior*. Columbus, Ohio: Charles E. Merrill Publishing, 1986, chaps. 2, 7.

Davis, Keith, and John W. Newstrom. *Human Behavior at Work*. 7th ed. New York: McGraw-Hill, 1985, chaps. 3, 16.

Donnelly, James H.; James L. Gibson; and John M. Ivancevich. *Fundamentals of Management*. 6th ed. Plano, Tex.: Business Publications, 1987, chap. 20.

French, Wendell L. *The Personnel Management Process*. 6th ed. Boston: Houghton Mifflin, 1987, chaps. 7, 8.

Griffin, Ricky W. *Management.* 2nd ed. Boston: Houghton Mifflin, 1987, chaps. 3, 17.

Heneman, Herbert G.; Donald P. Schwab; John A. Fossum; and Lee D. Dyer. *Personnel/Human Resource Management.* 3rd ed. Homewood, Ill.: Richard D. Irwin, 1986, chap. 4.

Megginson, Leon C. *Personnel Management: A Human Resources Approach.* 5th ed. Homewood, Ill.: Richard D. Irwin, 1985, chap. 12.

Reardon, Kathleen Kelly. *Gift Giving Around the World.* Palo Alto, California: Pass, partout, 1986.

Rue, Leslie W., and Lloyd L. Byars. *Management: Theory and Application.* 4th ed. Homewood, Ill.: Richard D. Irwin, 1986, chap. 3, pp. 71–73.

Schermerhorn, John R. *Management for Productivity.* 2nd ed. New York: John Wiley & Sons, 1986, chap. 20.

JOURNALS

Cressey, Donald R., and Charles A. Moore. "Managerial Values and Corporate Codes of Ethics." *California Management Review* 25, no. 4 (Summer 1983), pp. 53–77.

Donellon, Anne; Barbara Gray; and Michael G. Bougon. "Communication, Meaning, and Organized Action." *Administrative Science Quarterly* 31, no. 1 (March 1986), pp. 43–55.

"Ethics in Business Prize." *Harvard Business Review* 61, no. 1 (January-February 1982), pp. 142, 143.

Fritzche, David J., and Helmut Becker. "Linking Management Behavior to Ethical Philosophy—An Empirical Investigation." *Academy of Management Journal* 27, no. 1 (March 1984), pp. 166–75.

Henderson, Verne E. "The Ethical Side of Enterprise." *Sloan Management Review* 23, no. 3 (Spring 1982), pp. 37–47.

Horten, Thomas R. "For Superior Performance . . . How to Manage Oneself." *Management Review* 73, no. 1 (January 1984), pp. 2, 3.

Jansen, Erick, and Mary Ann Von Glinow. "Ethical Ambivalence and Organizational Reward System." *Academy of Management Review* 10, no. 4 (October 1985), pp. 814–22.

Kilmann, Ralph H.; Mary J. Saxton; and Roy Serpa. "Issues in Understanding and Changing Corporate Culture." *California Management Review* 28, no. 2 (Winter 1986), pp. 69–86.

Lodge, Cabot. "The Connection between Ethics and Ideology." *Journal of Business Ethics* 1, no. 2 (May 1982), pp. 85–98.

McCoy, Bowen H. "An Executive's Perspective on Ethics." *Management Review* 72, no. 7 (July 1983), pp. 20–24.

Moskowitz, Daniel B., and John A. Byrne. "Where Business Goes to Stock Up on Ethics." *Business Week*, October 14, 1985, pp. 63, 66.

Richman, Barry. "Stopping Payments under the Table." *Business Week*, May 22, 1978, p. 18.

Trevino, Linda Klebe. "Ethical Decision Making in Organizations: A Person-Situation Interactionist Model." *Academy of Management Review* 11, no. 3 (July 1986), pp. 601–17.

Waters, James A., and Peter D. Chant. "Internal Control of Managerial Integrity: Beyond Accounting Systems." *California Management Review* 24, no. 3 (Spring 1982), pp. 60–66.

Weber, James. "Institutionalizing Ethics into the Corporation." *MSU Business Topics* 29, no. 2 (Spring 1981), pp. 47–52.

WHAT THIS INCIDENT IS ABOUT:
Paternal benevolence from the executive suite
backfires, and policy changes must be made to
remedy the situation. The incident calls attention to
factors important in job satisfaction and the
relationship between job satisfaction and job
productivity.

35

The air-conditioned cafeteria

INCIDENT

In December 1985, the executive-management committee of the Berkshire Stove and Range Company made a recommendation to the company president that the employee cafeteria be air-conditioned. Its recommendation was based on the fact that the temperature in the foundry area and other production areas was often over 100 degrees Fahrenheit. In addition, since company profits for the fiscal year had been good, the committee felt that employees were entitled to share in the profits. The air-conditioned cafeteria would represent management's appreciation of the employees' good work.

At the end of another fiscal year, December 1986, the executive-management committee held a meeting and reviewed the company's operation for the past year. Again, profits were high, labor productivity was good, and labor turnover was low. The committee unanimously agreed that the employees deserved additional recognition for their fine work, and the group considered what might be done to show management's appreciation. Since the company cafeteria was air-conditioned during the past year on the committee's recommendation, several of its members wondered if employees appreciated this sort of action. The committee asked Oscar Thompson, the personnel director, to send a questionnaire to a sample of 50 employees and obtain their reaction to the air-conditioned cafeteria. The committee agreed to meet again in a month and hear a report from the personnel director.

The personnel director mailed a simple form to 50 employees containing the following request: "Please state your reaction to the recently air-conditioned cafeteria."

Of the 50 forms mailed, 46 were returned. The answers could be classified as follows:

Reaction		Total Number
a.	"I didn't know it was recently air-conditioned."	16
b.	"I never eat there."	8
c.	"If management can spend money like that, they should pay us more."	6
d.	"I wish the entire plant were air-conditioned."	8
e.	"That is a cafeteria for management people."	4
f.	"It's OK."	2
g.	Miscellaneous comments.	2

The rather negative survey results were not a complete surprise to Thompson. He knew that the executive-management committee was comprised of company vice presidents and other senior executives. Such individuals were, in his opinion, completely isolated in their analytic ivory towers and lacked the ability to identify with the needs and desires of foundry and production workers. Thompson knew of some companies that had adopted a philosophy that regarded the workers themselves as sources of ideas and that respected their ability to suggest changes for improvement. He was tempted to recommend that the company establish PIP teams, patterned after Texas Instruments' People Involvement Program. Thompson was not convinced, however, that such an approach would work with Berkshire Stove and Range employees. His reservations were compounded when he recalled overhearing a corporate vice president characterize T-groups, team building, and quality circles as fads and gimmicks. Thompson did know, however, that as a result of the survey responses, he was expected to make some policy recommendations to the executive-management committee at its next meeting. His problem was to decide what he would recommend.

CRITIQUES

KEITH DAVIS
Professor Emeritus of Management
Arizona State University

First, let us make some observations about management's action regarding air-conditioning the cafeteria in December 1985.

1. Management made the decision without any participation from employees or any effort to determine specifically what the most pressing employee needs were.
2. The underlying causes for management's action seem to have no direct relation to the action.
   a. The fact that production areas are hot does not necessarily require refrigerated eating areas. As a matter of fact, the opposite may be true. The contrast between the hot work areas and the cool area where one relaxes may be so great as to cause chilling, discomfort, and colds.
   b. A good profit year is not necessarily a proper reason for installing air-conditioning.

   Generally, action should be rationally related to causes.

Now, let us look at management's action in December 1986.

1. The personnel director apparently is not doing his job, because he has nothing particular to recommend and has to be instructed to follow up on what happened last year. He strongly needs to adopt a more *proactive* and less *reactive* strategy (that is, act to prevent problems before they occur, rather than react to patch up situations after problems develop). He will be a more proactive manager if he develops professional personnel policies and takes some initiative. One of his first steps should be designing and implementing policies and programs that improve employee participation.
2. Neither the personnel director nor the other executives seem to know how employees reacted to last year's expression of "appreciation." What has happened to communication in this organization?
3. The open-ended questionnaire is effective in disclosing several different responses that were unexpected. The proportion of returns was high for this sort of survey, but responses were overwhelmingly negative, suggesting that there may be some problems with employee attitudes and job satisfaction. (For information about job satisfaction, see Keith Davis and John W. Newstrom, *Organizational Behavior: Human Behavior at Work*, 7th ed., New York: McGraw-Hill, 1985, chapter 6.)

In this incident, management planning is weak, there is minimum employee participation, employee communication is deficient, and decision making is not rationally related to causes or employee needs. Consequently, satisfaction with the cafeteria (and probably other employment conditions) is poor. Although low job satisfaction does not guarantee declining productivity, it may have long-run negative effects unless the quality of management improves. To solve these problems, the personnel director needs to develop effective personnel policies and programs that build employee participation, improve communication in all directions, and work toward better job satisfaction. Sudden change is unlikely in this situation, but the personnel director can develop policies and programs that work toward long-run change for the better.

PAUL J. GORDON
Professor of Management
Indiana University

What recognition can management provide to show appreciation for employee contribution to a successful year? Or should the management orientation in posing the question this way be turned around? How effective is an unsolicited, unilateral show of appreciation if the recipient would prefer some part in decisions including the allocation of resources that affect his or her well-being?

Either way, should the sharing take place only in years of success? Should employees be rewarded if the circumstances leading to success had little to do with employee behavior? If some award is made, either as a recognition of past accomplishments or as a lively anticipation of future accomplishments, why and how does consultation (or at least a declaration of intention) fit into the picture?

If management were more fully developed as a science, one might say that selection of utilities (U) as desirable should lead to choice of actions (A) to be taken under conditions (C), and that these should produce outcomes (O) with probabilities (P) and risks (R). Then, in cases such as the present one, the rational manager would have little difficulty in making a highly rational decision. As in real life, however, rationality, information, prediction, and control, especially in the area of human behavior, are not fully developed.

Without giving technical criticism of the questionnaire technique, there might have been ways to avoid what is now a potential source of employee irritation and management embarrassment. The recognition, given with neither consultation nor declaration of intention by management, apparently has not had the reception that management would have preferred. Unfortunately, without some reasonable meeting of expectations, one or both parties can become aggrieved. Consultation might have avoided the 1985 gap, and it might have provided better general understanding on cafeteria usage and the allocation of money for improvements such as air-conditioning. This earlier experience, however, can provide a lesson for management in the coming year.

The important issues are to learn, if possible, why things are going so well; to assure continuity of a good situation; and to find policies and means for continued improvement. Information given in the case suggests that profits, productivity, and turnover are in good shape. If management can clarify the objectives (the future conditions that management seeks to create), and tie employee performance through some means and standards to these objectives, it may be started on a more adequate policy and system for incentives. The objectives, the standards, and the necessary details of administration must be well understood for the intended results to be achieved. This means adequate communication and may mean consultation and participation in the plan's developmental stages and administration. The ad hoc, unilateral decision may have done no harm, but nothing suggests that repetition will do any special good.

For Oscar Thompson, the personnel director, there are several points to consider, including possible corridor work, before offering policy and procedure recommendations to the executive-management committee at its next meeting.

The first question is whether he is correctly "reading" and understanding top management's views. Personnel directors must be wary of evangelizing on behalf of whatever might be touted as the current "quick fix" for the problems that were addressed last year under some other label.

Second, techniques that do not fit in the corporate value structure and do not relate to corporate performance will likely be short-lived. If techniques are to have credibility as part of the recognition or reward structure, there should be some self-evident relation to both managerial and employee motivation. If techniques are adopted without laying the groundwork with line managers or employees and without discussion of intent and possible effects, the cafeteria situation may be repeated. Worse, if room is left to speculate on the intent and the effects, action may be held suspect.

Third, a serious and unanswered question is that of why management wants to do anything.

The commentary to this point constitutes an agenda for some corridor work before the meeting. Alternatives at the meeting might include: (1) no action; (2) policy clarification with procedure subject to consultation; or (3) a joint labor-management task force's specific recommendations. Policy and procedure accepted as reasonable are more important than perfection. The ingredients of success are more in the "ambiente" than the technique! No need to repeat air-conditioning the cafeteria as a response to 100 degrees in the foundry!

OBSERVATIONS

While executive-committee members would not be expected to spend a lot of their time in the foundry, they do need to learn something about the attitudes and working conditions of employees at the operative level. Moreover, even minimum management interaction with the workers can be beneficial and informative. Many management development programs stress the importance of staying in touch with employees, being seen in the work area from time to time, and creating informal situations for management-employee interaction. Recently, *Supervisory Management* presented several items that employees responded to with improved work and company loyalty, including chief executive officer "brown bag" lunches with groups of employees and cooking by the plant manager at the supervisor's annual outing.

Professors Gordon and Davis suggest several projects for the personnel director of Berkshire Stove and Range Company, among which are improving employee participation, improving communication with employees, and improving his understanding of top management's views.

DISCUSSION ITEMS

1. Professor Gordon suggests that the following three alternatives might be considered at the next meeting of the executive-management committee: (1) no action, (2) clarification of policy with procedure subject to consultation, or (3) a joint labor-management task force appointed to make specific recommendations. Select your preferred option and discuss its advantages and disadvantages.
2. How should the management of the Berkshire Stove and Range Company use the information they have obtained from the opinion survey?
3. How is the issue of "resistance to change" relevant in this incident?

SUGGESTED READINGS

BOOKS

Arnold, Hugh J., and Daniel C. Feldman. *Organizational Behavior*. New York: McGraw-Hill, 1986, chaps. 6, 14.

Callahan, Robert E.; C. Patrick Fleenor; and Harry Knudson. *Understanding Organizational Behavior*. Columbus, Ohio: Charles E. Merrill Publishing, 1986, chaps. 3, 4, 7.

Davis, Keith, and John W. Newstrom. *Human Behavior at Work*. 7th ed. New York: McGraw-Hill, 1985, chap. 6.

Donnelly, James H.; James L. Gibson; and John M. Ivancevich. *Fundamentals of Management*. 6th ed. Plano, Tex.: Business Publications, 1987, chap. 10.

French, Wendell L. *The Personnel Management Process*. 6th ed. Boston: Houghton Mifflin, 1987, chap. 6.

Griffin, Ricky W. *Management*. 2nd ed. Boston: Houghton Mifflin, 1987, chap. 13.

Heneman, Herbert G.; Donald P. Schwab; John A. Fossum; and Lee D. Dyer. *Personnel/Human Resource Management.* 3rd ed. Homewood, Ill.: Richard D. Irwin, 1986, pp. 616, 637–47.

Megginson, Leon C. *Personnel Management: A Human Resources Approach.* 5th ed. Homewood, Ill.: Richard D. Irwin, 1985, chap. 13, pp. 302–6, 625.

Rue, Leslie W., and Lloyd L. Byars. *Management: Theory and Application.* 4th ed. Homewood, Ill.: Richard D. Irwin, 1986, chaps. 14, 17.

Schermerhorn, John R. *Management for Productivity.* 2nd ed. New York: John Wiley & Sons, 1986, chaps. 11, 12.

JOURNALS

Agnew, Neil, and John Brown. "Limited Potential: Human Relations Then and Now." *Business Horizons* 29, no. 6 (November-December 1986), pp. 34–42.

Beck, Charles E., and Elizabeth A. Beck. "The Manager's Open Door and the Communication Climate." *Business Horizons* 29, no. 1 (January-February 1986), pp. 15–19.

Bergerson, Allen W. "Employee Suggestion Plan Still Going Strong at Kodak." *Supervisory Management* 2, no. 5 (May 1977), pp. 32–36.

Cavanagh, Michael E. "In Search of Motivation." *Personnel Journal* 63, no. 3 (March 1984), pp. 76–82.

D'Aprix, Roger. "The Oldest (and Best) Way to Communication with Employees." *Harvard Business Review* 60, no. 5 (September-October 1982), pp. 30, 31.

Hunsaker, Phillip L. "Strategies for Organizational Change: The Role of the Inside Change Agent." *Personnel* 59, no. 5 (September-October 1982), pp. 18–28.

Judson, Arnold S. "The Awkward Truth about Productivity." *Harvard Business Review* 60, no. 5 (September-October 1982), p. 93.

Kesselman, Gerald A. "The Attitude Survey: Does It Have a Bearing on Productivity?" *Advanced Management Journal* 49, no. 1 (Winter 1984), pp. 18–24.

Milbourn, Gene, and Richard Cuba. "OD Techniques and the Bottom Line." *Personnel* 58, no. 3 (May-June 1981), pp. 34–42.

Palmer, Robin. "A Participative Approach to Attitude Surveys." *Personnel Management* 9, no. 12 (December 1977), pp. 26, 27ff.

Rothwell, William J. "Conducting an Employee Attitude Survey." *Personnel Journal* 62, no. 4 (April 1983), pp. 308–11.

Shetty, Y. K. "Key Elements of Productivity Improvement Programs." *Business Horizons* 25, no. 2 (March-April 1982), pp. 15–22.

Staw, Barry M. "Organizational Psychology and the Pursuit of the Happy/Productive Worker." *California Management Review* 28, no. 4 (Summer 1986), pp. 40–53.

Sullivan, Jeremiah. "A Critique of Theory Z." *Academy of Management Review* 8, no. 1 (January 1983), pp. 132–42.

Whittset, David A., and Lyle Yorks. "Looking Back at Topeka: General Foods and the Quality-of-Work-Life Experiment." *California Management Review* 25, no. 4 (Summer 1983), pp. 93–109.

WHAT THIS INCIDENT IS ABOUT:
Bonuses offered by airlines and other travel-related
enterprises to encourage repeat business can be a
thorny policy problem. This incident poses the
question of rightful claim to such bonuses. Who
should benefit: the employees who do the traveling
or the employers who pay the bills?

36

Travel policy dilemma

INCIDENT

Margie Clark, manager of the travel department for a large midwestern
company, was grappling with several issues posed by the frequent-flier
programs of the major airlines. Frequent-flier programs are designed by
the airlines to attract frequent business travelers and make them loyal
customers. In doing this, the airlines hope to increase traffic and fill otherwise empty seats.

Frequent-flier programs offer bonuses based on the number of miles
traveled on an airline by a traveler. The value of these bonuses varies.
Most of the programs have levels of gifts, beginning with the upgrading of
a coach ticket to first class when a traveler accumulates between 2,000 and
10,000 miles on an airline or has taken so many flights with the airline.
Free first-class tickets are the prize for flying 50,000 miles. At the top of
the scale, for example, the bonuses are free round trips to foreign destina-
tions such as London, Scandinavia, and Australia. Free luxury cruises are
also available, usually for two persons.

From her research, Clark learned that traveler response to frequent-
flier programs has exceeded the airlines' expectations. Nearly 6 million air
travelers were estimated by an airline source to be enrolled in the programs. Reportedly, a midwestern travel agency figured that the frequent-
flier employees of one company generated nearly $200,000 in bonuses from
the almost $8 million the company spent on airline tickets for its employ-
ees' business travel each year. The director for advertising and promotion
of another major airline said that the frequent-flier program is one of their
best marketing tools ever. "They are fixtures in our promotional package
and will be for a long time to come," he said. Clark concluded that the

value of the bonuses was not trivial and that the programs were not likely to be eliminated in the near future by the airlines.

Clark's dilemma centered on the issue of who has rightful claim to the bonuses: the employees, who do the traveling, or the employers, who pay the airline travel fares. On this question, the airlines' policy was clear. Ample evidence showed that although the airlines had designed the frequent-flier programs for business travelers, they structured them to reward the individuals who fly—not the company that pays. For example, a major airline recently bought a half-page advertisement in *The Wall Street Journal* with a lead statement in ¾-inch-high boldfaced letters asserting "Half of you are earning bonuses every. time you fly." The advertisement stated, "When you start collecting the bonuses you earn, you'll smile. Which will bring you back again and again . . ." and "You should collect the bonuses you earn by flying and you can do that by joining our frequent-flier program."

Clark found that airlines typically would not help employers who tried to get information about individuals' flight records. On this point, one airline representative said, "We tell them 'no.'"

Another issue contributed to Clark's problem. When a business traveler joined an airline's bonus program, she or he tended to fly with that airline exclusively to build up bonus points as rapidly as possible, although lower ticket fares were often available at competing airlines. Whenever this situation occurred, the higher fare costs accrued to the company paying for the ticket, but the bonus points accrued for the employee's benefit. Under these circumstances, the employer is at a disadvantage, while flying employees are benefiting, a result that Clark found little justification for.

Clark's information indicated that some companies let employees use the bonuses for personal travel, in accord with the obvious intent of the airlines. Other companies do the opposite and have straightforward policies declaring that employees are expected to use bonus benefits for future business travel. Clark discovered that federal employees were required by regulation to use bonuses for future business travel. It seemed that a federal employee who used bonuses for personal travel would be stealing government property.

As Clark reviewed the information that she had assembled, her dilemma deepened. Last week, top management had asked her (1) to recommend an operating policy for handling the problems posed by the frequent-flier programs and the bonuses generated by them, and (2) to recommend plans for implementing the policy. Clark's problem became critical when she glanced at her watch and realized that she was scheduled to report her recommendations to top management in only two hours.

CRITIQUES

EDWARD R. CLAYTON
Professor of Management Science
Virginia Polytechnic Institute
and State University

The critical issue in this case is how a company wants to treat its employees. Before discussing this issue, let's look at a similar situation and pose a question to the reader. Last month, a colleague of mine had gone to a professional meeting at the state's expense. The meeting was in a city that his wife wanted to visit; therefore, from his own money, he purchased her an airline ticket, and they flew to the meeting together. Their return flight was overbooked by the airline, and the airline asked for volunteers to wait for the next flight. He and his wife volunteered and consequently were bumped from their flight. As a reward, they were given two free tickets to any U.S. city.

Suppose this happened to you and when you reported for work the next day, the personnel manager asked for your free ticket and your spouse's free ticket because both of you qualified for a reduced fare based on company-paid travel. How would you react and what degree of company loyalty would this situation foster?

Given two flights to the same destination, a company usually prefers that employees take the cheaper flight. However, a cheaper flight may not always be the best flight in terms of factors other than cost. Further, flights to the same destination may have different fares due to time. How many all-night, red-eye special flights would management want their employees to take to save a few dollars?

Finally, most of the people that a company sends on business trips are high-level, responsible executives who often work long hours when they are out of town on business. By flying the same airline, they may get some special treatment that might make large amounts of travel more bearable.

In summary, Clark should recommend to top management that they (1) remind traveling employees by memo not to abuse their company with frequent-flier programs and to use their best judgment in scheduling travel, and (2) drop the matter from further consideration.

WARREN W. MENKE
Professor of Management
Clemson University

This incident clearly describes two basic issues:

1. The company pays for the airline tickets, but who should get the bonus?
2. Airline travel costs are inflated by an employee's exclusive use of one airline to collect bonus points.

These are both results of a third issue caused by an airline policy that infringes both upon a company's responsibility to minimize operating costs and upon its prerogative to distribute perquisites (bonuses) in line with company policy and goals.

The now inadequate company travel policy must be adjusted to meet the airlines' challenge so that the company can use the frequent-flier bonus to reduce future travel costs (as the federal government does). The company also needs to allay employee dissatisfaction about the loss of "their" bonuses.

Recognizing that employee dissatisfaction may be the most difficult problem, Clark should enlist the personnel department in an alliance to advertise and explain the new travel policy. Their goals should be to ensure that all employees learn about the new policy and the large amounts of company money represented by the airlines' bonuses. If these points are made effectively, there should be little employee reluctance to recognize and accept that it is the company's responsibility to both employees and stockholders to use such money for reducing travel costs.

The new policy's emotional impact may be mitigated by delaying its implementation from three to six months and by replacing the lost "perk" with a company-instituted one. It would be wise to announce and apply at least one half of the cost savings toward initiating some benefit for all employees and their families—for example, a company health spa, clubhouse, swimming pool, and the like.

Clark should also recommend that the travel policy be revised so that current airlines' "bonus" money can be used for reducing future travel expenses, that the travel department's responsibility as the only purchaser of tickets for company travel be defined, and that conditions and exceptions to the rule be defined.

As sole purchasing agent, the travel department should be responsible for buying tickets to satisfy the goal of reasonably meeting employee convenience, minimizing travel costs, and maximizing travel effectiveness. (The latter goal may require further policy definition because, for example, a business trip scheduled to correct a customer's complaint would probably preempt employee convenience and place a low priority on minimizing travel costs). The travel department could easily assume responsibility for keeping flight records. The large sums of money spent on travel could be used to negotiate with the airlines for reduced rates.

In summary, to meet the airlines' policy infringement without requiring their cooperation, a revised travel policy should be issued, advertised, and explained, and the travel department's responsibilities should be changed. The airline will still have the incentive to offer bonus points or discounts toward future fares, the company will reduce costs and regain control of their perquisites, and all employees will gain a new or improved benefit.

OBSERVATIONS

Would it be considered prudent for a firm's management to condone gift taking by employees who are authorized to expend the firm's assets in purchasing services from the same vendors who are giving the gifts? Whether the gifts are called "bonuses" or "side payments," is the result not the same? On the other hand, perhaps the marginal cost to the firm is relatively small compared to the motivational and other behavioral benefits accruing to the company's bonus-earning employees.

Professors Clayton and Menke present interesting critiques with rather opposite recommendations. This might have been expected, because actual companies have opposite policies regarding the use of bonuses. If bonuses are viewed as fringe benefits, can their discriminatory nature, in that only employees who travel by plane are eligible to receive the benefits, be justified?

DISCUSSION ITEMS

1. What would be the major features of an implementation plan for establishing company control of frequent-flier bonuses in Margie Clark's company—considering that traveling employees are accustomed to personal use of the bonuses?
2. Suppose the frequent-flier bonuses were given in cash. Would this modify your recommended policy toward their ownership and use? Explain.
3. To whom do the bonuses rightfully belong? Should this right be asserted? If so, how should it be done? If not, then why not?

SUGGESTED READINGS

BOOKS

Arnold, Hugh J., and Daniel C. Feldman. *Organizational Behavior*. New York: McGraw-Hill, 1986, chaps. 3, 12.

Callahan, Robert E.; C. Patrick Fleenor; and Harry Knudson. *Understanding Organizational Behavior*. Columbus, Ohio: Charles E. Merrill Publishing, 1986, chaps. 7, 11.

Davis, Keith, and John W. Newstrom. *Human Behavior at Work*. 7th ed. New York: McGraw-Hill, 1985, chaps. 3, 5.

Donnelly, James H.; James L. Gibson; and John M. Ivancevich. *Fundamentals of Management*. 6th ed. Plano, Tex. Business Publications, 1987, chap. 10.

French, Wendell L. *The Personnel Management Process*. 6th ed. Boston: Houghton Mifflin, 1987, chap. 20.

Griffin, Ricky W. *Management*. 2nd ed. Boston: Houghton Mifflin, 1987, chap. 13.

Heneman, Herbert G.; Donald P. Schwab; John A. Fossum; and Lee D. Dyer. *Personnel/Human Resource Management*. 3rd ed. Homewood, Ill.: Richard D. Irwin, 1986, chap. 15.

Megginson, Leon C. *Personnel Management: A Human Resources Approach*. 5th ed. Homewood, Ill.: Richard D. Irwin, 1985, chaps. 16, 17.

Rue, Leslie W., and Lloyd L. Byars. *Management: Theory and Application*. 4th ed. Homewood, Ill.: Richard D. Irwin, 1986, chaps. 5, 13.

Schermerhorn, John R. *Management for Productivity*. 2nd ed. New York: John Wiley & Sons, 1986, chaps. 3, 12.

JOURNALS

Altier, William J. "Task Forces: An Effective Management Tool." *Management Review* 76, no. 2 (February 1987), pp. 52–57.

Bishop, Kathleen A. "The Silent Signals." *Training and Development Journal* 39, no. 6 (June 1985), p. 36.

Bloom, Stuart P. "Policy and Procedure Statements that Communicate." *Personnel Journal* 62, no. 9 (September 1983), pp. 711–18.

Carter, Michael F., and Kenneth P. Shapiro. "Develop a Proactive Approach to Employee Benefits Planning." *Personnel Journal* 62, no. 7 (July 1983), p. 562.

Cole, Albert, Jr. "Flexible Benefits Are a Key to Better Employee Relations." *Personnel Journal* 62, no. 1 (January 1983), pp. 49–53.

Flanagan, William G. "More Sweets to the Suite." *Forbes* 127, no. 12 (June 8, 1981), pp. 107–10.

Foegen, J. H. "The Creative Flowering of Employee Benefits." *Business Horizons* 25, no. 3 (May-June 1982), pp. 9–13.

Horton, Thomas R. "Shaping Business Values." *Management Review* 73, no. 4 (April 1984), pp. 2, 3.

Kovach, Kenneth A. "New Directions in Fringe Benefits." *Advanced Management Journal* 48, no. 3 (Summer 1983), pp. 55–63.

Melohn, Thomas H. "How to Build Employee Trust and Productivity." *Harvard Business Review* 61, no. 1 (January-February 1983), pp. 56–61.

Meredith, Jack R. "The Importance of Impediments to Implementation." *Interfaces* 11, no. 4 (August 1981), pp. 71–74.

Platten, Donald C. "The Employee Benefits—Does the Company Also?" *Harvard Business Review* 61, no. 5 (September-October 1983), p. 20.

Tannenbaum, Arnold S., and Walter J. Kuleck, Jr. "The Effect on Organization Members of Discrepancy between Perceived and Preferred Reward Implicit in Work." *Human Relations* 31, no. 9 (September 1978), pp. 809–21.

Toy, Stewart. "A Storm Warning for Frequent Fliers." *Business Week* (November 10, 1986), p. 88.

WHAT THIS INCIDENT IS ABOUT:
Temporary employee transfers made under pressure
lead to individual apprehension and performance
problems in this incident, which explores the issues
of task organizing, motivation, communication, and
gaining acceptance of change.

37

Unexpected reassignment

INCIDENT

As Regional Hospital began phasing in the Medicare Prospective
Payment System (PPS), based on reimbursement for costs associated with
diagnostic-related groups, Edwin Barker, comptroller and head of the
business affairs department, realized they were in for a major transition.
Under this system, the hospital could not collect more for a treatment
procedure than the amount set by the federal government. If it kept costs
below established levels, the hospital could keep the difference as profit.
So Regional Hospital and its accountants scrambled to develop cost-track-
ing methods related to the more than 400 diagnostic-related categories. This urgent effort caused an overload in the hospital's insurance claims
office. Even though the section head scheduled all the overtime allowed
by the budget, the work backlog increased.

John Marks, an assistant hospital administrator whose specialty was
computer operations, analyzed the problem and recommended that
treatment-cost data and service-charge data be converted for computer
operations. A special conversion unit, headed by Marks, was established.
Completion of the conversion project within six months was necessary to
bring treatment costs in line and to meet audit requirements.

On Wednesday, the day after the special project unit was set up, Marks
asked Barker to assign three reliable clerks from his division to the special
project unit. General supervision of the clerks would be retained by their
regular division, but the clerks would receive technical supervision in the
new unit.

One of the clerks selected for the special project unit was Lin Buxby,
who had graduated from high school one year earlier with a good achievement record. She had vision problems corrected by contact lenses, a fact

reflected on her personnel record. The supervisor to whom she was first assigned called the personnel department about the matter and was assured that Buxby's eyesight should not handicap her for general clerical work. At her first formal appraisal, six months after being hired, Buxby's overall performance was rated as "good" by the supervisor. For this reason and others, she was selected as one of three clerks for the special project unit.

On Thursday, the three clerks were told about their temporary reassignment by Barker shortly before they were to begin. The type of work was not mentioned in his brief announcement. The reassignment was unexpected by them. Two clerks readily accepted the reassignment with comments such as "Our pay will be the same" and "We can still have lunch with our friends here because we're just going across the hall."

Buxby, however, was noticeably upset by the turn of events. She asked Barker, "Why can't I stay here? When can I return?" Her questions went unanswered.

When the three clerks arrived at the special project unit on Friday, a staff member explained the work, desks were chosen, and work was assigned. During the first coffee break, Buxby rushed back across the hall. Bursting into tears, she implored Barker to let her return and continue training in her original assignment. She said, "The confusion and pressure are too much. And we don't know what to expect next." Barker explained that the situation would soon settle down, that the experience would help her when she returned to her original position, and that she might make some overtime wages. Buxby seemed convinced and went back to work in the special project unit.

Two working days later, Marks called Barker and demanded that Buxby be replaced immediately. Marks said that Buxby was too slow, that she couldn't do anything right, and that Barker had sent an incompetent clerk to do a top-priority project. That call attracted Barker's attention, because he did not want to make that kind of an impression on the assistant hospital administrator. He was upset, surprised, and convinced that Buxby's poor performance was intentional. A replacement for Buxby was selected.

The next morning, Barker took Buxby's replacement to the special project unit, brought Buxby back to her original position, and talked to her. It appeared that Buxby didn't know why she had been replaced. When he referred to her being slow and making many mistakes, Buxby said, "No one said anything to me about making mistakes. But I knew I was slow. The lines on the data sheet ran together due to the columns on the coding sheets being only one fourth of an inch wide. Everything seemed to swim in front of my eyes. Trying not to make mistakes slowed me down. I told the supervisor about my trouble, and she said, 'I'll see what I can do.' The next thing I knew, you brought me back."

Barker concluded that everyone connected with the Buxby incident was partially responsible. He knew that Buxby had previously met the organization's personnel selection criteria, and that her work performance had been rated "good" in the formal performance appraisal. Yet, he was painfully aware that his assigning Buxby to the special unit had led to trouble: Buxby was embarrassed and reduced to tears, progress in the special unit was disrupted and delayed, and Marks had accused him of sending an incompetent clerk. Barker needed to decide how to restore Buxby's confidence in her ability, her standing as a "good" worker, and her status in the work group. He also wanted to identify the factors that most likely caused the trouble, and to develop policies to reduce the chance of similar employee difficulties recurring.

CRITIQUES

WILMAR F. BERNTHAL
Professor Emeritus,
Management and Organization
University of Colorado at Boulder

The most obvious approach to analyzing the incident is to view it as a breakdown in interpersonal relations and communication. The solution would then be to train managers in interpersonal skills and sensitivity.

Another approach is to view the incident as an illustration of a mechanistic approach to job enrichment, with a supervisor giving a worker doing a routine job an opportunity for personal growth and development on the job. The analysis would then point out the importance of considering individual differences when anticipating worker response to such a change and challenge.

A third view is that the incident may be a manifestation of a systems problem, in which managers act quite naturally in their given system roles, but the system may not be adequate for dealing with individual and interpersonal considerations. While all three approaches have merit, let's look at the systems elements first, to make sure we do not prematurely ascribe to managers' personalities what may be a result of structural arrangements in the organization.

In Regional Hospital, the administration of business affairs, such as accounting and processing insurance claims, is highly routinized, with employees implementing standardized procedures. When an administrative change is required by new environmental circumstances, such as the Medicare changes, the organization responds by having staff specialists, such as Marks's special project unit, develop new procedures.

In this setting, administrators tend to think in mechanistic terms. They use employees as interchangeable parts to serve system needs and train them to implement new procedures. They look to experts in the personnel department to help in selection and placement, to assure that employees are qualified to do the work. In such a system, it is only natural that the supervisor only checked with personnel in determining whether Lin Buxby could do general clerical work. Barker used only similar data in assigning her to the special project.

This management system, however, neglects other motivating factors that might affect employee behavior. Buxby, for example, may have special needs for a supportive work climate, in view of her visual handicap. To remove her from the security of a considerate training supervisor, routine work, and a happy relationship with co-workers, and to place her in a temporary, nonroutine job with less-sympathetic direction may undermine the self-confidence she needs to develop to function effectively.

The administrator thus faces a conflict between his right to assign workers (his bureacratic role) and his need to live with the consequences of these decisions. The system provides him with an initial screening of employees to ensure they are qualified to do a job, including working on the special project. However, it is only through sharing the problem with employees and permitting them to express their assignment preferences that he can elicit information on the motivational factors that cause one employee to seek the variety or challenge of a special assignment and cause another to prefer the shelter and security of an old, routine assignment. This is particularly true in assigning work to a person such as Buxby, who already feels handicapped.

At this point, Barker needs to do some "healing of relationships" with John Marks, who is anxious to have his project move forward, and with his clerks and their supervisor, whose cohesive group has been disrupted. In addition, he needs to formulate policies that will assure hospital administrators and employee groups that their interests will be considered in future work assignments.

With Marks, it should be sufficient to make a simple apology for the temporary disruption of his project and to assure him that the project will soon be under control. With his clerks and their supervisor, a meeting is necessary in which Barker takes responsibility for the strain caused by the incident. An effort to reestablish Buxby as an important member of the clerical group is also necessary, whether or not she returns to the special project.

Based on an open discussion with the clerks and their supervisor, Barker should formulate policies and procedures for making temporary work assignments and for reviewing the performance of workers temporarily separated from their primary units. Also, all employees, especially handicapped workers like Buxby, need to be familiar with the personnel department's services for helping them assess their strengths, limitations, and career potential, and in charting career paths and training programs that benefit both the organization and the worker.

To proceed with the special project, all clerks should be apprised of the project requirements and the experiences that can be gained from participating in it. All clerks, including Buxby, should have an opportunity to bid for such an assignment. Those whose preferences cannot be satisfied on this project should be considered as other opportunities arise.

HERBERT G. HICKS
Professor of Management
Louisiana State University

This incident vividly illustrates several things about persons working in organizations:

1. Members of organizations have feelings or emotions that can affect their performance more than pay.
2. Although organizations exist to accomplish certain objectives, these objectives may not be compatible with members' individual objectives.
3. Informal organizations spring up in the "shadow" of formal organizations. These informal organizations exist to satisfy the needs of members that are not satisfied by formal organizations.
4. Individual objectives of persons, as expressed in their membership in informal organizations, may be as powerful as their objectives in belonging to the formal organization.
5. Managers frequently ignore all of the above.

In the present case, the three clerks were treated as if they were machines with no individuality, emotions, or social bonds in the organization. As a prescription, Barker should have discussed the proposed transfer with the three affected persons, and he should have taken into account the first four points above.

It is quite likely that Buxby's increased visual difficulties in the new situation are partly psychosomatic. On the other hand, her physical problem would have been uncovered with appropriate discussion.

I disagree with Barker's conclusion that everyone was responsible. There is no evidence that anyone performed incompetently before this incident. I pin the blame squarely on Barker for failing to communicate adequately with his employees to discover their feelings about the new assignment.

Members of organizations are not unfeeling robots who can be mechanically manipulated. Every person has a unique personality, unique abilities, unique limitations, and unique needs and objectives. Furthermore, a person's emotions often cause behaviors that may seem to defy rational understanding by others. But, to one's self, one's actions always "make sense," based upon some facet of his or her internal motivation.

Effective management in the present incident probably would have prevented the problem. Then we never would have heard of Buxby's "eye trouble."

OBSERVATIONS

New employees are especially vulnerable while finding their place in the organization, establishing interpersonal relationships, and trying to identify in some meaningful way with the organization. Since reliable support structures are not yet formed, new employees tend to be sensitive to supervisory relationships. Managers and subordinates share the responsibility for developing productive and satisfying work relationships for new workers.

Professor Bernthal recognizes that the administrator's right to assign workers produces consequences that he or she must live with. Bernthal emphasizes examining structural arrangements in the organization. Professor Hicks focuses on the characteristics of persons and groups in organizations, finding that Edwin Barker failed to properly consider these behavioral factors.

DISCUSSION ITEMS

1. Discuss the personal and organizational goals that appear to govern the behavior of John Marks, Edwin Barker, and Lin Buxby in this incident. Identify sources of conflict and recommend solutions.
2. When in the chain of events connecting Buxby's initial hiring and her unexpected replacement on the special project unit could intervention have occurred in the unfortunate cascade of events? By whose actions? Explain.
3. Compare the three ways that Professor Bernthal views the incident. Which way has the most validity? Explain.

SUGGESTED READINGS

BOOKS

Arnold, Hugh J., and Daniel C. Feldman. *Organizational Behavior*. New York: McGraw-Hill, 1986, chap. 13.

Callahan, Robert E.; C. Patrick Fleenor; and Harry Knudson. *Understanding Organizational Behavior*. Columbus, Ohio: Charles E. Merrill Publishing, 1986, chaps. 4, 5, 9.

Davis, Keith, and John W. Newstrom. *Human Behavior at Work*. 7th ed. New York: McGraw-Hill, 1985, chaps. 20, 21.

Donnelly, James H.; James L. Gibson; and John M. Ivancevich. *Fundamentals of Management*. 6th ed. Plano, Tex.: Business Publications, 1987, chap. 13.

French, Wendell L. *The Personnel Management Process*. 6th ed. Boston: Houghton Mifflin, 1987, chaps. 9, 10, 16.

Griffin, Ricky W. *Management*. 2nd ed. Boston: Houghton Mifflin, 1987, chap. 10.

Heneman, Herbert G.; Donald P. Schwab; John A. Fossum; and Lee D. Dyer, *Personnel/Human Resource Management*. 3rd ed. Homewood, Ill.: Richard D. Irwin, 1986, chap. 3.

Megginson, Leon C. *Personnel Management: A Human Resources Approach*. 5th ed. Homewood, Ill.: Richard D. Irwin, 1985, chaps. 8, 10, 11.

Rue, Leslie W., and Lloyd L. Byars. *Management: Theory and Application*. 4th ed. Homewood, Ill.: Richard D. Irwin, 1986, chap. 17.

Schermerhorn, John R. *Management for Productivity*. 2nd ed. New York: John Wiley & Sons, 1986, chaps. 8, 11, 12.

JOURNALS

"Cheer Up, Stressniks: It's All in Your Mind." *Management Review* 72, no. 6 (June 1982), p. 56.

Coil, Ann. "Job Matching Brings out the Best in Employees." *Personnel Journal* 63, no. 1 (January 1984), pp. 54–60.

"Computer Shock Hits the Office." *Business Week*, August 8, 1983, pp. 46–49.

Feldman, Daniel C., and Jeanne M. Brett. "Coping with New Jobs: A Comparative Study of New Hires and Job Changers." *Academy of Management Journal* 26, no. 2 (June 1983), pp. 258–72.

Fetter, R. B., and J. L. Freeman. "Diagnosis-Related Groups: Product Line Management within Hospitals." *Academy of Management Review* 11, no. 1 (January 1986), pp. 41–54.

Gast, Michael F., and Paul J. Patinka. "Imprinting the Young Employee." *Business Horizons* 26, no. 4 (July-August 1983), pp. 11–13.

Gibb, Peter. "The Facilitative Trainer." *Training and Development Journal* 36, no. 7 (July 1982), pp. 14–35.

Harris, Phillip R., and Dorothy L. Harris. "Human Resource Management, Part I: Charting a New Course in a New Organization in a New Society." *Personnel* 59, no. 5 (September-October 1982), pp. 11–17.

Nelton, Sharon. "Beyond Body Language." *Nation's Business* 74, no. 6 (June 1986), pp. 73, 74.

Rafaeli, Anat, and Robert I. Sutton. "Expression of Emotion as Part of the Work Role." *Academy of Management Review* 12, no. 1 (January 1987), pp. 23–37.

Reed, David J. "One Approach to Employee Assistance." *Personnel Journal* 62, no. 8 (August 1983), pp. 648–52.

St. John, Walter D. "Successful Communication between Supervisors and Employees." *Personnel Journal* 62, no. 1 (January 1983), pp. 71–77.

Seers, Anson; Gail W. McGee; Timothy T. Serey; and George B. Graen. "The Interaction of Job Stress and Social Support: A Strong Inference Investigation." *Academy of Management Journal* 26, no. 2 (June 1983), pp. 273–84.

Shetty, Y. K. "Management's Role in Declining Productivity." *California Management Review* 25, no. 1 (Fall 1982), pp. 33–47.

Wexley, K. N., and E. D. Pulakos. "Sex Effects on Performance Ratings in Manager-Subordinate Dyads: A Field Study." *Journal of Applied Psychology* 67, no. 5 (October 1982), pp. 433–39.

Zajonc, R. B. "Emotion and Facial Efference: An Ignored Theory Reclaimed." *Science*, April 5, 1985, pp. 15–21.

Zaleznik, Abraham. "Managers and Leaders: Are They Different?" *Harvard Business Review* 64, no. 3 (May-June 1986), p. 48.

WHAT THIS INCIDENT IS ABOUT:
The problems faced by a union in its attempts to
establish and maintain strength provide the basis for
discussing such issues as union leadership, union-
management cooperation, giveback concessions, and
bankruptcy.

38

Union's dilemma

INCIDENT

The executive committee of Local Union No. 16 of the American
Machinists and Skilled Workers met in the local union hall to discuss strategies it would adopt during contract negotiations scheduled to convene in
the near future. There were additional items the union wanted to bargain
for, but the company management had already indicated it would adopt a
hard-line approach to the negotiations. Rumor had it that management was
talking about wage paybacks or givebacks. They were reportedly considering requesting that the union accept smaller wage rates for its members.
The most serious threat to the union was that management was considering
a reorganization through Chapter 11 of the bankruptcy laws—to destroy
the union. Consequently, certain union executive committee members felt
that management was in a stronger bargaining position than the union and
that additional contractual demands must be minimized. Other members
felt that certain problems should be addressed in the negotiations. One
problem concerned the company's promotion policies. It seemed that
every time the union elected a member to shop steward in a production
department, the company shortly promoted that individual to the rank of
foreman or supervisor. Overnight, the shop steward became a member of
management. Occasionally, a shop steward who was not too effective in
representing employees was allowed to remain a shop steward. However,
some of the best union members were now members of management.

The executive committee realized that a person offered the foreman's
position could hardly afford to turn down a pay raise of approximately one
third. Also, the union could not afford to subsidize each employee who was
offered such a job and turned it down. One committee member suggested
that only the incompetent should be elected shop stewards, but the idea

was rejected because all agreed that the shop steward occupied the most important post in the local union. Another suggestion was that the union bargain for a contract clause that would prevent management from promoting anyone who held the title of shop steward. Bill Peterson, union president, had reservations about the suggestion, because he felt the company would probably offer to promote the best shop stewards after they gave up their posts. In a way, the union would be training and selecting personnel for management positions. A final suggestion, which Peterson felt had merit, was that the union ask for veto power over all promotions to foreman or supervisor. He was afraid, however, that once management realized the consequences of such veto power, they would reject it immediately.

The executive committee asked that another meeting soon be held. Peterson would assess the validity of rumors regarding management's position relative to negotiations and would also make recommendations about the union's position at that time.

CRITIQUES

MAX S. WORTMAN, JR.
Professor of Management
University of Tennessee

Management is attempting a long-term effort to undermine the strength of the union. In the past few years, it has become increasingly common for management (particularly in states that are not prounion) to try undermining the union. Attempts range from covert efforts such as in this incident, to overt attempts to prevent union representation elections using unfair labor practices as outlined by the National Labor Relations Act (for example, management efforts to prevent the unionization of J. P. Stevens & Company).

Management is undermining union strength in several ways. First, effective union stewards are almost always promoted to foreman, thus taking away the backbone of an effective union (both as present first-line union leaders and as future union presidents and officers). Second, "converted" foremen are usually much tougher on their former union colleagues than foremen who have never served in a trade union. For example, former union officials frequently make extremely tough employers' association executives. Third, management has an unusual pay policy of one third more pay for foremen than stewards. Normally, foremen are salaried, while stewards are paid by the hour plus an extra amount per hour for performing the duties of steward. If a steward draws overtime, it is common for that individual to make more money than a foreman. The apparent overpayment of foremen in this incident is a clear symptom of an attempt to undermine the union. Fourth, management was willing to retain ineffective stewards in that position after it was determined that they were not effective. This weakens union participation in the contract's administration.

Yet, assuming that management is not trying to undermine the union, management may be weakening itself because of a potential prounion stance created from the continuous flow of neophyte union leaders. Furthermore, informal bargaining between prounion foremen and stewards may occur at the supervisory level, thus setting precedents that will weaken the management position in the long run. Lastly, management is relying on the union for both selection and training of foremen. Such a reliance gives the union control over the type of foremen selected.

What should the union do (assuming that management is trying to undermine it)? First, the union needs to strengthen the stewards' position by negotiating a stronger payment clause for the steward's duties. In this way, there would not be a wide pay differential between stewards and foremen—and there would not be as large an incentive to become a foreman. Second, the union should attempt to negotiate steward-foreman training programs. Perhaps these training programs could be taught by a union-management team or by an unbiased local community college faculty or at an industrial relations center at a nearby university. Third, the union should attempt to negotiate as many joint labor-management committees as possible, including safety and health committees, benefits committees, and productivity improvement committees. Through these joint efforts, the union would strengthen its position.

What should management do? It should assess its entire selection and training program to determine if it has a prounion bias that has spread throughout the managerial hierarchy. Then it should attempt to establish a strong selection program that consists of entry-level supervisors from internal and external sources. External sources could include management trainees from community colleges and universities. After they have been selected, a strong management development program should be instituted. By gaining control of the input for foreman selection and training, management should eliminate its prounion bias.

***

DANIEL A. WREN
Professor of Management
University of Oklahoma

Judging by the evidence in this incident, one could easily conclude that the "union's dilemma" is management's practice of promoting many shop stewards to managerial positions. Let us assume that the union leaders are correct in assuming that management is using the union as a training ground for supervisors (note that the "incompetent" stewards are left in place). Two explanations of management's promotion policy are possible: (1) Management promotes the good stewards and leaves the poor ones where they are to weaken the union; or (2) management is really in step with the thinking of its union member employees in recognizing the stewards' leadership qualities. Both of these explanations are believable, and there is no evidence to refute them.

If management is trying to weaken the union by this practice, there is little the union can do to stop it. The National Labor Relations Board, an agency of the federal government, has the authority, subject to courts of appeal, to determine what areas of labor-management relations are subject to collective bargaining and what areas are reserved exclusively to management, that is, "management's rights." The right to promote a person to management has so far remained a practice which is not subject to collective bargaining. Thus, the union would probably lose any charge of an unfair labor practice. In the second possibility, that is, management recognizing the leadership qualities of employees elected by the union members, both sides may benefit, and there is really no issue to resolve. Even though the new supervisors were formerly union members and officials, they could also become an effective part of management. We assume all too often that labor and management must conflict and that management is management and labor is labor and never the twain shall meet. This is not true. Labor and management have a common interest—management needs labor and vice versa. The new supervisors have experience as workers, have seen management from the worker's viewpoint, have gained the respect of co-workers, and may become effective supervisors who can promote the mutual interests of worker and manager.

Another issue is less apparent but poses the greatest concern for the union executive committee. This issue concerns the company's position about wages and job security in the coming negotiations. So far there are "rumors," but the union leaders have no hard evidence about what position management will take. Union leaders are typically well-informed people who should not be underestimated when it comes to intelligence and awareness of economic, social, and political trends. These leaders, like other informed citizens, see three trends influencing the future of unionism as an institution:

1. Due to a shift in our nation's economic structure from manufacturing to services, there has been a union membership stagnation as a percentage of the total labor force.
2. An economic recession has led many unions to make concessions in wage rates ("givebacks") and in rules concerning work methods (that is, giving management more flexibility in making work assignments).

3. The use of Chapter 11 bankruptcy proceedings to repudiate or renegotiate labor contracts.

In each of these instances, union leaders see themselves at a relative disadvantage in terms of bargaining power. In this incident, this is the real issue
that faces union leaders. At this moment, they are uncertain, insecure, and
jump at every rumor that floats through the grapevine.

The absence of specific facts about the company's financial situation
reduces our ability to address the issues directly. We know that the executive committee is concerned and they must feel their dilemma endangers
the union's survival. The most threatening situation would be a Chapter 11
bankruptcy filing, which would place the union in real jeopardy. Somewhat
less threatening is the possibility of wage givebacks; in this scenario, the
union would bargain to minimize these as much as possible and might
propose other concessions in lieu of wage givebacks.

What both labor leaders and management officials need to do is begin
some discussions and disseminate some information that will reduce the
current fear, uncertainty, and rumors. Misinformation is harmful to labor-
management relations. What is the company's financial situation? What are
the workers' wages when compared to, say, the industry average? Once
information about these items flows, then labor and management should sit
down and analyze how they can improve the situation. If, for example, the
company is paying employees far above competitors' wage costs, then wage
or other concessions may be necessary if the company is to compete more
successfully. If wage costs are in line, are there improvements in work
methods, equipment and machinery, or other items that labor and management could improve? For example, some companies use quality circles to
tap labor's brains for ideas and involvement in improving product quality,
reducing costs, saving time, and so forth.

The union's dilemma is also management's dilemma. Promoting shop
stewards is not the real issue, but it is one that can be discussed in the
absence of information about the coming negotiations. It is an unpopular
position to maintain that labor and management have a mutuality of interests and should strive to break down the barriers of "we" versus "them." In
situations such as this, there is only "we," and labor and management need
to put the issues in the open, where they can be constructively addressed.

OBSERVATIONS

This incident illustrates a number of problems unions face as they
attempt to establish and maintain their strength. Professor Wren identifies
various trends that influence the future of unionism and the bargaining

power of unions. The most threatening, in his view, is the increasing number of firms that are requesting reorganization under Chapter 11 of the Bankruptcy Code to allegedly cancel their union contracts. When Continental Airlines and Wilson Foods Corporation filed for bankruptcy in 1983, they were accused of trying to rid themselves of unwanted labor contracts. The trend has apparently accelerated as a result of a Supreme Court decision rendered in early 1984, which ruled that a company that files for bankruptcy can cancel a union contract, cut wages, and lay off workers without having to prove that the contract would have caused the company to go completely broke. A company must show, however, that the labor contract would have unduly burdened its prospects for recovery and that reasonable attempts were made to bargain with the union for deferred or smaller wage increases or other money-saving measures. Only then can the company be freed from its labor obligations.

Bankrupt companies have more latitude in union dealings than their solvent competitors. But there are limits to those powers, and the courts will attempt to define what they are. Also, apparently healthy companies using the bankruptcy law as an escape hatch from high-priced labor agreements may be short-lived due to the legislation being introduced in Congress to overhaul the Bankruptcy Code.

DISCUSSION ITEMS

1. Discuss some of the pragmatic reasons why management and the union might have difficulty in cooperating on the issues in this incident.
2. Bill Peterson, union president, has requested that another meeting of the executive committee be held. At that time, he will make recommendations about the union's position. What recommendations should he make? Justify your views.
3. Professor Wren notes three trends related to unionism occurring: (1) A shift in our country's economic structure from manufacturing to services; (2) concessions in givebacks; and (3) use of Chapter 11 bankruptcy laws to repudiate or renegotiate labor contracts. What is your prediction regarding the future of these trends? Justify your views.

SUGGESTED READINGS

BOOKS

Arnold, Hugh J., and Daniel C. Feldman. *Organizational Behavior*. New York: McGraw-Hill, 1986, chap. 4.

Bacharach, Samuel B., and Edward J. Lawler. *Bargaining Power, Tactics, and Outcomes*. San Francisco: Jossey-Bass, 1981.

Callahan, Robert E.; C. Patrick Fleenor; and Harry Knudson. *Understanding Organizational Behavior*. Columbus, Ohio: Charles E. Merrill Publishing, 1986, chap. 16.

Davis, Keith, and John W. Newstrom. *Human Behavior at Work*. 7th ed. New York: McGraw-Hill, 1985, chap. 17.

Donnelly, James H.; James L. Gibson; and John M. Ivancevich. *Fundamentals of Management*. 6th ed. Plano, Tex.: Business Publications, 1987, chaps. 11, 23.

Freeman, Richard B., and James L. Medoff. *What Do Unions Do?* New York: Basic Books, 1985.

French, Wendell L. *The Personnel Management Process*. 6th ed. Boston: Houghton Mifflin, 1987, chaps. 22–25.

Griffin, Ricky W. *Management*. 2nd ed. Boston: Houghton Mifflin, 1987, chaps. 1–3, 21.

Heneman, Herbert G.; Donald P. Schwab; John A. Fossum; and Lee D. Dyer. *Personnel/Human Resource Management*. 3rd ed. Homewood, Ill.: Richard D. Irwin, 1986, chaps. 16, 17.

Megginson, Leon C. *Personnel Management: A Human Resources Approach*. 5th ed. Homewood, Ill.: Richard D. Irwin, 1985, chaps. 18, 19.

Moore, Christopher W. *The Mediation Process*. San Francisco: Jossey-Bass, 1986.

Rue, Leslie W., and Lloyd L. Byars. *Management: Theory and Application*. 4th ed. Homewood, Ill.: Richard D. Irwin, 1986, chap. 15.

Schermerhorn, John R. *Management for Productivity*. 2nd ed. New York: John Wiley & Sons, 1986, chap. 18.

JOURNALS

"Bankruptcy as an Escape Hatch." *Time*, March 5, 1984, p. 14.

Blake, R. R., and Jane Mouton. "Developing a Positive Union-Management Relationship." *Personnel Administrator* 28, no. 6 (June 1983), pp. 23–31, 140.

Chaison, G. N., and M. S. Plovnick. "Is There a New Collective Bargaining?" *California Management Review* 28, no. 4 (Summer 1986), pp. 54–61.

Craver, C.B. "The Current and Future Status of Labor Organizations." *Labor Law Journal* 36, no. 4 (April 1985), pp. 210–25.

Glaberson, W. B. "The Bankruptcy Laws May Be Stretching Too Far." *Business Week*, May 9, 1983, p. 33.

Kirpatrick, David. "What Givebacks Can Get You." *Fortune* 114, no. 12 (November 24, 1986), pp. 60–72.

Kochan, T. A., and R. B. McKersie. "U.S. Industrial Relations in Transition." *Monthly Labor Review* 108, no. 5 (May 1985), pp. 28–29.

Kruse, S. A. "Giveback Bargaining: One Answer to Current Labor Problems." *Personnel Journal* 62, no. 4 (April 1983), pp. 286–92.

Labich, Kenneth. "America's Most Arrogant Union." *Fortune* 114, no. 11 (November 10, 1986), pp. 153–58.

Martin, Bob. "The Supreme Court's New Era—What's Ahead for Labor Law?" *Personnel Journal* 65, no. 10 (October 1985), pp. 92–98.

Mills, D. Q. "When Employees Make Concessions." *Harvard Business Review* 61, no. 3 (May-June 1983), pp. 103–13.

Mitchell, Daniel. "Alternative Explanations of Union Wage Concessions." *California Management Review* 29, no. 1 (Fall 1986), pp. 95–108.

Saporito, Bill. "Unions Fight the Corporate Sell-Off." *Fortune* 108, no. 1 (July 11, 1983), pp. 145–52.

Stone, D. C. "Can Unions Pick up the Pieces?" *Personnel Journal* 65, no. 2 (February 1986), pp. 36–40.

Summers, T. P.; J. H. Betton; and T. A. Decotiis. "Voting for and against Unions: A Decision Model." *Academy of Management Review* 11, no. 3 (July 1986), pp. 643–55.

Swann, J. P. "The Decertification of a Union." *Personnel Administrator* 28, no. 1 (January 1983), pp. 47–51.

WHAT THIS INCIDENT IS ABOUT:
This incident focuses on the difficult position of the
employee whose personal value system differs from
the organizational value system, and who desires to
do the right thing. Issues such as loyalty, obligations, moral imperatives, ethical behavior, and job
security are involved.

39

Whistleblowing

INCIDENT

Albert Higgenbotham, a 48-year-old middle manager for United Fibers,
Inc., with children in college, recently discovered that the company's
owners were cheating the government out of several thousand dollars in
taxes annually. Albert feels that he has an obligation to do something about
the situation, but he also has a sense of loyalty to the firm and to his
superiors. He also desires to keep his job. Thus far, Albert has not done
anything except worry.

Needing to talk with someone helpful and "safe," Albert thought of his
brother, Richard, who works at the same company as a quality assurance
manager. One Tuesday after work, Albert drove over to his brother's house
and accepted a seat on the patio and a beer. Wanting to ease into the
discussion of his concerns, Albert mentioned an item printed in that day's
newspaper entitled "Pentagon Whistleblower Wins Promotion and Legal
Fees." Albert had read the article carefully and had learned that years
earlier, whistleblower Earnest Fitzgerald had blown the whistle on a $2
billion cost overrun on the giant C-5A military transport plane project, and
because of his action, Fitzgerald was fired from the Air Force. The brothers exchanged views and agreed that it took great personal courage for
Fitzgerald to blow the whistle, to be ousted from his job, and then to
struggle through the long and expensive battle to obtain a reinstatement
order from the Civil Service Commission and back pay, and to win a legal
suit for recovery of $200,000 in legal costs he sustained. The brothers
agreed that volunteering for those experiences bordered on the heroic.
They speculated that Fitzgerald had expected better treatment than he
received.

While trying to work up to presenting his ethical problem to Richard,

Albert referred to several other examples of ethical puzzles and whistle-blowing in business organizations that he had read about. He mentioned the case of the B. F. Goodrich Company employee who was allegedly pressured by superiors to misrepresent test results on a new brake designed for military planes. Albert also recalled the case of a senior design engineer for Ford Motor Company who, after objecting to the hazardous design features of the Ford Pinto's gas tank and windshield, was demoted and terminated before suing the company. After relating these examples of conflict between employee personal values and company goals and practices, Albert shifted the conversation to his ethical problem, described it fully to Richard, and asked for his brother's thoughts.

Richard responded by describing his own ethical predicament to a dismayed Albert.

> Our company has been selling defective parachute cord to the federal government for the past six months. When my chief quality control inspector first discovered the parachute cord flaws and informed me, I immediately informed my superior. He suggested that my data must be erroneous and instructed me to run the tests again. I did. The results of the second round of tests were similar to the earlier ones. Learning the results, my superior told me that the statistical incidence of cord failure was acceptable to our company, that the parachute cord we were selling to the government was being stockpiled anyway, and that it probably never would be used. He suggested that I not worry unnecessarily. I have continued to worry a lot. It looks like you and I are in the same boat, brother. Do you think we should blow the whistle? If we do blow the whistle, what will be the consequences? What should we do?

Albert had no ready answers to Richard's questions. Indeed, Albert had come expecting to ask similar questions, and he was chilled to find Richard with similar problems. Albert felt pulled in three directions. First, there were his personal values, his own interests, and his sense of professional integrity. Second, he felt a sense of loyalty to the company and to its owners. Third, he felt a moral obligation to prevent serious injuries and injustice to the public. The pressures of these unresolved forces tugging at him were beginning to make Albert's stomach hurt.

At work, Albert had discreetly inquired and there seemed to be no company policy regarding actions an employee should take in the situation he and Richard were in. He needed to decide about blowing the whistle. Also, he needed a list of prudent guiding steps that he could take which might make it unnecessary to blow the whistle. Finally, before acting, he needed a comparison of desirable and undesirable consequences likely to be generated by his whistleblowing.

It wasn't easy to know the right thing to do, nor was it easy to know if it was worth doing or not. Albert did know that he needed relief from his uncertainty and indecision, and that his brother Richard did too.

CRITIQUES

DALTON E. McFARLAND
University Professor Emeritus of Management
University of Alabama—Birmingham

No one in an organization can escape the moral and ethical dilemmas inherent in all decisions. Yet the moral and ethical elements are often submerged in the daily work routines. In effect, expectations of proper conduct are largely built into the social system in the form of assumptions, directives, and policies. Because social systems can malfunction due to neglect, erosion, distortion, intentional deviancy, or other manifestations of poor management, corporate officers should monitor the company's moral climate and require all managers to review the ethical and moral aspects of their subordinates' performance. In the case of United Fibers, Inc., it is unlikely that such monitoring will occur if the allegedly questionable ethics of the owners and others can be substantiated.

Proper conduct normally is maintained through sanctions that can be brought to bear on deviant behavior. There are, however, many forces that frustrate this process. One is that some companies do not closely observe the moral and ethical aspects of employee behavior, believing that rules and policies are sufficient for regulating conduct. Taking ethical behavior for granted can be risky. Another inhibiting factor is that most people are touchy about discussions of morals and ethics. They are masters of avoidance techniques. People are also reluctant to judge one another, partly because they are uncertain in judgments of their own conduct, and partly because they know their own ethical shortcomings. In the case of United Fibers, Inc., the odds are against frank discussions of such problems because the owners' standards are questionable. They have fostered or tolerated cover-up attitudes in the organizational hierarchy. The company's organizational climate tends to discourage those who hope for better ethics.

Specific instances of improper conduct nevertheless have come to the attention of Richard and Albert Higgenbotham, and unless these issues are resolved, there will likely be a loss of organizational effectiveness. Small moral deviations often become larger problems; concerns become anxieties in morally sensitive managers. Episodes of misbehavior may seem unrelated, but they are important when they reflect patterns of continuous neglect of moral and ethical principles. Ethical or moral malfeasance is the obvious target of whistleblowing, but it should be treated not only by ethical standards but also by criteria of management competence and the company's long-run welfare.

Whistleblowing is the term applied to disclosing the misdeeds of superiors or colleagues to preserve ethical or morally acceptable behavior and to prevent or correct wasteful, harmful, or illegal acts. In the case of United Fibers, Inc., managers have been indoctrinated with a false emphasis on loyalty, which keeps managers from acting on their ideals. Thus, the concerns of Albert and Richard reveal a three-way conflict between loyalty to the company, to its owners, and to personal ideals and principles. Concerning the owners, the brothers ask, "Shall we be loyal to tax cheaters and thereby not make trouble for the company?" Richard's problem is different from Albert's problem, because in his case, immediate and serious harm is likely to happen to people because product defects are being covered up.

Whistleblowers always take great risks in reporting their observations and attempting to halt the mispractices of others. Frequently their fate is ostracism, loss of job, or even threats to lives or safety of themselves and their families. Even if they kept their jobs, the opprobrium of their co-workers would probably last beyond any correction that might occur. The opprobrium accorded to whistleblowers puts a higher value on loyalty than on conscience; team spirit is placed above the ethical and moral code.

Whistleblowing is a last-resort tactic. It is understandable that a person concerned with an ethical issue would approach whistleblowing with prudence. It is a test of character to realize that following one's conscience usually has economic or other costs. Because illegal and unethical acts are often the result of corporate structure or policy rather than the whims of individuals, firms can consider conducting workshops and training programs, and take concrete steps so that potential whistleblowers can communicate their reservations without penalties.

As a result of Watergate and other scandals, and the resulting demand for better ethics, people are increasingly willing to take the risks of whistleblowing. Some do it for reasons of conscience, others for self-preservation—the avoidance of complicity and penalties for participating in frauds, for example. The attitudes of managers show a reduced emphasis on the value of loyalty at all costs. People have learned to limit their sense of obligation and gratitude to their employers. The threat of severance is not taken lightly, but blind deference to authority is becoming rarer. Ambition for status and pay is no longer the motivation for loyalty that it once was.

It behooves Richard and Albert first of all to be sure of their facts. Then, they will have to take a hard look at their obligations and determine their priorities. To do nothing would make things worse by allowing wrongs to continue and risking great harm to others. The cause of their concern is likely to surface at some later time, with questions asked about their failure to sound the alarm. Loyalty to bad leadership pays penalties in the long run, and stands no chance of rewarding Richard and Albert.

Richard and Albert, if they are sure that the alleged wrongs are occurring, may decide that gaining a clear conscience at the cost of their jobs is the only way to reduce their anxieties. They could even lose good friends who fear that repercussions will hurt everyone and who resent upsetting a situation that they thought was working passably well. They could seek help from an attorney, a member of the clergy, or a trusted person close to the top of the company, but in the end, they are going to be alone and will likely be in the job market without good references.

WILLIAM J. WASMUTH
Professor of Management
Cornell University

Facing a potential whistleblowing situation, such as the one confronting Albert and Richard Higgenbotham at United Fibers, Inc., is indeed a stressful dilemma. Whistleblowers, as employees who believe their organizations are engaged in illegal, dangerous, or unethical conduct, almost always lack authority or power to make changes on their own. Equally frustrating, as in this case, there are only a limited number of companies that have policies regarding steps or appeals an employee can take, which might make it unnecessary to blow the whistle. The exceptions are those dozens of companies that have set up formal "ombudsman" systems in which a senior executive operating outside the normal chain of command is permanently available at the end of a hot line to deal with employee grievances and alarms on a confidential basis.[1] While this is a hopeful development, the most common outcome is that potential whistleblowers need relief from uncertainty, indecision, and a sense of desperation.

A widely read text, *Whistle-Blowing! Loyalty and Dissent in the Corporation*, has documented the experiences of 10 whistleblowers in varied American industries. All 10 were terminated. Only one was able to win reinstatement, while two others secured partial damages in court. The other seven have been unable to obtain reinstatement, damages, or vindication of their professional reputations.[2]

Given this experience, the risks to individuals who contemplate blowing the whistle are often so great it behooves them to vigorously explore other alternatives. The undesirable consequences likely to be generated by whistleblowing suggest that it pragmatically needs to be a strategy of last resort.[3] Ethically, this is unfortunate, since more than merely several dozen organizations, as noted above, should be able to keep appeal channels open to correct wrongdoing from within while protecting the complainants from reprisals. Hopefully, in the future, the many concessions

---

[1]Michael Brody, "Listen to Your Whistleblower," *Fortune*, November 24, 1986, pp. 77, 78.

[2]Alan F. Westin, *Whistle-Blowing! Loyalty and Dissent in the Corporation*, New York: McGraw-Hill, 1981, pp. 132–33.

[3]Exceptions would be those cases where individuals cannot categorically stand silent in the face of wrongdoing without worrying that they might be accomplices and thereby subject to disciplinary action.

made in reaching pragmatic versus ethical decisions will narrow or disappear. There is some progress in this direction as courts in roughly half the states have cut back the employer's traditional right to hire and fire at will, ruling that employees cannot be discharged for refusing to violate state laws or for revealing violations of those laws. Currently five states—California, Michigan, New York, Connecticut, and Maine—have passed statutes codifying such rights.[4] In the interim, however, there are certain assumptions and procedures that seem prudent in guiding the actions of persons such as Albert and Richard.

On a personal level, the work record of the prospective whistleblower is very important to possible success. Individuals recognized as good performers have more credibility than those perceived as activists "out to get the company" or as incompetents who are taking action to avoid discipline. While not explicit, the case implies that Albert and Richard have satisfactory work records.

Furthermore, it is implied that the two brothers, as managers, are not members of a professional association or labor union. They, therefore, are not protected by a collective bargaining contract which includes provisions for arbitration to protect employees against unfair dismissals. They assume all the risks of personal job security.

On a factual level, the prospective whistleblower needs to carefully assess and attempt to verify what he or she alleges to be the facts of management misconduct. Determining the accuracy of whistleblowing charges frequently is difficult; therefore, allegations are not always correct. In this case, the brothers are confronted by two different situations.

Albert is pondering a tax evasion situation which, if his facts are correct, is clearly illegal. The consequences of tax cheating, whatever the amount, are serious. However, the case information specifies that Albert "discovered recently that the owners were cheating the government." There is no indication of how this discovery was made. Albert needs to answer such questions as: Were his sources reliable? How confident is he that the information is correct? As a middle manager, why and how did he become privy to this information? Is he responsible in any way for the accuracy of the financial records, including tax returns? If not, who is responsible, and is there any reason Albert cannot discuss his discovery with that individual? Because Albert has not done anything except worry, his next step should be an attempt to verify the facts of his discovery and then consider the need to pursue internal appeals.

Richard's situation is somewhat different and, in many ways, more serious. If his facts are correct, and if there is statistical evidence to indicate they are, the issue is one of potential illegality and danger to people who use parachutes with defective cords. Furthermore, Richard has used

---

[4]Brody, "Listen."

internal channels by reporting to his superior and was told, in effect, to stop worrying and drop the issue. This is an inappropriate message, for it is largely worry over moral issues for persons like Richard that forces them to contemplate taking such risks. Richard, therefore, needs to pursue an additional internal appeal, primarily in an attempt to reconcile which quality standard is applicable—the one that guides the quality control inspector and Richard or the one that Richard's superior indicates is acceptable to the company and the government.

As with any sound grievance procedure, there are certain steps that whistleblowers should follow. The first step is to raise the protest and exhaust all internal steps before taking it to government bodies or the public. Management needs a chance to learn of and correct the problem before public exposure harms the company's reputation and sales. The courts, arbitrators, and administrative agencies generally require that employees initially use internal procedures if they want protection from retaliatory discharge. The only exceptions to this procedure might be circumstances such as when the company has a history of taking reprisals, where using internal procedures would unreasonably delay action to protect public safety, or where those in charge are clearly part of an illegal operation. In such cases the whistleblowers should seriously consider using a lawyer, preferably one who has had experience with white collar crime in a federal court. He or she can work in the capacity of an agent, thereby preserving the whistleblower's anonymity.

There are no indications of such exceptions applying to the brothers' appeal. Therefore, the first step they should take, should the factual investigation warrant further action, is to submit a written statement to their immediate superiors that explains their understanding of the existing policy or practice, their concerns or disagreements and reasons for them, and the consequences that could arise if the policy or practice is in violation and not changed. Documenting each step is important should further appeals become necessary within the company or to outside inspectors, agencies, or the courts.

If all internal appeals fail, Albert and Richard would then have to weigh the risks of "going public." Before doing so, they should learn what are the requirements and procedures for lodging a complaint with the relevant government agency and the time limits within which reports of alleged violations must be reported.[5] The risks of reprisals increase as appeals escalate. However, by adopting a strategy of first following internal procedures, supported by careful documentation along the way before going public, the legitimate whistleblower's odds of winning are improved, although by no means assured.

Despite what now appears to be unfavorable odds to prospective

---

[5]Westin, *Whistle-Blowing!* p. 162.

whistleblowers like Albert and Richard, their kind will no doubt continue to question and challenge perceived corporate wrongdoing. Since the 1960s, there has been an increased concern by employees, particularly professionals, about performing work that violates ethical standards.[6] Management is under increasing pressure to find ways to encourage and intelligently process such legitimate dissent.

Even more important, employers need to concentrate on avoiding the problems that give rise to whistleblowers' concerns; for example, establishing a policy to develop a final product review committee where dissenting choices, such as Richard Higgenbotham's, can be heard without reprisal. Openness in dealing with illegal, dangerous, or unethical issues is clearly a superior long-run strategy to one that attempts to conceal such issues.

OBSERVATIONS

Ideally, a successful whistleblowing episode would result in the wrong being righted and honor and a promotion being bestowed upon the whistleblower, or at least continued employment. The record, however, reflects the opposite results in many whistleblowing incidents. Outcomes are likely to fall short of righting misdeeds or illegal acts, instead dishonoring the whistleblower professionally and even socially, and ultimately leading to the whistleblower's unemployment. This picture may appear bleak; however, Professors McFarland and Wasmuth have discussed conditions that contribute to more successful whistleblowing results. Hopefully, in any case, the act of whistleblowing will at least provide some release for the individual from stress anxiety and will sustain the integrity of the whistleblower's personal value system. Considerable literature on the issues related to whistleblowing is available to persons either interested in the subject or needing guidance.

DISCUSSION ITEMS

---

1. Discuss the advantages and disadvantages of whistleblowing for the individual, management, the organization, and society.
2. Develop and present: (a) recommendations for establishing internal appeal channels for correction of wrongdoing from within the organiza-

---

[6]Ibid., p. 7.

tion, and *(b)* recommendations for policies and procedures to protect complainants from reprisals.
3. Differentiate whistleblowing from disloyalty to one's superiors and organization.

SUGGESTED READINGS

BOOKS

Arnold, Hugh J., and Daniel C. Feldman. *Organizational Behavior*. New York: McGraw-Hill, 1986, chaps. 14, 16.

Callahan, Robert E.; C. Patrick Fleenor; and Harry Knudson. *Understanding Organizational Behavior*. Columbus, Ohio: Charles E. Merrill Publishing, 1986, chaps. 4, 12.

Davis, Keith, and John W. Newstrom. *Human Behavior at Work*. 7th ed. New York: McGraw-Hill, 1985, chaps. 3, 16, part 6.

Donnelly, James H.; James L. Gibson; and John M. Ivancevich. *Fundamentals of Management*. 6th ed. Plano, Tex.: Business Publications, 1987, chap. 20.

French, Wendell L. *The Personnel Management Process*. 6th ed. Boston: Houghton Mifflin, 1987, chap. 8.

Griffin, Ricky W. *Management*. 2nd ed. Boston: Houghton Mifflin, 1987, chap. 16.

Heneman, Herbert G.; Donald P. Schwab; John A. Fossum; and Lee D. Dyer. *Personnel/Human Resource Management*. 3rd ed. Homewood, Ill.: Richard D. Irwin, 1986, chap. 5.

McCoy, Charles S. *Management of Values: The Ethical Difference in Corporate Performance*. Cambridge, Mass.: Ballinger Publishing, 1985.

Megginson, Leon C. *Personnel Management: A Human Resources Approach*. 5th ed. Homewood, Ill.: Richard D. Irwin, 1985, chap. 10.

Rue, Leslie W., and Lloyd L. Byars. *Management: Theory and Application*. 4th ed. Homewood, Ill.: Richard D. Irwin, 1986, chaps. 4, 5, 11.

Schermerhorn, John R. *Management for Productivity*. 2nd ed. New York: John Wiley & Sons, 1986, chaps. 3, 20.

Westin, Alan F. *Whistle-Blowing! Loyalty and Dissent in the Corporation*. New York: McGraw-Hill, 1981.

JOURNALS

Brody, Michael. "Listen to Your Whistleblower." *Fortune* 114, no. 13 (1986), pp. 77, 78.

Chewning, Richard C. "Can Free Enterprise Survive Ethical Schizophrenia?" *Business Horizons* 27, no. 2 (March-April 1984), pp. 5–11.

Chrisman, James J., and Archie B. Carroll. "Corporate Responsibility—Reconciling Economic and Social Goals." *Sloan Management Review* 25, no. 2 (Winter 1984), pp. 59–65.

Elliston, F. A. "Anonymous Whistleblowing." *Business and Professional Ethics Journal* 1, no. 2 (Winter 1982), pp. 39–58.

Ewing, David W. "Due Process: Will Business Default?" *Harvard Business Review* 60, no. 6 (November-December 1982), pp. 114–22.

Hauserman, Nancy R. "Whistle-Blowing: Individual Morality in a Corporate Society." *Business Horizons* 29, no. 2 (March-April 1986), pp. 4–9.

Henderson, Verne E. "The Ethical Side of Enterprise." *Sloan Management Review* 23, no. 3 (Spring 1982), pp. 37–47.

Keeley, Michael. "Values in Organizational Theory and Management Education." *Academy of Management Review* 8, no. 3 (July 1983), pp. 376–86.

McGowan, W. "The Whistleblowers' Hall of Fame." *Business and Society Review*, no. 52 (Winter 1985), pp. 31–36.

Parmerlee, Marcia A.; Janet P. Near; and Tamila C. Jensen. "Correlates of Whistle-blowers' Perceptions of Organizational Retaliation." *Administrative Science Quarterly* 27, no. 1 (March 1982), pp. 17–84.

Roush, John A. "Loyalty in the Inner Circle." *Business Horizons* 26, no. 5 (September-October 1983), pp. 55, 56.

Stevens, Charles W. "The Whistleblower Chooses Hard Path, Utility Study Shows." *The Wall Street Journal*, November 3, 1978, p. 1ff.

Williams, Oscar F. "Business Ethics: A Trojan Horse." *California Management Review* 24, no. 4 (Summer 1982), pp. 14–24.

Wilson, Glenn T. "Solving Ethical Problems and Saving Your Career." *Business Horizons* 26, no. 6 (November-December 1983), pp. 16–20.

Wuthnow, Robert. "The Moral Crises in American Capitalism." *Harvard Business Review* 60, no. 2 (March-April 1982), pp. 76–84.

WHAT THIS INCIDENT IS ABOUT:
Massive labor reductions are afoot, but no policy
exists to guide the attendant decisions; the morale
and livelihood of employees are without the protections of policy or long-term planning. The
incident involves robotics, automation and its
effects, technological unemployment and displacement, personnel planning, work force reduction,
and job rights.

40

Work force reduction
policy

INCIDENT

Five years ago, Wireweave, Inc., moved to a rural area 25 miles outside
a large southern city. The company, formerly situated in a midwestern
industrial city, chose this location primarily because of the lower wage
rates paid in the community, because of a nonunion tradition in the region,
and because of the favorable tax situation.

Wireweave, a manufacturer of wire products, has two major high-vol-
ume product lines—aluminum wire screen and dish racks. The dish racks
are supplied to several appliance manufacturers for use in automatic
dishwashers.

Because of intense industry competition, Wireweave's management
realized several years ago that if Wireweave were to continue manufacturing aluminum wire screen and dish racks and, in fact, to stay in business, it
would have to procure up-to-date equipment, become more automated and
computerized, and even use robots for some of the hottest and dustiest
jobs. After a two-year evaluation of production needs and an analysis of
technologically advanced manufacturing equipment including robots,
Wireweave purchased equipment that would modernize production and
replace 65 employees, representing about 33 percent of the total labor
force. Significant labor costs would be saved by this employment reduction. As a result, Steve Jackson, president of Wireweave, expected the
company to regain its competitiveness and profitability.

The following spring, shortly after installing the new equipment,

Jackson called in Muriell Fincher, personnel director, and told her that the company no longer could afford to employ the unneeded workers. He requested that she decide on an acceptable plan for reducing company employment by 65 persons, and he clearly stated the sooner the better in terms of company profitability. Jackson also asked that she recommend a specific operating policy covering future work force reductions.

Fincher had successfully handled some tough challenges as personnel director, but the latest assignments from Jackson were the most difficult ones she had faced. As Fincher considered relevant options and constraints, her deliberations were dominated by three factors: (1) the company's economic and ethical responsibilities to terminated employees, (2) the potential morale problems for employees who are retained, and (3) the pressure from Jackson for prompt decision and action.

CRITIQUES

JEFFREY R. CORNWALL
Assistant Professor of Management
University of Wisconsin—Oshkosh

Muriell Fincher has struck upon the two most important issues that must be addressed when facing such a decision: the company's responsibility to the workers and the impact on the workers that remain after the layoff.

Clearly organizations have a responsibility to consider their employees in matters such as these. Most would agree that a group that has such a direct stake in the outcome of such a decision should at least be considered in the decision-making process, and probably should be allowed some degree of input. Many options exist for corporations that are implementing permanent work force reductions. Workers in a given situation may have very specific needs associated with potential layoffs which a corporation can, and should, meet. At a minimum the company should facilitate the outplacement of workers by providing some of the following types of services:

1. Individual career counseling may be required by some workers. For some, this may have been the only job they have ever had and they may not know how to deal with the situation that faces them. Since Wireweave is new to this location, the need for this may not be as great.
2. Another service is sponsoring seminars on conducting a job search and writing résumés. Most workers can make the transition out of your company easier if they are given the proper tools.
3. Sometimes it is possible to assist workers in securing employment

elsewhere. If other areas are experiencing growth and need workers with skills your workers possess, both parties can benefit from such a strategy.

In addition, there are valid arguments for providing retraining for workers who are being displaced by technology. This is clearly the most costly strategy, but is also the most effective strategy for outplacement.

Efforts such as these not only fulfill the responsibility that the corporation has to workers for their service, but also will minimize the impact on the remaining workers. Such layoffs, even when handled in the best way possible, will have an impact on the loyalty, trust, morale, and performance of the workers who were retained. An equitable and honest approach can soften the blow. However, if handled poorly, as was the case in this incident, large layoffs can create a climate that will potentially offset any gains hoped for by the new technology.

Unfortunately this is all water under the dam for Wireweave. Steve Jackson made several key mistakes that make this a no-win situation for himself, Fincher, Wireweave, and the employees in question. There is no possible plan that would satisfy the first two factors being considered by Fincher. The reasons for this are clear.

First, Jackson should have considered the need for layoffs and the implication of these layoffs from the moment the decision was made to introduce the new technology. He had over two years to prepare, but waited until the implementation had already been completed. He treated this issue as an afterthought, even though it is clear that work force reductions were the goal of this project from the beginning. He had delegated to Fincher that which was his own responsibility all along.

Second, the impact on employees should be a part of the plan. The impact should be considered from the outset. Strategies such as those indicated above should be evaluated and integrated into the implementation of the new technology. In addition, costs involved in these strategies should be included in the calculations of total project costs. Wireweave may have moved south to avoid unions, but Jackson's inability to foresee the consequences of his actions, or rather inactions, has sown the seeds for a union to walk right in to his company.

Since part of her charge was to develop a policy for future layoffs, Fincher can at best convince Jackson of the need to follow a different path in the future. However, given the history of Wireweave, I doubt that she will get very far with this approach.

JANE HASS PHILBRICK
Adjunct Professor of Management
Georgia Southern College

Many manufacturing concerns face the problems inherent with technological change. This incident illustrates exactly what *not* to do.

Perhaps the most blatant mistake made by Wireweave was poor, if any, planning. Human resource planning is both a necessity and a social responsibility of organizations. It includes planning for future personnel needs in light of the rapid changes in technology that businesses face today.

When Wireweave began "planning" its relocation, forecasts of technological changes and attendant personnel requirements should have been made. Had such planning occurred, a variety of realistic, long-term employment options could have been presented to prospective employees. Many persons might have been willing to work flexible, part-time schedules or to job share. Such flexible working conditions would have made Fincher's assignment to reduce the employment force by one third immensely easier. From a systems standpoint, discharging so many employees will have an adverse economic multiplier effect on the whole community.

Fincher must try to undo some of the damage that will inevitably result from discharging employees. First and foremost, a specific operating policy for work force reduction must be formulated. Although employees will obviously be skeptical and suspicious, discussions between Fincher and employee representatives should begin at once. Although there is a tradition of nonunionization in the area, neglecting to include the employees in formulating a policy of work force reduction could lead to a unionization effort. The management literature suggests mixed reactions to technological changes in U.S. manufacturing industries. As evidenced by U.S. auto workers, efforts to minimize the impact of automation on workers have been successful when workers believe their job security and longevity are not at stake. The Coch and French studies in a pajama factory illustrate that worker involvement should lead to decreased resistance to change and increased commitment to solving the problem of company survival.

Some work-reduction measures could include provisions to:

1. Reduce employment gradually by not replacing employees who quit or retire.
2. Temporarily lay off employees based on seniority, with rehiring provisions and pension considerations.
3. Job share, that is, two employees share one job.
4. Train some workers, who would have been discharged, to monitor automated equipment.
5. Solicit help from the surrounding business community in relocating employees, and possibly provide financial help in the form of retraining.

Again, the lack of adequate planning by Wireweave must be emphasized. The fire-fighting approach to decision making that Jackson seems to promote can only lead to financial disaster for Wireweave and the community.

OBSERVATIONS

One dimension of the quality-of-work-life concept is job security. Thirty percent of Wireweave employees will lose their jobs based on the president's decision. Effects of technological unemployment run deep, causing loss of automobiles, homes, and even self-respect in prolonged cases. Because their training and abilities have become obsolete due to technological changes, many laid-off workers face the possibility of never being re-employed at comparable skill and wage levels. The English classify such workers as "redundant." In the United States, we sometimes describe them as "superfluous" or more ominously as "obsolete."

Corporate managers attempt to reduce the devastating effect of technological unemployment by long-range personnel planning, by phasing in new technologies, by retraining workers for jobs outside the company, and by establishing company job placement services to aid displaced workers. Ford Motor Company, for example, is reported to have continued similar services for laid-off workers for more than 15 months after closing a plant in California. At Wireweave, President Jackson gets low marks on social responsibility, Ms. Fincher gets no lead time, and the workers get jobbed.

DISCUSSION ITEMS

1. If you were the personnel director, would you follow orders and discharge the 65 employees or would you make recommendations for other action to reduce the company's work force? If the latter, then give your recommendations.
2. What is your evaluation of the president's proposed actions?
3. Compare technological unemployment and economic unemployment in terms of implications for workers, managers, and the economy.

SUGGESTED READINGS

BOOKS

Arnold, Hugh J., and Daniel C. Feldman. *Organizational Behavior*. New York: McGraw-Hill, 1986, chap. 10.
Callahan, Robert E.; C. Patrick Fleenor; and Harry Knudson. *Understanding*

Organizational Behavior. Columbus, Ohio: Charles E. Merrill Publishing, 1986. chap. 11.

Davis, Keith, and John W. Newstrom. *Human Behavior at Work*. 7th ed. New York: McGraw-Hill, 1985, chap. 13.

Donnelly, James H.; James L. Gibson; and John M. Ivancevich. *Fundamentals of Management*. 6th ed. Plano, Tex.: Business Publications, 1987, chaps. 4, 16, pp. 187–90.

French, Wendell L. *The Personnel Management Process*, 6th ed. Boston: Houghton Mifflin, 1987, chap. 5.

Griffin, Ricky W. *Management*. 2nd ed. Boston: Houghton Mifflin, 1987, chap. 6.

Heneman, Herbert G.; Donald P. Schwab; John A. Fossum; and Lee D. Dyer. *Personnel/Human Resource Management*. 3rd ed. Homewood, Ill.: Richard D. Irwin, 1986, chap. 7, pp. 356–63.

Megginson, Leon C. *Personnel Management: A Human Resources Approach*. 5th ed. Homewood, Ill.: Richard D. Irwin, 1985, chaps. 5, 10.

Rue, Leslie W., and Lloyd L. Byars. *Management: Theory and Application*. 4th ed. Homewood, Ill.: Richard D. Irwin, 1986, chaps. 6, 7.

Schermerhorn, John R. *Management for Productivity*. 2nd ed. New York: John Wiley & Sons, 1986, chap. 4.

JOURNALS

Anderson, Jerry W., Jr. "Social Responsibility and the Corporation." *Business Horizons* no. 4 (July-August 1986), pp. 22–27.

Baird, Lloyd; Ilan Meshoulam; and Ghislaine Degive. "Meshing Human Resources Planning with Strategic Business Planning: A Model Approach." *Personnel* 60, no. 5 (September-October 1983), pp. 14–25.

Bateman, J. Fred. "The Unending Revolution." *Business Horizons* 29, no. 4 (July-August 1986), pp. 2–8.

Beck, Robert N. "Visions, Values, and Strategies: Changing Attitudes and Culture." *The Academy of Management Executive* 1, no. 1 (February 1987), pp. 33–39.

Cornfield, Daniel B. "Chances of Layoff in a Corporation: A Case Study." *Administrative Science Quarterly* 28, no. 4 (December 1983), pp. 503–20.

Dobbins, Gregory H., and Stephanie J. Platz. "Sex Differences in Leadership: How Real Are They?" *Academy of Management Review* 11, no. 1 (January 1986), pp. 118–27.

Foulkes, F. K., and J. L. Hirsch. "People Make Robots Work." *Harvard Business Review* 62, no. 1 (January-February 1984), pp. 94–102.

Leonard-Barton, Dorothy, and W. A. Kraus. "Implementing New Technology." *Harvard Business Review* 63, no. 6 (November-December 1985), pp. 102–10.

Mucygk, Jan P. "Comprehensive Manpower Planning." *Managerial Planning* 30, no. 3 (November-December 1981), pp. 36–40.

Pakchar, Paul. "Effective Manpower Planning." *Personnel Journal* 62, no. 10 (October 1983), pp. 826–30.

Scarborough, Norman, and Thomas W. Zimmerer. "Human Resources Forecasting: Why and Where to Begin." *Personnel Administrator* 27, no. 5 (May 1982), pp. 55–61.

Scherba, John. "Outplacement as a Personnel Responsibility." *Personnel* 50, no. 3 (May-June 1973), pp. 40–44.

Thompson, Arthur A., Jr. "Strategies for Staying Cost Competitive." *Harvard Business Review* 62, no. 1 (January-February 1984), pp. 110–17.

"What Did We Learn from RIFs? Reduction in Force." *Management Review* 73, no. 1 (January 1984), pp. 53, 54.

"Will High Tech Create a Low-Skills Job Environment?" *Management Review* 73, no. 1 (January 1984), p. 52.

41

A corporate policy on AIDS

Ashley Derek, president of Derek Airlines, returned to his office after attending a two-day seminar sponsored by the National Association of Airline Executives. The seminar focused almost completely on the subject of how firms in the airline industry should be addressing the AIDS (Acquired Immune Deficiency Syndrome) problem. A message that all seminar speakers and discussants repeatedly conveyed was that it was most important for a firm to adopt a policy, or policies, indicating the position that the firm would take with respect to employees having, or suspected of having, AIDS.

After much thought and deliberation Derek began to draft a number of statements reflecting a wide variety of positions his firm might take for dealing with AIDS victims, and from which one complete statement expressing the actual position of the firm might be drawn. The position options that Derek developed were as follows:

- Derek Airlines reserves the right to require an examination by a medical doctor appointed by the company to determine if any employee has AIDS.
- The employment of any Derek Airlines employee diagnosed as having AIDS will immediately be terminated.
- Any Derek Airlines employee who becomes sick with AIDS will be encouraged to seek assistance for medical treatment at company expense.
- Any Derek Airlines employee diagnosed as having AIDS who has recovered from the initial sickness and wants to return to work will be permitted to do so as long as able to do so.
- As long as a Derek Airlines employee diagnosed as having AIDS is able to meet acceptable performance standards, and the condition is no threat

to others, the employee will be treated in all respects like any other employee.

- If warranted Derek Airlines will make reasonable work accommodations for any employee diagnosed as having AIDS so long as these work accommodations do not interfere with the business needs of the work unit. Flexible work time is an example.

Derek next attempted to formulate one clearly articulated statement that would reflect the actual position of the company regarding the AIDS problem. He started by writing, "It is the policy of Derek Airlines. . . . " It was at this point he called for assistance from some of his associates.

42

Failure to delegate

Frank Jones became supervisor of plant maintenance after 15 years as operator of a local electrical appliance repair shop. Spindle Rayon Mill had moved to the small southern community where Frank lived in 1973. Frank accepted a job on the construction crew and was later employed on an hourly basis to install and maintain the lights, air-conditioning, generator, steam plant, and miscellaneous equipment.

By 1980, floor space had tripled and the work force had increased by several hundred. Frank found that his responsibilities had grown commensurately. He was often required to work overtime, and he occasionally returned to the plant during the night to make necessary repairs. He performed his work conscientiously and was considered a devoted and loyal employee. It was necessary to add workers to his crew, and in late 1988, he was given a salary, the title of director of physical plant, and responsibility for the efforts of 16 employees.

It was noted, however, that Frank still preferred to repair the machines personally rather than direct his subordinates to do so. The plant manager told him one man could no longer perform all the required work and encouraged him to do less of the repair work and instead to select, train, and direct capable subordinates.

Frank tried. He even dressed like the other supervisors and organized his crew so that he could spend most of his time in the office. It was not long, however, before department heads were complaining that machinery needed repairs and that work schedules were disrupted due to inoperative machines. It was reported that when physical-plant repairmen were summoned, they were often incapable of completing the repairs without calling Frank. After a brief interval, Frank returned to his blue denims. One department head complained to the plant manager that Frank was possessive about the machinery and was deliberately not selecting and training qualified repairmen because he seemed to feel secure only if others regarded him as indispensable.

The plant manager considered what to do. He knew that Frank was not performing the supervisory function, yet he remembered the years and loyalty that Frank had devoted to the company. He believed that ethical considerations and policy issues required examination, and that an effective implementation plan was also needed.

43

Human obsolescence

For many years, the Springside Manufacturing Company employed six bookkeepers to keep the accounts current. Recently, however, bookkeeping procedures were computerized, and the need for bookkeepers no longer existed. Several company vice presidents met to determine what to do about six excess bookkeepers.

During the meeting, decisions were made to send one of the bookkeepers to a computer school, to accept the resignation of one, and to grant a leave of absence to one. Moreover, it was decided to use one of the bookkeepers on a temporary assignment in the typing pool because she was returning to school in two months, and to discharge the fifth person with 30 days' pay because he had been excessively absent from work during the past year.

The sixth bookkeeper was Jack Anderson, a loyal employee of 18 years. He had celebrated his birthday the previous week, and at age 61 he was looking forward to retirement in four years. Although Anderson's availability and credentials had been circulated to all company department heads, no one was interested in accepting him.

One vice president suggested that Anderson be discharged with 90 days' pay to provide him with some compensation while seeking other employment. Another vice president suggested that Anderson receive some menial job with the company for four years so that he could qualify for retirement. He argued that it would be unfair to discharge a man with Anderson's length of service so near to retirement. Discussion then centered upon such topics as obligation to employees, obligation to owners, public relations, appropriate policies for dealing with human obsolescence, and management responsibilities for displaced employees. The absence of a company policy addressing early retirement made the decision unnecessarily difficult. The two vice presidents decided to draft such a policy and submit it along with their recommendation about Anderson to the company president.

44

Management by suggestion

Driving into the parking lot of Gymnastic Gear, Inc., early Thursday afternoon, chief executive officer Doug Magill saw that the section reserved for on-the-go executives needing quick and frequent access to the building was fully occupied. Irritated, he jumped the sidewalk curb, parked along the right-of-way, and went to inspect the credentials of vehicles in the reserved section, which Magill himself had ordered installed to avoid the very problem he was experiencing. He noticed an unfamiliar luxury car without a company parking decal straddling the white line between two spaces.

As Magill turned to enter the building, head custodian Thaddeus Ralston said, "Good afternoon," and asked if there was a problem. Still somewhat piqued, Magill pointed to the offending car and said, "Thaddeus, I sure would like to know who parked in our reserved section. Tell whoever it is to come see me if they need parking assistance." Having vented his irritation, Magill continued to his office and began a scheduled staff meeting, forgetting the incident entirely.

Thirty minutes later, Magill's secretary signaled him on the intercom and indicated, in a rather strained voice, that he was needed in the outer office. When Magill stepped out, the scene that confronted him was disconcerting.

Ralston stood in a menacing position by the door with a suspicious look on his face. Next to him was a short man in a grimy white jumpsuit bearing the words "Ace Towing Service." And worst of all, the third figure in the room was grinding his teeth and glaring at Magill, clearly on the brink of an angry outburst. Magill recognized him instantly as Marty Holloway, the prominent gymnastics coach who had volunteered hundreds of hours in the past two years to consult with company technicians and designers on the specifications and applications of new gymnastics equipment.

"What's going on here, Thaddeus?" asked Magill, with the sinking feeling that he already knew what had happened.

"Well, Mr. Magill, after I saw you were upset about the car being in your way, I called the tow truck. That parking lot's my responsibility, since it's part of the grounds. While we were hooking up the dolly, this fella comes out all upset and says we're messing with his car. He said somebody told him it was OK to park there. So I brought him to see you, just like you said. Isn't that what you wanted?"

Holloway could contain himself no longer. "I came here to meet with one of your technicians, who told me I could leave my car where I did. Is this the way you treat people who are trying to contribute their time and expertise for your benefit? I'm surprised you didn't have me arrested while you were at it!"

Magill was dismayed. He never intended for a tow truck to be summoned or that the owner of the car, whoever it was, be humiliated and enraged. He hadn't really directed that any action be taken . . . or had he? Yet Ralston was a conscientious employee, simply trying to do his job to the best of his ability. Holloway was no scofflaw; he was an asset to the company, more valuable than some of the employees with parking privileges. His goodwill must somehow be restored.

"When I've handled this," Magill vowed to himself, "we'll develop policies to ensure that Gymnastics Gear, Inc., will never face this kind of problem again." Magill racked his brain for a course of action.

45

Policy implementation problems

Business had been good during the past year, and Harvey Daniels, president of Systems and Mechanical Research Associates, Inc., confidently expected a 200 percent increase in sales within two years. Knowing that many carefully selected professional persons would be required in the near future, Daniels authorized the director of personnel, William Seagle, to establish operating policies and procedures for formally recruiting and selecting professional personnel for the company.

Seagle, who had resolutely campaigned for a more centralized policy for hiring professional personnel, was visibly pleased with the president's decision. Without delay he devised and applied a set of modern personnel practices that gave the personnel department an important role of authority and responsibility in the hiring of professionals. To his great disappointment, however, the operating managers, including Daniels, continued to hire professionals informally.

Recently, David Hall was hired as chief research engineer, after his name was submitted to the president by the vice president of engineering. Hall, who was then unemployed, was invited to the home office for a personal interview. After spending three days with Hall, the company's top management unanimously agreed that he was an excellently qualified, technically competent person and was easy to get along with. Daniels then telephoned Hall's references. In every case but one, the candidate was given the best recommendation possible, and two of the firms stated they would be delighted to employ him again. These comments substantiated Daniel's own impression of Hall. Without losing any more time, Daniels offered Hall the job. Hall accepted the position and moved his family and possessions to a nearby city the following week.

After working for three months, Hall's contributions were so impressive that Daniels wondered how the company had been able to get along without him.

334

About the same time, Seagle became worried about some irregularities in Hall's background. In a routine manner, his office had set up a personnel folder after being notified of Hall's hiring and had initiated the data confirmation process: (1) the College of Engineering where Hall said he had taken his undergraduate and graduate work in mechanical engineering was contacted; (2) an attempt was made to assemble copies of publications that Hall had listed in his employment application; and (3) an effort was made to confirm the "highest previous salary earned" that Hall had reported. The personnel director was amazed to discover that: (1) Hall had never been enrolled in the institution from which he claimed two degrees; (2) one listed publication had never been published; and (3) Hall had overstated his highest previous salary by $7,000.

Seagle was uncertain how to proceed. His position as personnel director was seriously undercut by the operating managers; moreover, he felt that the president had no confidence in him. He wondered, "What should I do?" On the one hand, Hall's credentials were unquestionably flawed and overstated, perhaps even fraudulently so. Yet, Hall had proven impressively that he could do the job and, in so doing, he had earned the professional respect of the company president. Seagle was disconsolate. He felt vulnerable and unprotected. In trying to meet his responsibilities as director of personnel, Seagle was professionally stymied (1) by uncertainty over how to handle the critical information in Hall's personnel file; (2) by lack of acceptance for the centralized policy of hiring professional personnel; and (3) by need of a strategy for changing the "cart before the horse" hiring approach used by line managers—including the president.

46

Questionable policy

Otis Leach was sure he was going to die when he felt the handgun jabbed roughly into his back. Leach, night clerk at a convenience food store, decided to use the only two weapons he could find: his elbow and a fire extinguisher. With the gun at his back, Leach raised his elbow and swung around, knocking his assailant to the ground. He then sprayed the robber in the face with the powder from a nearby fire extinguisher. The man, gun in hand, ran from the building moaning. Police were called to the scene, but they were unable to find him.

While Leach was cited by some for his bravery, local law enforcement officials were not so inclined to commend him. Instead, the county sheriff stated publicly that the safest thing would have been to comply fully with the robber's requests and let him get out of there.

Lyndon Boggs, president of the convenience store chain that Leach worked for, was particularly concerned about the incident, because he realized he was negligent in instructing employees regarding what they should do in such situations. After consulting with crime prevention experts, he issued a policy statement to all employees, which read as follows:

> With respect to robbery attempts, your company has adopted a no-resistance policy. Store clerks are to cooperate fully when confronted with robbery attempts. Violators of this policy will be subject to termination.

Soon after the policy was circulated, a group of store managers, accompanied by Leach, met with the company president to protest the no-resistance policy. They indicated employee sentiment was that store clerks should have the prerogative of deciding what to do and that the policy was too restrictive. Leach was asked to express his views, and he indicated that he did not consider himself a hero, that he only wanted to protect his life so that he could support his wife and infant child. He related that when he felt the gun in his back and realized how nervous his assailant was, he was sure he would be killed even if he complied with the demands. He said he had cleaned the area around the extinguisher about an hour earlier and the idea to use it just popped into his head. Leach and others indicated they should be able to keep themselves from being killed, and that any attempt to implement the policy would be met with negative reactions from those affected by it.

Boggs agreed to reconsider his no-resistance policy in view of these employee sentiments.

47

Sensitive employment reference

As director of a large, nonprofit research organization that has an active affiliation with a large university nearby, James Ashworth just transferred an experienced administrative officer, Jennifer Lee, to one of the largest and most active departments. The department has a substantial budget and is supported by numerous research grants, both governmental and nongovernmental, that are administered by the university. Many of the department's professional staff, including its chief, hold faculty appointments at the university. Most of the technical support personnel are full-time employees of Ashworth's organization. The department's two top-level technical personnel are Lee and the supervisory technician, Tom Cook. Both are Ashworth's employees.

Shortly after assuming her position, Lee discovered several suspicious operations involving the supervisory technician's areas of responsibility. Cook was a 15-year veteran of the department who had advanced to his present position through six promotions. In addition, he had received numerous performance awards and commendations over the years. Cook had close personal relationships with the department chief and with one of the department's primary supply contractors.

Ashworth appointed a committee of three to investigate the irregularities that were called to his attention by Lee. The committee was zealous and its investigation appeared to be more of an inquisition than an inquiry. The material developed by the committee was incomplete and inconclusive, however. It contained many assumptions, conclusions, and speculations that were neither supported nor denied by the facts. While the information looked bad for Cook, Ashworth did not have sufficient evidence to prosecute him or to remove him.

When Cook was confronted with the evidence, he claimed that he was being used as a scapegoat for the university's professionals. He claimed to be following their orders. He threatened to involve "a lot of important people" in the research organization and at the university if action was taken against him. Ashworth gave Cook an extended leave with pay, at the end of which he was permitted to resign. Ashworth also replaced the department chief.

While Cook was on leave prior to resigning, his attorney, a former U.S. attorney and local political figure, contacted Ashworth concerning the kind of employment reference his client would receive. He stated that his client was being used as a scapegoat and that his future employment should not be jeopardized by a bad employment reference, especially because nothing prejudicial was ever proven. The attorney felt it would be better for all concerned if his client could secure other employment smoothly.

Shortly after the attorney's visit, an investigator from a federal agency contacted Ashworth concerning a full-scale investigation being conducted as a preliminary step in employing Cook in a "sensitive" position with their agency. The investigator asked for a confidential employment reference for Cook.

Ashworth desired to preserve his reputation for professional honesty and fairness, while discharging his professional obligations and avoiding exposure to libel charges. Normally, he gave laudatory employment references with confidence and pleasure. But in this instance he would have liked to have had a policy for handling negative employment references because he needed to decide about the employment reference request for Cook. The ethical considerations, policy issues, and legal implications presented formidable challenges to Ashworth.

48

Smokers versus nonsmokers

Although there were only 7 smokers among the 25 finance department employees at Big Orange Insurance, Inc., they were spread throughout the common work area; their respective skills made it impractical to group them together. Because they objected to smoking, two nonsmoking employees began a grievance procedure, while other nonsmokers filed claims against the company's employee health plan for visits to allergists, respiratory specialists, and other practitioners, which they insisted were caused by the "polluted" work environment. Absenteeism attributed to these ailments also increased, and departmental output suffered accordingly. Nonsmokers' complaints intensified despite informal attempts to mediate the disputes.

Beverly Bennett, finance department director, finally was forced to raise the issue at the biweekly interdepartmental meeting. She outlined the problem, adding that she used to smoke and that she had no particular sympathy or animosity for either faction.

The facilities director said, "We can't help you, Beverly. Partitions won't stop the smoke from collecting below the ceiling and drifting through the work area, and the ventilation system in your wing is top of the line. There's no way to improve the air circulation. Besides, it sounds to me as if the density of the smoke is less important to your nonsmokers than asserting their rights. They won't be satisfied with changes that just make the smoke more tolerable."

Brad Langley, vice president for administrative operations at Big Orange, conducted the meeting, and asked if others around the table were experiencing similar problems. He had never considered rules of conduct while at one's desk as an appropriate issue for attention at this level, but the finance department situation was serious.

The personnel director said he simply refused to hire personnel department employees who wanted to smoke in the office. "What they do at lunch is their own business, but in our department, there is no smoking— period." The data processing director explained that the sensitive electronic equipment in his area had special temperature and atmospheric requirements, which dictated that employees who wanted to smoke step outside. "Unfortunately, that means we have high-paid technicians and systems analysts loitering outside several times each day," he said. Others indicated that their areas had no real problem with smoking, because employees were in private offices or cubicles rather than concentrated in common areas.

Vice president Langley did not know how to proceed. He recalled an item that had appeared in the newspaper the previous week. The Civil Aeronautics Board (CAB) had vacillated over their decision to ban smoking on flights of less than two hours. An airline representative had told the CAB that the airlines were trying to accommodate everyone. She said, "This is a very emotional subject. We are the party in the middle between smokers and nonsmokers." Langley appreciated their dilemma; he felt exactly like the party in the middle of someone else's battle. He hesitated to develop a policy on an issue that differed among departments and that seemed to have no common solution. Still, the situation in the finance department was becoming critical. He recalled that several major firms had recently established policies leading toward "smoke-free" organizations. To Langley, however, the ethical considerations and policy implications of such action were troublesome.

49

Span of control

The owner and chief executive officer of Electronic Systems, H. F. Olson, an avid reader of professional management literature, became intrigued with concepts emanating from the behavioral sciences. Particularly impressive to him were the ideas expressed by such men as Chris Argyris, A. H. Maslow, and Douglas McGregor. Recorded attempts to put into practice McGregor's so-called "Theory Y" were especially intriguing. Olson decided he should try to modernize his company's management style in accordance with these concepts. He retained the services of a consultant, whose name he associated with these management concepts.

The consultant made many suggestions regarding job enlargement, decentralization, delegation, participation, and reorganization of work patterns. Most of the recommendations seemed to relate to the company's organization structure. The consultant noted that organizations structured in accordance with classical management theory provided a narrow span of control. This is necessary because of the close supervision that is presumably given to subordinates. However, recent notions regarding a subordinate's ability and desire to exercise self-direction and control reduce the necessity of close supervision. Under this concept, the span of control can be wide and the number of managerial levels reduced.

Olson was not completely convinced that a wide span of control and fewer levels really reflected the views of the behavioral scientists as opposed to the views of the traditionalists. Electronic Systems was at present organized so that above the first-line supervisor level there were 20 department heads, five division heads, three vice presidents, the executive vice president, and the president.

Olson called a meeting of his four vice presidents to review the formal organization structure of Electronic Systems and the consultant's suggestions, and to prepare a written policy guide for modernizing the company's management style and for reorganizing the company.

50

Suggestion system policy

OFFICE OF THE PRESIDENT
Memorandum
Date: Friday, November 25, 1988
From: Bob Adams, president
To: John Sullens, vice president for human resources

Employee suggestion systems have been around for a long time. The positive financial impact of suggestion systems is significant in some organizations, according to my reading. For example, the National Association of Suggestion Systems estimates that 80 percent of the 500 largest U.S. corporations have such programs, and that employee suggestions save the nation's companies more than $500 million a year.

The negative aspect of the suggestion system is that employees may become disgruntled about how the company runs the system. You may recall that two United Airlines employees charged in court that United stole their suggestion for a reduced-fare plan for employees of all airlines, that United successfully implemented the plan, and that United cheated them out of hundreds of thousands of dollars that they had coming under the company's suggestion system. They cited a provision of United Airlines' suggestion system rules that stated, "An employee is entitled to 10 percent of a typical year's profits resulting from an idea submitted through the suggestion system and successfully implemented."

During the trial, expert witnesses testified that in a typical year of operations under the reduced-fare plan, United earned $3 million attributable to the plan, of which 10 percent, or $300,000, rightfully belonged to the two employees who submitted the suggestion. The jury found that the company acted in bad faith by failing to pay off under the suggestion system, and assessed $1.8 million in damages against the airline, which a judge later reduced to $368,000.

We can't afford to risk such financial peril! It's critical, therefore, that you promptly review our suggestion system rules and policies and that you give me recommendations on the following issues. Include advantages and disadvantages associated with your policy recommendations.

1. *Calculation of award amount:* Should we offer a flat amount of money for each accepted suggestion, or should the award be based on a percentage of the savings (earnings) during some period? What percent? What period?
2. *Maximum award:* Should we have a maximum limit on the payoff for any single suggestion (perhaps $10,000), or should it be open-ended?
3. *Time of award payment:* Should we pay the award in full when the suggestion is accepted or as the savings (earnings) are realized annually?
4. *Joint award allocation:* When two or more employees combine on a suggestion, how should we allocate the award among them?
5. *Originality:* Should we pay off for suggestions that help us, even if they aren't original with the employee(s) making the suggestion?
6. *Impetus award:* Are you in favor of an "impetus award" in the range of $100–$500 to recognize a suggestion that hastens an action initiated by the company before receipt of the suggestion?
7. *Written rules:* Do you think we need to spell out in writing every aspect of our suggestion system, or will an informal approach be more conducive to employee participation?
8. *Proof of knowledge:* Should we require all employees to sign a form stating that they have read and understand the suggestion system's rules (if we decide to write them up)?
9. *Another limitation:* Should an employee be limited to suggestions relating only to his or her area of the organization?
10. *An exclusion:* Should our marketing function and financial policy (including product and service pricing) be excluded from the suggestion system?
11. *Evaluation:* Do you have any suggestions on a procedure for evaluating suggestions?
12. *Abandonment:* Maybe dropping the suggestion system would be easiest. What do you think?

We are reviewing all aspects of our suggestion system policy. Our attorney recommends abandonment. Let me hear from you as soon as possible. Treat this as a "hot" item.

ABOUT OUR CRITIQUE WRITERS

SHEILA A. ADAMS, Ph.D. (University of Washington), is an associate professor of management, and chairperson, department of management and marketing, University of North Carolina—Wilmington. Her previous positions include assistant professor of management at Arizona State University; instructor at the University of Puget Sound, the University of Nevada—Reno, and Reno Junior College of Business; and director of the Bureau of Business and Economic Research at the University of Nevada—Reno. Her publications include numerous articles and cases in professional journals and books. Her current teaching and research interests are business policy, organizational effectiveness, and power/conflict.

WILLIAM P. ANTHONY, Ph.D. (Ohio State University), is a professor of management and former chairman of the management department of the College of Business at Florida State University. He has published more than 30 articles and 9 books in management, supervision, and labor relations. He has also consulted with and lectured to a wide variety of business, governmental, and other not-for-profit organizations throughout the United States on management topics.

WILMAR F. BERNTHAL, D.B.A. (Indiana University), is professor emeritus of management and organization at the University of Colorado—Boulder. He has taught at Valparaiso University and Indiana University, and he has published numerous articles in management journals. He is a fellow in the Academy of Management. His major fields of interest are organization theory, organizational behavior, and business and society.

BERNARD J. BIENVENU, D.B.A. (Harvard University), is the Lether Edward Frazar Honor Professor of Management and Administrative Studies Emeritus at the University of Southwestern Louisiana. He is presently active in consulting, particularly in the fields of supervisory and management development, and is a frequent speaker at professional association meetings and conferences. He has published numerous articles and is author of the book *New Priorities in Training—A Guide for Industry*, published by the American Management Association. He has served as a visiting professor at a leading business school in France, and he has lectured on management in many African countries. He is past president of the Southwestern Management Association and the Southern Management

Association. His major areas of interest are policy and strategy, motivation and morale, management development, and management of education and public institutions.

ROBERT BOISSONEAU, Ph.D. (Ohio State University), is a professor of health care administration at the Center for Health Services Administration, College of Business, Arizona State University, Tempe. He also teaches in the department of management. He has spoken at many national health meetings and published widely in allied health and health administration literature. He has received numerous grants and has served as a consultant to both HEW's Bureau of Health Manpower and the Michigan Department of Mental Health. He was a hospital administrator at Detroit Memorial Hospital and at the Ohio State University Hospitals, and was a faculty member in health administration programs at Ohio State and the University of Missouri—Columbia. Boissoneau served as the first dean of the College of Human Services at Eastern Michigan University. His major areas of interest are health administration, education in the health professions, and internal hospital organization and management.

ELMER H. BURACK, Ph.D. (Northwestern University), is a professor of management and former management head, College of Business, University of Illinois—Chicago. He has also taught at the Illinois Institute of Technology, Northwestern University, and San Diego State University. He has published numerous articles in professional journals and books, including *Managing Change* (1979), *Growing: Careers for Women* (1979), *Human Resource Planning* (1979), and *Organizational Analysis* (1975). His latest book, *Planning Strategies for Succession and Management Development*, is in press (1987). He has been on the editorial review board of the *Academy of Management Journal* and has served as chairman or president of: the personnel division and health care division of the Academy of Management, the Human Resource Management Association of Chicago, the Midwest Human Resource Planners Group, and the Illinois Management Training Institute. He has also served as vice chairman of the Governor's Advisory Council on Employment in Illinois, and is a consultant to various institutions.

LINDA McGEE CALVERT, Ph.D. (Louisiana State University), is an associate professor of management at the University of Houston—Clear Lake. She was president of the Southwest Academy of Management (1987–88) and is actively engaged in the Management Consultation Division of the Academy of Management. Her major areas of interest are management theory, organizational behavior, and women in management.

JOHN M. CHAMPION, Ph.D. (Purdue University), is a professor of management and administrative sciences at the University of Florida. Prior to returning to full-time teaching and research, he held an administrative position as chairman of the university's graduate program in health and hospital administration. He has also taught at Purdue and Georgia State University. He serves as management consultant to a number of hospitals and businesses, and he has conducted and participated in many training and management development programs. In addition to numerous journal articles, he is the author of *General Hospital—A Model* (1976) and coauthor of *Critical Incidents in Management* (6th ed., 1989). He is a member of the American Psychological Association, the Academy of Management, and the Southern Management Association.

EDWARD R. CLAYTON, Ph.D. (Clemson University), is professor of management science at Virginia Polytechnic Institute and State University. He is the author of numerous papers and articles on operations research and information systems. He is a consultant to several firms on business applications of computer systems and mathematical programming. He is a coauthor with L. S. Moore of *GERT Modeling and Simulation Fundamentals and Applications* (1978). His major fields of interest are simulation, mathematical programming, and computer applications to business problems.

JEFFREY R. CORNWALL, D.B.A. (University of Kentucky), is an assistant professor of management at the University of Wisconsin—Oshkosh. He has published in the *Journal of Management* and in *Human Relations*. He is actively involved in the Entrepreneurship Center of the University of Wisconsin—Oshkosh. His areas of interest include organizational technology, business policy, entrepreneurship, and business ethics.

LARRY L. CUMMINGS, D.B.A. (Indiana University), is the J. L. Kellogg Distinguished Research Professor in the Kellogg Graduate School of Management, Northwestern University. He has taught at Indiana University, Columbia University, and the University of British Columbia. He has published more than 80 articles and is coauthor of 13 books including *Readings in Organizational Behavior and Human Performance* (1973), *Organizational Decision Making* (1970), *Performance in Organizations* (1973), and *Research in Organizational Behavior*, volumes 2–6 (co-editor, 1980–84). He is consulting editor, Richard D. Irwin Series in Management and the Behavioral Sciences. He is a fellow and past president of the Academy of Management. He is a fellow in the Division of Industrial and Organizational Psychology of the American Psychological Association and is a fellow in the American Institute for Decision Sciences.

JAMES H. DAVIS, Ph.D. (Ohio State University), was a professor emeritus of business administration in the College of Administrative Science at Ohio State at the time he wrote his critique. During the time he was an active academician he published a number of significant publications including the *Handbook of Sales Training* (1954) and *Sales Management* (1954 coauthor). He served as a consultant to a number of government agencies and industrial firms.

KEITH DAVIS, Ph.D. (Ohio State University), is professor emeritus of management at Arizona State University. He has taught at Ohio State, Indiana University, and the University of Texas. He has published over 150 professional articles, and his books include *Organizational Behavior: Human Behavior at Work* (7th edition, 1985), *Readings and Exercises in Organizational Behavior* (7th edition, 1985), *Personnel Management and Human Resources* (2d edition, 1985), and *Business and Society* (5th edition, 1984), winner of an Academy of Management book award. He is a fellow in the Academy of Management and the International Academy of Management, and a contributor to more than 100 books. Four of his books have been translated into other languages. He was a national Beta Gamma Sigma Distinguished Scholar in 1975–76 and visiting professor at the University of Western Australia in 1974.

SHEILA DAVIS, Ed.D. (University of Massachusetts—Amherst), is an assistant professor of organizational behavior at Ohio State University. She teaches courses in career development, organizational development, and the history of organizational behavior and management thought, and a course that she developed entitled "Women and Organization." Davis is also an organizational and training consultant and has worked with the McDonnell-Douglas Corporation, the Shering Corporation, and various Ohio agencies. Her research interests are in the interaction of organizational variables with gender. She has published articles in research and practitioner journals on various aspects of this topic.

ANDRÉ L. DELBECQ, D.B.A. (Indiana University), is dean of the Leavey School of Business and Administration at the University of Santa Clara. His research has focused on managerial decision making, organizational innovation, and organizational structures. He is a fellow in the Academy of Management and has served on its board of governors, and as chair of the Public Sector and Organization and Management Theory Divisions. He has authored or coauthored three books and more than 80 articles in management and decision making.

MAX L. DENSMORE, Ph.D. (Michigan State University), is a professor of business administration at the F. E. Seidman Graduate School of Business, Grand Valley State College. His primary interests are policy, strategy, planning, and control. He formerly taught at the University of Alabama and the University of Dayton. He is a past chairperson of the health care administration division of the Academy of Management. He has written in numerous publications and is active in consulting.

W. JACK DUNCAN, Ph.D. (Louisiana State University), is a professor of management and associate dean of the graduate school of management at the University of Alabama—Birmingham. He is a fellow of the Academy of Management, past member of the academy's board of governors, and a past chairperson of its Management Education and Development Division. He is past president of the southwest division of the academy and president-elect of the Southern Management Association. He is the author of several books, including *Management: Progressive Responsibility in Administration* (1983), and has written numerous articles for *Academy of Management Journal*, *Academy of Management Review*, *Management Science*, *Human Relations*, *Public Administration Review*, and others. He has held visiting professorships at the International Business Institute in Switzerland and at Northeastern University.

ROBERT R. ENGEL, Ph.D. (University of Iowa), is an associate professor of foundations and higher education at the University of Iowa's College of Education. At the University of Iowa he has also been assistant dean of liberal arts, assistant director of summer sessions, associate dean for academic affairs, and assistant to the president. He has served on the board of trustees of Rust College, and is a member of the board of trustees of Cornell College. His published works include "Preparing for Planning: An Outline for Smaller Colleges and Universities" (with John D. Kraus, Jr.), *Association of American Colleges*, December 1978; "Board of Trustees and Academic Decision Making" (with Paul Achola), *Review of Educational Research*, Spring 1983; "Curriculum Reform: Applications from Organization Theory" (with Lelia Helms and Catherine Hahn), *Journal of Research and Development in Education*, Spring 1984; and numerous other articles and monographs.

ALAN C. FILLEY, Ph.D. (Ohio State University), is a professor of management at the University of Wisconsin. He has taught at the University of Georgia as a distinguished visiting scholar, Ohio State, and the University of North Dakota. He is a contributor to major business journals and is the author of *The Compleat Manager* (1978) and *Interpersonal Conflict Resolution* (1975), and coauthor of *Managerial Process and Organizational Behavior* (1976). He has coedited *Management in Perspective* (1965) and *Studies in Managerial Process and Organizational Behavior* (1972). His major fields of interest are organizational behavior, organization theory, and organizational intervention.

WILLIAM M. FOX, Ph.D. (Ohio State University), is a professor of industrial relations and management at the University of Florida. He has held faculty positions at Ohio State, Texas Tech University, and the University of Washington. He was a Fulbright Lecturer in Finland in 1957–58, and a Fulbright Senior Research Scholar in Japan in 1974–75. In addition to publishing numerous articles, he edited *Readings in Personnel Management from Fortune* (1957 and 1963); wrote *The Management Process: An Integrated Functional Approach* (1963); and recently completed a new book entitled *Effective Problem Solving in Groups* (1987). He conducted studies in leadership under contract to the Office of Naval Research in 1970–74. He is past president of the Southern Management Association and past chairman of the organization and management theory division of the Academy of Management in which he is a fellow.

STEPHEN G. FRANKLIN, Ph.D. (University of Oklahoma), was an associate professor of business administration, Graduate School of Business Administration, Emory University, Atlanta, Georgia, at the time he wrote his critique. Among his publications is *Principles of Management*, 8th edition (1982), on which he was a coauthor.

WILLIAM C. FREDERICK, Ph.D. (University of Texas), is a professor of business administration in the Graduate School of Business at the University of Pittsburgh, where he teaches courses dealing with the relations between business and society and conducts research on corporate social policy and management values. He has served as a management education consultant to private foundations and businesses in the United States and abroad, and in 1980–81 he was the Charles Dirksen Professor of Business Ethics at the University of Santa Clara. He is coauthor of *Social Auditing: Evaluating the Impact of Corporate Programs* (1976) and *Business Society: Management, Public Policy, Ethics* (1984); and he edited *Research in Corporate Social Performance and Policy* (vol. 9, 1987).

R. EDWARD FREEMAN, Ph.D. (Washington University), is a visiting associate professor of business administration, the Darden School, University of Virginia. Prior to that appointment he was an associate professor in the department of strategic management and organization in the School of Management at the University of Minnesota. His doctorate is in philosophy. He is the author of *Strategic Management: A Stakeholder Approach* (1984). His current research is on ethics and strategy, stakeholder theory of the firm, and game theory.

CYNTHIA V. FUKAMI, Ph.D. (Northwestern University), is an associate professor of management in the College of Business Administration at the University of Denver. She has conducted and published research in many areas of human resource management and organizational behavior, including turnover and absenteeism, dual careers, employee transfers, organizational commitment, and union attitudes. She is a member of the editorial board of the *Academy of Management Journal*, representative at large for the Organizational Behavior Division of the Academy of Management, and a member of the board of directors of the Organizational Behavior Teaching Society.

C. B. GAMBRELL, JR., Ph.D. (Purdue University), is dean of the new School of Engineering of Mercer University in Macon, Georgia. Most recently he was executive vice president and provost at West Coast University. He was previously vice president for academic affairs at the University of Central Florida. He has taught at Purdue University, Stanford University, Arizona State University, Clemson University, Lamar University, and the University of Central Florida. He has published numerous articles in business and professional journals, and he is an active consultant to government and industry. His major areas of professional interest are organization and management, economic analysis, human factors, work study, and productivity.

THOMAS Q. GILSON, Ph.D. (Massachusetts Institute of Technology), is an arbitrator and lecturer in the College of Business Administration at the University of Hawaii, where he formerly served as associate dean and professor of industrial relations. Prior to that, he was a professor and chairman of the management department at Rutgers University. He also has served on the faculties of the Massachusetts Institute of Technology, Clark University, and the Newark College of Engineering. He has had business experience as a personnel director and as a training director. He is the author of several books and many journal articles. His major areas of interest are management development, collective bargaining, organizational behavior, and personnel administration.

ROBERT T. GOLEMBIEWSKI, Ph.D. (Yale University), is research professor of political science and management at the University of Georgia. He taught at Princeton University and the University of Illinois, and was a visiting lecturer in industrial administration at Yale and visiting professor in the faculty of management, University of Calgary, during the last six fall semesters. His significant publications include *Behavior and Organization* (1962), *The Small Group* (1962), *Men, Management, and Morality* (1965), *Organizing Men and Power* (1967), *Managerial Behavior and Organization Demands* (1967), *Perspectives in Public Management* (1968), *Sensitivity Training and the Laboratory Approach* (1970, 1973, and 1977), *Renewing Organizations* (1972), *Cases in Public Management* (1973 and 1976), *Individual Learning and Change in Groups* (1976), *Public Administration as a Developing Discipline*, vols. 1 and 2 (1978), *Approaches to Planned Change*, vols. 1 and 2 (1979), *Mass Transit Management* (1981), *Humanizing Public Organizations* (1985), and *Stress in Organizations* (1986).

PAUL J. GORDON, Ph.D. (Syracuse University), is a professor of management at the Indiana University Graduate School of Business. He was 1969 president of the Academy of Management in which he is a fellow. He also is a fellow of the International Academy of Management and honorary fellow of the American Academy of Medical Administrators. Listed in *Who's Who in America* and *Who's Who in the World*, his professional interests are in complex organizations and strategic management.

WALTER T. GREANEY, JR., L.L.M., Ph.D. (Harvard University), was a professor of management in the School of Management at Boston College and a practicing attorney at the time he wrote his critique. He specialized in the fields of taxation and public finance, banking, and corporate finance.

ROBERT M. GUION, Ph.D. (Purdue University), is a professor of psychology at Bowling Green State University and is a licensed psychologist. He was 1972–73 president of Division 14 of the American Psychological Association and the 1982–83 president of Division 5 of the American Psychological Association. He is the author of *Personnel Testing* (1965). He has taught and conducted research at the University of California, the University of New Mexico, and the Educational Testing Service. He is a consultant and contributor to journals in personnel, psychology, and business. His major fields of interest are employee selection, employee motivation, and measurement theory.

OGDEN H. HALL, Ph.D. (Louisiana State University), was a professor of allied health auxiliaries at the Louisiana State University Medical Center at the time he wrote his critique. He taught at the University of New Orleans and at Virginia Polytechnic Institute and State University. He has served as president of the Eastern Management Association and the Southern Management Association. He has been active in the Academy of Management and the American Institute for Decision Sciences, having served on the governing board and council, respectively. His consulting activities include industrial, educational, governmental, and health services organizations. His major fields of interest are organizational and interpersonal communications, management of learning systems, and organization development.

RICHARD I. HARTMAN, D.B.A. (Indiana University), is a professor of management and chairman of the department of business management and administration at Bradley University. Formerly, he taught at the University of Georgia and Indiana University. He has published in *Human Resource Management, Personnel Journal, Personnel Administrator, Industrial Management*, and *Industrial Engineering*. He is also coauthor of two books and a number of business cases. His major fields of interest are organization theory, personnel management, and business policy.

JAMES O. HEPNER, Ph.D. (University of Iowa), is a professor and director of the Washington University Health Administration Program in St. Louis. He is an experienced hospital administrator and has served as a national consultant in health services administration to the surgeon general of the United States Air Force. He is a fellow in the American College of Healthcare Executives and currently serves on their board of governors, a member of the American Public Health Association, and an honorary fellow in the American Academy of Medical Administrators. He also has been a consultant to the Department of Health and Human Services. He is the author of five books: *The Health Strategy Game* (1973), *Personnel Administration and Labor Relations in Health Care Facilities* (1969), *Health Planning for Emerging Multi-Hospital Systems* (1978), *Hospital Administrator–Physician Relationships* (1980), and *Hospital Labor Relations* (1987).

HERBERT G. HICKS, Ph.D. (University of Alabama), is a retired professor of management, Louisiana State University. In addition to numerous articles, his books include *The Management of Organizations* (4th ed., 1981), *Management: Organizations and Human Resources* (2d ed., 1976), *Modern Business Management* (1974), *Organizations: Theory and Behavior* (1975), and *Business: An Involvement Approach* (1975). He has served as president of the Southern Management Association, the Southwest Division of the Academy of Management, and the National Academy of

Management, of which he is now a fellow. His major fields of interest are management consulting, organization theory, administrative theory, and general management.

PHYLLIS G. HOLLAND, Ph.D. (University of Georgia), is an associate professor of management at Valdosta State College. She previously taught at Georgia State University. She is coauthor of *Strategic Management: Concepts and Experiences* (1986), and her articles on family business have appeared in *Business Horizons* and *The Director*. She is the author of a number of cases which appear in strategic management texts, and is currently working with the Georgia Department of Education to establish strategic planning in local school systems.

A. T. HOLLINGSWORTH, Ph.D. (Michigan State University), is professor of management and dean of the School of Business at Monmouth College in West Long Branch, New Jersey. He has held faculty and administrative positions at the University of North Carolina at Asheville, the University of South Carolina, the University of Petroleum and Minerals, Saudi Arabia, Southern Illinois University—Carbondale, and Florida Atlantic University. He has published articles in journals such as the *Journal of International Business Studies, Journal of Retailing, Business Horizons, Journal of Small Business Management, Personnel Journal*, and *The Journal of Applied Psychology*. He has coauthored a number of books, including *A Practical Approach to the Management of Small Business*. He has also consulted extensively with a variety of national and international organizations.

ANNE SIGISMUND HUFF, Ph.D. (Northwestern University), is an associate professor of strategic management and director of the office for Information Management at the University of Illinois, Champaign-Urbana. Her research focuses on the cognitive processes of strategy reformulation, and on strategy formulation as the result of group interactions.

JAMES E. INMAN, J.D. (University of Akron), is a professor of business law and director of graduate programs in business in the College of Business Administration at the University of Akron. He previously served for six years as editor of the *Akron Business and Economic Review* and four years as a staff editor of the *American Business Law Journal*. He is a member of the Ohio bar and the American Business Law Association. For over a decade, he has served as a labor arbitrator for the northeastern Ohio steel industry. He is author of the *Regulatory Environment of Business*

(1984) and coauthor of the *Legal Environment of Business* (1983). He has written articles appearing in *Business Law Review, Atlanta Economic Review,* and *American Business Law Journal.* He also lectures in management seminars on government regulations and environmental affairs of business.

R. DUANE IRELAND, Ph.D. (Texas Tech University), is the W. A. Mays Professor of Entrepreneurship and Strategic Management and chairman, department of management, in the Hankamer School of Business, Baylor University. He also serves as a research associate in the Business School's Center for Entrepreneurship. An active member of the Academy of Management, he served (from 1984–87) as the secretary and newsletter editor for the Academy's Business Policy and Planning Division. His major fields of interest are strategic management, organization theory, and entrepreneurship. He has published in a range of journals, including the *Academy of Management Journal,* the *Academy of Management Executives,* the *Strategic Management Journal, Administrative Science Quarterly, Decision Sciences, Human Relations,* and the *Journal of Management Studies.* His consulting activities have focused on performance coaching and counseling and the effective management of project teams.

JOHN H. JAMES, D.B.A. (Indiana University), is an associate professor of management at the University of Florida. His publications include *Critical Incidents in Management* (coauthor, 6th ed., 1989), *Long-Range Planning for Small Business* (coauthor, 1964), and articles in various management journals. Professional activities include having been chairman of the constitution and bylaws committee of the Academy of Management, and chairman of the southeastern chapter of the Institute of Management Sciences. In addition to teaching at both the graduate and undergraduate levels, he has participated in a number of management development and supervisory training programs for managers in business, government, and health care organizations.

MAX B. JONES, Ph.D. (University of North Carolina), is a professor of management and chairman of the department of management at Old Dominion University, and he was 1971 president of the Southern Management Association. He has taught at North Carolina State University—Raleigh, the University of North Carolina, and the College of William and Mary. He is on the Roster of Arbitrators for the Federal Mediation and Conciliation Service and has served as a consultant to public and private sector organizations.

CHARLES R. KLASSON, D.B.A. (Indiana University), is a professor of business organization and policy at the University of Iowa. He served as the executive associate dean at Iowa for seven years. Prior to that, he held positions at the University of Texas and Arizona State University. He serves as a consultant to various federal agencies and currently is doing work on competitive response strategies of U.S. banks and airlines. He has served as a management consultant for 25 years, including work for AT&T regarding their divestiture of operating companies.

TERRY L. LEAP, Ph.D. (University of Iowa), is a professor of management in the College of Commerce and Industry at Clemson University. He teaches courses in personnel management and has published a research monograph on *Health and Job Retention*. His research includes articles published in the *Harvard Business Review, Industrial and Labor Relations Review, Human Relations, Labor Law Journal*, and *Employee Relations Law Journal*. Professor Leap also serves as a consultant and guest speaker for private and public sector organizations.

CYRIL C. LING, D.B.A. (University of Wisconsin—Whitewater), was a professor of management in the College of Business Administration, University of Wisconsin—Oshkosh, at the time he wrote his critique. Prior to this assignment, Ling served as senior vice president and director of educational development for the Bank Administration Institute, a research and development organization for commercial banking. He has also headed the staff of the American Assembly of Collegiate Schools of Business, has been actively involved in management development programs, has edited two journals, and authored *Personnel Management* (1963). He is a member of Beta Gamma Sigma, Sigma Iota Epsilon, and the Academy of Management.

JAMES P. LOGAN, Ph.D. (Columbia University), is a professor of management at the University of Arizona. Formerly he was a visiting fellow at the Western Australian Institute of Technology. He served on the faculty of the Graduate School of Business, Columbia University, and as a visiting professor at IMEDE in Lausanne, Switzerland. His publications include coauthor of *Strategy, Policy and Central Management* (1984) and *Management of Expanding Enterprises* (1955). His major fields of interest are business policy, strategic planning, and long-range planning.

FRED LUTHANS, Ph.D. (University of Iowa), is the George Holmes Professor of Management at the University of Nebraska at Lincoln. He taught at the U.S. Military Academy at West Point while serving in the Armed Forces. He has published 15 books and about 100 articles in applied and academic journals and research reports. His book *Organizational Behavior Modification*, coauthored with Robert Kreitner, won the American Society of Personnel Administration award for the outstanding contribution to human resource management. His articles are widely reprinted and have brought him the American Society of Hospital Personnel Administration award. The consulting coeditor for the McGraw-Hill Management Series, he also serves on a number of editorial boards. He served on the editorial board of the *Academy of Management Review* for six years. He has been active in the Academy of Management in which he was elected a fellow in 1981. He has been its vice president, program chair, and president.

KARL O. MANN, Ph.D. (Cornell University), is a professor of industrial relations and acting chairman of the department of management and industrial relations at Rider College. Previously he served as a faculty member at the American University, Duquesne University, and the University of Toledo. His numerous publications in personnel management and labor relations include a book of *Readings in Labor Relations*. His major areas of interest are personnel management, labor relations and collective bargaining, and compensation administration.

MARK J. MARTINKO, Ph.D. (University of Nebraska), is a professor of management in the College of Business at Florida State University. He has published numerous articles and books and conducted a variety of workshops in both the United States and abroad focusing on leadership, motivation, and organizational development. He is currently a member of the editorial board of the *Academy of Management Review* and is an active participant in both the Academy of Management and Southern Management Association.

VIRGINIA G. MAURER, J.D. (Stanford University), is an associate professor of business law and legal studies at the University of Florida. Previously she served as special assistant to the president at the University of Iowa. She has published widely in law reviews and business journals. She is vice president of the Southeastern Business Law Association and coeditor of the *Business Law Journal*. Her major areas of interest are antitrust and trade regulation, commercial and consumer law, and law and economics. In 1984 she chaired the Task Force on Student Conduct at the University of Florida, which addressed issues of sexual coercion and harassment on the university campus.

DALTON E. McFARLAND, Ph.D. (Cornell University), has taught at Michigan Technological University, Michigan State University, and, since 1972, at the University of Alabama—Birmingham, where he is now University Professor Emeritus of Management. He is engaged in a variety of research, consulting, and public service projects. He is author of *Management: Foundations and Practices* (5th ed., 1979), *Management and Society* (1982), and other books, articles, and research monographs. He is a fellow in the Academy of Management, the International Academy of Management, and the Society for Applied Anthropology. In 1974, he was honored as a Beta Gamma Sigma Distinguished Scholar in Business, and in 1978 as a Distinguished Alumnus, Western Michigan University.

JOSEPH F. McGRAW, M.S. (University of Colorado), is dean, Division of Business at Troy State University—Montgomery. His experience includes a partnership in a manufacturing concern and 27 years as a personnel officer with the United States Air Force.

WARREN W. MENKE, Ph.D. (Purdue University), is a professor of management at Clemson University. He has a doctorate in electrical engineering and spent 18 years in industry, the last 10 in engineering management for the Sperry Gyroscope Company. He has taught quantitative management courses at the University of Florida and Clemson University. He has published in *Management Science, Management Accounting, The Florida Entomologist, Ecology,* the *IEEE Transactions on Systems, Man, and Cybernetics,* and the *Accounting Review.* His major interests are reflected in his research in simulation modeling for policy decisions. He is a registered professional engineer, a member of AIDS, TIMS, IEEE, and the following honor societies: Eta Kappa Nu (EE), Sigma Xi (Science), Sigma Pi Sigma (Physics), and Alpha Iota Delta (Decision Sciences).

THOMAS A. NATIELLO, Ph.D. (Michigan State University), is a professor of management and health administration and the director of the Institute for Health Administration and Research at the University of Miami, where he heads the Graduate Health Administration Program. He has conducted research in a variety of organizations, and was chairman and founder of the Health Care Administration Division of the Academy of Management. He has served as a consultant to various agencies of the U.S. Department of Health and Human Services and to other public and private organizations. His major fields of interest are organization structure and design, evaluation of health care and other human services, organizational policy, and contingency theory.

FRANK P. NUMER, J.D. (University of Miami), was a professor of business administration at Robert Morris College when he wrote his critique. His industrial experience has included being manager of management development for the R.C.A. Service Company, and positions with Westinghouse, Inc., and the H. J. Heinz Company. He has had wide consulting experience, having given management development seminars in Pennsylvania, Ohio, Indiana, Illinois, Florida, New York, and Kentucky. His major areas of interest have been in the areas of business policy, labor management relations, law, and management development.

JOHN A. PEARCE II, Ph.D. (Pennsylvania State University), is holder of the LeRoy Eakin Endowed Chair in Strategic Management and chairman of the management department at George Mason University. He previously taught at Penn State, West Virginia University, and the University of South Carolina. Professor Pearce is coauthor of eight books, including *Strategic Management: Strategy Formulation and Implementation*. He has also authored or coauthored more than 100 refereed articles and papers. Pearce serves on the editorial boards of the *Academy of Management Review* and the *Journal of Management Case Studies*, is the consulting editor in strategic management for the *Journal of Management*, and the advisory editor for the Random House, Inc., series on management. Pearce has been an officer of several associations of scholars and researchers including the Academy of Management, the Decision Sciences Institute, and the Southern Management Association.

LYNN H. PETERS, Ph.D. (University of Wisconsin), is a professor of management at San Diego State University. He is author of *Management and Society*, and is listed in both *Who's Who in America* and *American Men and Women of Science*. He was an officer of the Academy of Management and is a member of the Academic Senate of the California State University and Colleges. He is directing a statewide external degree program in hotel and restaurant administration for the Consortium of California State University. His major areas of interest are business and society, organization theory, and organizational change.

JANE HASS PHILBRICK, Ph.D. (University of South Carolina), is a management systems consultant in Savannah, Georgia. She has adjunct faculty status at Savannah State College and Georgia Southern College. While teaching at the University of Florida, she was named Outstanding Faculty Member by Mortar Board. Her articles have been published in psychology, economics, and personnel journals. As a management consultant, she focuses on small business computer applications.

ROSEMARY PLEDGER, D.B.A. (Texas Tech University), was dean of the School of Business and Public Administration at the University of Houston—Clear Lake at the time she wrote her critique. Pledger served as past president of the Academy of Management (1979). Her major areas of interest included management theory, organizational behavior, personnel management, and women in management.

LYMAN W. PORTER, Ph.D. (Yale University), is a professor of management in the Graduate School of Management at the University of California, Irvine. He was dean of that school from 1972–83. Prior to joining that faculty in 1967, he served 11 years on the faculty of the University of California, Berkeley. He has published widely, and is the coauthor of five books. He is coeditor of the *Annual Review of Psychology* and is a member of the editorial boards of several journals. He served as president of the Academy of Management in 1973–74, and president of the division of industrial organizational psychology of the American Psychological Association in 1975–76. He is a fellow in the American Psychological Association. His major fields of interest are job attitudes, organization communication, organization politics, and management education.

DENNIS F. RAY, Ph.D. (University of Florida), is a professor of management and head of the department of management at Mississippi State University. Prior to his appointment at Mississippi State in 1966, he taught at the University of Alabama and the University of Florida. He has served as editor of the *Journal of Management*, business manager of the Academy of Management publications, and both as a member of the board of governors and secretary-treasurer of the Academy of Management. He is a consultant to numerous government agencies including the U.S. Department of Agriculture. His major areas of interest are organizational behavior and management theory.

STEPHEN P. ROBBINS, Ph.D. (University of Arizona), is a professor of management at San Diego State University. He is the author of eight books, his most recent including *Organization Theory* (2nd ed., 1987); *Essentials of Organizational Behavior* (2nd ed., 1988); *Management* (2nd ed., 1988); and *Personnel: The Management of Human Resources* (3rd ed., 1988). His major areas of interest are conflict management, organizational politics, and training of managers in developing their interpersonal skills.

DANIEL D. ROMAN, Ph.D. (University of Southern California), is professor emeritus of management science, George Washington University. He has taught at the American University, Florida State University, and California State University—Northridge, and has served as visiting professor at Ohio State University, Bradford University in England, and the University of Southern California. He has published many articles on the management of science and technology. He is the author of *R&D Management: The Economics and Administration of Technology* (1968), *Science Technology and Innovation: A Systems Approach* (1980), *International Business and Technological Innovation* (1983), and *Managing Projects: A Systems Approach* (1986). He has served as a consultant to industrial organizations and government agencies and such international organizations as UNESCO in Paris, the International Institute for Management of Technology in Milan, the Organization of American States in Brazil and Peru, the International Institute for Applied Systems Analysis in Vienna, and the Bradford Management Center in Bradford, England. He is past national chairman of the academic advisory committee for the National Association for Purchasing Management (NAPM) and director of the NAPM certification program. His major fields of interest are management theory and practice, production, and the management of science, technology, and innovation.

VIDA SCARPELLO, Ph.D. (University of Minnesota), is an associate professor of management at the University of Georgia. She is coauthor of *Personnel/Human Resource Management* (1988) and teaches graduate courses in compensation administration, labor relations, organization theory, behavior, design, and change. She has held professional positions in industry in the areas of labor relations and compensation administration and consults in areas of organizational change and human resource management. Her research activities focus on job satisfaction and its relationship to performance and turnover.

JOHN R. SCHERMERHORN, JR., Ph.D. (Northwestern University), is a professor of management at Southern Illinois University at Carbondale, where he has previously served as a department head and associate dean. He has also taught at Tulane University, the University of Vermont, and the Chinese University of Hong Kong. He is the author of *Management for Productivity* (1986) and senior coauthor of *Managing Organizational Behavior* (1985). He is an active researcher and consultant to organizations in the United States and abroad. He is past chairperson of the Management Education and Development Division of the Academy of Management.

LAWRENCE L. SCHKADE, Ph.D. (Louisville State University), is Ashbel Smith Professor of Information Systems and Management Sciences, and the director of the Center for Research in Information Systems at the

University of Texas at Arlington. He has served on the faculties of the University of Texas at Austin and Louisiana State University, and as Ford Foundation Professor at the Instituto Tecnologico de Monterrey, Mexico. His books include *The General Theory of Systems Applied to Management and Organization* (1980) and *Statistical Analysis for Administrative Decisions* (1984), and he has published research articles in several journals. He is past president and a fellow of the Decision Sciences Institute, a fellow of the American Association for the Advancement of Science, and the recipient of a Distinguished Scholar Award for Beta Gamma Sigma and the American Assembly of Collegiate Schools of Business. His special fields of interest include system theory, organization decision making, and information systems.

LYLE F. SCHOENFELDT, Ph.D. (Purdue University), is a professor of management and director, College of Business Administration (CBA) Fellows Program at Texas A&M University. He previously taught at Rensselaer Polytechnic Institute and the University of Georgia. His principal research is in the area of management identification and development of management talent. He has had more than 40 publications in his field and is on the editorial boards of the *Journal of Applied Psychology, Personnel Psychology*, and *Applied Psychological Measurement*. Among his honors, Dr. Schoenfeldt won the Cattell Award of the Society of Industrial and Organizational Psychology, American Psychology Association, for his ideas on prediction of managerial success.

DAVID B. STARKWEATHER, Dr. P.H. (University of California—Los Angeles), is a professor of health services management at the University of California—Berkeley. He holds faculty appointments in the School of Public Health and the School of Business Administration. His previous positions include those of associate director and director, Palo Alto Stanford Hospital Center. His publications include numerous cases and articles in professional journals. His current research is centered upon hospital mergers and health care markets. He is a trustee of Herrick Memorial Hospital in Berkeley, California, and past chairman of the accreditation Commission for Graduate Education in Health Services Administration.

A. J. STRICKLAND, Ph.D. (Georgia State University), is a professor of strategic management at the University of Alabama. He is the author of numerous textbooks in strategic management. He has written *Strategic Management: Concepts and Cases* (with Arthur A. Thompson, Jr.), *Readings in Strategic Management* (with Arthur A. Thompson, Jr., and William E. Fulmer), *Tempomatic IV: A Management Simulation* (with Charles R. Scott, Jr.), and *Micromatic: A Strategic Management Simulation* (with Tim Scott).

MARILYN L. TAYLOR, D.B.A. (Harvard University), is associate professor of strategic management in the University of Kansas School of Business. She is author of several articles, a number of cases, and coauthor of a book. She is active in several professional organizations and is currently on the editorial board of two journals. Professor Taylor is active with the business community as director of the field studies program for the University of Kansas and teaches actively in several executive development programs.

HENRY L. TOSI, Ph.D. (Ohio State University), is a professor of management at the University of Florida. He has held faculty positions at the University of Maryland, the University of California—Irvine, and Michigan State University. He is a fellow of the Academy of Management, has been president of its midwest division (1972), and has served as chairman of its Organization Behavior Division. His books include *Management by Objective: Research and Applications* (1974), *Management: Contingency, Structure, and Process* (1982), *Organizational Behavior* (1977), and *Theories of Organization* (1983). He has written more than 50 articles appearing in the *Academy of Management Journal, Journal of Business, Administrative Science Quarterly,* and other journals. He is a member of the editorial review board of *Administrative Science Quarterly*.

RALPH N. TRAXLER, JR., Ph.D. (University of Chicago), is a professor of management (corporate strategy) in the School of Business at Savannah State College. Previously he served on the faculties of Emory and Henry College, the University of Florida, and Emory University. He was dean of the College of Business and Management Studies at the University of South Alabama and dean of the School of Management and Business Sciences at Oklahoma City University. He is active as a consultant with a specialized interest in management development. His other fields of interest are business history, business organization, and policies.

SHARON TUCKER, Ph.D. (University of Chicago), is a principal with Hay Management Consultants. She was previously at Washington University and Southern Illinois University at Edwardsville. She is coauthor with Walter Nord of *Implementing Routine and Radical Innovations*. She is also the author of articles and book chapters on women in management and organizational politics, and is past chair of the Women in Management Division of the Academy of Management.

MARY ANN VON GLINOW, Ph.D. (Ohio State University), is an associate professor of management and organization at the University of Southern California. She has been active in the Academy of Management, having served on the board of governors, and chaired a Task Force on Ethics in the Organizational Behavior Division. That ethics work resulted in a newsletter devoted to ethical "rights and wrongs and ambiguities" that was sent to the Academy of Management membership. In addition to ethics, she works in two other areas: currently writing a book on *Managing High Technology and Professional Employees*, and very active in research on Korea and the People's Republic of China.

WILLIAM J. WASMUTH, D.B.A. (Indiana University), is a professor of human resources and personnel management at the New York State School of Industrial and Labor Relations at Cornell University. He is faculty advisor of a regional rehabilitation management training project, and has recently served as chairman of the extension department. His books include *Human Resources Administration: Problems of Growth and Change* (1970), *Organizational Cases and Intrigues: Dynamics of Supervision* (1974), and *Effective Supervision: Developing Your Skills through Critical Incidents* (1979). He has designed a number of management training simulation programs including CHARMS (Cornell Hotel and Restaurant Management Simulation) (1981). He is an active management consultant and has had considerable experience in industry. He is a member of the Industrial Relations Research Association. His major fields of interest are organization growth and change, personnel management, training and development, organization structure and innovation, and supervision.

WILLIAM B. WERTHER, JR., Ph.D. (University of Florida), is the chair professor of executive management in the School of Business Administration at the University of Miami. He also serves as a labor arbitrator with the American Arbitration Association and the Federal Mediation and Conciliation Service. He is the author of *Personnel Management and Human Resources* (2nd ed.) with Keith Davis, in addition to 4 other books, 70 articles, and a score of arbitration awards. His experience includes work as an advisor to more than 60 organizations throughout North America in the areas of corporate strategy, productivity, and human resource management.

STUART A. WESBURY, JR., Ph.D. (University of Florida), is president of the American College of Healthcare Executives. Prior to that appointment he was director and professor, section of health services management in the School of Medicine at the University of Missouri—Columbus. He has had hospital administration experience as director of the University of Florida's Shands Teaching Hospital and Clinics. He is a fellow in the

American College of Healthcare Executives and a former member of the Advisory Editorial Board of *Hospitals and Health Services Administration*. He is a past chairman of the board of directors of the Association of University Programs in Health Administration.

J. CLIFTON WILLIAMS, Ph.D. (Purdue University), is the H. R. Gibson Professor of Management at Baylor University. His prior positions at Baylor included director of graduate studies in industrial psychology, chairman of the psychology department, dean of the graduate school, and administrative vice president. The author of two management textbooks and numerous other publications, he is also president of Leadership Systems Corporation, a publisher of management development materials, and he has served as a management consultant for many years.

MAX S. WORTMAN, JR., Ph.D. (University of Minnesota), is a professor of management at the University of Tennessee. He previously taught at Virginia Polytechnic Institute and State University, Iowa State University, University of Minnesota, University of Iowa, and University of Massachusetts. He has been editor and associate editor of the *Academy of Management Review*, and he has served on the editorial review boards of the *Journal of Management, Journal of Collective Negotiations in the Public Sector*, and *Human Resources Planning*. He has written more than 100 articles and papers and written or edited 9 books including: *Administrative Policy* (1975, 1980), *Defining the Manager's Job* (1975), and *Emerging Concepts in Management* (1975). He was a Ford Faculty Research fellow in 1963–64. He has served as a consultant to federal, state, and local governments, including the U.S. Equal Employment Opportunity Commission, U.S. Civil Service Commission, and the U.S. Navy. He has served in many capacities in the Academy of Management and the International Personnel Management Association.

DANIEL A. WREN, Ph.D. (University of Illinois), is a professor of management at the University of Oklahoma. He taught at Florida State University prior to moving to Oklahoma, and he has been active in the Southern Management Association and is a fellow of the Academy of Management. In addition to numerous articles in professional journals, he is the author of *The Evolution of Management Thought* (3rd ed., 1987) and the coauthor (with Dan Voich, Jr.) of *Management: Process, Structure, and Behavior* (1984).

Incident Analysis Classification Matrix (See Chapter 2 for an elaboration of the Incident Analysis Sequence Process.)

	Decision-Making	Policy Formulation	Policy Implementation	Policy Violation
1. A Sexual Harassment Policy	S	M	S	S
2. Abusive Discharge Suit	M	M	S	
3. An Exam for Mrs. Smith	M	M	S	
4. Assembly Line Protest	M	S		
5. Conflict of Interest	M	S	S	M
6. Consultant's Report	M			
7. Contradictory Staff Advice	M	S	S	
8. Dual Lines of Authority	M	M	M	S
9. Effective Leadership	M	M		
10. Employee Complaint	M	S		
11. Employee Raiding	S	M	S	
12. Equal Employment Reaction	M	S	M	
13. Equal Pay for Comparable Worth	M	S	M	
14. False Reports	M	S	M	M
15. Heroic Banker	M	M	S	M
16. Illegal Drug Policy	S	M	S	M
17. Implementing Strategic Change	S		M	
18. Indigenous Leader	S	M	M	

19. Invasion of Privacy	S	M	M	S
20. Moonlighting Policy	S	M	S	M
21. Moral Question	S	M	S	
22. Perceived Pay Inequity	M	S	S	
23. Performance Appraisal Policy	S	S	M	M
24. Policy under Pressure	M	M	S	
25. Production Slowdown	S	S	S	M
26. Public versus Private Interests	M	S		
27. Quality Circle Consequence	M	S	S	
28. Questionable Purchasing Practices	M	S	S	
29. Resistance to Change	S	M	S	
30. Résumé Falsification	S	S	M	M
31. Reverse Discrimination	S	M	M	S
32. Robot Repercussion	S	M	M	
33. Stress Management	S	M	S	
34. Stringless Gift?	M	M	S	
35. The Air-Conditioned Cafeteria	M	S	S	
36. Travel Policy Dilemma	S	M	M	
37. Unexpected Reassignment	S	M	S	
38. Union's Dilemma	M	S		
39. Whistleblowing	M	M	S	
40. Work Force Reduction Policy	S	M	S	